The Book of Acts

The Book of Acts

CATHOLIC, ORTHODOX, AND EVANGELICAL READINGS

Edited by Charles Raith II

THE CATHOLIC UNIVERSITY OF AMERICA PRESS
Washington, D.C.

The paper used in this publication meets the minimum requirements of American
National Standards for Information Science—Permanence
of Paper for Printed Library Materials, ANSI Z39.48–1984.
∞

Design and composition by Kachergis Book Design

Congress Cataloging-in-Publication data available
from the Library of Congress
ISBN 978-0-8132-3167-9

Contents

Illustrations

Preface

In the fall of 2016, eighteen scholars—six Catholics, six Orthodox, and six Evangelicals—gathered at John Brown University in Siloam Springs, Arkansas, to read and engage the book of Acts together. The conference, titled "Engaging the Book of Acts, Engaging One Another: Catholics, Orthodox and Evangelicals," was sponsored by the Paradosis Center for Theology and Scripture, whose mission includes "bringing together Catholics, Orthodox and Evangelical Christians to have meaningful theological exchanges, centered on Scripture and rooted in the Great Tradition, so that we may more fully understand and live out the traditions (cf. 2 Thes 2:15) passed down to us from the beginning." There were six sessions, each session beginning with a main paper from either a Catholic, an Orthodox, or an Evangelical on a pericope of Acts. The main paper was followed by two response papers from representatives of the other two traditions. This structure created two levels of dialogue: first (and foremost), the text of Acts; and second, the main paper. All the speakers were encouraged to allow their ecclesial traditions to bear fully—to the extent possible—upon their readings of Acts. The engagement was full of light and at times not without heat! But everyone involved walked away with a richer reading of Acts and a better appreciation for how we can help one another more fully embody the Christian faith. The same will be true for the reader of this volume.

The conference and this volume could not have occurred without the help of many people, more than can be mentioned here. Many thanks go to the Paradosis Conference student leadership team—Adam, Sharon, Shannon, Alan, Josh, Elizabeth, and Micah—who did a splendid job meeting the needs of speakers and attendees. Thanks are also due to the board and associates of the Paradosis Center for their continual support and guidance. I also want to thank John Martino at the Catholic University of America Press for his efforts in getting this work to see the light of print. Last, I want to thank Jeff and Ryan for their encouragement throughout the life of the Paradosis Center and the way they desire and seek after Christian unity and peace.

Abbreviations

Modern editions

ANF	*The Ante-Nicene Fathers*. Edited by Alexander Roberts and James Donaldson. 1885–1887. 10 vols. Repr., Peabody, Mass.: Hendrickson, 1994.
CCSL	Corpus Christianorum: Series Latina
GCS	Die griechischen christlichen Schriftsteller der ersten [drei] Jahrhunderte
GNO	Gregorii Nysseni Opera. Edited by Werner Jaeger. Leiden: Brill, 1952–.
NPNF[1]	*A Select Library of the Nicene and Post-Nicene Fathers of the Christian Church*, Series 1. Edited by Philip Schaff et al. 14 vols. Buffalo, N.Y.: Christian Literature, 1887–1894. Repr., Peabody, Mass.: Hendrickson, 1994.
NPNF[2]	*A Select Library of the Nicene and Post-Nicene Fathers of the Christian Church*, Series 1. Edited by Philip Schaff et al. 14 vols. Buffalo, N.Y.: Christian Literature, 1887–1894. Repr., Peabody, Mass.: Hendrickson, 1994.
PG	Patrologia Graeca [= Patrologiae Cursus Completus: Series Graeca]. Edited by Jacques-Paul Migne. 162 vols. Paris, 1857–1886.
PL	Patrologia Latina [= Patrologiae Cursus Completus: Series Latina]. Edited by Jacques-Paul Migne. 217 vols. Paris, 1844–1864

Ancient Works

Comm. Jo.	Origen, *Commentarii in evangelium Joannis*
Enarrat. Ps.	Augustine, *Enarrationes in Psalmos*
Ep.	*Epistulae*
Eun.	Gregory of Nyssa, *Contra Eunomium*
Haer.	Irenaeus, *Adversus haereses*
In Cant.	Gregory of Nyssa, *In Canticum Canticorum*

Or.	Gregory of Nazianzus, *Theological Orations*
Rom.	Ignatius of Antioch, *Epistle to the Romans*
Tim.	Plato, *Timaeus*

Mishnah, Talmud, and Rabbinic Literature

ʿArak.	ʿArakin
Pesaḥ.	Pesaḥim
S. ʿOlam Rab.	Seder ʿOlam Rabbah
Šabb.	Šabbat

The Book of Acts

INTRODUCTION

Reading Acts Together as Catholics, Orthodox, and Evangelicals

Charles Raith II

"Acts is a 'charter' document of Christian self-identity and legitimation, written, not for a specific 'Lukan community,' but rather for a general audience of early Christians living in the ancient Mediterranean world."[1] Wrestling with the book of Acts forces Christians back to their initial heritage, back to the beginning of their common Christian identity. In Acts we have the story of the newly birthed church—a church birthed through the washing and renewal of the Holy Spirit and continually guided by that very same Spirit. It is the church that all ecclesial communities recognize as the fount of their heritage. Reading Acts together as Catholics, Orthodox, and Evangelicals has the feel of a gathering of relatives coming together for some special occasion and reading a story about their common great-great-great-grandparents. They may have difficulty at times recognizing one another as relatives when they gaze only at one another. But they must acknowledge their family ties through their mutual recognition that those great-grandparents are *their* great-grandparents. And once this fact is recognized—that we are relatives with the *same* origin—we can no longer treat one another as strangers and aliens but rather as family, however estranged we might judge one another to be.

Our shared commitment to our origins—to the church of the "way" presented to us in Acts—forces us out of, in David Yeago's words, "a let bygones be bygones" attitude toward ecclesial affiliation.[2] This attitude is the

1. Mikeal C. Parsons, *Luke*, Paideia: Commentaries on the New Testament (Grand Rapids: Baker Academic, 2015), 4; Richard Bauckham, ed. *The Gospel for All Christians* (Grand Rapids: Eerdmans, 1998), 46.

2. David S. Yeago, "The Spirit, the Church, and the Scriptures: Biblical Inspiration and Interpretation Revisited," in *Knowing the Triune God: The Work of the Spirit in the Practices of the Church*, ed. James J.

very opposite of the pursuit of unity. Politeness toward one another can be a source of the problem, for it can fuel a complacency about our divisions.[3] The truth is that we come together all believing that our present identities as Catholics, Orthodox, and Evangelicals are in some way in continuity with the church of Acts. But we have to acknowledge that we cannot all actually be in continuity, given the divisions (and not just differences) that exist among us. Recognizing this fact could result in coming together and having a family squabble over who most looks like great-great-Grandpa Minick. Or our coming together, if done in charity (as is the case with the contributors of this volume), could result in overall family enrichment as we share those family traits with one another that our own communities might have forgotten or possibly never knew existed. Our togetherness rather than our separateness enables each of us to more fully reflect the richness of our heritage.

I am depicting here in metaphorical terms the phenomenon of "receptive ecumenism." Paul Murray describes receptive ecumenism as "putting at the forefront of the Christian ecumenical agenda the self-critical question, 'What, in any given situation, can one's own tradition appropriately learn with integrity from other traditions?'"[4] Murray claims that receptive ecumenism is not about being *less* Catholic, Orthodox, Anglican, Reformed, or otherwise, but rather about becoming *more* of these by learning from the other. It is less a losing of identity and more a "finding and freeing of a richer, fuller identity."[5]

We do not come to Acts, then, *in spite of* our present identities as Catholics, Orthodox, and Evangelicals. Gazing upon the original "charter" doc-

---

Buckley and David S. Yeago (Grand Rapids: Eerdmans, 2001), 78. See also Walter Cardinal Kasper: "The Bible, for both our church communities [Catholic and Protestant (and I add Orthodox)], is the fundamental document of our faith and I have the impression that we can make further fundamental progress by involving scripture study more fully in dogmatic questions" (*That They Might All Be One: The Call to Unity Today* [London: Continuum, 2004], 131).

3. Peter Leithart, *The End of Protestantism: Pursuing Unity in a Fragmented Church* (Grand Rapids: Baker Academic, 2016), 4.

4. Paul D. Murray, "Receptive Ecumenism and Catholic Learning—Establishing the Agenda," in *Receptive Ecumenism and the Call to Catholic Learning: Exploring a Way for Contemporary Ecumenism*, ed. Paul D. Murray (Oxford: Oxford University Press, 2008), 12.

5. Murray, "Receptive Ecumenism," 17, 24n. For this reason, Murray criticizes in the name of receptive ecumenism the dichotomy posed by R. R. Reno, "The Debilitation of the Churches," in *The Ecumenical Future*, ed. Carl E. Braaten and Robert W. Jenson (Grand Rapids: Eerdmans, 2004), when he states, "The ecumenical process is stalled because the churches cannot square the circle. They cannot articulate their identities as churches, while at the same time admitting that they suffer ecumenical need for unity with others" (47). Murray's suggestion is that by becoming more fully Anglican, Baptist, Reformed, Lutheran, or otherwise, these ecclesial communities will move toward one another, toward unity.

ument is not a practice of nostalgia, nor is it an attempt to occlude the developments of this original identity over time. We are not called to simply reduplicate the church of Acts, as if the church in Acts were the only legitimate form; nor could we reduplicate it if we tried. Yet neither are we called to reinvent the wheel, as if our present embodiment of the faith need not have anything to do with the original. Reading Acts through our contemporary ecclesial lenses, then, enables us to see the seeds of more developed ideas, judgments, and practices that have informed our present identities. At the same time, the legitimacy of any of the present identities as Catholic, Orthodox, and Evangelical depends upon a demonstration of some sort of family resemblance to the original. We are called to be the recipients of the "traditions passed down from the beginning" (2 Thes 2:15). Even if one wants to claim the same family *name*, deploring one's heritage and setting off on one's own path may result in little to no family ties. The approach in this volume, then, runs contrary both to a modern biblical studies approaches that would lock the church's original identity in the past and to a modern theologically progressive approach that would collapse contemporary identity into the present and hoped-for future. The past both legitimizes and fuels the present, while the present does not simply reduplicate the past but faithfully carries on the traditions through a doctrinal developmental process natural to a *living* faith.

While Acts provided its Christian audience a foundational self-understanding, an outward, evangelistic imperative is intrinsic to this self-understanding: "[The book of Acts] motivated and equipped believers to bear faithful witness to the apostolic gospel."[6] Our ordering of ourselves as Christians—in our beliefs and practices—is intrinsic to our bearing witness in the world. An inward focus is necessarily also an outward focus; the church as "mother" and the church as "mission" are not two competing callings but rather reflect the single calling to be the body of Christ. The church cannot accomplish its mission without being rightly ordered internally. But that right internal ordering necessarily entails a church on a mission.

Reflecting the intrinsic connection between mother and mission, we find peppered throughout Acts moments of Christian unity founded in Christian charity that Luke presents as part of the Christian apologetic. In

6. David G. Peterson, *The Acts of the Apostles*, Pillar New Testament Commentary (Grand Rapids: Eerdmans, 2009), 38; Richard N. Longenecker, *The Expositor's Bible Commentary*, vol. 10, *Luke-Acts*, ed. Tremper Longman III and David E. Garland, rev. ed. (Grand Rapids: Zondervan, 2007), 676–78.

Beverly Roberts Gaventa's words, "Luke portrays the church's relentless witness through its preaching and teaching, but *the church's witness also takes the form of mutual responsibility in a community of believers*."[7] This comes as no surprise in light of Jesus's words, "By this all people will know that you are my disciples, if you have love for one another" (Jn 13:35 ESV), as well as Jesus's prayer, "[I pray] also for those who will believe in me through their word, that they may all be one, just as you, Father, are in me, and I in you, that they also may be in us, so that the world may believe that you have sent me" (Jn 17:20–21 ESV). When we broach the topic of unity and its evangelistic impact, however, we are forced to deal with what modern ecumenism has deftly recognized: our divisions as Catholics, Orthodox, and Evangelicals undermines the Christian evangelistic imperative.[8] It is no coincidence that the modern ecumenical movement was birthed by the modern missionary movement. Reflecting on the church in Acts thus occasions acts of penance for the ways we have wandered into disunity. We must grieve over our sin if we are to proceed toward the healing of its effects.

This is not to say the fledging church of Acts was not without its tensions, especially as people of the "Way" worked through the implications of their faith in Jesus Christ for their Jewish heritage: "Luke situates the Christian community within the larger Jewish debate about self-identity. . . . Luke understands the Way to be a movement within first-century Judaism."[9] The tension was, in broad strokes, a two-sided struggle: how Jewish *should* you have to be in order to be Christian, on the one hand, and how Jewish *can* you be and be Christian, on the other. Wrapped up in this issue was the question of what to do with the gentiles, the "outsiders" who wanted to follow Jesus as the Christ. How did the early church wrestle with these issues? What judgments did they make that might inform the struggles we face in the present day? How did they maintain unity in the Spirit in the midst of forces pulling the new believers in different directions? These are all questions whose answers may inform our present ecclesial tensions.

We begin our journey through Acts with the pivotal moment of Christ's ascension into heaven. In chapter 1, Fr. John Behr tackles Acts 1 and the ascension of Christ and argues that Christ's ascension into the heavens is a

7. Beverly Roberts Gaventa, *Acts*, Abingdon New Testament Commentaries (Nashville: Abingdon, 2003), 41.

8. For a recent introduction to "modern ecumenism," see R. David Nelson and Charles Raith II, *Ecumenism: A Guide for the Perplexed* (London: Bloomsbury T&T Clark, 2017).

9. Parsons, *Luke*, 7.

victory march and a divine enthronement, one that unites heaven and earth as the single creation of God. Fr. Behr engages Douglas Farrow's work on the ascension and claims, contra Farrow's tendency to posit an Origenist spiritualizing tendency against an Irenaean incarnational approach, that the actual corporeal ascension of Christ and the "spiritualizing" approach of the ascent of the mind are united through their emphasis on ascent as transformation. For Fr. Behr, the body in which Christ undergoes the passion and then ascension is made, through the passion, to share in the properties of the divine nature, with the result that we no longer recognize Jesus according to the flesh but according to the divine, which requires the ascent of the mind. Hans Boersma responds with an affirmation of Fr. Behr's thesis that the Origenist spiritualizing tendency and the Irenaean incarnational approach are not in opposition to one another but share an eschatology that "regards temporal and spatial realities as being in need of transformation so as to be fitted for the eschaton." Boersma believes that a healthy dose of "Christian Platonism" and its idealist view of matter—something he finds particularly in Jonathan Edwards—is necessary to provide a proper theological and metaphysical support of the ascension. Douglas Farrow, after affirming the notion of the ascent of the mind, pinpoints the real difference between himself and Fr. Behr and Boersma: to ascend means to grasp Jesus Christ in *both* natures. It is *not* a matter of passing through the human to the divine. Farrow reaffirms his suspicion of Origen as a reliable guide on this point, not because of his affirmation of the ascent of the mind but because of the way he conceives the ascension of Jesus Christ in relation to his humanity.

In chapter 2 David Jeffrey takes up Acts 2 and the outpouring of the Holy Spirit. Reflecting on his own story to illustrate the difficulties Christians experience in making sense of the glossolalia in Acts, Jeffrey wonders, "Are Pentecostals 'evangelical'?" This provides him the opportunity to clarify at length what it means for him as an Anglican to be "evangelical." Jeffrey connects the events of Acts 2 and in particular tongues to the strongly missiological emphasis of the church, which he finds present in the "Gregorian" tradition (as opposed to the "Calvinist" tradition) of Anglican interpretation of this passage. Jeffrey seeks to avoid making glossolalia a mark of exclusion, distinguishing Christian from non-Christian, and emphasizes instead that the phenomenon of Acts 2 is *xenoglossia*—and thus is missional character. Fr. Thomas Guarino complements Jeffrey's reading by highlighting the "birth of the church" in Acts 2. Fr. Guarino connects the unity displayed at Pentecost to the attempts at Vatican II to enflesh the unity of Christians in its pronouncements, and further connects this unity with effective testimony to the gospel. Fr. Eugen Pentiuc responds by clarifying that there is not "an" or "the" Orthodox approach to Pentecost in Acts 2, and makes the reserved statement that "the *general* view among Orthodox believers is that glossolalia was a *temporary* gift given to the church in its infancy." Fr. Pentiuc emphasizes the interplay between Scripture and tradition in Orthodox thought and practice, and thus he looks at the role that Acts 2 plays in the Byzantine liturgical tradition. Through this analysis, he pushes back against a clear-cut distinction between glossolalia and xenolalia, finding in the liturgical sources a place for a "second baptism" if understood as a deepening of or recommitment to one's initial baptism.

In chapter 3 Matthew Levering addresses Stephen's stoning, recorded in Acts 7. Levering sees in Stephen's speech a pattern for all Christians to follow when facing their own death. Stephen both looks back and looks forward in the face of death. He looks back and describes not only his own life but the life of Israel; he looks forward in faith and hope and sees not only his own victory but also that of Jesus and all those he gathers to himself. Thus for Levering, Stephen illustrates that we never die as individuals; rather "our dying belongs to the history of God's people, so that the history of Israel and of the church is *our* history." Levering recognizes that some have viewed Stephen's speech as anti-Jewish, and thus he contextualizes the speech within Jewish Scripture to show its thoroughgoing Jewishness. Dale Coulter responds by focusing on the role of memory in the formation of God's people and the role of the Spirit in taking us up into the people—the latter being a point he feels Levering overlooks. Coulter wants to see the "baptism in the Spirit" as shorthand for the full manifestation of the grace of God in the life of the community: "Stephen's speech and his vision are Spirit-induced events." The speech and vision correspond to the Protestant emphasis on faith as simultaneously an illumination of the mind and igniting of the heart. While acknowledging his gratitude for Levering's essay, Marcus Plested focuses on the Orthodox appropriation of Stephen's death, which identifies Stephen as proto-martyr and proto-deacon. But even within these descriptions, unique to Orthodoxy, claims Plested, is Stephen as exemplar mystic. The Orthodox tradition is especially interested in Stephen's vision and his proclamation of that vision for others to participate in it.

In chapter 4, Ralph Wood addresses the thorny topic of Paul's conversion as recorded in Acts 9. Wood acknowledges that there is no such thing as a "view" from nowhere, and that any approach to the topic will necessarily be contextualized. Thus Wood takes a unique approach to the topic by looking at different depictions of Paul's conversion in patristic, medieval, Renaissance, and modern theology and art. He begins by pairing an early icon of Paul's conversion with Chrysostom's sermons, highlighting the *theosis* dimension in their depictions. He then pairs Thomas Aquinas's explanation of Paul's conversion in the *Summa theologiae* with Pieter Bruegel the Elder's *The Conversion of Paul,* highlighting their emphasis on the divine activity over the human. Next Wood pairs Erasmus's account with Michelangelo Merisi da Caravaggio's *Conversion of St. Paul* and *The Conversion on the Road to Damascus,* and wonders whether both "missed" the heart of the matter by depicting Paul's conversion in humanistic terms. Last, Wood pairs Karl Barth's account of Paul's conversion with William Blake's *Conversion of St. Paul,* highlighting their "uncompromising christological account" of the Damascus road event, which put them out of step with their times. Gary Jenkins responds by picking up where Wood leaves off: the conversion experience of Friedrich Nietzsche. While Jenkins accepts Wood's conclusion about "St. Friedrich Nietzsche," Jenkins questions Wood's Barthian prism for reading Acts 9 (and Nietzsche), and in particular "that what confronted St. Paul made him radically other than what he had been." Instead, Jenkins draws on the Orthodox tradition of the mystery of human nature elevated to the divine as an appropriate framework for understanding Paul's conversion. Fr. Thomas Weinandy responds by thinking through what Paul "the artist" would have *himself* "seen" within his own conversion experience. Fr. Weinandy argues that Paul's own interpretation of his conversion provides a hermeneutical key for understanding much of his theology found in his letters.

In chapter 5 Robert Wilken addresses the so-called Council of Jerusalem in Acts 15. Wilken emphasizes the ecclesial nature of the early church, that it was a corporate body with distinct offices, rituals, reverence for tradition, and formulas of belief. Wilken notes that the meeting in Acts 15 is actually the third time leaders met to make important decisions on behalf of the church; the first shortly after Christ's ascension, and the second regarding the feeding of widows. The events in Acts 15, however, pertained to gentile converts and the place of Jewish law in their conversion (i.e., circumcision and food laws). Wilken argues that while the response on circumcision was clear, these first Christians, who were "pious and observant Jews," did not throw off their Judaism but gave "a solution in Jewish terms" to the issues of veneration of idols, marriage practices, and meat improperly slaughtered. Thus for Wilken, Acts 15 can been read as illustrating the abiding significance of Judaism for Christians. Wilken concludes, "The church continues to be dependent on the witness of Israel." Bradley Nassif responds by engaging Wilken's interpretation in conjunction with present Orthodox-Jewish relations. Nassif departs from Wilken's more optimistic vision by affirming the Orthodox position that witness to Jewish people remains a missionary mandate today. He further uses the opportunity of the Council of Jerusalem in Acts 15 to address the issues of "authority" and "ecclesiology" in conjunction with the subsequent councils that were held in the Byzantine Empire from 325 to 787 C.E. Nassif hopes that by doing so, Catholics and Evangelicals may understand at least *why* the Orthodox Church sees itself as faithfully preserving the tradition in an unbroken succession of truth. Gerald McDermott appreciates Wilken's emphasis that "the olive tree of Israel still supports (present tense) the grafted-in gentile branches," but he questions Wilken's conclusion that the Council of Jerusalem made circumcision no longer required of any disciples of Jesus, and that the Jew-gentile distinction had ended. Rather, the council merely decided a point rabbis had been teaching for some time: gentiles were not required to become Jews to participate in God's promises. Moreover, kosher laws, argues McDermott, were still applicable to Jesus-following Jews (though not gentile followers). McDermott concludes that Jewish and gentile followers of Jesus have "unity in God, diversity in persons and roles."

In chapter 6, Fr. Andrew Louth analyzes Paul's speech on Mars Hill in Acts 17. Fr. Louth begins by acknowledging the general lack of engagement with this passage in the Fathers, though he finds an interesting perspective in Clement of Alexandria. For Clement—the "godfather" of apophatic theology—the "unknown god" is not so much a god that has been overlooked but rather is God, unknown by nature. This leads Fr. Louth to Dionysios, who took his queues from Clement in expounding on the God who is unknowable by nature. Dionysios's method of interpretation, however, went beyond what we usually think of as interpretation by his *becoming* the historical Dionysios the Areopagite found in Acts 17. Fr. Louth argues that "the identity he finds with the Athenian judge is a corollary of the identity his master Paul finds with Christ." He goes on to demonstrate the centrality of

Scripture is to Dionysios's apophatic-kataphatic approach to theology, and how this theology is meant not to give a collection of truths for developing an objective understanding of God's relation to the world but to lead us into the mystery of God in Christ. Fr. Louth concludes by analyzing how Dionysios's approach becomes embodied in the liturgy.

Fr. Brian Daley begins with a similar acknowledgment regarding the surprising lack of engagement from the Fathers, both Greek and Latin, with this "thrilling" scene of Paul at Mars Hill in Acts 17. Fr. Daley proceeds to expand on Fr. Louth's summary of the patristic material by looking at the first six centuries of interpretation. Donald Fairbairn takes up Fr. Louth's two main points—the inscription is best read as "to an unknowable God," and Dionysios's act of inserting himself into the text of Acts 17—and addresses the "significant tensions" that exist within Evangelicalism on these points. None of the Protestant commentators Fairbairn consults even mention the possibility of translating the inscription as "to an unknowable God," which reflects for Fairbairn the general unease with the *via negativa* within "professional" Evangelical exegetes. Fairbairn finds this in great tension, however, with the actual practice of rank-and-file Evangelicals. Fairbairn also worries that the Evangelical individualistic approach to Scripture reverses the Dionysian approach: instead of inserting one into the text, one instead applies the text to his or her life.

CHAPTER 1

Acts 1 and Christ's Ascension into Heaven

Fr. John Behr (Orthodox)

The LORD says to my lord:
"Sit at my right hand,
till I make your enemies your footstool."
The LORD sends forth from Zion
    your mighty scepter.
    Rule in the midst of your foes! . . .
The Lord has sworn
    and will not change his mind:
"You are a priest forever,
    after the order of Melchizedek." (Ps 110: 1–2, 4)

When the apostle and evangelist Luke gives his first account of the ascension of Christ, in the last lines of his Gospel, it is set very much in priestly terms: "while he blessed them, he parted from them, and was carried up into heaven. And they returned to Jerusalem with great joy, and were continually in the temple blessing God" (Lk 24:51–53).[1] He is a priest for ever after the order of Melchizedek, making a priestly offering for us at the heavenly altar. Melchizedek, of course, has no genealogy: he mysteriously appears to Abram—bringing out bread and wine as the priest of God Most High (Gn 14)—never to appear again, but recalled by this psalm and then by the author of Hebrews in chapter 7. He neither ascended or descended—he just appears.

Others, however, have ascended to the heavens: Enoch walked with God, and then "was not, for God took him" (μετέθηκεν, "translated" Gn 5:24), and Elijah was caught up to the heavens in a chariot in the whirlwind (2 Kgs 2:11).

1. Scripture quotations are from the RSV, with slight changes.

Yet, when Christ ascends, something unprecedented happens: He is seated at the right hand of God himself, and he is established as King:

> God has gone up with a shout,
> the LORD with the sound of a trumpet.
> Sing praises to God, sing praises!
> Sing praises to our King, sing praises!
> For God is the king of all the earth;
> sing praises with a psalm!
> God reigns over the nations;
> God sits on his holy throne. (Ps 47:5–8)

Christ's ascension into the heavens is therefore a victory march and a divine enthronement. It is an ascension that, moreover, causes surprise in the heavens themselves:

> Life up your heads, O gates!
> and be lifted up, O ancient doors!
> that the King of glory may enter.
> Who is the King of glory?
> The LORD, strong and mighty,
> The LORD, mighty in battle!
> Lift up your heads, O gates!
> and be lifted up, O ancient doors!
> that the King of glory may enter.
> Who is the King of glory?
> The LORD of hosts,
> He is the King of glory. (Ps 24:7–10)

According to Irenaeus, the gates that ask, "Who is this King of glory?" are the principalities and the angelic ranks: they ask a first time because, having descended invisible to his creatures, he now ascends in the flesh; and so they are told: He is "the LORD, strong and mighty in battle." [2] But when they ask a second time, they then respond themselves: "He is the LORD of hosts, the King of glory!" As close as the angelic ranks are to God in heaven, not even they knew his eternal counsel, his primordial decrees, established from the beginning and brought to completion or perfection at the end—the things that, as Peter says, even the angels long to look into (1 Pt 1:12).[3]

2. Irenaeus, *Demonstration of the Apostolic Preaching* 84, in Irenaeus of Lyons, *On the Apostolic Preaching*, trans. John Behr, Popular Patristics Series (Crestwood, N.Y.: St. Vladimir's Seminary Press, 1997).

3. See especially Gregory of Nyssa, *Homilies on the Song of Songs* 8, in Gregory of Nyssa, *Homilies on*

Christ's ascension into the heavens—a victory march and a divine enthronement—surprises not only the heavenly beings but also his disciples on earth. For this is not what the disciples were expecting when they asked the risen Christ: "Will you now [finally!] restore the kingdom to Israel?" (Acts 1:6). King David ascended to his throne, and took possession of the kingdom; Christ's triumphal entry into Jerusalem, a few weeks earlier, might have seemed like a political coup, but it proved not to be: "My kingdom is not of this world," not of this *kosmos* (Jn 18:36). It might not be of this cosmos, but it is certainly to include the earth, for it was possession of the land that was promised to the patriarchs, and this remains to be fulfilled.[4] King David ascended to his throne, and took possession of the kingdom, but that throne was only on earth, and his kingdom was earthly. As Peter points out in his great speech on the day of Pentecost: "David did not ascend into the heavens" (Acts 2:34). Christ ascending in the flesh into the heavens not only surprises the heavenly host but also unites heaven and earth as the single creation of God.

From this heavenly throne, the incarnate Christ, the Son of God, awaits the subjection of all things to him.

> Why do the nations conspire,
> and the people plot in vain?
> The kings of the earth set themselves,
>   and the rulers take counsel together,
>   against the LORD and his anointed, saying:
> "Let us burst their bonds asunder,
>   and cast their cords from us."
> He who sits in the heavens laughs;
>   the LORD has them in derision.
> Then he will speak to them in his wrath,
>   and terrify them in his fury, saying,
> "I have set my king
>   on Zion, my holy hill."
> I will tell of the decree of the LORD:
> He said to me, "You are my son,
>   today have I begotten you.

the Song of Songs, trans. Richard A. Norris, Writings from the Greco-Roman World 13 (Atlanta: Society of Biblical Literature, 2012).

4. For this point, see Irenaeus of Lyons, *Against the Heresies* 5.30.4 and 5.32.1–2, in *ANF* 1:504, 505–6.

> Ask of me, and I will make the nations your heritage,
> and the ends of the earth your possession.
> You shall break them with a rod of iron,
> and dash them in pieces like a potter's vessel." (Ps 2:1–9)

Christ reigns, and now the enemies, seeing the truth of God, wage war with a new intensity, fighting with the only means they know, producing simulacra of the truth (brilliantly analyzed by Douglas Farrow in his work *Ascension Theology*).[5] Yet the victory is already won, so that Christ reigns until all his enemies are placed under his feet, so that he, in turn, can then subject all things to God, who will thus be all in all (1 Cor 15:24–28).

With Christ enthroned, as the Son, at the right hand of God, the problem posed to David, through the mouthpiece of Nathan, is finally resolved:

> Thus says the Lord: Would you [David] build me a house to dwell in? . . . The LORD declares to you that the LORD will make *you* a house. When your days are fulfilled and you lie down with your fathers, I will raise up your offspring after you, who shall come forth from your body, and I will establish his kingdom. He shall build a house for my name, and I will establish the throne of his kingdom for ever. I will be his father and he shall be my son. . . . And your house and your kingdom shall be made sure for ever before me; your throne shall be established for ever. (2 Sm 7:5, 11–16)

As Douglas Farrow points out, the question here is: "Who would establish whose house—David, Yahweh's or Yahweh, David's?" And Farrow answers: "In the event—the event of one who makes *himself* the temple of the Spirit, and is ultimately brought by the Spirit into the Father's presence—both are true."[6]

Christ has ascended to the right hand of God himself, or perhaps rather, as we will see, as himself the Right Hand of God (Acts 2:33). Is the right hand of God a place within our spatiotemporal cosmos? Clearly not—and we don't need Galileo to tell us that! For the angels already ask: "Why do you stand looking up into the heavens? This Jesus, who was taken up from you into heaven, will come in the same way as you saw him go into heaven" (Acts 1:11). He will come in the same way—that is, on the clouds, for as Christ himself, when asked, "Are you the Christ, the Son of the Blessed One?" replied: "I am, and you shall see the Son of Man seated at the right hand of the Power [on high] and coming with the clouds of heaven"

5. Douglas Farrow, *Ascension Theology* (London: Bloomsbury, 2011), 89–121.
6. Farrow, *Ascension Theology*, 7n14.

(Mk 14:62). It is as the apocalyptic Son of Man, foreseen by Daniel, that Christ is enthroned, and in this way he will come.

In his book *Ascension Theology*, a brilliant reclaiming of the theme and reality of "ascension" in Christian theology, Farrow contrasts two different ways of approaching the ascension of Christ (and ourselves in him) that he sees in the early church and its subsequent history. On the one hand, there is a kind of demythologizing of the idea that a corporeal substance could pass into a realm that is by definition only for spiritual substances. For Origen, the language of ascent and descent cannot be taken in a spatial sense:

> And so, let the Word of God depart toward the one who sent him, leaving the world behind and going to the Father, as we seek to understand the words at the end of the Gospel according to John, "do not touch me, for I have not ascended to the Father," in a mystical sense, thinking of the ascension of the Son to the Father with sanctified insight as an ascension of the mind rather than of the body.[7]

This ascension of the mind correlates, in the common reading of Origen, to a Platonic dualistic worldview—that we are minds trapped in bodies, needing to be liberated from material reality through a spiritualizing process, through our ascension in mind above material reality and its temporal history. Farrow sees this "internalizing" approach lingering through subsequent theological developments: the eucharistic controversy of the Middle Ages, the Reformation, and the Enlightenment, to the position of Schleiermacher that the teaching about Christ's resurrection, ascension, and parousia "cannot be laid down as properly constituent parts of the doctrine of his person," to today, when the ascension is largely forgotten.[8] Although Farrow recognizes that this is "a decisive break with the past rather than a mere turning," he comments:

> But it is nonetheless true that it involves a genuine extension of the Origenist tradition as mediated by Augustine. For what emerges here is not so much a rejection of the doctrine of the ascension as the first really thoroughgoing attempt to interpret it in terms of *the effect Jesus has on us*, rather than in terms of events that belong to his own personal history.[9]

7. Origen, *On Prayer* 23.2, in Alistair Stewart-Sykes, trans., *Tertullian, Cyprian, and Origen, On the Lord's Prayer*, Popular Patristics Series (Crestwood, N.Y.: St. Vladimir's Seminary Press, 2004).

8. Cf. Farrow, *Ascension Theology*, 156, referring to Schleiermacher, *Christian Faith* §99.

9. Farrow, *Ascension Theology*, 26–27; he adds on 29: this "follows a long history of quietly marginalizing the human Jesus, which in my judgment is the chief characteristic of the Origenist option."

Yet this demand for ascending with the mind is a persistent theme throughout the patristic tradition, evident even in those strove against the supposed "Origenist" teachings, such as Maximus, as Farrow notes. As Maximus himself puts it:

> For those who seek the Word of God according to the flesh, the Lord does not ascend to the Father; but to those who seek him out according to the spirit through lofty contemplations, he ascends to the Father. Therefore, let us not constantly hold here below him who for our sake came to be here below out of his love for humanity, but rather let us come to be with him above, with the Father, leaving the earth and all things about the earth.[10]

Against this spiritualizing approach to the ascension, Farrow calls upon Irenaeus, as one who, in his struggles against the Gnostics and gnosticizing tendencies, defended the reality of the human being, body and soul, and the reality of the ascent into heaven of the incarnate Word—in the flesh—and us in him, to share in the glory of the Father

In this approach, the ascension is the fulfillment of created creaturely reality in God. Farrow describes this, in a very precisely constructed phrase, as "a transformative relocation into a time and space and mode of life defined by full participation in the Trinitarian economy."[11] With this definition, Farrow wants to ensure two things. First, that in the ascension, "God does something quite new with and for the man Jesus, as a basis for that which he intends to do with and for us." And, second, "that this something ... is not contrary to his or our creaturely participation.... The ascension is not merely removal *from* a place but also *to* a place," not a progressive spiritualization.[12] As Farrow puts it, Christ

> moves, not upwards in space, but from the old creation to the new. He moves from Egypt and Golgotha and Olives—those places in which we ourselves become old, says Irenaeus, because of transgression—to the place in which righteousness reigns and all the life-giving promises of God are fulfilled. As the Incarnate one, our saviour, Jesus, is always at the right hand of God; indeed he *is* the right hand of God. Yet his entry into the new creation is also his entry into the full dispensation of

10. Maximus the Confessor, *Centuries on Theology* 2.47, in Maximus the Confessor, *Two Hundred Chapters on Theology*, trans. Joshua Sales, Popular Patristics Series (Crestwood, N.Y.: St. Vladimir's Seminary Press, 2015).

11. Farrow, *Ascension Theology*, 44.

12. Farrow, *Ascension Theology*, 45.

the divine power he mediates as saviour, and from this perspective his ascension is rightly spoken of as an exaltation *to* God's right hand.[13]

Farrow stresses word "transformative" in his definition of the ascension to explain the relation between the old and the new. The ascension, he says, "does not entail admission to an already existing place but the creation of a new one. . . . The creation of a new time and place and mode of life and that not *ex nihilo* (out of nothing) but *ex vetere* (out of the old one)." And this transformation, he adds, is already evident in the relation between Isaiah and Genesis; it is an "eschatological discontinuity yet without sacrificing the element of continuity."[14] The place to which Jesus goes, in Farrow's words,

> is really a place, yet it is not one to which we can refer on our own terms, cosmological or otherwise. It is not somewhere in this world, a *Lebensraum* attainable by political or technological conquest; nor yet is it somewhere in addition to this world, an "outside" to which one escapes. Rather it exists by virtue of the transformation or reconstitution of this world in the Spirit. Hence it can be referred to only indirectly. Which is to say, from the place and time in which we ourselves remain it can be recognized only by faith, and can be touched only sacramentally.[15]

This is, he says, "the marriage of heaven and earth, [which was] foreseen by the prophets and witnessed to by the apostles and martyrs of Jesus Christ, entails the complete deconstruction and regeneration of earthly reality."[16] As such, we cannot think about the place now occupied by Jesus as a distant place, whether spatially or temporally (in the sense of "a far-off future, gradually approaching"), nor an interior place, or even one that is "sacramentally interior" ("hidden somehow in the spiritual interstices of the cosmos, which may be pried open by liturgical manipulation").[17] According to Farrow, these "common misconceptions arise from a *non*-eschatological way of thinking," "misguided attempts to say what cannot be said." "All that can be said," according to Farrow,

> is that the time and place which Jesus occupies are those in which and by way of which, God's sovereign act of recreation is extended through him to all times and places. And what kind of act is that? One that we can never hope to describe, cer-

13. Farrow, *Ascension Theology*, 46.
14. Farrow, *Ascension Theology*, 47.
15. Farrow, *Ascension Theology*, 47.
16. Farrow, *Ascension Theology*, 47.
17. Farrow, *Ascension Theology*, 48.

tainly, but one whose foundation—the cross and resurrection—we have already witnessed and whose consequences we will all experience at the parousia.[18]

"Where I am going you cannot come," declares Jesus. And Farrow adds—we cannot comprehend or locate where he is going on any map we have. But, he adds, this doesn't mean that all we can do is return to an "Origenist model," or one in which Jesus is "thought to be atopic or atemporal (that is, without place or time of his own, beyond those of his life from Bethlehem to Golgotha)." Nor is it "acosmic"—merely "the meaning of the Christ event"—in some kind of spiritual psychology. Rather,

> an eschatological approach to the doctrine of the ascension insists with Scripture and creed on bodily ascension. It is Irenaean and incarnational, hence completely committed to speaking about every dimension of creaturely existence. At the same time it remains stubbornly independent of any merely natural cosmology or anthropology which, without knowledge of the resurrection or ascension, must lack knowledge even of its own limitations.[19]

Farrow rightly emphasizes the eschatological and transformative dynamic of the ascension. But, before we agree too hastily that the patristic tradition is divided into two tendencies—an Origenist spiritualizing tendency and an Irenaean incarnational approach—we should look a bit more deeply, for the emphasis on transformation is evident in both, and might help us not only understand each but also what is meant by each. Perhaps there is more in what is meant by saying that the Word assumed (or takes up) a body.

Returning to Origen, he consistently connects Christ's lordship with his exaltation on the cross: "the Son became king through suffering the cross."[20] In the last section of the last book of *Commentary on John*, treating the departure of Jesus—"where I am going you cannot follow me now," yet, "I go to prepare a place for you" (Jn 13:36; 14:2)—Origen expounds more fully what is meant by this exaltation, in striking terms:

> Now I think God also highly exalted this man when he became obedient *unto death, and the death of a cross*. For the Word in the beginning with God, God the Word, was not capable of being highly exalted. But the high exaltation of the Son of Man

18. Farrow, *Ascension Theology*, 48.

19. Farrow, *Ascension Theology*, 49.

20. Origen, *Commentary on John* 1.278, in Erwin Preuschen, ed., *Origenes Werke*, vol. 4, *Der Johanneskommentar*, GCS 10 (Leipzig: Hinrichs, 1903); translation from Origen, *Commentary on the Gospel of John*, trans. Ronald E Heine, Fathers of the Church 80, 89 (Washington, D.C.: The Catholic University of America Press, 1989). Further quotations are taken from this translation.

which occurred when he glorified God in his own death consisted in the fact that he was no longer different from the Word but was the same with him [ἡ δὲ ὑπερύψωσις τοῦ υἱοῦ τοῦ ἀνθρώπου, γενομένη αὐτῷ δοξάσαντι τὸν θεὸν ἐν τῷ ἑαυτοῦ θανάτῳ, αὕτη ἦν, τὸ μηκέτι ἕτερον αὐτὸν εἶναι τοῦ λόγου ἀλλὰ τὸν αὐτὸν αὐτῷ]. For if *he who is joined to the Lord is one spirit,* so that it is no longer said that *they are two,* even in the case of this man and the spirit, might we not much more say that the humanity of Jesus became one with the Word when he who did not consider *equality with God* something to be grasped was highly exalted? [Phil. 2:6] The Word, however, remained in his own grandeur, or was even restored to it, when he was again with God, God the Word being man.[21]

The unity of the God-man is effected upon the cross, for after it, and in its light, we can no longer differentiate between human and divine properties: we no longer know Christ by a set of fleshly properties, but now we know him as the Word of God. It is on the cross that we finally see the true form and divinity of the Son of God, and from this moment on no longer "see" Jesus with our bodily perception, for, as Paul says, "even though we once knew Christ according to the flesh, we know him thus no longer" (2 Cor 5:16).

It might sound rather "adoptionist" and even seems to anticipate Diodore of Tarsus and Theodore of Mopsuestia.[22] But it is, nevertheless, what we are in fact given to see in the Synoptic Gospels, and especially in the Letter to the Hebrews and Revelation. It is also something that is found not only in earlier writers but also in the later Orthodox tradition. According to Ignatius of Antioch, for instance: "Our God Jesus Christ, now he is in the Father, is all the more visible."[23] More visible than he was before—not less—even though we no longer see him in the flesh.

The most striking similarities are with Gregory of Nyssa, often held to be the most "Origenist" of the Cappadocian Fathers, yet recognized, at the Seventh Ecumenical Council, as "being called by all the father of the fathers."[24] In *Against Eunomius* 3.3, Gregory expounds the statement of Peter in Acts that "God made him both Lord and Christ, this Jesus whom you crucified" (Acts 2:36), and does so largely through the word from Peter's

21. Origen, *Commentary on John* 32.324–26.

22. See John Behr, *The Case against Diodore and Theodore: Texts and Their Contexts,* Oxford Early Christian Texts (Oxford: Oxford University Press, 2011). See the passages preserved of Theodore preserved by Leontius (LT 2–6, *Case,* 284–91).

23. Ignatius of Antioch, *Epistle to the Romans* 3, in Alistair Stewart, trans., *Ignatius of Antioch: The Letters,* Popular Patristics Series 49 (Crestwood N.Y.: St Vladimir's Seminary Press, 2013), 69. Further quotations from Ignatius's letters are from this translation.

24. *Acta,* sixth session, vol. 5; Mansi 13:293e.

speech a few verses earlier, that Jesus was "exalted by the Right Hand of God" (Acts 2:33), reading the dative as expressing agency, rather than "to the right hand" as most modern translations do.[25]

According to Gregory, Eunomius takes the Son's suffering upon the cross as a mark of distinction between him and the impassible Father; but for Gregory it instead reveals "the supreme exercise of his power" rather than "an indication of weakness," showing that "the God made manifest through the Cross ought to be honored just as the Father is honored."[26] Moreover, he continues: "We say that the body also, in which he accepted the passion, being combined with the divine nature, was by that commingling made into that which the assuming nature is." With regard to Peter's words, Gregory points out that it is not as though there are two subjects here, but rather, "Scripture says that two things have been done to a single person, the passion by the Jews, the honor by God, not as though there was one who suffered and another who was honored by the exaltation."[27] This is shown even more clearly, for Gregory, when Peter says he was "exalted by the Right Hand of God." As Gregory explains: "The Apostle said that the humanity [τὸ ἀνθρώπινον] was exalted, being exalted by becoming Lord and Christ; and this took place after the passion."[28] He then continues in stronger terms:

> He who says *exalted by the Right Hand of God* clearly reveals the unspeakable economy of the mystery, that the Right Hand of God, who made all things that are, who is the Lord by whom all things were made and without whom nothing that is subsists, himself raised to his own height the human being [τὸν ... ἄνθρωπον] united to him, making him also, by the commixture, to be what he is by nature: he is Lord and King, and the King is called Christ; these things he made him too.... And this we are plainly taught by the voice of the Peter in his mystic discourse, that the lowliness of the one crucified in weakness (and weakness, as we have heard from the Lord, indicates the flesh [Mt 26.41]), that, by virtue of its mingling with the infinite and boundless [nature] of the Good, remained no longer in its own measures and properties, but by the Right Hand of God was raised up together, and became Lord instead of servant, Christ the King instead of a subject, highest instead of lowly, God instead of man.[29]

25. Gregory of Nyssa, *Against Eunomius* 3.3, in GNO 2:107–33; translation from William Moore and Henry Austin Wilson, in *NPNF*² 5:172–81, where it is numbered, according to the older numeration, as *Against Eunomius* 5; the sections are also numbered differently there. Further quotations are from this translation.

26. Gregory of Nyssa, *Eun.* 3.3.30–34.

27. Gregory of Nyssa, *Eun.* 3.3.42.

28. Gregory of Nyssa, *Eun.* 3.3.43.

29. Gregory of Nyssa, *Eun.* 3.3.44.

Again, this might also sound like some kind of adoptionism, but it is not. Rather, to paraphrase Gregory's argument here and throughout *Against Eunomius* 3.3: through the passion, Christ, as human, becomes that which as God he always is. The exaltation, effected this way, raises Christ's human nature (or as Gregory says "the human being")—that which he assumes—to be what Christ is by nature: the body in which he undergoes the passion is made, through the passion, to share in the properties of the assuming nature.

Jesus Christ is, as Gregory repeatedly asserts in this text, "the God revealed through the cross": where the cross stands, as it were, as a synecdoche for all the events of the passion—the crucifixion, resurrection, ascension, and bestowal of the Spirit—all of which are held together by John: Christ ascends in glory upon the cross, and from the cross bestows the Spirit (Jn 19:30).[30] The cross stands as a synecdoche, for it is the last publicly visible image of Christ on earth: For the resurrected Christ doesn't appear publicly to all, and even those to whom he does appear don't at first recognize him. There is always some stage through which they have to pass before they recognize him.

The cross, then, is our lens and prism for understanding the revelation of God in Christ; as a lens it brings into focus "the God revealed through the Cross," and as a prism, it enables us to look at the different aspects involved in the passion, never forgetting that they all hold together as one single mystery. If we were to attempt to theologize apart from the cross, to see God revealed in Christ apart from the passion (after which we no longer know him in the flesh) we will end up defining divinity in human terms. If we, for instance, attempt to look behind the cross to see Jesus before the passion, as if the passion had never happened (rather unhistorical in its attempt to be historical), we will end up seeing Jesus as he appears in his human properties, as the son of the carpenter from Nazareth; we will not "see," or rather intellectually contemplate, the Word of God, and so will not be doing theology. This is Gregory's chief complaint about Apollinarius:

On a true interpretation Christ is both man and God: in respect of sight he is man; in respect of rational thought, God. That is not what Apollinarius says: in his con-

30. See John Ashton, *Understanding the Fourth Gospel*, 2nd ed. (Oxford: Oxford University Press, 2007), 347–48: "Now the expression παραδιδόναι τὸ πνεῦμα ["to hand over the Spirit," cf. Jn 19:30] allows him to fuse Easter and Pentecost as well, hinting that there is no need to think of the latter as a distinct and separate event."

clusions he characterizes the divine by reference to what is seen rather than what can be known by the mind.[31]

To define incarnation in terms of the divine coming to be in human form, within the spatiotemporal framework of this cosmos, misses the mark.

If, on the other hand, we do not attempt to look behind the cross, but look *through* the cross, we see the unchanging identity of the crucified one throughout his life, from his birth from the Virgin and throughout his ministry. This is, of course, the same hermeneutic needed to read Scripture and encounter the Word of God: If we stay at the level of the letters, the flesh, we will never come to contemplate the Word. The transformative aspect of the ascension (as part of the spectrum of colors refracted by the prism of the cross) is indeed vital, as Farrow rightly argues. Ascension is "from a place and to a place," but this place is not now defined in terms of our spatiotemporal cosmos; it is not so much a place *at* the right hand, in a spatial sense, but rather *as* the Right Hand of God. Christ *is* the "place" of God—"I go to prepare a place for you" (Jn 14:2)—for in him dwells the fullness of divinity bodily (Col 2:9), and indwelling in a transformative manner.

Origen's image of a piece of iron placed in the fire gives a vivid sense of what is involved in this transformation.[32] A piece of iron, which is identified by certain properties (cold and hard), when placed in a fire loses all those properties, while yet remaining the iron that it is, to become identified by the properties of the fire (hot and fluid). So also the human nature of Jesus (identified by certain sense-perceptible, spatiotemporal, human properties) is no longer known by these properties, but rather by the properties of God, being beyond space and time; it is revealed, as we have seen, in and through the transformation and exaltation effected through the cross, when this is understood by intellectual contemplation rather than physical sight, and as he passes out of physical sight.

As the fire assumes the iron into itself, and transforms it into itself—the iron remains iron, but is only known by the properties of fire—the fire is now, in turn, embodied as it were in the iron. Divinity likewise has, through

31. *Refutation of the Views of Apollinarius* 23, in Gregory of Nyssa, *Antirrheticus* (GNO 3.1:191, lines 24–27): οὐκοῦν κατὰ τὸν ἀληθῆ λόγον καὶ ἄνθρωπος ἐστι καὶ θεός, τῷ ὁρωμένῳ ἄνθρωπος, τῷ νοουμένῳ θεός. ὁ δὲ οὐ τοῦτό φησιν, ἐν τῷ συμπεράσματι τῷ φαινομένῳ τὸ θεῖον, οὐ τῷ νοητῷ ὁριζόμενος; translation from St. Gregory of Nyssa, *Refutation of the Views of Apollinarius,* in *Anti-Apollinarian Writings,* trans. Robin Orton (Washington, D.C.: The Catholic University of America Press, 2015), 189.

32. Origen, *On First Principles* 2.6, in Origen, *On First Principles,* ed. and trans. John Behr, Oxford Early Christian Texts (Oxford: Oxford University Press, forthcoming).

the ascension, assumed the human nature of Christ into itself: it now has a body, it is incarnate, but in a body that is no longer subject to the spatiotemporal constraints of our cosmos; it is, rather, the very body of God, beyond all space and time.

If this is the case, then the supposed "Origenist" emphasis on the ascent of the mind and the Irenaean emphasis on incarnation are not opposed to each other, but correlative. We must not, as Gregory of Nyssa urges against Apollinarius, define the divine in terms of appearance in the flesh, but rather raise up our minds to understand the reality that lies eternally before us, hanging on the cross and passing over into God. Christ, seated at the right hand of God, *is* the Right Hand of God, who, together with the Spirit, are the Hands of God bringing the creature, made from mud, to perfection, sharing in the power and glory of God and transformed by that participation.

At the right hand of God, and as the Right Hand of God, he will come as we saw him depart, on the clouds as the Son of Man. And the true witnesses of this are the martyrs: As Ignatius says, on the way to his martyrdom:

> Birth-pangs are upon me. Suffer me, my brethren; hinder me not from living, do not wish me to die. . . . Suffer me to receive the pure light; when I shall have arrived there, I shall become a human being. Suffer me to follow the example of the passion of my God.[33]

He will receive the light, born into life, and become a "human being": I would suggest that the Greek word here—ἄνθρωπος—bears the weight of its Semitic counterpart, the "Son of Man," so that Ignatius expects to become a Son of Man, just as did Enoch.[34] He, moreover, also begs the Roman Christians to be silent, so that he may be "a word of God" and not merely a "cry."[35] Christ will return as we saw him depart, and "we know that when he appears we shall be like him, for we shall see him as he is" (1 Jn 3:2). Let us, then, as Gregory the Theologian exhorts us, lay aside "the earthbound carnality of our minds," and ascend with Christ in our minds, so as to be transformed with him in our body.[36]

33. Ignatius, *Rom.* 6.

34. See 1 Enoch 70–71. George W. E. Nickelsburg and James C. VanderKam, trans., *First Enoch: A New Translation* (Minneapolis: Fortress, 2004).

35. Ignatius, *Rom.* 2.

36. See Gregory of Nazianzus, *Or.* 29.18, in St. Gregory of Nazianzus, *On God and Christ: The Five Theological Orations and Two Letters to Cledonius*, trans. Frederick Williams and Lionel Wickham, Popular Patristics Series (Crestwood, N.Y.: St. Vladimir's Seminary Press, 2002).

RESPONSE

Ascension of an Immaterial Body

With Contributions from Nicholas of Cusa, Jonathan Edwards, and Gregory of Nyssa

Hans Boersma (Evangelical)

In the year 1454, the German theologian Nicholas of Cusa (1401–1464) sent a twofold gift of encouragement to the monks of the Benedictine community at Tegernsee: a newly penned book of his, *De visione Dei*, along with an icon, likely of the face of Christ.[37] At the beginning of his treatise, Cusa asks the monks to engage in an experiment:

> I am sending, to your charity, a painting that I was able to acquire containing an all-seeing image, which I call an icon of God.
>
> Hang this up some place, perhaps on a north wall. And you brothers stand around it, equally distant from it, and gaze at it. And each of you will experience that from whatever place one observes it the face will seem to regard him alone. To a brother standing in the east, the face will look eastward; to one in the south, it will look southward; and to one in the west, westward. First, therefore, you will marvel at how it is possible that the face looks on all and each one of you at the same time.... Next, let the brother who was in the east place himself in the west, and he will experience the gaze as fastened on him there just as it was before in the east. Since he knows that the icon is fixed and unchanged, he will marvel at the changing of its unchangeable gaze.[38]

Nicholas draws attention to the fact that no matter where a monk may place himself with respect to the icon, the face depicted in it appears to look at him directly. Of course, as both Cusa and the Benedictine monks are aware, in reality the Christ figure looks not just on one individual, but on every

37. Most of the material in this essay appeared in a variant form in Hans Boersma, *Seeing God* (Grand Rapids: Eerdmans, 2018), chapter 14.

38. Nicholas of Cusa, *On the Vision of God*, preface. All translations of Nicholas of Cusa, *On the Vision of God*, are from *Selected Spiritual Writings*, trans. and ed. H. Lawrence Bond (Mahwah, N.J.: Paulist Press, 1997)

one of the monks at the same time, regardless of where they place themselves in relation to the icon. With this experiment, Cusa draws our attention to the meticulous and loving providential care of God for each and every one of us.

In this response to Fr. Behr's chapter, I will attempt to provide support for one of its main arguments, namely, that the Origenist spiritualizing tendency and the Irenaean incarnational approach are not opposed to one another but share an eschatology that regards temporal and spatial realities as being in need of transformation so as to be fitted for the eschaton. I have long been convinced that it is not only Irenaeus who—against all gnosticizing of God's good creation—had a high view of embodiment, but that all the required ingredients for a positive evaluation of the body are present in the Christian Platonist tradition of East and West. It is not only Irenaeus but also the tradition following in the footsteps of Origen in the East and of Augustine in the West that maintained that Christ had bodily ascended to the right hand of the Father and that his ascended body is the firstfruits and guarantee of our bodily resurrection on the day of judgment.[39] We need the Christian Platonism that has characterized much of the tradition, in order to provide proper theological and metaphysical support for the doctrine of the ascension as well as for a proper understanding of embodiment and creation more broadly understood.

I don't know whether Fr. Behr will welcome my Christian Platonist support of his argument that Irenaeus's and Origen's approaches are complementary rather than contradictory. My thesis goes beyond what he argues in his chapter; in particular, I will look to the idealist tradition of Christian Platonism to defend the spiritualizing tendency of the Origenists, and Fr. Behr may or may not follow me in this. The view I will put forward is that expressed by Nicholas of Cusa and others in the Christian Platonist tradition, namely, that it is God's gaze in Christ that lovingly calls creation into being and sustains it in its created form, both in this temporal life and in the future resurrection. Whatever Fr. Behr's stance may be on this, on the idealist understanding of matter, or on the Christian Platonist tradition within which this idealism has its place, my overriding point is the following: An idealist view of matter, which lies deeply embedded within Christian Platonism, allows us to view

39. It seems to me that Douglas Farrow's disjunction of the Irenaean incarnational approach and the Origenist spiritualizing tendency does not do proper justice to the incarnational element that characterizes almost all of the Christian tradition. See my review of Douglas Farrow's *Ascension Theology* (London: T&T Clark, 2011) in *First Things*, August/September 2011, 62–63.

the Origenist and Irenaean approaches as complementary rather than contradictory, which is one of the key points Fr. Behr makes in his chapter. And I will add the further corollary that this metaphysical understanding of creation provides us with an invaluable tool in defense of the embodied character of the ascension and hence of the resurrection of the body—though it entails a view of matter and of the body that radically rejects the modern seclusion of the natural, material order as something independent and separate from the life of God in Jesus Christ.

It is with good reason that Nicholas of Cusa asked the monks of Tegernsee to subject themselves to the gaze of Christ. He was convinced that it is only God's vision that sustains our embodied being. After a few introductory chapters, Nicholas turns his treatise into the form of a prayer, and he addresses the God who looks on him (as well as on the monks of Tegernsee):

> Lord, in this image of you I now behold your providence by a certain sensible experience. For if you do not abandon me, the vilest of all, you will never abandon anyone.... By no imagining, Lord, do you allow me to conceive that you love anything other than me more than me, for it is I alone that your gaze does not abandon. And since the eye is there wherever love is, I experience that you love me because your eyes rest most attentively on me, your humble servant. Your seeing, Lord, is your loving.[40]

Cusa is enthralled with God's vision of himself and of all reality. God's face is a face whose "eye reaches all things without turning" and in so doing loves all things.[41] This love of God causes Cusa in turn to love God. It feeds him and kindles his desires, so that he drinks of the dew of gladness, which becomes a "fountain of life" inside him.[42] The end result of God's seeing is the communication of immortality and, thus, "eternal happiness."[43]

For Nicholas, the *visio Dei* of the title of his book is, in the first place, a subjective genitive. It speaks of God's all-seeing, unchangeable gaze of hu-

40. Nicholas of Cusa, *On the Vision of God* 4.9–10.

41. In typically Platonic fashion, Cusa maintains that God always and only looks on us in providential love and mercy, communicating to us immortality and happiness. When we miss out on the loving glance of God it is not because God is not looking on us in love but simply because by our free will we have decided to look away from his face. Thus Nicholas comments that God never changes his eyes or his gaze: "If you do not look upon me with the eye of grace, I am at fault because I have separated myself from you by turning away toward some other, which I prefer to you" (*On the Vision of God* 5.14). Similarly, Nicholas suggests: "And the more one strives to look on you with greater love, the more loving will one find your face. Whoever looks on you with anger will likewise find your face angry" (*On the Vision of God* 6.19).

42. Nicholas of Cusa, *On the Vision of God* 4.12.

43. Nicholas of Cusa, *On the Vision of God* 4.12.

manity in love and mercy. To be sure, the treatise also speaks of our vision of God, but on Nicholas's understanding, our vision of God is invariably predicated on his vision of us.[44] We cannot see God without his first seeing us. In fact, since Nicholas explicitly identifies God's gaze with his providential love, it would not be too far of a stretch to suggest that Nicholas believed in a *creatio continua* of sorts, in which the created order perdures only inasmuch as it is upheld by the loving gaze of God.[45] Cusa confesses: "I exist only insomuch as you are with me. And since your seeing is your being, therefore, because you regard me, I am, and if you remove your face from me, I will cease to be."[46] Our vision of God is always only in response to God's vision of us. Put differently, if God's vision of the world is the emanation of creation from the being of God, our vision of him constitutes our deifying return to him.

Nicholas discusses also the vision we have of God. He bases it in the beauty of the face of God, which attracts our loving gaze: "Every face has beauty, but none is beauty itself. Your face, Lord, has beauty, and this having is being. It is thus absolute beauty itself, which is the form that gives being to every form of beauty. O immeasurably lovely Face, your beauty is such that all things to which are granted to behold it are not sufficient to admire it."[47] God's face, according to Nicholas, is beauty itself. We see this "face of faces" in veiled fashion by looking into the faces of those around us.[48]

44. Cf. Jean-Luc Marion's comment: "Je peux bien dire que je vois Dieu, mais cela ne se peut que si Dieu, ce Dieu qui reste un Dieu caché, me le concède; et il ne donne d'être vu par quelqu'un d'autre, qu'en le lui donnant, donc en voyant lui-même et d'abord ce quelqu'un qui, alors, éventuellement le verra. Il faut pour qu'un visage voie le visage de Dieu, que se visage, Dieu le tourne d'abord vers ceux qui le regardent" ("I may well say that I see God, but this can only be if God, this God who remains a hidden God, grants it to me. And he only lets himself be seen by someone else by giving himself to him, so by himself first seeing this someone who will thus eventually see him. For a face to see the face of God, God must first turn this face towards those who look at him") ("Voir, se voir vu: L'Apport de Nicolas de Cues dans le *De visione Dei*," *Bulletin de Littérature Ecclésiastique* 117, no. 2 [April 2016]: 7–37, at 18–19).

45. Marion notes that for Nicholas of Cusa God's gaze is always already a loving gaze: "L'intentionnalité [du regard de Dieu] n'aboutit pas à l'objectité, ni ne vise un objet, mais déploie l'amour et vise un aimé, qui peut alors devenir en retour un amant" ("The intentionality [of the gaze of God] does not lead to 'objecthood,' nor does it aim at an object, but extends love and aims at a beloved, who can then in turn become a lover") ("Voir, se voir vu," 35).

46. Nicholas of Cusa, *On the Vision of God* 4.10. Cusa similarly comments a little later: "Your seeing is nothing other than your bringing to life, nothing other than your continuously imparting your sweetest love" (*On the Vision of God* 4.12). Again, he states: "You are visible by all creatures and you see all. In that you see all you are seen by all. For otherwise creatures cannot exist since they exist by your vision. If they did not see you who see, they would not receive being from you. The being of a creature is equally your seeing and your being seen" (*On the Vision of God* 10.40).

47. Nicholas of Cusa, *On the Vision of God* 4.10.

48. Nicholas of Cusa, *On the Vision of God* 4.10.

But the eye seeks to see the light that is beyond all visible light. As a result, the eye "knows that so long as it sees anything, what it sees is not what it is seeking."[49] Only when we enter into the cloud—a picture derived from the Christian Platonist tradition reaching back via Dionysius to Gregory of Nyssa—do we see the invisible light of the beauty of God: "The denser, therefore, one knows the cloud to be the more one truly attains to the invisible light in the cloud."[50] For Nicholas of Cusa, the notion of "invisible light" bespeaks the recognition that God can be found only after we willingly enter into the cloud and in doing so acknowledge what Cusa terms the "coincidence of opposites" (*coincidentia oppositorum*)—the deeper the obscurity of the cloud, the more clearly we see the brilliance of the light of God's face.[51]

The eighteenth-century Reformed philosopher-theologian Jonathan Edwards (1703–1758) had a theological and metaphysical approach similar to that of Nicholas of Cusa. I have no evidence that Edwards was actually familiar with Cusa's treatment of the beatific vision. Nonetheless, had he read Cusa's *De visione Dei,* I suspect he would have been enthralled by it. Edwards's own theological approach, like that of Cusa, was deeply grounded in the Christian Platonist tradition, probably mostly as a result of his reading of the Cambridge Platonists. The result is that Edwards, too, thought of the beatific vision as being caught up in God's loving gaze on us. For Edwards, as for Cusa, the beatific vision means that we enter ever more gloriously into the light of God's face.[52] It is hardly surprising that previous scholarship

49. Nicholas of Cusa, *On the Vision of God* 6.21.

50. Nicholas of Cusa, *On the Vision of God* 6.21.

51. Cf. Nicholas's comment: "I admit that darkness is light, ignorance knowledge, and the impossible necessary. . . . We are admitting, therefore, the coincidence of contradictories, above which is the infinite. But this coincidence is a contradiction without contradiction, and it is an end without end" (*On the Vision of God* 13.53). It is important to recall that for Nicholas this vision of God is presented in a profoundly trinitarian and christological fashion—and here he clearly advances beyond Dionysius. Moving inside the cloud (or beyond the wall of the coincidence of opposites), the believer enters Paradise, where he encounters Jesus as the Tree of Life. Turning to him in prayer, Nicholas writes, "O Jesus, you are the Tree of Life in the paradise of delights. For none can be fed by that desirable life except from your fruit. . . . Just as everyone is bound to you, O Jesus, by a human nature common to oneself and to you, so one must also be united to you in one spirit in order that thus in one's nature, which is common with you, Jesus, one can draw near to God, the Father, who is in paradise. Therefore, to see God the Father and you, Jesus, his Son, is to be in paradise and everlasting glory. For outside paradise one cannot have such a vision since neither God, the Father, nor you, Jesus, are able to be found outside paradise. Therefore, every human being who has attained happiness is united to you, O Jesus, as a member is united to its head" (*On the Vision of God* 21.92).

52. This is not to deny obvious (and significant) differences between Edwards and Cusa. For Edwards, the history of redemption takes on much greater prominence than for Cusa. Edwards's theology of vision does not use the "cloud" language of the apophatic tradition (and does not revel in its paradoxical

has detected similarities between Edwards and Maximus the Confessor as well as between Edwards and Gregory Palamas.[53] The similarities are genuine in my opinion, as are the similarities with regard to the vision of God between Cusa and Edwards, because the Puritan pastor deliberately grounded his theology within the patristic and Neoplatonic traditions.

One statement of Cusa, in particular, would have held great appeal to Jonathan Edwards: "In that you see all you are seen by all. For otherwise creatures cannot exist since they exist by your vision."[54] For Edwards, as for Cusa, the creature exists only by God's vision. Our existence from moment to moment is the result of being seen by God. Edwards, like Cusa, was convinced that it is only in and through divine perception that created reality has being. As he puts it in his "Notes on Knowledge and Existence": "All existence is perception. What we call body is nothing but a particular mode of perception; and what we call spirit is nothing but a composition and series of perceptions, or an universe of coexisting and successive perceptions connected by such wonderful methods and laws."[55] The result is that, for Edwards, the only substance that truly exists is God himself. As Edwards comments in his notebook "Of Atoms": "The substance of bodies at last becomes either nothing, or nothing but the Deity acting in that particular manner in those parts of space where he thinks fit. So that, speaking most strictly, there is no proper substance but God himself (we speak at present with respect to bodies only). How truly, then, is he said to be *ens entium* [being of beings]."[56] Put differently, for Edwards, there are no created substances apart from the one substance that only and truly exists, namely, God himself. On Edwards's understanding, only the idealist notion that "to be is to be perceived" (*esse est percipi*) would suffice to counter properly

language). For Edwards, unlike for Cusa, the beatific vision is not just spiritual but also bodily in character (see Hans Boersma, "The 'Grand Medium': An Edwardsean Modification of Thomas Aquinas on the Beatific Vision." *Modern Theology* 33, no. 2 [2016]: 187–212). Furthermore, Edwards's occasionalism makes him resistant to free will, whereas for Cusa it is precisely free will that causes us to turn away from the vision of God and lapse into nonbeing.

53. See Michael Gibson, "The Beauty of the Redemption of the World: The Theological Aesthetics of Maximus the Confessor and Jonathan Edwards," *Harvard Theological Review* 101, no. 1 (2008): 45–76; Michael J. McClymond, "Salvation as Divinization: Jonathan Edwards, Gregory Palamas and the Theological Uses of Neoplatonism," in *Jonathan Edwards: Philosophical Theologian*, ed. Paul Helm and Oliver Crisp (Burlington, Vt.: Ashgate, 2003), 139–60.

54. Nicholas of Cusa, *On the Vision of God* 10.40.

55. Jonathan Edwards, "Notes on Knowledge and Existence," in *Works of Jonathan Edwards* (hereafter cited as *WJE*), vol. 6, *Scientific and Philosophical Writings*, ed. Wallace E. Anderson (New Haven: Yale University Press, 1980), 378.

56. Jonathan Edwards, "Of Atoms," *WJE* 6:215.

the baleful impact of materialism. For Edwards, matter simply doesn't exist, except in the sense that God's loving gaze continually calls forth the ideas of his mind. The notion of a material substance, a substratum that underlies the properties that we perceive with the senses, seemed nonsensical to Edwards.

Edwards staunchly opposed the materialism of Thomas Hobbes, which to many in the eighteenth century held great appeal. To Edwards, it was not adequate to counter materialism by resorting to a division of reality into form and matter. Edwards would have regarded Aristotelian hylomorphism as incapable of countering the materialism of modernity. For Edwards, Thomas Aquinas would have been far too Aristotelian. Aquinas, following the Stagirite on this score, had emphasized the importance of sense perception and had treated empirical objects as consisting of substance and accidents. As a result, he had argued by way of analogy from empirical sense data to the existence of God. Edwards nearly turned this Thomist approach to analogy upside down. William S. Morris puts it as follows:

> Edwards argued that rationally we must conceive of God as substance, and argue by analogy from God to the creature. For the creature exists only in God, and the substantiality of any material thing is only substance by participation. Edwards argued from reason and idea to sense, not from sense to reason and idea. He argued from the creator to the creature, not from the creature to the creator. We know the shadow by the substance, and not the substance from the shadow. Spirit is substance, and body is shadow. In metaphysics, reason argues *to* sense, rather than *from* sense. God is known immediately, not mediately and by inference.[57]

One may or may not agree that idealism implies the rejection of Thomas's doctrine of analogy. One may well argue that also with idealist and Platonist convictions, it is possible to argue rationally from the shadows to the substance. Still, Morris's overall point is well taken: for Edwards, the creature only has existence in God, and Edwards's metaphysics was deeply influenced by Platonic assumptions, one of which is the immateriality of empirically observable realities. Morris puts it well when he comments: "If he [Edwards] had had to choose between Plato and Aristotle for philosophic mentor, he would politely have turned aside from the Stagirite."[58]

Since Edwards holds that creation exists from moment to moment sim-

57. William Sparkes Morris, *The Young Jonathan Edwards: A Reconstruction* (New Haven: Jonathan Edwards Center at Yale University; repr., Eugene, OR: Wipf and Stock, 2005), 427–28.

58. Morris, *Young Jonathan Edwards*, 428.

ply by being perceived, the created order does not have independent stability for him. Created beings are constantly in flux, and it is only through God's sovereign and loving gaze that created things have continuity in their being. Creation, explains Seng-Kong Tan, is for Edwards a "continuous *ex nihilo* operation."[59] Created entities have their being only in God's *creatio continua*, that is to say, in his continuous perception of them. Edwards—and on this point he undoubtedly differed from Nicholas of Cusa—grounded his metaphysical idealism in his deeply held Calvinist conviction of the sovereignty of God. It is only the will of God, according to Edwards, that allows for the continuity of created objects and for the stability and reliability of the world around us: "When I call this an arbitrary constitution, I mean, that it is a constitution which depends on nothing but the divine will; which *divine will* depends on nothing but the *divine wisdom*. In this sense, the whole course of nature, with all that belongs to it, all its laws and methods, and constancy and regularity, continuance and proceeding, is an *arbitrary constitution*."[60]

Oliver Crisp rightly terms Edwards's approach *occasionalist*, meaning that God "continually creates the world *ex nihilo* moment-by-moment" and that "God is the only causal act in the world," so that "creaturely 'acts' are merely the 'occasions' of God's activity."[61] Crisp compares God's continuous creation in Edwards to watching a movie:

> When watching a movie at the cinema we appear to see a sequence of actions across time represented in the projected images on the silver screen. But in reality, the images are a reel of photographic stills run together at speed to give the illusion of motion and action across time. Similarly with occasionalism: the world seems to persist through time, but in fact it does not. "The world" (meaning here, the created cosmos) is merely shorthand for that series of created "stills"—that is, the complete, maximal, but momentary states of affairs—God brings about in sequence, playing, as it were on the silver screen of the divine mind.[62]

By closely linking his immaterialist metaphysics to his Calvinist occasionalism, Edwards devised a rather distinctive version of idealism. After all,

59. Seng-Kong Tan, "Jonathan Edwards's Dynamic Idealism and Cosmic Christology," in *Idealism and Christian Theology*, ed. Joshua R. Farris, S. Mark Hamilton, and James S. Spiegel, Idealism and Christianity 1 (New York: Bloomsbury Academic, 2016), 239.

60. Jonathan Edwards, *WJE*, vol. 3, *Original Sin*, ed. Clyde A. Holbrook (New Haven: Yale University Press, 1970), 403; italics original. Cf. Tan, "Jonathan Edwards's Dynamic Idealism," 241.

61. Oliver D. Crisp, "Jonathan Edwards's Ontology: A Critique of Sang Hyun Lee's Dispositional Account of Edwardsian Metaphysics," *Religious Studies* 46, no. 1 (2010): 1–20, at 10.

62. Crisp, "Jonathan Edwards's Ontology," 10.

we encounter other forms of idealism in earlier Christian Platonists such as Gregory of Nyssa and Nicholas of Cusa. Neither of them lapsed into the monergism that characterizes Edwards's thought. To be sure, Edwards's idealism and his occasionalism make for a logical fit, but the Christian Platonist background of immaterialism suggests that idealism does not necessarily entail occasionalism.

To my knowledge Edwards never connected his idealist view of matter with questions of the ascension of Christ or of the body's eternal future. Some have hinted that Edwards may have seen some connection between his idealism and his eschatology. Robert Caldwell suggests that "Edwards's reflections on the 'physics' of heaven and the nature of the saints' glorified bodies there remain some of the most fascinating (if not the most speculative) reflections in all of his writings."[63] Indeed, Edwards speculates, for instance, that in heaven the bodily senses will allow the saints to converse with people at "a thousand miles' distance."[64] The bodies of the saints will be attuned, maintains Edwards, to every physical pleasure, though in such a way that this pleasure will contribute also to spiritual pleasure.[65] These eschatological musings certainly make for interesting reading. And though Edwards nowhere provides a metaphysical underpinning for these eschatological observations, it seems to me he easily could have done so. In the remainder of this chapter I will suggest that it is precisely his idealist view of matter that would have provided him with a framework for these eschatological speculations with regard to the body and sense perception.

In order to make this argument, I will turn briefly to the fourth-century Cappadocian Gregory of Nyssa (ca. 335–ca. 394), who as a Christian Platonist was deeply influenced by Origen, and whose view of matter—and of the human body in particular—was quite similar to the later understanding of Jonathan Edwards. To be sure, Nyssen never argued that that to be is to be perceived. In that sense, the icon's gaze would not have held the same theological significance for him as it later did for Nicholas of Cusa and for Jonathan Edwards. Nonetheless, Gregory of Nyssa, like Edwards, was an immaterialist, and he developed the implications of his metaphysics specifically with regard to the human body, as he recognized the possibilities

63. Robert Caldwell, "A Brief History of Heaven in the Writings of Jonathan Edwards," *Calvin Theological Journal* 46, no. 1 (2011): 48–71, at 66.

64. Edwards, "Miscellanies" No. 263, in *WJE*, vol. 13, *The "Miscellanies," a–500*, ed. Harry S. Stout (New Haven: Yale University Press, 1994), 369. Cf. Caldwell, "Brief History of Heaven," 6.

65. Edwards, "Miscellanies" No. 233, in *WJE* 13:350–51. Cf. Caldwell, "Brief History of Heaven," 67.

that his immaterialism held out for an articulation of the resurrection of the body.

Gregory, much like Edwards, regarded the human body as fluid and malleable. Its characteristics could, and did, change over time. As he struggled to restrain his emotions at his sister Macrina's deathbed, he recognized that his saintly sister's body had begun to take on angelic form: "It was as if by some dispensation an angel had assumed a human form, with whom, not having any kinship or affinity with the life of the flesh, it was not at all unreasonable that the mind should remain in an unperturbed state, since the flesh did not drag it down to its own passions."[66] His sister, he insists, was rapidly losing her gendered character on her deathbed: "The subject of the tale was a woman—if indeed she was a 'woman,' for I know not whether it is fitting to designate her of that nature who so surpassed nature."[67] Gregory's destabilizing of his sister's gender does not turn her from a woman into a man. Nyssen proposes instead that bodily gender does not have ultimate, eschatological significance. He considered his sister's virtue to be of such an exalted character that he observed in her the realization of the Lord's promise that we will be like the angels (Lk 20:35–36). Gender differentiation, for Gregory, is something that only fits our postlapsarian situation, which is a life of food and drink, sexual activity, the passions more broadly, as well as mortality.[68] The resurrection body—angelic in character as it is—is not characterized by any of this.

Gregory's insistence on the fluidity of gender is the direct result both of his Christology and—immediately linked to it—his understanding of virtue. Nyssen refuses to give autonomy to the natural world of our postlapsarian state. Our bodies—the "tunics of hide" of Genesis 3:21 to which Gregory repeatedly alludes—do not have the kind of stability that our modern concept of *pura natura* might cause us to expect. Bodies as we know them today are deeply compromised as a result of the fall, and it is only when they are reconfigured in Christ that they take on their proper identity as God meant

66. Gregory of Nyssa, *The Life of Macrina*, in Anna M. Silvas, *Macrina the Younger, Philosopher of God*, Medieval Women: Texts and Contexts 22 (Turnhout: Brepols, 2008), 132.

67. Gregory of Nyssa, *Life of Macrina*, 110.

68. To be sure, Gregory does explain in *On the Making of Man* that already in Paradise God created human beings as male and female, but God did so because he foreknew the fall and wanted Adam and Eve to be prepared for their postlapsarian mode of existence. See Gregory of Nyssa, *On the Making of Man* 17.4, in *NPNF*[2] 5:407 (quotations of this work are from this source); Hans Boersma, *Embodiment and Virtue in Gregory of Nyssa: An Anagogical Approach*, Oxford Early Christian Studies (Oxford: Oxford University Press, 2013), 100–109.

them to be. That is to say, it is the christological telos that determines, for Gregory, the true identity of the human body. The christological eschaton, not some observable, purely natural order, tells us what the body is meant to be. Therefore, when Nyssen explains the proverbial saying that the young man must embrace the feminine figure of wisdom (Prv 4:8), he insists with an appeal to Galatians 3:28 that the gendered language of Proverbs 4 must not be taken literally: "It is clear that the eagerness for this kind of marriage is common to men and women alike, for since, as the apostle says, 'There is neither male nor female,' and Christ is all things for all human beings, the true lover of wisdom has as his goal the divine One who is true wisdom, and the soul, clinging to its incorruptible Bridegroom, has a love of true wisdom which is God."[69] The human body will be reconfigured in the hereafter so as to be conformed to Christ. It is a transformation that will involve the loss of gender, but emphatically not of the body. The body—though changed—will find its ultimate destiny in the fullness (πλήρωμα) of Christ.[70]

Gregory maintains that this bodily transformation hinges on growth in virtue. It is his admiration for his sister Macrina's saintly character that makes him recognize that she has undergone a physical transformation from a female to an angelic body. Similarly, in his *Homilies on the Song of Songs,* Nyssen maintains that when through a life of virtue we more and more identify with Christ, we actually "put him on," as Saint Paul words it (Eph 4:24; Col 3:10).[71] Along with the bride of the Song, we take off the postlapsarian tunic of hide (Song 5:3), and replace it with the garment of Christ:

> Whoever has taken off the old humanity and rent the veil of the heart has opened an entrance for the Word. And when the Word has entered her, the soul makes him her garment [ἔνδυμα] in accordance with the instruction of the apostle; for he commands the person who has taken off the rags of the old humanity "to put on the new" tunic that "has been created after the likeness of God in holiness and righteousness" (Eph 4:24); and he says that this garment [ἔνδυμα] is Jesus (cf. Rom 13:14).[72]

69. Gregory of Nyssa, *On Virginity* 20.328.2–9, in Virginia Woods Callahan, trans., *Ascetical Works,* Fathers of the Church (Washington, D.C.: The Catholic University of America Press, 1967), 64.

70. Gregory links the fullness (πλήρωμα) of Christ with the creation of "man" in the image of God (Gn 1:27a). He distinguishes this universal, christological "man" from the provisional creation of human beings as "male and female" (Gn 1:27b). See Gregory of Nyssa, *On the Making of Man* 16.8–9. See Boersma, *Embodiment and Virtue,* 104–5.

71. For more detail, see Boersma, *Embodiment and Virtue,* 87–92.

72. *Homilies on the Song of Songs* 11, in Gregory of Nyssa, *Homilies on the Song of Songs,* trans. and ed. Richard A. Norris, Writings from the Greco-Roman World 13 (Atlanta: Society of Biblical Literature, 2012), 347.

Jesus is the new garment that replaces the tunics of hide that God gave human beings after the fall (Gn 3:21), and we put on this new tunic through a life of holiness and righteousness. As we become like Christ (in virtue), we put on Christ as our new garment, so that our postlapsarian bodily constitution changes. In other words, for Gregory it is not only the case that a change can be observed in our virtues, but the change involves an actual physiological transformation. Putting on Christ means, for Gregory, that we replace the fallen, passible life with the eschatological impassible existence that becomes ours in and through identification with Christ. As they identify with Christ, human beings undergo an ontological—and this implies for Gregory also a physical—change in their bodily makeup.

This bodily change—effected in Christ through a life of virtue—is possible, for Gregory, inasmuch as he holds lightly to the continuity of matter. Peter Bouteneff rightly observes that for Gregory, "the difference between the body's coarseness in the present life, and the 'lighter fibres' with which our body will be spun in the resurrection ... rests within the moral realm. For Gregory conceives of matter itself as essentially formless, not to say immaterial."[73] Like Edwards would later do, so Gregory here appeals to the divine will as that which makes it possible for material objects to come into being out of nothing.[74] Saint Gregory maintains that there is nothing material that underlies the various properties of an object that we perceive by means of the senses: "If, then, colour is a thing intelligible, and resistance also is intelligible, and so with quantity and the rest of the properties, while if each of these should be withdrawn from the substratum, the whole idea of the body is dissolved; it would seem to follow that we may suppose the concurrence of those things, the absence of which we found to be the cause of the dissolution of the body, to produce the material nature."[75] For Gregory, what we call "matter" is simply the convergence of a bunch of properties, which themselves are intelligible, not material.[76] Such an idealist

73. Peter C. Bouteneff, "The Problem of the Body in the Anthropology of St. Gregory of Nyssa," in *Gregory of Nyssa: Homilies on the Beatitudes: An English Version with Supporting Studies: Proceedings of the Eighth International Colloquium on Gregory of Nyssa (Paderborn, 14–18 September 1998)*, ed. Hubertus R. Drobner and Albert Viciano, Supplements to Vigiliae Christianae 52 (Leiden: Brill, 2000), 418.

74. Gregory of Nyssa, *On the Making of Man* 23.5.

75. Gregory of Nyssa, *On the Making of Man* 24.2.

76. Cf. James S. Spiegel, "The Theological Orthodoxy of Berkeley's Immaterialism," *Faith and Philosophy* 13, no. 2 (1996): 216–35; Richard Sorabji, *Time, Creation and the Continuum: Theories in Antiquity and the Early Middle Ages* (1983; repr., Chicago: University of Chicago Press, 2006), 290–91; Stephen H. Daniel, "Berkeley's Christian Neoplatonism, Archetypes, and Divine Ideas," *Journal of the History of Philosophy* 39, no. 2 (2001): 239–58; Kirill Zinkovskiy, "St Gregory of Nyssa on the Transformation of Physical

view of matter allows for an eschatological view of the body as something rather ethereal, reconstituted in angelic form in the nongendered fullness of Christ.

As I already mentioned, Gregory did not ground the malleability of the body in God's contemplation of human beings the way that Edwards did. Nor did Gregory's synergistic approach to virtue allow for the Calvinist occasionalism of Edwards's idealism. And unlike Gregory, Edwards never linked his immaterialist metaphysic with his speculations regarding the expanded possibilities of sense perception in heaven. It is not clear to me why he did not do so. As our excursus on Gregory of Nyssa's theology illustrates, Edwards's immaterialism could have been of great metaphysical support for his eschatological speculation. In particular, immaterialism allows one to hold on to the Irenaean incarnational approach—and so to the confession that it is Christ's actual body that is in heaven at the right hand of the Father, as well as to the confession of our own bodily resurrection in and through him—in combination with the spiritualizing tendencies of Gregory of Nyssa and others. For Gregory, the heavenly reality of the eschaton necessitates a spiritualizing of the body. But it is not a spiritualizing that leaves the body behind. Instead, it is a spiritualizing that is predicated on the continuation of the body, transformed and made perfect in the eschatological reality of Jesus Christ. Or, as Nicholas of Cusa might have put it, it is when God's vision of us in Jesus Christ transforms us—body and soul—that even our physical senses are healed, so as to obtain powers of contemplation such as "no eye has seen, nor ear heard, nor the heart of man imagined" (1 Cor 2:9 ESV). The ascension of Christ, on this understanding, was truly a bodily ascension. But the body is no longer conceived of in modern terms, as a self-sustained, independent entity that continues uninterruptedly through time—and perhaps into eternity—unaffected by the loving gaze of God in Christ. Instead, the body is a fluid, malleable convergence of intelligible properties conceived and perceived by God, in and through Christ, and brought to its perfection through participation in him.

Elements—in Nature and Holy Eucharistic Gifts," in *The Beauty of God's Presence in the Fathers of the Church: The Proceedings of the Eighth International Patristic Conference, Maynooth, 2012*, ed. Janet Elaine Rutherford (Dublin: Four Courts Press, 2014), 150–60.

RESPONSE

Passing Over into God?

Douglas Farrow (Catholic)

I thank Fr. Behr for his engagement with my book, and I welcome this exchange, in which I expect to learn more about his approach to theology as well as to the matter at hand. We have long shared an interest in patristic theology, and we have never before had the opportunity to discuss it in person. Thanks also, then, to Dr. Raith and his colleagues at John Brown University for this opportunity.[77]

Let me begin by stating unequivocally that I am no Apollinarian. The God-man had, and has, both a human body and a rational soul; the unassumed would otherwise remain the unhealed, as Gregory of Nazianzus famously observed. I believe in the redemption of the mind, in other words, and in the ascent of the mind. For it belongs to the very nature of the *intellectus,* particularly the human *intellectus,* to ascend from lower truths to higher, and from created things to knowledge of God the creator.[78] Further, it belongs to the *intellectus,* when it is in receipt of that *gratia elevans* that exceeds the *gratia creans* by which it came to be in the first place, to rise to the knowledge of God *in se,* and so to beatitude—a beatitude possible only when God makes himself the means of knowledge as well as the end of knowledge, which he does in and through the incarnation. Moreover, I agree with Gregory of Nyssa (who in turn was in agreement with Irenaeus) that the ascent of the mind is an epektasic ascent, an ascent that is at once both a true resting in God and a perpetual advance in the enjoyment of God.

What exactly are we arguing about then? I want to get at that by be-

77. First conference note: Expectations were not disappointed, and a conversation has been struck that will not be hindered, we trust, but enhanced by the very preliminary exchange that appears in the present volume. Quotations of Fr. Behr are taken from the uncorrected draft originally sent to me.

78. Atheism is a sin against man as well as a sin against God; that is one reason why the psalmist calls the atheist a fool.

ginning where Fr. Behr ended, namely, with a quotation from Gregory of Nazianzus's Third Theological Oration. Gregory is defending the doctrine of the Holy Trinity and the deity of the Son. Here is the passage, supplied at length:

> For we have learned to believe in and to teach the deity of the Son from the great and lofty utterances [of Scripture].... But in opposition to all these [examples], do you reckon up for me the expressions which make for your ignorant arrogance, such as *"My God and your God"* [etc.] ...? For every one of these points, taken separately, may very easily ... be explained to you in the most reverent sense, and the stumbling-block of the letter be cleared away—that is, if your stumbling at it be honest, and not wilfully malicious. To give you the explanation in one sentence: What is lofty you are to apply to the Godhead, and to that nature in him which is superior to sufferings and incorporeal; but all that is lowly to the composite condition of him who for your sakes made himself of no reputation and was incarnate—yes, for it is no worse thing to say, was made man—and afterwards was also exalted. *The result will be that you will abandon these carnal and groveling doctrines, and learn to be more sublime, and to ascend with his Godhead, and you will not remain permanently among the things of sight, but will rise up with him into the world of thought, and come to know which passages refer to his* [divine] *nature, and which to his assumption of human nature.* For he whom you now treat with contempt was once above you. He who is now man was once the Uncompounded. What he was he continued to be; what he was not he took to himself. In the beginning he was uncaused; for what is the cause of God? But afterwards for a cause he was born. And that cause was that you might be saved, who insult him and despise his Godhead—because of this, that he took upon him your denser nature, having converse with flesh by means of mind. *While his inferior nature, the humanity, became God, because it was united to God, and became one person because the higher nature prevailed in order that I too might be made God so far as he is made man.*[79]

So: The one who denies the deity of Christ is accused of carnal readings of Scripture and earthbound opinions about Christ. Rightly so. He does not rise to a true and godly understanding. To ascend with the mind means here to grasp Jesus Christ in both his natures, that which is caused (the human) and that which is uncaused (the divine). Remaining carnal and earthbound means to presuppose that this cannot be, that it is not so, and to refuse to allow Scripture to show otherwise.

Now, I don't think Fr. Behr supposes me to be in danger of Arianism as

79. Gregory of Nazianzus, *Or.* 29, On the Son, §§17–19, in *NPNF*[2] 7:307–8 (punctuation and capitalization altered; emphasis added).

well as Apollinarianism. What he is concerned about is my attack on the tradition of ascension of the mind. But which tradition? That is what we must get clear. He notes my rejection of the trajectory that in the West leads to the likes of Hegel and of Schleiermacher, who do not grasp the doctrine of the two natures or, at all events, refuse it and seek some other way of ascent. Fr. Behr (though he has good things to say about this part of chapter 2 of *Ascension Theology*, as of chapter 6) does not note what I argue in chapter 7; that is, my agreement with Gregory that God is humanized so that man might be deified, "in order that I too might be made God so far as he is made man."

So far as he is made man? Yes, precisely. The true ascent of the mind takes place only when we keep in view this *mirifica commutatio*, to use a Latin expression. It is not simply a matter of passing from the humanity to the divinity, but of entering into and remaining within the exchange, the communion of being and knowing and doing between the caused and the Uncaused that is made possible by the incarnation. Put more simply, as Irenaeus did in his *Demonstratio*, the true ascent—not only of the mind but of the whole person, body and soul—takes place for us as the Spirit leads us to the Son and the Son presents us to the Father and the Father bestows on us a share in the eternal life and beatitude of God. And the Spirit-led *mens* or *intellectus*, which, taken together with the will (*voluntas*) and with the capacity not just for desire but for deliberate love, is far the noblest part of us—the part that our bodies must and, in the resurrection, will follow and obey—rises up to this beatitude by degrees, as Irenaeus also taught, and the Cappadocians too.

When this ascent is happening—an ascent not to be confused with the ascension of Jesus Christ, though strictly dependent upon it, for that ascension, *the* ascension, is how the Son completes his presentation of man to the Father—Scripture is not read carnally; that is, with the blinkers of unbelief. It is read in and with the church, and with understanding.[80]

I take it there is much agreement here. Surely this is not what concerns Fr. Behr. But, being in the Eastern tradition, he quite naturally worries about my rejection of certain elements of Eastern theology, in which I find some of the roots of a problem now primarily Western, namely, the tendency to treat the ascension of Jesus as merely a cipher for the ascent of man. He

80. Wherever we find this sort of thing in the fathers, we are hearing riffs on Romans 8 as well as on John 14–16, Hebrews 12, and so forth.

worries, that is, about what he sees as my divide-and-conquer approach to the patristic tradition, and about my criticism of the ascension of the mind motif as we find it on the Origenist side of that tradition. He himself treats what I call the Irenaean and the Origenist elements as complementary—conjunctive not disjunctive. He even implies that there is a certain carnality in seeing them as disjunctive.

Well, I didn't cut class yesterday and fly for several hours to darkest Clintonian Arkansas just to confirm for you that I am partial to Irenaeus! There is a serious question here respecting the unity of tradition. I would not be a Catholic if I didn't believe in that unity. But no one can deny that tradition evolves, and that it evolves in part through the creative suffering of serious tensions, some of which raise questions of heterodoxy. Origen was and remains a site of such tensions. Was it not Arius's radicalization of Origen's subordinationism that finally provoked the Nicene crisis?

Origen was a great man, a great scholar, a devoted and long-suffering Christian. He was never sainted, and is not in the proper sense of the word a father, though many of the Fathers (including Gregory of Nyssa) were nurtured by his work, and some followed him down false paths as well as true. I do not think that one divides or belittles the patristic tradition by pointing out that there are false paths to be found in Origen as well as true. This indeed belongs to the tradition. Origen's views fell eventually outside the bounds of orthodoxy on the Trinity and the incarnation as well as on eschatology. That does not make him a heretic, of course, but it does make him an unreliable guide. Gregory of Nyssa, who may also have been a father of fathers, in the looser sense, and was in the proper sense a father himself—though hardly *the* father of the Fathers—was the worse, on my view, for being a less discriminating reader of Origen than was Gregory of Nazianzus.

But let us turn, for a moment, from this disagreement about Origen and Gregory of Nyssa to establish two more points of agreement, or what I hope might be agreement; for if we are to get to the heart of the matter we must move beyond acknowledgment that the intellect is built to ascend, both by philosophical reason to the First Cause and, by the further and distinct grace of revelation, to knowledge of the Holy Trinity.

First: The revelation of God in Christ, without which the true ascent of the mind is not possible, requires attention to the whole life and ministry of Christ, which is centered upon, though not concluded on, the cross. What is concluded on the cross, I would say, or at all events in the descent to the dead, is the self-offering of the Son from within the depths of human alienation from God; thereafter that self-offering would be made, not in the attendant humiliation, but in the exaltation of divine deliverance and reward.

Second: There is an *itinerarium mentis* cultivated by tradition, as theology and prayer, indeed as prayerful theology, that involves seeking to know Christ according to the Spirit—the Holy Spirit—rather than according to the flesh—unaided or "carnal" reason—and so to know also the Father as Father. This *itinerarium* belongs to the ecclesial exaltation of Christ precisely in his obedient suffering of humiliation. Without pursuit of it neither theology nor prayer is authentically Christian.

So where, if these things be granted, is the disagreement? Does it reduce to a question about how tradition in general is handled, or about Gregory of Nyssa in particular? Or does it extend to a question about how *the humanity of Christ* is handled, hence also about the nature of the salvation and perfection of the human being? This is what I would most like Fr. Behr to clarify for me.

Now I have said that my attack on Origen was not an attack on the ascent of the mind. It was an attack, rather, on a certain view of the ascension of Jesus Christ, a view that regards the latter, not as the glorification of the incarnate Word, but as a retraction or marginalization of his humanity so that his divinity could appear uncompromised. It is entirely understandable that the Arian crisis should prompt some of the Nicene defenders to press the ascension into this service, but Gregory of Nazianzus holds no such view.[81] There are many in the Origenist tradition, however, who do operate with a retraction theory of some sort, for the simple reason that (like Origen) they do not see humanity, bodily humanity, as something capable of union and communion with God. They are inclined, therefore, to treat the incarnation as something perfected on the cross, where the body is eliminated; and to understand what follows after as the restoration of the soul of Jesus to heaven and of the Logos to his former divine glory.[82] For them the cross is glorious just because it marks the point at which the Logos turns back, and the cosmos with him, to its divine origin, forsaking the world of the flesh: not the world of the flesh insofar as it lacks the Spirit (though that is the view of Paul, John, Irenaeus, et al.) but the world of the flesh, full stop.

81. Nor does Augustine, in his mature thought, or the other leading fathers, Latin or Greek.

82. I make this distinction because Origen makes it, though those I am calling "Origenists" may not. See Douglas Farrow, *Ascension and Ecclesia* (Edinburgh: T&T Clark, 1999), 89.

Fr. Behr is not an advocate of such views, but I worry that he leaves openings for them. If I understand him correctly, he does see the incarnation as an event that is only perfected on the cross, and he does treat the resurrection and ascension primarily as a transformation in the way the incarnate one relates to us and is perceived by us. Talk of this transformation very quickly becomes epistemological rather than eschatological. It is not about what happens to Jesus but about what happens to the way we see or know Jesus. And where Jesus himself is concerned, the transformation in question seems to become ontological, though it is sometimes difficult to tell whether it is ontological or epistemological. At all events, it is about Jesus becoming God rather than man—"God instead of man," in Gregory of Nyssa's language.[83]

Fr. Behr will have to forgive me if my paraphrase of his frequently elliptical (and frankly puzzling) account is a rather clumsy one, but I think I hear him saying that the incarnation does not entail a divine person dwelling among us in two natures, having taken from Mary our human nature in addition to his divine nature, but rather God taking to himself a human life, which is lived out from conception to cross, and through "the cross" or "the passion"—understood as a single, if complex, transformative event that appears to some observers only as the darkness of death but to others as (also) the joy and light of resurrection—is glorified, such that it now exists in God and has in some fashion the unity and permanence of God. If I am hearing rightly, bodily resurrection and ascension just *are* this "passing into God" of the crucified one. They are the unification, the divinization, the rendering eternal of the life and death of Jesus.

But perhaps I am not hearing rightly, for this view is neither biblical nor orthodox. There may be perfectly orthodox ways of reading *Contra Eunomius* 3.3.44; indeed, I think there are. But they do not include—not unless the mystical reading of mystical discourses covers a multitude of sins—asserting that the resurrection and ascension of Jesus is the divine

83. Here again is the text of *Eun.* 3.3.44 supplied by Fr. Behr: "He who says *exalted by the Right Hand of God* clearly reveals the unspeakable economy of the mystery, that the Right Hand of God, who made all things that are, who is the Lord by whom all things were made and without whom nothing that is subsists, himself raised to his own height τὸν ἄνθρωπον united to him, making him also, by the commixture, to be what he is by nature: he is Lord and King, and the King is called Christ; these things he made him too. And this we are plainly taught by the voice of Peter in his mystic discourse, that the lowliness of the one crucified in weakness (and weakness, as we have heard from the Lord, indicates the flesh [Mt 26:41]), that, by virtue of its mingling with the infinite and boundless [nature] of the Good, remained no longer in its own measures and properties, but by the Right Hand of God was raised up together, and became Lord instead of servant, Christ the King instead of a subject, highest instead of lowly, God instead of man."

Word causing his human nature to "pass into God" or to abandon "its own measures and properties" for divine measures and properties. Does that not fall under the censure of Gregory of Nazianzus, who insists that the human nature of Jesus retains its properties?[84] Is it not contrary to the teaching of the apostles and Fathers generally? Unless, of course, all that is meant by such a claim is that the mortal is made immortal and glorious, the lowly made lordly, by the will of the Father and the action of the Spirit and the combined action and passion of the incarnate Word.[85]

Fr. Behr, however, wants to read Gregory of Nyssa with Origen rather than with Nazianzen. He quotes Origen's assertion that "the high exaltation of the Son of Man which occurred when he glorified God in his own death consisted in the fact that he was no longer different from the Word but was the same with him."[86] He then paraphrases by asserting that "the unity of the God-man is effected upon the cross, for after it, and in its light, we can no longer differentiate between human and divine properties." Whether there is "a hint of adoptionism" here is a question we may safely answer in the affirmative. Origen, as already said, is very far from the later mark of Chalcedon when it comes to the two natures of the Word, and indeed the person of the Word. Things are otherwise with Gregory of Nyssa, and with Fr. Behr also. But the latter seems quite comfortable with the kenoticism of the Origenist tradition, which (in the West) extends as far as Hegel and even Barth, who is quite explicit in treating the incarnation as something that happens between conception and cross and is complete on the cross, such that all the weight falls thereafter on revelation of the crucified one as Lord. I tried to show in *Ascension and Ecclesia* how problematic it is to treat the natures as two simultaneous movements (one of descent and the other of ascent), and thus to reduce the person of the incarnate Son to a contrapuntal composition that plays itself out in history and is repeated endlessly in eternity.

84. See Douglas Farrow, *Ascension Theology* (London: T&T Clark, 2011), 39–40, per Gregory's letter to Cledonius.

85. I say "action and passion" because it is not quite right, in my view, to say (as the Wikipedia entry on Fr. Behr has him saying) that "when Christ dies as a human being, he demonstrates his divinity as God—he raises his own body." The resurrection of Jesus is an act of the Father in answer to Jesus's prayer, and of the Spirit, who is the Lord and Giver of life (cf. Douglas Farrow, "Resurrection and Immortality," in *The Oxford Handbook of Systematic Theology*, ed. John Webster, Kathryn Tanner, and Iain Torrance [Oxford: Oxford University Press, 2007], 212ff.). Nor is it quite right to say that the revelation of "the same glory which he shared with the Father from all eternity ... is located solely on the Cross"—though if we are speaking of *that* glory, rather than the messianic glory (per Ps 2 or 24 or 110, etc.), then a case can certainly be made that it is concentrated on the cross, and there revealed in supereminent fashion.

86. Origen, *Comm. Jo.* 32.324–62.

Things are not quite so bad as all that in Barth,[87] nor, I trust, in Fr. Behr, but it is quite plain that he too regards the natures as movements and the incarnation as a process that is completed by the cross, which means that there really is nowhere for the incarnate one to go in his resurrection and ascension, and nothing for him to do but to pass into God. What that means for Jesus is not explained here, nor what it might imply about our own eventual deification. What it means for us at the moment is that we can now see him as God and so read Scripture correctly. If "we do not attempt to look behind the cross"—or for that matter *beyond* the cross—but rather "look through the cross, we see the unchanging identity of the crucified one throughout his life, from his birth from the Virgin and throughout his ministry." And this is "the same hermeneutic needed to read Scripture and encounter the Word of God" in it. From the point of fullness—the cross—everything should become clear.

Now Fr. Behr wants to use "the cross" as synecdoche, such that it has reference also to the resurrection, ascension, and Pentecost. This usage, unfortunately, serves up a great many ambiguities, even generating some uncertainty as to whether and how the resurrection is a real event for Jesus, something entirely distinct from the suffering of the cross. It also allows Fr. Behr to evade the biblical claim that it is only in the light of the resurrection that the *cross* itself is seen clearly.[88] Did Paul insist, "We preach Christ, and him crucified"? Certainly, but he also preached Jesus and the resurrection (see 1 Cor 1:23; Acts 17:18 [with vv. 30–31]). In Scripture these are the two basic elements of a complex narrative, privileged in various ways according to the requirements of the context, but they are distinct elements that are, and must be, distinctly proclaimed. Consider, for example, the Philippians hymn that says: "He became obedient unto death, even death on a cross. Therefore God has highly exalted him ..." (Phil 2:8–9 RSV).[89] *Therefore*, not therein. We need not and should not deny that he was exalted therein. The Gospel of John is careful to include a therein. But the "there-

87. Though see the latter part of my discussion of Barth in *Ascension and Ecclesia*, 242ff.

88. I agree with Robert Wilken's claim in *The Spirit of Early Christian Thought* (New Haven: Yale University Press, 2003), xv, that "the Resurrection of Jesus is the central fact of Christian devotion and the ground of all Christian thinking." (This does not prevent Wilken, by the way, from being a great admirer of Origen.) And here it should also be observed, *pace* Fr. Behr, that the resurrected one *is* seen physically, and seen publicly, as the Gospels and Acts and 1 Corinthians make clear.

89. Thus Gregory, in the passage quoted above from *Or.* 29, says that the Son was made man "and afterwards was also exalted." As I have argued elsewhere, the exaltation takes place in two stages, as resurrection and as ascension, per Luke's own account.

fore" has preeminence in the Gospel narrative and hence also in theology. And the exaltation in question is not, in the first instance, the revelation of Jesus as God, but the establishment of Jesus as Lord. It is first of all eschatology, and only afterward epistemology. It is the triumph of the Christ before it is a revelation of the divinity of the Christ.

It is understandable in the wake of the Arian crisis that eschatology would be turned to epistemological and ontological ends—understandable and acceptable, for we already find this in the Gospels. "My Lord and my God!" says Thomas when he sees and touches the risen Christ. In seeing and touching, he knows this man in his humanity as his Lord—both in the titular messianic sense, "Son of God," already granted by Nathaniel at Jn 1:49, and in the ontological sense of John's prologue, as "God the Son," to use later language. I am not contesting this ascent of the mind of the disciples, which took place even before the ascension of their Lord. I am contesting treatments of the ascension of the Lord that do not know how to affirm his risen body as a real human body, home to a real rational soul, both of which are at last at home with God, treatments that do not know how to "see" or "touch" it either theologically or anthropologically, and that therefore falsify the ascent of the mind as an intellectual movement away from his humanity to his divinity, and/or as a retreat to his humanity as it appears on the *via crucis* or on the cross itself. We require eschatology first, ontology and epistemology afterward. The reduction of eschatology to ontology or epistemology is not so much an exigency in the face of Arianism as a sign of nervousness about the Semitic character of the Scriptures, which anticipate a real future for human beings qua human beings.[90]

Of course Jesus's death on the cross, as the supreme act of his love both for the Father and for the world, is a revelation (for those with eyes to see) of his greatness and glory, and the chief cause of his exaltation by the Father. But his death on the cross, though a "lifting up" (by man, against God, and by God for man) is not, taken by itself, his glorification. It does glorify him, for by this very means he glorifies the Father on behalf of man and the

90. Second conference note: Having now heard Hans Boersma talk about "transformation," a word he seems content to use in a rather abstract fashion, I begin to wonder whether he too is somewhat nervous about biblical eschatology. Much mischief is made of Paul's contrast in 1 Cor 15 between the σῶμα ψυχικόν and the σῶμα πνευματικόν—a contrast with which Irenaeus works creatively, and without too much mischief, in *Haer.* 5.36—which must not be turned into some idea of "plastick nature" that, in the final analysis, is indistinguishable from Origenism. But here, too, a further conversation must be had. For my part, I have tried to indicate the basic features and principles of eschatological transformation in "Resurrection and Immortality" and in chapters 3, 5, and 7 of *Ascension Theology.*

Father glorifies him in turn. But how? By showing us what Jesus has done? Yes. By showing us who it is who has done this—that Jesus and the Father are one God? Again, yes. But Jesus himself is the object of this glorification, and his glorification is first of all the reward he reaps in the resurrection and ascension and heavenly session and, ultimately, in his parousia and in the kingdom that shall have no end. It is the reward of a man for the sake of other men. This cannot be thought properly on Origen's schema, and it cannot be thought properly on Barth's actualist schema either.

Fr. Behr's own schema, as it appears in this paper, seems to me much closer to Barth's than to Origen's. But I remain uncertain what he means when he says, "to define incarnation in terms of the divine coming to be in human form, within the spatiotemporal framework of this cosmos, misses the mark." I should have thought it necessary (even on his schema) in order to hit the mark. It is much easier to understand why he wants to say that the place to which the ascended one goes "is not now defined in terms of our spatiotemporal cosmos, it is not so much a place at the right hand, in a spatial sense, but rather *as* the Right Hand of God." Of course, I do not myself say that it can be defined in term of the cosmos as we know it; that is something I expressly deny. But I also deny that the ascended one requires no space, whether because in substance his humanity is now indistinguishable from his divinity or because that substance is spaceless and timeless except for the space and time it had during his sojourn in the land of sepulture. If Fr. Behr means to say either of those things, he sets himself against both Scripture and tradition in a most impossible fashion.[91]

Again, I am not sure why Fr. Behr says: "So also the human nature of Jesus (identified by certain sense-perceptible, spatiotemporal, human properties) is no longer known by these properties, but rather by the properties of God, being beyond space and time; it is revealed, as we have seen, in and through the transformation and exaltation effected through the cross, when this is understood by intellectual contemplation rather than physical sight, and as he passes out of physical sight." If all he means is that it is only as crucified, resurrected, and ascended, only as the source of the life-giving Spirit of God now poured out from heaven, that Jesus is known and believed to be God even by those who have not seen or touched him, who would dispute it? But that is not all he means, to judge by what he says next.

91. Denial that the ascended Christ can be situated in terms of our spatiotemporal cosmos is perfectly compatible with affirmation that he remains spatial and temporal in the mode of the new creation; see *Ascension and Ecclesia*, 263–64, and *Ascension Theology*, 48–49.

Divinity likewise has, through the ascension, assumed the human nature of Christ into itself: it now has a body, it is incarnate, but in a body that is no longer subject to the spatiotemporal constraints of our cosmos; it is, rather, the very body of God, beyond all space and time

... We must not, as Gregory of Nyssa urges against Apollinarius, define the divine in terms of appearance in the flesh, but rather raise up our minds to understand the reality that lies eternally before us, hanging on the cross and passing over into God.

This seems to me not to defeat Apollinarian thinking but merely to turn it inside out, much as Eutyches did. God has a body; it just isn't a body such as ours. God has his "man" or manhood; it just isn't a man or manhood like ours. It's something that happened and still happens, to which we ourselves can ascend by perceiving it rightly.

"If this is the case," concludes Fr. Behr, "then the supposed 'Origenist' emphasis on the ascent of the mind and the Irenaean emphasis on incarnation are not opposed to each other, but correlative." Well, I should like to believe that they are correlative, but they aren't. Irenaeus is interested in the descent of the Word and the resultant ascent of man, in body and rational soul. Origen is interested in the descent of the Word in order to liberate the rational soul from its bodily entanglement; which is not the gospel. As for Gregory of Nyssa, where he is insufficiently disentangled from the erroneous elements in Origen he is the worse for it. It is respect for the tradition, not disrespect, that compels one to say so. For the antisomatic is just as "carnal" as the antispiritual.[92] It is a refusal of the continuity between creation and redemption—the continuity Irenaeus affirmed and Origen denied, when he rejected the former's robust answer to the Gnostics and made out the material creation to be no more than a reform school for the soul.[93]

To sum up: A mystical theology of the cross that makes of Jesus's resurrection and ascension revelatory dimensions of the crucifixion rather than restorative and rewarding events for the man Jesus simply will not do. While I do not suppose Fr. Behr to be offering us just that, I can't help but wonder whether he *is* offering us an equivalent (within the Orthodox sphere) to

92. The flesh (σάρξ), being made by God, is good in itself, as is the entire body (σῶμα). Relying on these good gifts and on natural abilities, rather than relying on God, is of course bad, as is pandering to the disordered passions that bodily needs presently stir up. Such is what the prophets and apostles have in mind when they refer negatively to "the flesh." But they and we look for the redemption of the body, flesh and all; not to look for that redemption is an offense against the Spirit.

93. In Western terms, it is a rejection of the principle, later articulated by Thomas, that grace perfects nature rather than destroying it (*gratia non tollit sed perficit naturam*).

the incarnational actualism of Karl Barth, if not to the constructs by which certain post-Barthians and some Rahnerians have attempted to collapse the immanent into the economic Trinity, eliminating any consideration of that eternal Word by which God utters himself to and for himself without yet uttering himself to and for the creature.[94] Those who move in that direction inevitably wind up making God and the creature mutually defining, which means in the end defining one or the other away. I hope that Fr. Behr can and will clarify for us that he is in no danger of that; that there is a Son, a Logos, who is Logos from and to all eternity, whose freely assumed humanity is entirely distinct from his divinity; and that it is not man qua man, but man qua sinner, that must be undone by the cross.[95]

94. "The Word by which the Creator of all says itself" (Anselm, *Monologion* 31) is the same Word through which God calls creation into existence, but in that call the Word is spoken differently; that is, it is directed *ad extra*. So even if we take the incarnate Word to be one and the same with the Word of creation, as I believe Fr. Behr does, we may not take either creation or incarnation to be constitutive of God, though we must (as the *homoousion* attests) take God himself to be constitutive of the incarnation. See my critique of Robert Jenson on this point in "Robert Jenson's *Systematic Theology*: Three Responses," *International Journal of Systematic Theology* 1, no. 1 (1999): 89–95; see further *Ascension and Ecclesia*, 281ff.

95. Third conference note: Were men born to die? Tolkien explores this question at some length, and with great insight, in his *Athrabeth Finrod ah Andreth*, which was helpfully brought to our attention. The anthropology and cosmology of that document, and its sense of the transformation human nature has undergone through the fall and of that which it will yet undergo in its redemption, are quite different from Fr. Behr's, unless I miss my guess. Perhaps the document itself would supply a good starting point for a future Catholic/Orthodox/Evangelical discussion.

CHAPTER 2

Acts 2, Translating Pentecost

Whitsun Readings

David Lyle Jeffrey (Evangelical)

> Where is that fire which once descended
> On thy Apostles?
> —George Herbert, "Whitsunday"

I envy those who have never experienced religious embarrassment. As it happens, my volunteering to undertake to comment on Acts 2:1–13 owes directly to an embarrassing event in my teenage years, and a grudging recognition that it is probably time for me to repent. At the age of sixteen I went to a Pentecostal camp meeting. I was accompanied by three Pentecostals who had urged me to attend. One of those, I also confess, was a very shy but pretty new immigrant from Northern Ireland, and the idea of sitting next to this red-haired lass was sufficiently appealing that, despite parental warnings about tent meetings, I pled permission to go. My parents were Baptists of the Scots sort—strict and particular Baptists—and though they recognized the much larger Pentecostal Assembly as in some sense "Evangelical," they were convinced that the Holy Spirit was granted to a believer at baptism, that, like baptism itself, it happened only once, and that the idea of a second blessing or "baptism in the Holy Spirit" was a kind of contrivance. In particular they thought that the Pentecostal enthusiasm for "speaking in tongues" was an emotionally induced casting off of spiritual discipline and self-restraint such as could only confound proper worship in "good order and of a sound mind." Naturally, for the most part I shared their view; I even teasingly asked the red-haired lass if the Holy Spirit was helping her to do better in French class. But I was certainly—if complicatedly—interested in discovering what we might have in common.

This essay is dedicated to my friend W. Ward Gasque, scholar, teacher, and encourager.

A couple hundred or so rural people on a wood-chip-covered floor, with an electric organ madly stirring them up, can make a lot of noise, even in a tent. I don't remember anything from the sermon; what I do remember—vividly—is the entire crowd having gone forward for a "second blessing" in waves, invitation after invitation, with the organ all the while wailing away. Finally, only one person was left in his seat: me. I was terrified. Grown men, dancing in circles, hand in hand like in a Breughel painting, babbling away, and yes, there at the center, standing on a chair, arms in the air, and speaking volubly in tongues (none of them French), was the shy red-haired Irish girl. The hour-long ride home afterward seemed like an eternity. When I let my companions off at the house of the girl's parents, her older sister broke the silence to say, "We are sorry you are not a believer."

That's a hard line for a sixteen-year-old Baptist, and it has stayed with me. Might it be that some of us Evangelicals were not fully "believers"? I reread Acts. It seemed clear to me that what happened at Pentecost was not a prototype for what happened in the tent that night. Later I could see that instances of "speaking in tongues" such as Paul refers to in 1 Corinthians 14 were of an order more akin to it, but that also left me with difficult questions. Why did Evangelicals of my type accept the singular miracle in Acts 2 and not seek the other manifestation of speaking in tongues?

In college, I would be gratified to learn that even C. S. Lewis found glossolalia "an embarrassing phenomenon." And yet he left me, despite many other intriguing comments in his Pentecost sermon for Whitsunday in Mansfield College Chapel, Oxford, with an uncertain sense of how to square the event of Pentecost itself with the practice of glossolalia, for he did not in that sermon sufficiently separate them. Yet he stressed that the Pentecost event, and the speaking in tongues recorded in Acts 2:1–13, "is built into the very fabric of the birth story of the Church." He further observed that "it is this very event that the Lord had told the church to wait for—almost in the last words he uttered before his ascension."[1] C. S. Lewis was far and away the most read writer among my peers at Wheaton; I took him, as did most, to be an Evangelical authority, and for that and other reasons was still left with my question, Are Pentecostals Evangelical? without a satisfying answer.

During the time of our last gathering, as we reflected together on a number of pericopes in John's Gospel, I was conscious that our brothers and

1. C. S. Lewis, "Transposition," in *The Weight of Glory and Other Addresses* (New York: Macmillan, 1949), 16; his reference is to Acts 1:8.

sisters in the Catholic and Orthodox theological traditions were unsure of what the "big *E*" for Evangelical means in cases such as my own. Not that there are not almost as many shades of emphasis and opinion among Catholics and Orthodox as among those denoted at Paradosis as "Evangelical," but in the disparate churches of the Reformation such mutations have proliferated more variously, if for no other reason than that tradition itself is often disdained by Evangelical pastors and lay leaders in favor of what some presume to be a direct address to the *ipse verbum* of the biblical text.[2] No representative of the big-*E* theologians in our last conclave, however, exhibited any such presumption. Studies and commentaries were routinely consulted by Evangelical participants—including the writings of Catholic and Orthodox theologians from the second century to the twenty-first.

The oddly unrepresentative character of Evangelical scholarly work, then, is a curious element in our gathering once again; you may make of that what you will. In my case, I feel that this time I ought to show my particular colors more openly lest I be accused (as I have been before now) of being a papist wolf in Evangelical sheep's clothing, or even perhaps a lurking Jesuit under a Wesleyan Methodist wig—an accusation leveled more than once, by the way, at representatives of the great Evangelical Revival of the eighteenth century, such as the Wesleys and George Whitefield.[3] In fact, like them I have worshiped as an Anglican for more than forty years, many of those as an Anglo-Catholic of the high-on-the-candle, smells-and-bells variety. How then can I permit our impresario Charles Raith to present me as an "Evangelical"? And why have I not protested? Is it that I am embarrassed that the Anglican Church has its origins in the testicular ambitions of that injudiciously talkative "defender of the faith" King Henry VIII? More

2. David Bebbington has famously suggested that Evangelicals of whatever variety will share four emphases: Biblicism, crucicentrism, conversionism, and activism, but the term is used far more loosely than that nowadays. In any case, I find the six-point taxonomy of J. I. Packer to be closer to the longer lineage I wish to stress here. Packer's list is "(1) the supremacy of Scripture as God-given instruction, a sufficient, self-interpreting guide in all matters of faith and action; (2) the majesty of Jesus Christ our sin-bearing divine Saviour and glorified King, by faith in whom we are justified; (3) the lordship of the Holy Spirit, giver of spiritual life by animating, assuring, empowering and transforming the saints; (4) the necessity of conversion, not as a stereotyped experience but as a regenerate condition, a state of faith in Christ evidenced by repentance and practical godliness; (5) the priority of evangelism in the church's agenda; (6) the fellowship of believers (the faith-full) as the essence of the church's life." J. I. Packer, "The Anglican Commitment to Comprehensiveness," *Virtue Online*, June 2010, http://www.virtueonline.org/anglican-commitment-comprehensiveness-jipacker. The second and third points are particularly important for orthodox Anglicans, and these draw us closer than some Evangelicals to our common roots in Scripture and the Paradosis.

3. See David Lyle Jeffrey, ed., introduction to *English Spirituality in the Age of Wesley*, ed. David Lyle Jeffrey (1987; repr., Vancouver, B.C.: Regent College Publishing, 2000), 12–14.

than a few friends have asked me why I don't make a clean breast of it and petition to become a "big *C*," a Roman Catholic, the full Monty. Is it perhaps because I am avoiding other embarrassments?

So here is my confession, brothers and sisters: I am at best a "small-*e*" evangelical in our contemporary world. My embarrassment now is greatest with the injudicious use of that term itself by media moguls, entertainers, and professional "Evangelicals" alike; from Joel Osteen to Benny Hinn they make me twitch. The sense of "Evangelical" that still attracts me, indeed as powerfully now as it did when I was baptized, is more akin to that employed by Franciscans in the thirteenth century to refer to *imitatio Christi* and the *vita apostolica,* the life modeled by Christ and the apostles in the four Gospels and Acts, and proclaimed by them as liberating good news to anyone willing to take up the cross and actually follow Jesus (see Lk 9:23). I find this sense of the term strikingly similar to the usage of the eighteenth-century British "Evangelical" revival under the Wesleys, Whitefield, John Newton, Charles Simeon, and others. As it happens, I certainly recognize also a will to *imitatio Christi* in believers of many other ethnic and theological traditions, and it is why I am so grateful to be included in this gathering, for I think it is in that simple, radical sense of our universal calling that we may *all* aspire to an "Evangelical" life. In that light, I should like to focus my remarks on Acts 2:1–13 in such a way as to retrieve insights from Christians across the centuries, and then, out of my own small-*e* evangelical resources, modestly bear witness some notable Anglican reflections on this most evangelical of biblical texts, excepting only the Great Commission (Mt 28:18–20; Mk 16:16–18; cf. Acts 1:7–8), which it so clearly echoes.

First, however, we should consider the general American usage of the term. Whatever we may think of various distortions of the word *Evangelical* in our own time, I want to suggest that where Acts 2:1–13 is concerned, the broadly Evangelical (as distinct from specifically Pentecostal) perspective on this passage draws on two genealogies. The first and most obvious of these in America descends from Calvin. Though Calvin strongly affirms that the gift of the Holy Spirit was to the apostles and not their hearers, hence involving real, miraculous translation in order that gentiles might hear the gospel,[4] he clearly distinguishes this unique moment from oth-

4. John Calvin, *Acts of the Apostles* 1.2.4, in John Calvin, *The Acts of the Apostles,* trans. W. J. G. McDonald, ed. David W. Torrance and Thomas F. Torrance, Calvin's New Testament Commentaries 6 (Grand Rapids: Eerdmans, 1965), 50–53.

er manifestations of the Spirit as they are mentioned in Paul's letters (e.g., Rom 10:10; 1 Cor 12), claiming that all such miracles have now "ceased ... and have rightly lasted only for a time."[5] This stance, and Paul's aversion (1 Cor 12:3; 14:1–19) to potential abuses of glossolalia (tongues), have led many in the broadly "Reformed" Evangelical tradition, including Plymouth Brethren,[6] Dispensationalists,[7] Baptists, and Presbyterians,[8] to resist the characteristic Pentecostalist tendency to make a generic connection between the original gift of tongues at Pentecost (hence their denominational name) and the charismatic glossolalia Paul refers to as the "tongues of angels" (1 Cor 13:1), which are now typically an expected proof of the "second blessing" earnestly sought after in most Pentecostal churches. Maintaining this conflation among Pentecostal theologians can involve a distinction between what Roger Stronstad calls "the charismatic theology of Luke" and the pneumatology of Paul, between seeing the gift of tongues as an eschatological and missiological portent and its repeated experience as a sign of divine presence in believers' lives and worship.[9] In particular, according to Stronstad, "the sole distinctive element in Pentecostalism is its insistence that glossolalia is the essential evidence for the baptism in the Spirit."[10] Both Lukan and Pauline understandings are required, Pentecostals claim, for a holistic experience of the "power of the Spirit" in the life of the believer. Meanwhile, pronounced aversion to any literal understanding of the miracle in Acts 2 among liberal Protestants since F. C. Baur has

5. John Calvin, *Institutes* 2.4.19.6, in John Calvin, *Institutes of the Christian Religion*, trans. Henry Beveridge, 2 vols. (Grand Rapids: Eerdmans, 1981).

6. E.g., F. F. Bruce, *Commentary on the Book of the Acts*, New International Commentary on the New Testament (Grand Rapids: Eerdmans, 1954), 53–58.

7. E.g., S. Lewis Johnson, "A Symposium on the Tongues Movement Part II: The Gift of Tongues and the Book of Acts," *Bibliotheca Sacra* 120, no. 480 (1963): 309–21; Richard N. Longenecker, *Acts*, Expositor's Bible Commentary (Grand Rapids: Zondervan, 1995). Among Baptists, conservatives still tend to reflect similar opinions—e.g., David S. Dockery, "The Theology of Acts," *Criswell Theological Review* 5, no. 1 (1990): 43–55; among less conservative Baptists this perspective is often still present, even if more nuanced, e.g. Mikeal C. Parsons, *Acts*, Paideia: Commentaries on the New Testament (Grand Rapids: Baker Academic, 2008), 49–51, who gives a balanced account vis-à-vis the Pentecostal emphasis. G. K. Beale, "The Descent of the Eschatological Temple in the Form of the Spirit at Pentecost," *Tyndale Bulletin* 56, no. 1 (2005): 73–102, evades the linguistic issue via typology.

8. E.g., Beverly Roberts Gaventa, *Acts*, Abingdon New Testament Commentaries (Nashville: Abingdon, 2003).

9. Roger Stronstad, *The Charismatic Theology of St. Luke: Trajectories from the Old Testament to Luke-Acts*, 2nd ed. (Grand Rapids: Baker Academic, 2012), esp. 59–65. In a study that also focuses on Lukan distinctives, Graham H. Twelftree, *People of the Spirit: Exploring Luke's View of the Church* (Grand Rapids: Baker Academic, 2009), gives an Evangelical reading that nonetheless finds in Luke not only one but several "Pentecostal" appearances of the Holy Spirit (69–80).

10. Stronstad, *Charismatic Theology of St. Luke*, 2.

become increasingly conventional in the Reformed tradition; this has led some to rationalist and psychological accounts of the event.[11] (These are paralleled by similarly reductionist accounts among some Roman Catholics when charismatic phenomena has occurred in Roman Catholic environments.)[12]

The second genealogy of evangelical commentary on our passage is actually pre-Reformation, and it draws largely, though not exclusively, on Catholic sources from the Latin fathers and acquires a notably British lineage through and beyond the medieval period. Whereas Calvin emphasized the typological connection between the confusion of tongues at Babel and the profusion of understanding through those languages at Pentecost,[13] the Latin fathers[14] all comment on this passage, as does Gregory of Nazianzus,[15] by connecting it to the giving of the law at Sinai, thus following Jewish tradition.[16] The stress here is on covenant renewal and continuity, therefore, more than on typological contrast.[17] In the dispensation of

11. E.g., S. MacLean Gilmour, "Easter and Pentecost," *Journal of Biblical Literature* 81, no. 1 (1962): 62–66; Ernest Best, "The Interpretation of Tongues," in *Speaking in Tongues: A Guide to Research on Glossolalia*, ed. Watson E. Mills (Grand Rapids: Eerdmans, 1986), 295–312; cf. Anthony C. Thiselton, "The 'Interpretation' of Tongues: A New Suggestion in the Light of Greek Usage in Philo and Josephus," *Journal of Theological Studies* 30, no. 1 (1979): 15–36. Virginia H. Hine, "Pentecostal Glossolalia: Toward a Functional Interpretation," *Journal for the Scientific Study of Religion* 8, no. 2 (1969): 211–26; Gary Gilbert, "The List of Nations in Acts 2: Roman Propaganda and the Lukan Response," *Journal of Biblical Literature* 121, no. 3 (2002): 497–529; cf. Bruce M. Metzger, "Ancient Astrological Geography and Acts 2:9–11," in *Apostolic History and the Gospel: Biblical and Historical Essays Presented to F. F. Bruce*, ed. W. Ward Gasque and Ralph P. Martin (Exeter: Paternoster, 1970), 124–33; Christopher Forbes, "Early Christian Inspired Speech and Hellenistic Popular Religion," *Novum Testamentum* 28, no. 3 (1986): 257–70; also Forbes, *Prophecy and Inspired Speech in Early Christianity and Its Hellenistic Environments* (Peabody, Mass.: Hendrickson, 1997); but cf. Robert H. Gundry, "'Ecstatic Utterance' (N.E.B.)?" *Journal of Theological Studies*, n.s. 17, no. 2 (1966): 229–307; also James D. G. Dunn, *Jesus and the Holy Spirit* (London: SCM, 1975), 247. W. Ward Gasque, *A History of the Interpretation of the Acts of the Apostles* (1975; repr., Peabody, Mass.: Hendrickson, 1989), remains indispensable to a wider historical overview, but Mark J. Cartledge, "The Nature and Function of New Testament Glossolalia," *Evangelical Quarterly* 72, no. 2 (2000): 135–50, is a very helpful update on this pericope.

12. E.g., Anthony Archer, "Teach Yourself Tongue-Speaking," *New Blackfriars* 55, no. 651 (1974): 357–64.

13. John Calvin, *Acts of the Apostles* 2.2.

14. E.g., Jerome in *Ep.* 78.12; Augustine in *Contra Faustum* 32.12 and *De catechizandibus rudibus* 23.41; and Leo the Great's *Sermo de Pentecoste*.

15. Gregory of Nazianzus, *Or.* 31.

16. S. ʿOlam Rab. 5; Šabb. 86a–88a; ʿArak. 1.9; Pesaḥ. 68b. Something of the depth of Augustine's recognition of Pentecost as central to the identity of the Church is also evident in his ecclesiological reading of Ps 44 (45), where at v. 10 he relates the diversity of colors in the robes of the Bride as referring to the variety of languages in which the gospel is preached (*Enarrat. Ps.* 44.24 [CCSL 38:512]).

17. In his monumental work *On the Holy Spirit*, St. Basil actually omits to discuss the gift of tongues. But the dramatic character of the Pentecost event, as well as its typological possibilities, produced in other early Fathers an *enchiridion symbolorum*: the tongues of fire were related by St. Cyprian to the smoke

grace to the gentiles here begun, the meaning of the Pentecost event was understood to be emphatically missiological, thus a signal that the gospel was to be brought to all nations, and in particular in their own vernacular languages. In this context it is necessary to observe that vernacular languages were used from the earliest times by Christians, even in worship. As Origen put it, "Everyone prays and sings to God as best he can, in his mother tongue."[18] Eusebius suggests that by the early fourth century the Christian Scriptures had been translated into several languages.[19] John Chrysostom refers to the Gospel of John's having been translated into local languages not only in Egypt and Ethiopia but as far away as Persia and India, and there is abundant evidence that early Christians living and worshiping in multilingual communities enjoyed the services of translators working to provide local versions of sermons given in Greek.[20] The observation of Irenaeus that there are "many brethren in the Church ... who through the Spirit speak all kinds of languages" is perhaps an early suggestion that evangelists to the gentile nations might be empowered by the Holy Spirit to learn the language of their target culture at miraculous speed.[21] For the Venerable Bede, language learning was a feature of the church indicated clearly in the miracle, that "when it had spread to the ends of the earth [the church] was to speak in the languages of all nations," and that a duty of the church was in therefore in studious humility to recover "the unity of all languages which the pride of Babylon had shattered."[22] But in the early English tradition itself there was a division between those who eschewed commentary on

---

and fire on Sinai and to the burning bush (*Treatises* 101.555); St. Cyril of Jerusalem relates the tongues of fire to the fiery sword that barred Adam and Eve from Eden (*Catechetical Lectures* 17.15). Cyril also relates the wind to God's breath at Creation (17.12), and regards the gift of tongues at Pentecost as a reversal of Babel; cf. Gregory of Nazianzus, *Or.* 41.16.

18. Origen, *Contra Celsum* 8.37.

19. Eusebius, *Theophania* 3.28; cf. 4.7, 4.9.

20. John Chrysostom, *Homilies on the Gospel of John* 2.5. Chrysostom seems to have thought that the glossolalia referred to by St. Paul were in fact a speaking in other known languages (*Homilies on the First Epistle of Paul to the Corinthians* 35.4). For a fuller account, see Rick Strelan, "'We Hear Them Telling in Our Own Tongues the Mighty Works of God' (Acts 2:10)," *Neotestamentica* 40, no. 2 (2006): 295–319; also Simon Tugwell, "The Gift of Tongues in the New Testament," *Expository Times* 84, no. 6 (1973): 137; cf. J. Everts, "Tongues or Languages? Contextual Consistency in the Translation of Acts 2," *Journal of Pentecostal Theology* 4, no. 8 (1994): 71–80. Jaroslav Pelikan, *Acts*, Brazos Theological Commentary on the Bible (Grand Rapids: Brazos, 2005), 52–53, comes down on the side of those who stress the ἀκούομεν ἕκαστος (we hear) and suggests that the event is an instance of glossolalia.

21. Irenaeus, *Haer.* 3.4.2–4, in *ANF* 1:531. In his notes, J. B. Lightfoot sides with Irenaeus: *The Acts of the Apostles: A Newly Discovered Commentary*, ed. Ben Witherington III and Todd D. Still (Downer's Grove, Ill.: IVP Academic, 2014), 88–89.

22. Bede, *Acts of the Apostles* 2.3–4, in *The Commentary of the Venerable Bede on the Acts of the Apostles*, trans. Lawrence T. Martin (Kalamazoo, Mich.: Cistercian, 1989), 29.

Acts 2 and those like Aelfric in the late tenth century, who enthusiastically discusses Pentecost thirteen times in his *Catholic Homilies*.[23] Aelfric, as Kees Dekker has noted, is more sensitive to linguistic and translation issues than many in his time.[24]

Yet it may well be that the most important influence on the strongly missiological orientation of English commentary on Acts 2 has been Pope Gregory the Great, the commissioner of the apostolic mission to the "Angles" in AD 597, and in so many ways the father of English Christianity; Bede is among the many British theologians who, until the twelfth century, regularly call him "our Apostle."[25] In one of his homilies Gregory observes,

> For you have heard that the Holy Spirit appeared in fiery tongues upon the disciples and gave them knowledge of all languages. What truly is signified by this miracle, except that the Holy Church, filled with the same Spirit, was about to speak with the voice of all nations? Those who tried to build a tower against God have lost the communion of one language; however, in those who feared God with humility all languages are united.[26]

For Gregory there was a "hidden language" common to all whom the Spirit had gifted, so that, "with the proper guidance by the Spirit the variety of human languages [thus] formed no impediment to God's truth."[27] Gregory tells the story of a boy who recovered from apparent death, claimed to have been in heaven and there given the gift of tongues—which he demonstrated by speaking Bulgarian and Greek to his examiners.[28] Notably, for Gregory there was no privileged *lingua sacra*, whether Hebrew, Greek, or his own

23. See the discussion by Kees Dekker, "Pentecost and Linguistic Self-Consciousness in Anglo-Saxon England: Bede and Aelfric," *Journal of English and Germanic Philology* 104, no. 3 (2005): 345–72. For those who eschewed commentary, see, e.g., *Vercelli Homilies*; *Homilies* of Wulfstan; the earliest liturgies all lacking it. For Aelfric's homilies, see *Aelfric's Catholic Homilies*, vol. 1, *The First Series*, ed. Peter Clemoes, Early English Text Society, s.s. 17 (Oxford: Oxford University Press, 1997); and *Aelfric's Catholic Homilies*, vol. 2, *The Second Series*, ed. Malcolm R. Godden, Early English Text Society, s.s. 5 (London: Oxford University Press, 1979).

24. Dekker, "Pentecost and Linguistic Self-Consciousness," 348.

25. The first biography of Gregory I, the Whitby *Life* (AD 700) precedes by almost two centuries the Roman *Life*, and his dominance in Bede's *Ecclesiastical History* (ca. AD 731) attest to Gregory's special veneration and distinctive association with the evangelization of Britain; Bede calls him "our Apostle" (*Ecclesiastical History of the English People* 2.1). For a fuller account of the preeminence of Gregory as the shaping force in British Christian self-understanding before the Norman conquest, see Paul Hayward, "Gregory the Great as 'Apostle of the English' in Post-conquest Canterbury," *Journal of Ecclesiastical History* 55, no. 1 (2004): 19–57.

26. Gregory, *Homiliae in evangelia*, ed. Raymond Étaix, CCSL 141 (Turnhout: Brepols, 1999), 259–60; cf. *Moralia in Iob* 2.7.8 12.

27. Dekker, "Pentecost and Linguistic Self-Consciousness," 350.

28. Gregory, *Dialogues* 4.27.9–14.

vernacular Latin; any language might readily declare the glory of God.[29] As Bede after him would put it, all nations and languages of the world are called to praise him together;[30] this sentiment was echoed a millennium later in the great missiological hymn of Charles Wesley "O for a thousand tongues to sing my great Redeemer's praise," in which Wesley prays the Spirit's aid "to spread through all the earth abroad, the glories of thy Name." Far more than is generally recognized by English-speaking Protestants, the spirituality of Gregory the Great and his reading of Acts 2 established major lineaments in Britain especially that would continue long after him; from Bede's story of Caedmon (an example of a miraculous gift of language and translation) through the *Lay Folks Mass Book* and vernacular liturgies of York and the English catechism of Archbishop Thoresby of York (d. 1373) to the tremendous work of British mission societies in the nineteenth century in which language learning enabled biblical translation worldwide.[31] Evangelical proclamation in the vernacular of every tribe and nation is in this sense, I would suggest, a residual reflex of the Gregorian expectation and example.[32] The de-emphasis on sacred languages as a necessary medium for transmitting the text of the Bible itself, so characteristically English, has deep roots and wide branches; the Gregorian tradition extends to the formation of such groups as Wycliffe Bible Translators, still very much active today.

Christian Cooper has drawn to our attention another medieval element that presages modern Evangelical and missiological understandings of the significance of Acts 2:1–13. In an essay on Margery Kempe, whose fifteenth-century book describes two instances of miraculous translation brought on by her intercessory prayers, Cooper notes that *xenoglossia* (what actually happened in Acts 2) appears as a spiritual gift many times in Euro-

29. Robert Stanton, *The Culture of Translation in Anglo-Saxon England* (Cambridge: D. S. Brewer, 2002), 70–73.

30. Bede, *Liber hymnorum, thytthmi, varia preces*, ed. J. Fraipont, CCSL 122 (Turnhout: Brepols, 1955), 424–25.

31. *The Lay Folks Mass Book; or, the manner of hearing Mass, with rubrics and devotions for the people in four texts, and offices in English according to the use of York, from manuscripts of the Xth to XVth century*, ed. Thomas Frederick Simmons (Canon of York), Early English Text Society (London: Trübner, 1879); *The Lay Folks' Catechism; or, the English and Latin versions of Archbishop's instructions for the people . . .*, ed. Thomas Frederick Simmons and H. E. Nolloth, Early English Text Society (London: Kegan Paul, Trench and Trübner, 1901).

32. E.g., William Carey, Samuel Marshman, Robert Morrison, and James Legge. I am currently engaged in research on the Gregorian tradition in British Christianity, both acknowledged and passively assumed.

pean Christendom during the Middle Ages.[33] In male recipients the miracle invariably enables public preaching in a foreign-language environment. In female recipients of the gift, mystics who were essentially illiterate are given the gift of comprehending, writing, or speaking Latin. Examples of both types abound. The Dominican Vincent Ferrer (d. 1419), preaching in his native Valencian in 1405, was reportedly understood by a "large, multilingual crowd" in Greek, German, Sardinian, and Hungarian, as well as later in the Celtic of Brittany, where even women and children understood him. Similar miraculous xenoglossia are recorded for St. David and several other Welsh saints, as well as St. Norbert, St. Dominic, and more.[34] Among women, the Benedictine Elizabeth of Schönau, St. Catherine of Siena, St. Umilita of Faenza, and St. Bridgit of Sweden all received some order or other of instantaneous ability to read and understand Latin. The lives of many of these male and female saints were staple reading during the English spiritual awakening in the age of Richard Rolle, Walter Hilton, Julian of Norwich, and Dame Margery—roughly the age of Wyclif—and they had the effect of making vernacular translation appear to be a Spirit-prompted obligation, part of the Great Commission mandate and charism. It is no accident that both Wyclif and his associates Hereford and Purvey appealed to Gregory the Great in this context, much as had Alcuin before them.[35] In *Piers Plowman,* a popular religious poem contemporary with Wyclif, similar sentiments occur, and in the Chester cycle of Corpus Christi plays of a few years later, the Pentecost play (aptly enough called the Fishmongers Playe, no. 21), after the installation of Matthias as the twelfth apostle, has all twelve kneel and sing the "Veni, Creator Spiritus," which prompts God the Father to comment on what the giving of the Holy Spirit will mean to the

33. Christine F. Cooper, "Miraculous Translation in 'The Book of Margery Kempe,'" *Studies in Philology* 101, no. 3 (2004): 270–98.

34. Cooper, "Miraculous Translation," 273–75.

35. In the prologue, "blessed Gregory" is appealed to as an authoritative support for translation: *The Holy Bible, Containing the Old and New Testaments, with the Apocryphal Books in the Earliest English Versions Made with the Latin Vulgate of John Wycliffe and His Followers,* ed. Josiah Forshall and Sir Frederic Madden (Oxford: Oxford University Press, 1850); the prologue also appeals to Jerome's work translating from Hebrew and Greek texts, as well as to more proximate authorities, such as Robert Grosseteste, chancellor of Oxford and father of the English Franciscans, in making their case for vernacular translation (chap. 15); throughout Wyclif's *De veritate sacrae scripturae,* ed. R. Buddenseig, 3 vols. (London: Wyclif Society, Trübner, 1905–1907). Gregory the Great always heads his list of exegetes (along with Jerome, Ambrose, Chrysostom, and Bonaventure) who recognize that Scripture exhibits "a new grammar and new logic" (novam grammaticam et novam logicam) often obscured in Latin (vovas sensus terminorum scripture, qui nusquam originantur ex libris gramatice), 1.42. On Alcuin, for a brief account see Douglas Dales, "The Legacy of Bede," in *Alcuin: Theology and Thought* (Edinburgh: James Clarke, 2013), 19–30.

apostles as “Throughout the world they shall gonne, / My deeds to preche many one.”[36] When the tongues of fire appear, an angel tells the apostles the purpose of tongues:

> And through the Ghooste that I yow bring
> Yee shall have understanding
> Of every lond speaking,
> Whatsoever the saye.[37]

Philip quickly discovers that though till now he has been a monoglot Hebrew, he can suddenly speak any language at will, whether in its formal or patois version.[38] Though these are only popular forms of biblical commentary and paraphrase, they indicate how firmly Gregory’s understanding of the nature and purpose of tongues at Pentecost had become normative.

What I have called here the Gregorian genealogy or tradition comes into tension with the Calvinist tradition of interpretation of Acts 2:1–13 after the Reformation: The Puritan divines, such as Baxter, Sibbes, and Owen, all influenced by Calvin, largely eschew commentary; Anglican preachers such as John Donne, George Herbert, and Lancelot Andrewes on the other hand, all of whom drew upon earlier, especially patristic exegesis, take it up in liturgical preaching and reflection. It is the Gregorian tradition, persevering with vigor despite the divisions of the Reformation, which I now take to have most shaped understanding of Acts 2 in an Evangelical direction. This postulate may be briefly illustrated by a brief examination of the views of Lancelot Andrewes (1555–1626), seventeenth-century bishop of Winchester, a leading light in the 1604 Hampton Court Conference, and most eminent among the translators of the King James Bible authorized by King James I. Andrewes, as many of you know, was an excellent scholar, able to read and write in fifteen languages, and, as the poet T. S. Eliot was to discover, he was one of the most eloquent expositors of Holy Scripture ever to preach in England. Though today he would more likely be thought of as an Anglo-Catholic, he represents well the “Gregorian” Evangelical voice of a better time. His eleven volumes of published works include fifteen sermons preached on Pentecost Sunday, or “Whitsunday,” as it was long called in English tradition, fourteen of which were delivered before King James I

36. *The Chester Mystery Cycle*, ed. R. M. Lumiansky and David Mills, Early English Text Society, s.s. 3 (London: Oxford University Press, 1974), vol. 2, lines 207–9, 247–50.

37. Lumiansky and Mills, *Chester Mystery Cycle*, 247–50.

38. Lumiansky and Mills, *Chester Mystery Cycle*, 279–82.

between 1600 and 1621.[39] (The last sermon, for 1622, was never preached.) Only two of these sermons were direct expositions of our text in Acts 2:1–13, but all are interconnected with Andrewes's pneumatology. I want to consider briefly here the two sermons specifically on our text, and also his tenth Whitsunday sermon, on Lk 4:18–19. In all of these strongly trinitarian expositions Andrewes stresses the *initiatory* character of Pentecost, as the moment of the "the first dedication of Christ's Catholic Church on earth," "the first publishing of the Gospel," and "the first proclaiming of the Apostles' commission."[40] For him, the annual liturgical celebration of Pentecost is provided so as to occasion fulsome thanks for a gift of God "so great and so wonderful as there were not tongues enough upon earth to celebrate it" (sermon 1), and for him it serves as a culmination of all other liturgical feasts in the year as to their theological meaning and trajectory.[41] This had since the eighth century been a festal emphasis peculiar to the British, among whom Whitsun was, after Easter, the most public of festivals in many places, with pageants, dancing, and parades through the streets, originally featuring the catechumens dressed in white (hence one meaning of "Whit"), while the vestments of the clergy were also white, in contrast with the usual red elsewhere.[42] The heightened annual celebration underscores for Andrewes that there are many other gifts of the Holy Spirit, all intended for the common good and growth in holiness of the whole church, engraving, as it were, the whole of the narrative of our redemption and ongoing sanctification—which, like Wyclif before him, he calls "the Law of Christ"—on the hearts of believers. He draws thus on the Fathers both Greek and Latin to show a continuity between the first Pentecost at Sinai and the one in Acts 2, citing the connection made by Cyprian and others, where fifty days following the Passover in Exodus the law was given, and then describing the portent of that event as perfected in the gospel:

39. *The Sermons of Lancelot Andrewes*, vol. 2, *Paschal and Pentecostal*, ed. Marianne Dorman (Edinburgh: Pentland, 1993); see also *The Works of Lancelot Andrewes*, ed. J. Bliss and J. P. Wilson, 11 vols. (Oxford: Oxford University Press, 1841–1854).

40. Andrewes, *Paschal and Pentecostal*, 206. Cf. Twelftree, *People of the Spirit*, 75, who in a way quite representative of both modern Evangelical and Pentecostal commentators, rejects the "birthday of the Church" claim more commonly expressed by Anglicans.

41. In Catholic tradition elsewhere, by contrast, it has usually been the Feast of Corpus Christi that is taken to recapitulate the liturgical year.

42. *Albho*, the proto-Indo European word for *white*, yields up the original Greek term for Britain, *Albion* (Pliny), probably for the white cliffs of Dover, but also Lat. *albus*; f. *alba*, while the ancient name now applies only to Caledonia, Gaelic *Alba*.

Reckoning from Christ our Passover fifty days, that the Law was given at Sinai, the very same day does the new Law go out of Sion, as the prophet Isaiah foretold, *exibit de Sion Lex*, which is nothing else but the promulgation of the Gospel.[43]

To this he adds, drawing on John Chrysostom, that just as Pentecost had become associated with the initiation of the grain harvest,

In like sort we see that this very day, the Lord of the harvest so disposing it ... his first workmen, the Apostles, did put in their first sickle into the great harvest, *whereof the world is the field*, and the several furrows of it, *all the nations under heaven*.[44]

Pentecost is thus the inauguration of worldwide evangelism, gathering in sheaves from the fields "white unto harvest" as the Lord indicated. To these analogies he adds a third, from Augustine, drawing attention to the number of Pentecost, fifty, "being all a long [in] the law the number of Jubilee, which was the time of forgiving of debts, and restoring men to their first estates ... [and] which is now an act of God's most gracious general free pardon of all the sins of all the sinners of the world."[45] Andrewes thus provides a synthesis of the Pentecostal register connecting the law of Jubilee (Leviticus 25) with Isaiah's Jubilee prophecy and the quotation of it by Jesus at the outset of his ministry:

The Spirit of the Lord is upon me because he has anointed me to preach the gospel to the poor; he has sent me to heal the brokenhearted, to proclaim liberty to captives and recovery of sight to the blind, to set at liberty those who are oppressed; to proclaim the acceptable year of the Lord. (Lk 4:18–19; cf. Is 61:1–2)

The Jubilee was a proclamation of good news to all people, especially to those most in need of it; so too, Pentecost is a Jubilee proclamation of the "good news of great joy which will be to *all* people" (Lk 2:10) foretold by the angels to poor shepherds. Thus, for Andrewes, the "true Jubilee" is the gospel itself.[46]

Andrewes explains the suitability of Lk 4:18–19 as a Gospel reading for Pentecost by saying that from this coming of the Holy Spirit upon Jesus came the coming of the Holy Spirit upon the apostles, and indeed "upon us all."[47]

43. Andrewes, *Paschal and Pentecostal*, 210.
44. Andrewes, *Paschal and Pentecostal*, 210.
45. Andrewes, *Paschal and Pentecostal*, 211.
46. Andrewes, *Paschal and Pentecostal*, 301.
47. Andrewes, *Paschal and Pentecostal*, 302.

All our anointings are but drops from His anointing; all our missions and commissions, but quills, as we say, out of this commission here.... As he sent me, I send you. By that and no other commission did they, or do we, or will any come....

Why came the Spirit upon Christ? To send Him. Send Him to what? *Ad evangelizandum*. And why came the Spirit upon the Twelve this day, but for the very same end?

To proclaim what? *The acceptable year of the Lord*, that is, the Jubilee.[48]

In short, Andrewes ties the meaning of Pentecost directly to the divine purpose in Jubilee emancipation, and the proclamation of the gospel of liberty by Isaiah and by Jesus is therefore to be followed by a worldwide evangelical mission with the same purpose, a purpose not restricted to one year, as under the law, but is to be a perpetual Jubilee, proclaimed everywhere and always in all tongues. Thus, Andrewes notes, Paul speaks of the Jubilee as an age of grace, saying, "Behold, this is the day; behold now is the acceptable time," and he continues:

Whereby we are given to understand that Christ's jubilee, though it began when Christ first preached this sermon [in Nazareth], yet it ended not with the end of that year as did Aaron's, but was *Evangelium aeternum*; as also *perpetui jubilaei*, that does last and will last as long as the Gospel will be preached by himself, or others sent by Him, to the end of the world, *the time of restoring all things*.[49]

I suggest that this collocation by Andrewes offers a distinctively British Evangelical understanding of the Luke-Acts texts, and that it is largely representative of Whitsun exegesis in England from the time of Bede to the mid-nineteenth century.

For Andrewes, as would be the case for all normative Christianity, we are first regenerated by the Holy Spirit in our baptism, but it does not stop there. Rather, it is confirmed in the imposition of hands, and renewed continuously through acts of repentance, prayer, and in many other mysterious ways, so that by the Holy Spirit we are

taught all our life long that we know not, put in mind of what we forget, stirred up in what we are dull, helped in our prayers, relieved in *our infirmities*, comforted in our heaviness; in a word, *sealed to the day of our redemption*, and *raised up again in the last day*.[50]

48. Andrewes, *Paschal and Pentecostal*, 301–2.
49. Andrewes, *Paschal and Pentecostal*, 308.
50. Andrewes, *Paschal and Pentecostal*, 253 (sermon 5).

If we do not find in ourselves "a new heart and a new spirit," and that we are "renewed in the spirit of our mind," this ought to occasion in us an examination of conscience to discern by what impediments we are suppressing the work of the Spirit in us. Repentance ought to follow, so as to restore our fellowship. We ought thence to "lay no bars to keep him from us" and "use all good means to allure Him to us."[51] In short, there is also something Pentecostal in Andrewes's sense of our need for regular renewal, for the continuous operation of the Holy Spirit in our lives, opening up the channels of our minds and hearts to the Spirit again and again.[52]

In his second sermon on our text (1608) Andrewes stresses that the gifts of the Spirit are received communally, "given and received for the good of others."[53] This is the principle he finds to govern not only the gift of foreign languages but also the gift of clarity and eloquence that occurs when beleaguered believers are arraigned, as he has it, "in every judgment place, in every consistory."[54] Here, of course, he recalls the promise of Jesus that this would be one of the gifts of the Holy Spirit, that his disciples would be given the words to speak in their hour of need (Lk 12:11–12). As for the foreign languages, "so many sundry tongues to so many nations," that singular yet significant gift at Pentecost has resulted in a commitment to worldwide evangelism, that "by speaking all tongues, they have gathered a Church that speaks all tongues; a thing much tending to the glory of God." Here, like Gregory, he refers to the reversal of Babel, observing that as a result of Pentecost people all over the world "send up so many tongues, there to praise his name ... as a concert of many instruments might yield a full harmony."

In which, we behold the mighty work of God; that the same means of tongues, which was the destroying of Babel, the very same is here made to work the building of Sion; that means that scattered them from the tower of confusion, the very same

51. Andrewes, *Paschal and Pentecostal*, 256.

52. Andrewes also warns, however, that just because some have the apparent gift of tongues, it does not follow that it is a gift of the Holy Spirit, for it might come from an unholy spirit, even the "devil from hell" (Dorman, *Paschal and Pentecostal*, 215). This warning seems apt in the light of current psychological studies that record episodes of what appear to be demonic possession in which victims in a fit can suddenly speak "perfect Latin." See Richard Gallagher, "As a Psychiatrist, I Diagnose Mental Illness. Also, I Help Spot Demonic Possession," *Washington Post*, July 1, 2016, https://www.washingtonpost.com/posteverything/wp/2016/07/01/as-a-psychiatrist-i-diagnose-mental-illness-and-sometimes-demonic-possession/.

53. Andrewes, *Paschal and Pentecostal*, 220.

54. Andrewes, *Paschal and Pentecostal*, 221.

to reduce them to the fold of unity; that so the curse might be taken away, and a blessing come in place, the confused tongues being united into God's glory.[55]

We hear the voice of the great bishop still echoing.[56]

Andrewes concludes his second sermon for Pentecost with an observation that is well worthy of more extended reflection than I can give it here, but let me mention it. He directs us to verse 4: "And they were all filled with the Holy Spirit and began to speak with other tongues, *as the Spirit gave them utterance*."[57] Here he seems clearly to caution against undisciplined, ecstatic speech, insisting that what proceeded from the mouths of the apostles was "not the crudities of their own brain, idle, loose, undigested gear, God knows; no, but pithy and wise sentences." The Spirit, he says, gave them to speak "*magnalia; great and high points*; not *trivialia, base and vulgar stuff*, not worth the time it wasted."[58] That baser sort of speaking is not Spirit directed, he says, and it actually robs the hearer of what he is due. It is clear that Andrewes is alluding to the need for Spirit-directed discernment, rather than popular entertainment, in preaching in any language. As a bishop, of course, he had to be concerned with more than his own preaching.

If I have looked to the great preacher and translator Lancelot Andrewes to provide a rigorous Evangelical understanding of Acts 2:1–13, I do not mean thereby to suggest that he has been an influential model for address to our text by all who now call themselves "Evangelical." Indeed, to most North American Evangelicals he and the other seventeenth-century Anglican divines who were like him are almost completely unknown. This is a pity, for Andrewes was Evangelical in the radical sense; he believed that in the Gospels and Acts of the Apostles, not to mention the Epistles, we are set a standard far higher than that exhibited in the world around us, and that what enables the holiness to which we are called is the direct action of the Holy Spirit upon us. He believed further than in the bestowing of

55. Andrewes, *Paschal and Pentecostal*, 221–22.

56. See Malcolm Guite, "The Word and the Words: Andrewes, Donne, and the Theology of Translation," in *The King James Bible at 400: Assessing Its Genius as Bible Translation and Its Literary Influence*, ed. David G. Burke, John F. Kutsko, and Philip H. Townec (Atlanta: Society of Biblical Literature, 2013), 373–83.

57. Punning on "cloven tongues," Andrewes connects the cloven tongues of fire with the diversity of speech following: "to that end clove he their tongues; to make many tongues in one tongue, to make one man to be able to speak to many men of many countries, to every one in his own language" (Dorman, *Paschal and Pentecostal*, 216); this may be a suggestion that he remembered the distinctive Wycliffite translation of Acts 2:3–4, in which, despite the Latin "dispertae linguae / variis linguis" of the Vulgate from which Purvey worked, the rendering was "diuerse tonges / diuerse langages."

58. Andrewes, *Paschal and Pentecostal*, 222.

tongues at Pentecost the apostles and their audience were not given a one-off demonstration of the Spirit's power, but rather a template for apostolic mission *ad aeternum*. For Andrewes, as for Gregory the Great, the abiding significance of the gift of tongues at Pentecost is to tell us that we have work to do, work beyond our own shire; that work is to bring the gospel where it has not been heard, there to make it known in the mother tongue of people very unlike ourselves.

A concluding distinction: All of this pertains to Pentecost itself, a moment in salvation history from which Evangelicals have taken their identity, though not their name. In other words, xenoglossia rather than glossolalia is paramount in Evangelical understandings of the "gift of tongues," and many have noted with C. S. Lewis that with respect to the glossolalia in 1 Corinthians 12 and 14, from which Pentecostals seem to take their identity but not their name, that "St. Paul himself seems rather to have been embarrassed by it . . . and labours to turn the desire and attention of the Church to more obviously edifying gifts."[59] But to end on this note would be to beg my question at the beginning, Are Pentecostals (who major in this spiritual gift of glossolalia above others) Evangelical?

Well, both the National Association of Evangelicals and J. I. Packer say yes, just as much as Anglicans, so to that degree my youthful wonderment has been officially mooted. In any case, I now think that was not the best question. In the context of our confusions and cultural syncretisms, it might today be at least as appropriate to ask, Are Evangelicals sufficiently Pentecostal? Some would go so far as to ask, Are today's Evangelicals really Christian? (The answer, I hope, is "many of us are"—though too few in the radical sense intended by the first Franciscans, Lancelot Andrewes, or the great Evangelicals of the British revival.) As I have been reading biblical scholarship by Pentecostals on Luke-Acts and sympathetic modern Evangelicals such as Graham Twelftree, it has been impossible for me to overlook so much evidence that we Evangelicals have formed our opinion of Pentecostal scholarship—and on the work of the Holy Spirit in the life of the believer—on too exclusively a Pauline platform. Pentecostal scholarship has been asking, in the words of Robert P. Menzies, for the "church universal to take a fresh look at Luke's two-volume work"[60] and showing

59. See note 1: Lewis, "Transposition," 16. Cf. Luke Timothy Johnson, "Glossolalia and the Embarrassments of Experience," *Princeton Seminary Bulletin* 18, no. 2 (1997): 117.

60. Robert P. Menzies, "Luke's Understanding of Baptism in the Holy Spirit: A Pentecostal Dialogue with the Reformed Tradition," *Journal of Pentecostal Theology* 16, no. 1 (2008): 86–101. This irenic essay

with some persuasiveness that Luke's theology of the Spirit is different from Paul's in stressing not the soteriological but rather a charismatic dimension by which the church is given a prophetic gift aimed at service. This view, that the gift of the Spirit is a "prophetic enabling,"[61] Menzies finds consistent with Second Temple Judaism's expectations of messianic anointing, as is suggested in the verse from Joel (2:28) to which Peter appeals in his sermon. Pentecostals continue to speak of two baptisms in the Spirit, "one that is soteriological and initiates the believer into the body of Christ (1 Cor. 12:13) and one that is missiological and empowers the believer for service (Acts 1:8)."[62] For Anglicans and Catholics, I would note, there are clear overlappings of the second baptism with traditional understandings of the sacraments of confirmation and ordination.

As to the emphasis on the second baptism in the Spirit, by which the Pentecostal movement has been so marked since its inception, there has been appearance lately in many Christian denominations of explicit linkages between glossolalia (prayer "in the tongues of angels"), and both sanctification in the traditional sense, and *theosis* in the specifically Orthodox sense. In this latter reflection, glossolalia is seen as a participation in the divine life, a process based on the incarnation, "the provision of the means for that which occurred at Pentecost" and which develops through the maturing Christian life.[63] Both of these are recent clarifications of Pentecostal doctrine, which draw the movement, theologically at least, somewhat closer to Catholic and Orthodox positions, even as they constitute a challenge to traditional Reformed Evangelical perspectives.

There remains a caution of course: An exclusive emphasis on glossolalia can obscure the fact that in Pentecost itself the miracle was clearly *heteroglossa* (Gk. ἑτέραις γλώσσαις) or *xenolalia*, the speaking of known foreign languages intelligibly. This miracle bespeaks, as Gregory and others after him so clearly saw, the universality of the claims of the gospel for all the world. For many Evangelicals (including traditional Anglicans), the risk in emphasizing glossolalia as necessary for authentic Christian life is that it

---

is adapted from his *The Development of Early Christian Pneumatology, with Special Reference to Luke-Acts*, Journal for the Study of the New Testament Supplement Series 54 (Sheffield: Sheffield Academic, 1991).

61. Menzies, "Luke's Understanding," 92.

62. Menzies, "Luke's Understanding," 100.

63. Mark J. Cartledge, *Charismatic Glossolalia: An Empirical Theological Study* (Aldershot: Ashgate, 2002), is another "crossover" study by a contemporary Evangelical sympathetic to the Lukan emphasis in Pentecostalism. His invaluable survey of literature in the field in chapter 4 is a slight revision of his "The Nature and Function of New Testament Glossolalia," *Evangelical Quarterly* 72, no. 2 (2000): 135–50.

can seem too excluding, becoming a criterion by which believers are distinguished from nonbelievers.[64] This, in fact, seems to have been St. Paul's concern with the Corinthians, that the gift of glossolalia can become a means of exclusion not warranted by the gospel itself. In his two-volume work, Luke is acutely conscious, as perhaps we might expect a particularly observant gentile physician to be, of the presence of the Holy Spirit manifesting himself both throughout the Jewish Scriptures and most immediately in the lives of those around the Lord whose transformation into apostles he so carefully records; on the other hand, Luke's focus from beginning to end, Acts 2 included, is on the "good tidings of great joy which shall be to *all* people" (Lk 2:10; cf. 28:23–28), and there can hardly be anything more evangelical than that.

64. Christopher Forbes, *Prophecy and Inspired Speech in Early Christianity and Its Hellenistic Environment* (Peabody, Mass.: Hendrickson, 1997), 173–74.

RESPONSE

Vatican II and Analogical Thinking

Msgr. Thomas G. Guarino (Catholic)

At a recent meeting of Evangelicals and Catholics Together, the organizer of our conference, Dr. Charles Raith, told me that Dr. David Jeffrey would like a response that is both fully Catholic as well as fully ecumenical. Since David's paper is about Acts 2 and Pentecost, the day traditionally denominated as the "birth of the church," my response will, indeed, be centered on the church and on Catholicism in particular. In light of the recent commemoration of the fiftieth anniversary of Vatican II, I would like to reflect on how the council sought to enflesh the unity of Christians—and so to move closer to that unity displayed at Pentecost itself.

This may not appear to be a direct response to David's paper. But one aspect of his talk concerns the contemporary meaning of Pentecost for Christian believers. It is with this theme in mind that I recall John XXIII's famous prayer convoking Vatican II on Christmas Day 1961: "Renew your wonders in our time, O Lord, as in a new Pentecost, and grant that Holy Church may be united in unanimous and intense prayer."

How did Vatican II attempt to instantiate the unity of Pentecost for today's divided Christians? How did the council seek to exemplify Gregory the Great's claim, cited by Jeffrey, that there is a "hidden language" common to all whom the Spirit has gifted? Jeffrey cites Bishop Lancelot Andrewes, who sees in Pentecost "the inauguration of worldwide evangelism." Vatican II, similarly, said the worldwide mission of the church was "fully confirmed on the day of Pentecost." But the council also acknowledged that this global witness to Jesus Christ is deeply injured by ecclesial divisions. Only the restoration of unity among Christians—the unity witnessed at Pentecost—would provide effective testimony for the world today. These ideas form the substance of my response.

I do not expect either Evangelical or Orthodox theologians to agree with all my points. But I do think that all will find Catholicism's theological moves at the council—not always clearly understood—to be of interest and continuing relevance.

Let me state my central argument at the outset: Despite the often-heard claim that Catholicism definitively abandoned scholasticism at Vatican II, in fact, the theologians and bishops at the council used some of scholasticism's most important tools to reevaluate, in particular, Protestant churches, and to view them in much more positive light than had been the case heretofore—advancing Christian unity in the process.

Orthodoxy is also included in this reevaluation although even in the original schema *De ecclesia*, distributed in the fall of 1962, it is stated that throughout the second millennium—from Gregory VII in 1074 to Pius XII in 1953—the "Oriental communities" are "saepe et constanter" (often and constantly) called "churches" in the properly theological (and not simply sociological) sense of that word.[65] This indicates that even the original schema *De ecclesia*, though ultimately rejected, acknowledged the uniqueness of Orthodoxy.[66]

Nonetheless, prior to Vatican II, Catholicism had little *official* use for ecumenical dialogue, whether with Orthodoxy or with Protestantism. It is true that the Vatican tacitly supported the Malines Conversations in the 1920s, discussions between Catholics and Anglicans led by Cardinal Désiré Mercier and Lord Halifax. The theme of those conversations, "united not absorbed," was animated by the hope that Anglicanism could maintain its unique liturgical and theological traditions even while restoring the link to Rome that had characterized the English church in the first millennium.[67]

Despite Malines, the official line of Catholicism was quite clear, having been expressed in a 1928 encyclical by Pope Pius XI titled *Mortalium animos*. Pius spoke of ecumenically involved Protestant communions as purveying "a false Christianity, *ab una Christi Ecclesia admodum alienae*" (entirely foreign to the one church of Christ). Indeed, the encyclical comes very close to saying that the name "Christian" is appropriated by these communions illegitimately. Further, the pope bans Catholics from attending ecumenical

65. *Acta synodalia sacrosancti concilii oecumenici Vaticani II* (Vatican City: Typis Polyglottis Vaticanis, 1971), v. I/4, 12–122 at 88n6.

66. A few years after the council concluded, in 1971, Paul VI, in a letter to Patriarch Athenagoras, stated that between the Roman Catholic Church and the Orthodox churches "there already exists a communion which is almost complete—though still short of perfection." See E. J. Stormon, ed., *Towards the Healing of Schism* (Mahwah, N.J.: Paulist Press, 1987), 232.

67. See Lord Halifax, ed., *The Conversations at Malines 1921–1925* (London: Philip Allan, 1930).

meetings and warns of "pan-Christians"—those who wish to reduce Christian beliefs to a lowest common denominator.

Although this line was softened a bit by the Holy Office in 1949, allowing some well-trained priests and even an occasional layman to attend ecumenical meetings—although with strict episcopal supervision—the general sense on the eve of Vatican II was that ecumenism was to be avoided by Catholic theologians.[68] Yves Congar, the great ecumenist and conciliar theologian—who himself had been disciplined in 1937 for writing a book that spoke of the authentic gifts of Protestantism[69]—was glum about the prospects for ecumenism at the start of the council. He confided to his conciliar journal in July 1960, when preparations were already underway, that Vatican II was taking place twenty-five years too early. A generation of bishops needed to be theologically prepared for new movements within the church.[70] In fact, Congar's fears would prove unfounded for, as everyone knows, the council made very strong ecumenical overtures—and these were supported by the vast majority of the conciliar bishops. How was this turnabout theologically achieved?

Many are familiar with the argument that the council demolished scholastic theology in favor of biblical, patristic, and pastoral approaches. One representative of this point of view, John O'Malley, has written a generally good book on the council titled *What Happened at Vatican II*. But on the issue of scholastic thought, he overplays his hand. For example: "Vatican II . . . largely eschewed Scholastic language. . . . In so doing it largely abandoned the Scholastic framework that had dominated Catholic theology since the thirteenth century."[71]

But is this true? Did Catholicism abandon scholasticism at Vatican II? It certainly abandoned scholastic language, which is barely to be found in the documents. But what about scholastic and Thomistic *ideas*? In just this regard, I would like to cite, once again, Yves Congar, one of the principal theo-

68. For the Instruction, *Ecclesia Catholica* (*De motione oecumenica*), see *Acta apostolicae sedis* 42 (1950): 142–47. Language admonishing "dissident" Christians to return to Catholicism may be found throughout the document.

69. Yves Congar, *Divided Christendom* (London: Centenary, 1939). Congar would later write a book encouraging Catholic acknowledgment of the unique traditions of Orthodoxy. See Congar, *After Nine Hundred Years* (1954; repr., New York: Fordham University Press, 1998).

70. Yves Congar, *My Journal of the Council*, trans. Mary John Ronayne and Mary Cecily Boulding (Collegeville, Minn.: Liturgical Press, 2012), 4.

71. John W. O'Malley, *What Happened at Vatican II* (Cambridge, Mass.: Belknap Press of Harvard University Press, 2008), 46.

logical architects of Vatican II. Writing in 1967, just a couple of years after the council's conclusion, he states: While the references to Aquinas at Vatican II are not numerous, nonetheless "it could be shown … that St. Thomas, the *Doctor communis,* furnished the writers of the dogmatic texts of Vatican II with the *bases and structure* [les assises et la structure] *of their thought.* We do not doubt that they themselves would make this confession."[72]

Where do we find Aquinas's thought offering the "bases and structure" of the conciliar documents? And how does this instantiate John XXIII's desire that the council, in some sense, represent a "new Pentecost"?

For apposite examples, I would like to turn to the council's Dogmatic Constitution on the Church, *Lumen Gentium,* and its draftsman, Gérard Philips. Philips, a Flemish theologian, professor of theology at the University of Louvain in Belgium, was a pivotal thinker at Vatican II, although he remains unknown in large sectors of the English-speaking world. His official (and ungainly) title was Adjunct Secretary of the Theological Commission. (He was "adjunct" because the secretary of the commission was Sebastian Tromp, the Dutch Jesuit who was instrumental in writing the original schemas that were largely rejected by the council fathers. While Philips was elected as "adjunct secretary" in December, 1963, Tromp remained as secretary of the commission.) This situation might have caused tension, but as Congar writes in his journal: Philips has gained Tromp's confidence; during breaks, the two men always converse in Dutch. "That makes things a lot easier."[73]

Gustave Thils, another theologian from Louvain, who also served as a *peritus* on the Theological Commission, says that Philips was so deeply involved in the conciliar documents that one might call him the *homo conciliaris* par excellence.[74] He was deeply respectful toward every position advanced by the bishops on the commission. This was so much the case that one joke circulating among the *periti* described Philips's method as follows: When a bishop would approach him with an obscure point expressed in coarse Latin, Philips would (allegedly) reply: I have not clearly understood Your Excellency's concerns, but I shall certainly take them into account![75]

72. Yves Congar, "La théologie au Concile: Le 'théologiser' du Concile," in *Situation et tâches présentes de la théologie* (Paris: Cerf, 1967), 53 (emphasis added; translation mine).

73. Congar, *My Journal of the Council,* 509.

74. Jan Gootaers, ed., *Primauté et collégialité: Le dossier de Gérard Philips sur la Nota Explicativa Praevia (Lumen gentium, chap. III)* (Leuven: Leuven University Press, 1986), 10.

75. Gootaers, *Primauté et collégialité,* 10.

In studying Philips's diary (and other writings), I have come to believe that he was providentially placed on the Theological Commission of Vatican II. He was a moderate progressive, aligned with the *nouvelle théologie* and its turn to biblical and patristic thinking, but he also fully understood the concerns of the traditionalist minority among the bishops. He was a modest man, with a finely honed theological intelligence. As Congar says in his diary, Philips often says, "si Patres velint" (if the conciliar fathers so desire), giving the impression that they have made the decision. In actual fact, "he [Philips] leads the Fathers where he wants."[76]

Examples of Participation and Analogy at the Council

But on to the meat of the issue. How did Vatican II reevaluate Protestant churches—and so advance Christian unity—on Thomist grounds? It is my claim that Philips used the themes of *participation and analogy* in order to reorient the Catholic Church in its relationship with Protestant churches. In fact, it used these same tools when explaining several theological points in the dogmatic constitution *Lumen Gentium*.

One example of this may be found in Vatican II's treatment of the universal priesthood of the baptized. This issue, brought to the fore by the Reformation, was largely ignored by the Council of Trent (1545), which concentrated its energies on defending the ministerial priesthood.

At Vatican II, the original (rejected) schema *De ecclesia* spoke of the universal priesthood as only metaphorical and to be clearly distinguished from the *sacerdotium veri nominis*. But the gathered bishops reacted negatively to that phrase. Could not Vatican II say a positive word about the universal priesthood of all the baptized, especially given the affirmations about the priesthood of the faithful found in the Bible (citing 1 Peter)?

Philips argues that only Jesus "has by full right the name of priest"—only he is, as Thomas Aquinas calls him, the *verus sacerdos*[77]—even though this attribute or name is extended to others.[78] All Christians, both the ordained and the faithful, *participate* in the one priesthood of Jesus Christ. Although neither Philips nor *Lumen Gentium* uses the language of *formaliter*

76. Congar, *My Journal of the Council*, 510.

77. Thomas Aquinas, *Summa contra gentiles* 4.36.

78. Gérard Philips, *L'Église et son Mystère* (Paris: Desclée, 1968), 2:268.

et substantialiter, we can say that both priesthoods—the ministerial and that of the baptized faithful—participate in Christ's priesthood formally and substantially. In other words, to use the classical language, the priesthood belongs *per se et per essentiam* to Jesus Christ, while Christ's ministers and faithful possess this attribute *per participationem*. Participation in any attribute or perfection—in this case, the priesthood of Jesus Christ—is the ontological foundation for analogical naming. This approach clearly owes a good deal to the method of Aquinas himself.[79]

Philips was well aware of the precision needed on just this point. Three months after *Lumen Gentium* was promulgated (on November 21, 1964), he writes that *Lumen Gentium* is the church's "first official doctrinal declaration on the subject of the *universal priesthood* of the faithful."[80] This *novum* in conciliar history had to be expressed with exactness. To achieve this end, Philips used the classical tools of participation and analogy to explain how both the ministers and faithful truly participate in Christ's priesthood, although in essentially different ways.

Philips used the same method when talking about Mary the Mother of God, in chapter 8 of *Lumen Gentium*. Vatican II was crystal clear. Jesus Christ is the unique and sole mediator between God and men. (If one would like to see the influence of the Reformation on *Lumen Gentium*, one can surely find it in the drumbeat of affirmations insisting that Christ is the "one mediator" or "sole mediator" between God and humanity.)

So, Vatican II's Dogmatic Constitution on the Church teaches:

> There is but one Mediator as we know from the words of the apostle, "for there is one God and one mediator of God and men, the man Christ Jesus, who gave himself as a ransom for all" (I Tim. 2:5–6). The maternal duty of Mary toward men in no wise obscures or diminishes this unique mediation of Christ, but rather shows His power. For all the salvific influence of the Blessed Virgin on men originates, not from some inner necessity, but from the divine pleasure. It flows forth from the superabundance of the merits of Christ, rests on His mediation, depends entirely on it and draws all its power from it. In no way does it impede, but rather does it foster the immediate union of the faithful with Christ.[81]

79. I have treated at length the priesthood and analogical reasoning at Vatican II in "*Essentia et non gradu tantum differant*: A Note on the Priesthood and Analogical Predication," *The Thomist* 77, no. 4 (2013): 559–76.

80. Gootaers, *Primauté et collégialité*, 190.

81. Vatican Council II, *Lumen Gentium*, November 21, 1964, no. 60. The full text is available at www.vatican.va.

Mary's mediation, the council makes abundantly clear, relies on the unique mediator, Christ himself. At the same time, Christians are deeply linked to Mary and to all the saints who (according to Catholic teaching) unceasingly pray for us and accompany us on our journey to the Holy Trinity. This is the Catholic understanding of the creedal affirmation concerning the "communion of saints." Analogically speaking, then, Mary and the saints have *some* mediatorial role—but, once again, only by participation. As *Lumen Gentium* limpidly states:

> For no creature could ever be counted as equal with the Incarnate Word and Redeemer. Just as the priesthood of Christ is shared in various ways both by the ministers and by the faithful, and as the one goodness of God is really communicated in different ways to His creatures, so also the unique mediation of the Redeemer does not exclude but rather gives rise to a manifold cooperation which is but a sharing in this one source.[82]

The one mediator, the mediator between God and men *per se and per essentiam*—just as the one priest *per se and per essentiam*—is Christ Jesus the Lord. But others may participate in these attributes—substantially and formally, but always secondarily—and so may be properly called mediators (and priests). This kind of scholastic *language* is not found at Vatican II and so, from the linguistic point of view, the council did indeed abandon scholasticism—precisely in the interest of contemporary intelligibility. But the scholastic *ideas* of participation and analogy are deeply embedded in *Lumen Gentium*. Indeed, they provide the keys for understanding several of the council's fundamental affirmations.

A final example may be taken from another well-known section of the Dogmatic Constitution on the Church, a section that manifests the conciliar desire for Christian unity—and so for the unity of Pentecost itself.

Everyone knows that Vatican II said the church of Christ "subsists in" the Catholic Church.[83] Everyone knows as well that the exact meaning of this term has been debated for over fifty years, a state of affairs that Philips himself had anticipated. It is my contention that, with this language—and we now know that the term *subsistit in* was suggested by Sebastian Tromp, one of the most traditional theologians on the Theological Commission—classical Thomist tools were also at work. Philips himself remarks, in his

82. *Lumen Gentium*, no. 62.
83. *Lumen Gentium*, no. 8.

article published just three months after *Lumen Gentium* was formally promulgated, that one task of the dogmatic constitution was to determine the precise relationship of the people of God "with Catholics, with separated Christians, with non-Christians and even with unbelievers."[84] But how does one express unity with others without ignoring distinctions? How does one speak of similarity in difference? One traditional way has been through participation and analogy.[85]

Philips admits that the term *subsistit in* is difficult to translate. He then tries to explain its meaning:

> The expression means that the Church of Christ is fully present [*pleinement présente*], it is *en vigueur*, in the ecclesial organization of which the supreme head is Rome. It is not stated that it [the Church of Christ] "*est*" [is] the Roman Church and nothing more ... because there exist outside of this visible institution some elements of the Church of holiness and truth. This shows the ecumenical consciousness that was attained by almost all the conciliar Fathers. For them, the divisions among Christians became a problem which they refused to avoid.[86]

Now, I don't expect either Orthodox or Evangelical theologians to agree with Philips's statement. But I ask them to take note of how far the council progressed beyond *Mortalium animos* of 1928. Other churches, insofar as they possess elements of holiness and truth, are regarded as participating in the church of Christ with varying levels of intensity. We are a long way here from the claim that ecumenically involved Protestant churches purvey a "false Christianity," entirely foreign to the one church of Christ. Nor do other churches participate in the church of Christ in only a metaphorical sense. Rather, other churches *formally and substantially* participate in the church of Christ—to a greater or lesser extent—depending on the *elementa* (such as sound doctrine and the sacraments) that are present within them. If I may again invoke the classical phrases, the Catholic Church is *per se et per essentiam* the church of Christ while other churches are the church of Christ *per participationem*.[87]

So, while Vatican II does not ignore the differences between Catholi-

84. Gootaers, *Primauté et collégialité*, 190.

85. I have treated this issue at greater length in "Analogy and Vatican II: An Overlooked Dimension of the Council?" *Josephinum Journal of Theology* 22 (2015): 44–58.

86. Gootaers, *Primauté et collégialité*, 189–90.

87. The language of *per participationem* is intended to accent the perfections of holiness and truth that actually exist in other Christian churches. This language should not be understood as depriving other churches of their proper autonomy and identity.

cism and Protestantism, it also makes clear that the Catholic Church does not, so to speak, "suck out all the oxygen" from the church of Christ (which very well might have been the case if the council had simply stated, "The Church of Christ *is* [*est*] the Catholic Church"). While Christ's church exists fully within Catholicism, it may certainly be found, in varying degrees, in other churches as well.

My central point is this: The analogy of attribution is used at Vatican II, at several junctures, to explain similarity in difference—thereby bringing divided Christians closer to the unity represented by Pentecost. In the case at hand, other churches formally and substantially participate in the objective means of sanctification and truth that characterize Christ's church. This accent on participation and analogical attribution helped the council to offer a decidedly positive evaluation of, particularly, Protestant churches. The council changed the optic through which other Christian churches were viewed. No longer was the accent on differences, thereby sanctioning a dialectical approach. Now, the council could say that, despite differences with Catholicism, other churches participate actually and essentially in the church of Jesus Christ.

Another Kind of Analogy?

I have been discussing what might be called the "analogy from above," that is, examining the churches from the viewpoint of the objective means of sanctification and sound doctrine that exist within them. But does *Lumen Gentium* also allow us to speak of another kind of analogy, an analogy, so to speak, "from below"? By this I mean: Are Christians also bound together—and so approach more clearly the unity of Pentecost—by what might be called an "analogical relationship of discipleship"?

One part of *Lumen Gentium* reads:

> They are fully incorporated in the society of the Church who, possessing the Spirit of Christ accept her entire system and all the means of salvation given to her, and are united with her as part of her visible bodily structure and through her with Christ, who rules her through the Supreme Pontiff and the bishops. The bonds which bind men to the Church in a visible way are the profession of faith, the sacraments, and ecclesiastical government and communion. He is not saved, however, who, though part of the body of the Church, does not persevere in charity. He remains indeed in the bosom of the Church, but, as it were, only in a "bodily" manner

and not "in his heart." All the Church's children should remember that their exalted status is to be attributed not to their own merits but to the special grace of Christ. If they fail moreover to respond to that grace in thought, word and deed, not only shall they not be saved but they will be the more severely judged.[88]

The council here makes clear that a man may possess the entirety of Christian doctrine and the full complement of sacraments but if lacking in charity is not fully incorporated into the church. Indeed, as the text says, if someone "fails to respond to [Christ's] grace in thought, word and deed" he will not only not be saved but will also be more severely judged. The council makes clear, then, that what is *most important* in the church of Christ is responding to Christ's grace with a life of committed discipleship.

This point is intensified by the council's Theological Commission in its response to a proposed amendment. To the proposal that *Lumen Gentium* no. 8 be emended to read that the church of Christ "*subsistit* integro modo *in Ecclesia catholica,*" the commission references *Lumen Gentium,* no. 14 (cited above), with its claim that men and women are fully incorporated into the church who "possessing the Spirit of Christ" accept her entire system and all the means of salvation given to her.[89]

The intended teaching here (of both *Lumen Gentium,* no. 14, and the Theological Commission) is that one is *fully* a member of the church of Christ not simply by possessing the entire complement of the objective means of sanctification and truth but, most foundationally, by *possessing the Spirit of Christ,* without which one cannot be saved (citing Rom 8:9).

Given these affirmations, can we perhaps speak of an analogical relationship that binds together all Christian disciples? This is to say: while from an "objective" point of view, we have different relationships to the church of Christ, from a "subjective" point of view—holiness of life and committed discipleship—we also have very different relationships to the church of Christ. And this unity-in-difference is determined by one's participation in the new life of Christ's grace.

Consequently, Catholics who are not living Christian discipleship are clearly *not* "full members" of the church (*non plene incorporantur*).[90] As the council says, they may be "bodily members" but not "in the heart." Follow-

88. *Lumen Gentium,* no. 14.

89. For the proposed amendment and the response of the Theological Commission, see *Acta synodalia* III/6, 81. I am grateful to Fr. Joseph A. Komonchak, who pointed me toward this response of the commission. See also, *Acta synodalia* III/1, 188.

90. *Acta synodalia* III/1, 203nG.

ing the same logic, can one not fairly conclude that other Christians may be fully members of the church "in the heart" even though only partially related "in the body"?

If I may invoke a personal example: For many years I have been involved in the ecumenical initiative Evangelicals and Catholics Together (ECT), founded by Richard John Neuhaus and Chuck Colson in 1994. From a Catholic point of view, Evangelicals lack some of the means of salvation (e.g., the Eucharist). However, as Christians who "possess the spirit of Christ" and seek to live as committed disciples, they are nonetheless, following the logic of *Lumen Gentium*, incorporated members of the church "in the heart."

Can we conclude, perhaps, to two complementary ecclesiological analogies operative at Vatican II: an "objective" one, dealing with doctrine and the sacraments, and a "subjective" one, dealing with discipleship and holiness of life? This, I think, is a fruitful area for continuing exploration.

Conclusion

In this brief response to the fine paper of Professor Jeffrey, I have sought to make two points: First, Thomism and scholasticism did not magically disappear at Vatican II. The council certainly used a new vocabulary—precisely to allow the force and vigor of Christ's message to speak to the contemporary world. Nonetheless, as we have seen, Yves Congar, almost immediately after the council ended, insisted that Aquinas's thought structured the dogmatic texts of the council. But Congar himself offered no further explanation for this assertion. I have tried to show that the Thomist tools of participation and analogy were put to significant use in *Lumen Gentium*, markedly accenting the fraternal communion of Catholics with other Christians, and so helping to bring the church of Christ closer to that day of Pentecost when Christians, were fully united. Second, I have hinted that perhaps *Lumen Gentium*, with its accent not only on sound doctrine and the means of salvation but also on holiness and discipleship supports another kind of analogy—an analogy, so to speak, "from below." The dogmatic constitution states that they are fully incorporated into the church who not only possess the fullness of objective truth but also actively respond to Christ's new life of grace in thought, word, and deed. May we speak, then, of an analogy of all believers who formally and substantially participate in Christ's life of discipleship, a kind of "personal" analogy that would be complementary to the "objective" analogy?

For Bishop Lancelot Andrewes, Dr. Jeffrey remarks, "the abiding significance of the gift of tongues at Pentecost is to tell us that we have work to do, work beyond our own shire." Vatican II recognized with crystal clarity that much *theological* work needed to be done if Christians were to draw closer together, so that the unity of Pentecost could be realized in our day.

RESPONSE

"Retranslating" the Pentecost

Fr. Eugen J. Pentiuc (Orthodox)

From the outset: I learned a lot from David Jeffrey's highly informed presentation with respect to the subtle differences between Evangelical and Pentecostal theological perspectives on Acts 2 (not to mention the distinction between "small *e*" and "capital *E*" in the key term *evangelical,* as well as the roots of the Evangelical movement).

I wish I were—at least in part—a historian so as to respond with the same language to our esteemed presenter. Admittedly my knowledge of the minute distinctions listed in the essay is very limited. Nevertheless, I am an unapologetic student of the Bible and Semitic languages with a keen eye oriented to our primary biblical text, namely, the second chapter of Acts—and with a special interest in the history of interpretation. Or as the great semiotician Umberto Eco might have warned us, "Interpretation and over-interpretation."

As Jeffrey justly remarks, the plurality of Evangelical views obtains a cognate with those of us of the Orthodox persuasion. There is no such thing as "an" or "the" Orthodox view (singular), but rather various views that, more or less, can be classified under a wide and multicolored Orthodox umbrella. An example may suffice here: with respect to the relationship between Scripture *and* tradition, the waves are moving back and forth from what Thomas Torrance coined *sola patristica* (as a calque on *sola Scriptura*) to an increasing role given to Scripture (St. Gregory of Nyssa [*On the Holy Trinity, and of the Godhead of the Holy Spirit*]) speaks of the "centrality of Scripture" *within* tradition—a tenet that remained often underserved in the East, though ironically reified in the West after Vatican II), with a vast vista of gray area between.

However, "the"—if I may default to the use of the definite article—Orthodox view on the "centrality of Scripture" has nothing at all to do with

Scripture's self-sufficiency and its auto-use as a self-interpreting guide in matters of faith and action, as enunciated in J. I. Packer's list of evangelical tenets (see Jeffrey's essay).

From an Orthodox perspective, then, Scripture is spread everywhere within what we call "tradition." And the latter does not limit itself to the "apostolic tradition" (as in Jeffrey's essay), but it concerns the *entire* church's life under the guidance of the Holy Spirit.

Thus, overlooking the organic outgrowth of the "apostolic tradition" to the church's tradition (despite all the sots and thralls of human weaknesses) is to somewhat limit the work of the Spirit (inasmuch as humans can limit the Spirit) to the single and singular Pentecost event. and, with it, the lifespan of its direct witnesses, namely, those of the apostolic period. This limitation of the Spirit's work in the church consciously downplays or even effaces the contribution of the postapostolic generations to the alphabet of faith.

As an Orthodox student of the Bible—or perhaps to speak more clearly, as a student of the Bible who belongs to the Orthodox Church—I was truly impressed by the raft of patristic texts used in this essay. I think that adding some Byzantine liturgical hymns to Jeffrey's patristic texts is well-warranted, and hopefully, hermeneutically enriching to our common effort to grasp as much meaning as we can from Acts 2. Parenthetically, I might mention that I am currently working on a sequel to my last published book, *The Old Testament in Eastern Orthodox Tradition,*[91] tentatively titled *Hearing and Seeing the Scriptures: Liturgical Exegesis of the Old Testament.*

The Pentecost event narrated in Acts 2 has played a significant role within the Byzantine religious decor, leaving bold and important traces at the very level of liturgical terminology. Thus, an entire cycle of the liturgical year and its corpus—consisting of hymns and rubrics is called the *Pentekostarion* (along with the other two main cycles and corresponding literary corpora, the *Octoechos* and *Triodion*).

The Byzantine liturgical period *Pentekostarion* places special emphasis on the typological relationship between Easter and Pentecost, both events exemplifying Jesus's logion: "There are some standing here who will not taste death before they see that the kingdom of God has come with power" (Mk 9:1 RSV). In fact, the two events in Christ's salvific work, the resurrection and the descent of the Holy Spirit, were marked by powerful acts

91. Eugen J. Pentiuc, *The Old Testament in Eastern Orthodox Tradition* (Oxford: Oxford University Press, 2014).

and phenomena: earthquake, fire, wind (the same arsenal may be found in Elijah's quest for God: see 1 Kgs 19:11–12; cf. Ps 50:3; Is 66:15, 18). Nevertheless, the late fourth-century pilgrim-nun Egeria[92] mentions a Pentecost celebration in Jerusalem, followed surprisingly by the feast of Ascension.[93]

I would like now to turn to the text of Acts 2 (as part of *Ecclesiae innitia in Ierusalem* [Jerome], while making a few comments on Jeffrey's highly informative essay.

Acts 2:1–13: A Closer Look

Acts 2:1:

And when the day of Pentecost was fully come, they were *all* with one accord in one place. (KJV)

Καὶ ἐν τῷ συμπληροῦσθαι τὴν ἡμέραν τῆς Πεντηκοστῆς, ἦσαν ἅπαντες ὁμοθυμαδὸν ἐπὶ τὸ αὐτό.

How many people were empowered by the Holy Spirit on the Pentecost Day: 12, 120, 13, or "all believers"? Acts 2:1 simply states that "they were all [πάντες] with one accord in one place." A few manuscripts add "the apostles" (οἱ ἀποστόλοις) surmising in conjunction with Acts 2:14 that the twelve apostles (with Matthias taking the place of Judas, Acts 1:26) were the primary beneficiaries of the descent of the Holy Spirit. This inference is enforced by a liturgical Byzantine hymn, "When You did send down your Spirit, O Lord, while the Apostles were seated, the children of the Jews beheld and were astonished with amazement."[94] There is another hermeneutical option suggested by St. John Chrysostom, namely, that "all" in Acts 2:1 would hint at the 120 disciples of Acts 1:15. This interpretation may be found also in a liturgical Byzantine hymn stating that "the Holy Spirit came and rested upon the disciples' heads."[95] Note disciples, *not* "apostles"—and more than twelve!

Interestingly, in some Orthodox icons (going back as early as the sixth-century illuminated manuscript of the Syrian Rabbula Gospel)[96]

92. Egeria, *Peregrinatio* 43.1–3, 4–6.

93. Until the fifth century, Pentecost and Ascension were celebrated on the same day. See Robert Cabié, *La Pentecôte: l'évolution de la cinquantaine pascale au cours des cinq premiers siècles* (Tournai: Desclée, 1965).

94. Great Vespers of Pentecost, Plague Fourth Tone.

95. Great Vespers of Pentecost.

96. According to its colophon, the Rabbula Codex was copied by the monk Rabbula in St. John

Mary[97] appears in the center of the apostolic semicircular group.[98] Significantly, not only at the visual but also at the aural or what we might call the "sonic" level of the liturgical tradition Mary appears as *the* main beneficiary of the Pentecost miracle.[99] This may be a visual interpretation of the gloss in Acts 1:14 where "Mary the mother of Jesus, and … his brothers" were praying with Jesus's disciples in one place.[100] Mary's presence makes sense because from an Orthodox theological perspective, Mary experienced a Pentecost of sorts on the day of the Annunciation, when the Holy Spirit enabled her to become the vessel of Logos's very incarnation (Lk 1:26–38).

These interpretive possibilities show that the Pentecost event was *not* limited—in any way—to a narrow group of πνευματικοὶ, "spiritual," individuals, in the Pauline understanding of the word.

Moreover, another Byzantine hymn suggests that "*all* believers" (from *all* times) are, via the apostles, the true beneficiaries of the Pentecost event:

> Now the Comforting Spirit has been poured out upon all flesh [see Jl 2:28/3:1]; for beginning with the choir of the Apostles, from them he extended grace to the believers by participation. And he confirms his mighty descent by the distribution of tongues in the likeness of fire to the disciples, unto the praise and glory of God.

Monastery at Beth Sabga (Mesopotamia) in the year 586. This is perhaps the earliest iconic depiction of the Pentecost. I may add that Pentecost is not (yet) found among the biblical events painted in the early Christian Roman catacombs.

97. The Virgin Mary in the midst of the apostles with her arms stretched in prayer symbolizes the Church. See Marie-Louise Thérel, *Les symboles de l' "Ecclesia" dans la création iconographique de l'art chrétien du IIIe au VIe siècle* (Rome: Edizioni di Storia e Letteratura, 1973).

98. Claudine A. Chavannes-Mazel notes, "The iconography of Pentecost, however, was established somewhat later. Although the descent of the Holy Ghost was a crucial event in the legitimation of Christendom, it was an event without much human activity, taking place while the participants sat still and prayed. Despite the mighty wind and fiery tongues, the filling of the apostles with the Holy Ghost—the key moment—is difficult to picture because of its static character. For this reason, as we shall see, in rendering the event the dogmatic import was soon to overshadow the historical narrative." "Paradise and Pentecost," in *Reading Images and Texts: Medieval Images and Texts as Forms of Communication; Papers from the Third Utrecht Symposium on Medieval Literacy, Utrecht, 7–9 December 2000*, ed. Mariëlle Hageman and Marco Mostert (Turnhout: Brepols, 2005), 121.

99. After the iconoclastic period (eighth to ninth centuries), Pentecost was represented as an exclusively *male* event in both Eastern and Western iconography. For instance, Mary is absent from the Pentecost icon from Mount Sinai, dated by Kurt Weitzmann to the ninth or tenth century. See Kurt Weitzmann, *The Monastery of Saint Catherine at Mount Sinai: The Icons*, vol. 1, *From the Sixth to the Tenth Century* (Princeton: Princeton University Press, 1976), 73–76 and pls. xxx, xcix–ci); cf. Chavannes-Mazel, "Paradise and Pentecost," 124. Mary's place will be taken later on (e.g., seventeenth-century Russian icons of Pentecost) by an "empty chair" in the middle of the apostolic semicircle, chair representing Christ, the divine Teacher. Nevertheless, Mary will return in later Western depictions of Pentecost.

100. Kurt Weitzmann, "*Loca Sancta* and the Representational Arts of Palestine," *Dumbarton Oaks Papers* 28 (1974): 31–55, argues that the illumination could have been a reproduction of a monumental composition, once extant in the chapel of the Holy Spirit in Sion Church in Jerusalem.

Wherefore, noetically illumined in our hearts, and made steadfast in faith by the Holy Spirit, we beseech that our souls be saved.[101]

An aside: "noetically" is a delightful play on our father in the faith "Noah," as well as mere "intellectual activity."

Summing up then: the figures in the Byzantine Pentecost icon that were *not* present at the descent of the Holy Spirit (Luke, Mark, and Paul, and the symbolic character "King Kosmos" representing the entire world) plead for a more inclusive interpretation of Pentecost cast.[102]

Acts 2:4:

And they were all filled with the Holy Spirit, and began to *speak with other tongues*, as the Spirit gave them utterance. (KJV)

Καὶ ἐπλήσθησαν ἅπαντες πνεύματος ἁγίου, καὶ ἤρξαντο λαλεῖν ἑτέραις γλώσσαις, καθὼς τὸ πνεῦμα ἐδίδου αὐτοῖς ἀποφθέγγεσθαι.

Acts 2:6:

Now when this was noised abroad, the multitude came together, and were confounded, because that *everyone heard* them *speak* in *his own language*.

Γενομένης δὲ τῆς φωνῆς ταύτης, συνῆλθεν τὸ πλῆθος καὶ συνεχύθη, ὅτι ἤκουον εἷς ἕκαστος τῇ ἰδίᾳ διαλέκτῳ λαλούντων αὐτῶν.

Heterolalia/Xenolalia versus Glossolalia

To a certain extent, I do agree with David that in Acts 2 we have a case of *xenolalia* (speaking in foreign languages)—to be differentiated from *glossolalia* (speaking in tongues)—a special gift (χάρισμα) highly esteemed by the church in Corinth in Paul's day and more recently in Christian ecclesial communities as diverse as "Charismatic Catholic" and Southern Pentecostals.

On the one hand, the Byzantine liturgical hymns assigned for the Sunday of Pentecost support David's main point that the event at Pentecost was indeed unique. Thus:

Today all the nations beheld strange things in the city of David . . . all [the apostles] began to articulate strange and foreign words, doctrines strange and new, strange and new teachings of the Holy Trinity.[103]

101. Pentecost, Vespers, Third Prayer "With bent knees. . . ."

102. On the iconography of Pentecost, see André Grabar, "Le schéma iconographique de la Pentecôte," in *L'art de la fin de l'antiquité et du Moyen Age* (Paris: Klincksieck, 1968), 1:615–27 (originally published in Russian in *Seminarium Kondakovium* 2 [Prague, 1928], 223–39).

103. Sunday of Pentecost, Vespers, Sticheron.

The "language miracle" as described by Luke differs from the glossolalia mentioned by Paul in 1 Corinthians 12 and 14. If the former phenomenon refers to speaking in foreign languages intelligible to the hearers (see Acts 2:6, 8), the latter points to a special gift, speaking in tongues, commonly unintelligible, which required an interpreter.

On the other hand, there are few little brushes I would like to add to the glossolalia tableau masterly painted by Jeffrey in his essay. First, may I note that there is no clear-cut distinction in New Testament between xenolalia and glossolalia. For instance, Acts 2:13 suggests a case of confusing glossolalia. Some of the attendees did not make any sense of what the apostles were in fact saying, while many foreigners understood them in their own dialects; the former thought that the apostles were "drunk." According to 1 Corinthians 14:23, glossolalia could be mistaken as "madness" by unbelievers.

Moreover, Paul praises himself that he could speak in tongues better than any Corinthian (1 Cor 14:8). In the light of this statement, it is very difficult to believe that someone in his entourage—Luke, for example—would have been unfamiliar with glossolalia. Contra, for Luke, glossolalia is *the* or at least *a* sign of the Holy Spirit at work (see Acts 10:48; 19:6).

Acts 2:13 seems to be at odds with verse 6: "Everyone [ἕκαστος] heard them speak in his own language," unless Luke wants to convey something similar to Matthew 28:17: When the apostles saw the risen Lord, "they worshiped him; but some doubted." The sudden switch from "worship" to "doubt" parallels the Lukan gloss "some of them thought the apostles were drunk": the plight of human mutability! In order to downplay the apparent contradiction between verse 6 and verse 13, a Byzantine hymn identifies the skeptical in verse 13 with the "heathens": "The heathen imagined the diversity of tongues to be drunkenness."[104]

Another detail supporting the lack of clear-cut distinction between xenolalia and glossolalia is the use of the adjective "different" (ἕτερος) for both phenomena, "miracle language" (cf. Acts 2:4: ἑτέραις γλώσσαις) and glossolalia (1 Cor 14:21: ἑτερογλώσσοις). Probably there were multiple views on glossolalia during the apostolic period, running from "unintelligible" speech to xenolalia (speaking in foreign languages never known before). So Jeffrey's insistence on clear-cut distinction is a little bit of a generalization or an overly determined reading to a preconceived conclusion.

Trying to sum up the possible relations between Luke (Acts 2) and Paul

104. Sunday of Pentecost, Vespers, Second Plague.

(1 Cor 12; 14), Hans Conzelmann lists three options: (1) two sources (one depicting glossolalia in a Pauline sense and one describing a "language miracle") were combined; (2) an ecstatic episode interpreted as a "language miracle"; and (3) the "language miracle" alone being the basis of the tradition recorded in Acts 2.[105]

A last remark on the topic of xenolalia: Juxtaposing verse 6 with verse 13, one may conclude that the "language miracle" occurred at the crisscrossing of "speaking" and "hearing." The apostles were empowered by the Holy Spirit to speak in foreign languages (xenolalia) so that those present at the Pentecost could grasp their message (v. 6). Yet not all of the "hearers" understood them; some of them, as mentioned above, mistook the apostles as drunk (v. 13). This view goes against Calvin's interpretation mentioned by Jeffrey in his essay that the "language miracle" on Pentecost day was limited to the "speakers" (i.e., the apostles speaking in foreign languages) and had nothing to do with the "hearers." Yet verse 13 suggests that the "language miracle" was a bit more intricate, involving *both* speakers *and* hearers. As in other biblical recordings, a miracle happens at the intersection of God's intervention and human free acceptance—a synergetic process, that is.

Orthodox Views on Xenolalia and Glossolalia

What, then, is the Orthodox view, or rather *views*, on glossolalia? According to Fr. George Nicozisin, "The Orthodox Church does not rule out Glossolalia. She simply does not regard it as one of the important ones. Better to 'speak five words that can be understood ... than speak thousands of words in strange tongues' [1 Cor 14:18–19]."[106]

Besides the conspicuous silence from Justin Martyr on this topic, John Chrysostom and for that matter the monks of Athos, whose stories abound in examples of communication with the heavenly realm, have nothing to say about glossolalia as a Christian charism.

Jeffrey makes this trenchant remark: "The risk in emphasizing glossolalia [by the Pentecostals] is that it can seem too excluding, becoming a *criterion* by which *believers are distinguished from nonbelievers*." In striking contrast with the too-descriptive attitude of some of the past Western spiritual

105. Hans Conzelmann, *Acts of the Apostles*, Hermeneia (Minneapolis: Fortress, 1988), 27.

106. George Nicozisin, "Speaking in Tongues: An Orthodox Perspective," Greek Orthodox Archdiocese of America, September 3, 2005, http://www.goarch.org/ourfaith/ourfaith7112.

cast and modern Pentecostals who make of glossolalia a criterion of differentiation between genuine and nominalist Christians, there is the "silence" of the Eastern "desert fathers" (see the *Philokalia* for examples), who were reluctant, out of humility, to speak about the gifts of the Holy Spirit poured on them.[107] The same may be said, in a qualified way, of the Western fathers.

For Elder Ilie Cleopa of Romania, a preeminent figure of the twentieth-century Orthodox ascetic life, glossolalia, as a gift of the Holy Spirit, had a temporary character, being given to the church during her infancy.[108]

Interestingly, in the Orthodox Church, great elders and healers exercised various charismas of the Holy Spirit. To mention just a very few: Seraphim of Sarov (died early nineteenth century), St. John Kronstadt (died early twentieth century), Elder Paisios (1924–1994), and Elder Porphyrios (1906–1991). However, these saintly figures who received spiritual charisms underwent a long preparation of asceticism during which they were cleansed from propensities to sin. This is another point of contention with the Pentecostal view on glossolalia as "spontaneous" gift not requiring any spiritual preparation.

Jeffrey writes in his paper: "Pentecostals continue to speak of two baptisms in the Spirit, 'one that is soteriological and initiates the believer into the body of Christ (1 Cor 12:13) and one that is missiological and empowers the believer for service (Acts 1:8).' For Anglicans and Catholics, I would note, there are clear overlappings here with the sacraments of confirmation and ordination."

Thus if I may reiterate and expand on what I've stated from the outset, there is no one definitive, authoritative, monolithic Orthodox view on glossolalia. The *general* view among Orthodox believers is that glossolalia was a *temporary* gift given to the church in its infancy.

107. Archimandrite Zacharias notes, "Many of the Desert Fathers had this culture of hiding their charismas. One great ascetic received three monks in his cell. He wanted to observe their practice, so he pretended to be asleep. The three monks, thinking that their host was sleeping, encouraged each other, and then started praying. . . . But they had waited for their host to fall asleep and they had themselves pretended to be asleep, so that everything could be done in secret, without losing the reward of our Father Who sees in secret and rewards openly. Every precaution is taken so as not to lose the ethos of humility. This is the great culture of the Orthodox Church, and we must not lose it!" Archimandrite Zacharias, "On the Gift of Speaking in Tongues," in *The Hidden Man of the Heart (1 Peter 3:4): The Cultivation of the Heart in Orthodox Christian Anthropology* (Dalton, Pa.: Mount Thabor Publishing, 2008), Orthodox Christian Information Center, http://orthodoxinfo.com/inquirers/on-the-gift-of-speaking-in-tongues.aspx. See also Thomas Hopko, "The Gift, the Gifts, and Glossolalia," *Ancient Faith Podcast*, July 10, 2011, http://www.ancientfaith.com/podcasts/hopko/the_gift_the_gifts_and_glossolalia.

108. Elder Cleopa of Romania, *The Truth of Our Faith: A Discourse from Holy Scripture on the Teachings of True Christianity* (Athens: Uncut Mountain Press, 2000), chap. 18 passim.

In his paper "Personal Experience of the Holy Spirit according to the Greek Fathers," Metropolitan Kallistos Ware of Diokleia makes a notable remark.[109] In 1890, the Anglican priest Alexander Boddy came as a pilgrim to the great Solovetsky Monastery on the White Sea, north of Russia. There he was especially impressed by an iconographic depiction of the descent of the Holy Spirit at Pentecost. Years later, in 1907, upon the visit of T. B. Barratt, the parish of Alexander Boddy experienced an outpouring of the Holy Spirit. Most likely the impression of the Pentecost icon left on Boddy was still vivid on that occasion. Metropolitan Ware concludes his story thus:

> A formative event in the history of British Pentecostalism turns out in this way to have, as one of its sources, the iconography of an Orthodox monastic church.... This unexpected connection between Orthodox Christianity and the origins of the twentieth-century Pentecostal movement in Britain naturally leads us to ask: can we discover other links, on a more specifically theological level, between Orthodoxy and Pentecostalism? How far is the Christian East sympathetic to a "charismatic" understanding of the spiritual life?[110]

And Metropolitan Kallistos shows that there have been examples of church fathers in Eastern Christianity (e.g., Symeon the New Theologian, Macarius, Mark the Monk, and John Climacus) whose views were close to the modern Pentecostals, who see in glossolalia a continuous, long-lasting charism, a second baptism of sorts (to stretch the thought: a type of chrismation or confirmation, perhaps?), a distinguishing mark of genuine believers.

In addition to this rather surprising remark coming from the pen of a preeminent Orthodox theologian, Jeffrey wisely notes:

> As to the emphasis on the *second baptism* in the Spirit by which the Pentecostal movement has been so marked since its inception, there has been appearance lately in many Christian denominations of explicit linkages between glossolalia (prayer "in the tongues of angels"), and both sanctification in the traditional sense, and *theosis* in the specifically Orthodox sense.

Let us take a closer look at the Eastern church fathers just mentioned above.

Symeon the New Theologian (949–1022) speaks of a "continuous" work

109. Kallistos Ware, "Personal Experience of the Holy Spirit according to the Greek Fathers" (paper presented at the European Pentecostal/Charismatic Research Conference, Prague, September 10–14, 1997), posted online at *Silouan* (blog), August 5, 2008, http://silouanthompson.net/2008/08/personal-experience/.

110. Ware, "Personal Experience."

of the Holy Spirit in the believers. "Each of us, Symeon notices, is called by God to experience the indwelling presence of the Spirit 'in a conscious and perceptible way.'"[111] And then the New Theologian goes on rhetorically,

> Do not say, It is impossible to receive the Holy Spirit;
> Do not say, It is possible to be saved without Him.
> Do not say that one can possess Him without knowing it.
> Do not say, God does not appear to us.
> Do not say, People do not see the divine light,
> Or else, It is impossible in these present times.
> This is a thing never impossible, my friends,
> But on the contrary altogether possible for those who wish.[112]

Quite close to Symeon's view, yet not so poignantly stated, are the views of Mark the Monk (fifth century), Macarius the Great of Egypt (300–391, known to John Wesley), and John Climacus (seventh century). All these speak of a "second baptism" accompanied by external signs: shedding tears (Mark and John Climacus), contemplation of fire, and the obligatory, ineluctable light (Macarius and later Gregory Palamas).

In Macarius's *Homilies* there is even an allusion to speaking in tongues: "As for the apostles, they cried out willy-nilly. Just as a flute [note: apostles], when air is blown through it, gives out the sound that the flute-player wants, so it is also with the apostles and those who resemble them. When they were 'born from above' (Jn 3:3,7) and received the Paraclete Spirit, the Spirit spoke in them as He wanted."[113] The comparison here with the apostles suggests that the charism of speaking in tongues outlived the first Pentecost, and continued during the later church phases. I note that this is a quite isolated passage, which should be taken with caution. On the other hand, the *Homilies* often condemn an unintelligible speech (perhaps against the Messalians): "Those who draw near to the Lord ought to make their prayers in quietness and peace and great tranquility, not with unseemly and confused cries."[114]

John Climacus, as with Symeon the New Theologian, speaks of a "second baptism," namely, the "gift of tears," which is "higher" than the first baptism in sacramental water:

111. *Hymn* 27.125.
112. *Hymn* 27.125–32.
113. Quoted in Ware, "Personal Experience."
114. Quoted in Ware, "Personal Experience."

> The tears that come after baptism are greater than baptism itself, though it may seem rash to say so. Baptism washes off those evils that were previously within us, whereas the sins committed after baptism are washed away by tears [a process]. The baptism received by us as children we have all defiled, but we cleanse it anew with our tears. If God in His love for the human race had not given us tears, those being saved would be few indeed and hard to find.[115]

Climacus's contemporary St. Isaac of Nineveh (Isaac the Syrian) also speaks of "baptism of tears."[116]

More than anyone else in his guild, Symeon the New Theologian offers a central place in his mystical theology to the contemplation of the light, which is, of course, God himself. Symeon describes the one who sees the divine light in terms used by modern Pentecostals:

> A person who has within him the light of the most Holy Spirit, unable to endure it, falls prostrate upon the ground; and he cries out and shouts in terror and great fear, for he sees and experiences something that surpasses nature, thought and imagination. He becomes as one whose entrails have been set ablaze: devoured by fire and unable to bear the scorching flame, he is beside himself, and he cannot control himself at all. And though he sheds unceasing tears that bring him some relief, the fire of his longing is kindled to yet fiercer flames.... When he is entirely aflame and becomes as light, then is fulfilled the saying, "God is joined in unity with gods and is known by them."[117]

Not surprisingly, Symeon's writings are popular among the contemporary Orthodox faithful who came in contact with the charismatic movement!

In Metropolitan Kallistos's opinion, Macarius and Symeon speaking in great detail of the outward signs of the "second baptism" (i.e., tears, vision of divine light, and speaking with tongues) may serve as Orthodox testimony in any future Orthodox-Pentecostal dialogue.

115. *Ladder*, Step 7. Quoted in Ware, "Personal Experience."

116. *Ascetical Homilies* 14 and 37 [35]. See *The Ascetical Homilies of St. Isaac the Syrian*, trans. Holy Transfiguration Monastery (Boston: Holy Transfiguration Monastery, 1984), 82–83, 174.

117. Symeon, *Practical and Theological Chapters* 3.21. The final phrase is from St. Gregory of Nazianzus. Quoted in Kallistos Ware, "Personal Experience."

The Descent of the Holy Spirit in Byzantine Liturgical Hymns

I would like to conclude my response with some Byzantine liturgical hymns that see the descent of the Holy Spirit from a theological-poetic perspective. As a furtive look at the hymnic material, there are three main ideas the liturgists want to underscore with respect to Pentecost.

Purification

The Spirit of salvation, O Lord, who was conceived in the loins of the Prophets because of their fear of you and was brought forth upon the earth, does purify the hearts of the Apostles, and is renewed in an upright manner in the faithful.[118]

Wisdom

Through the descent of the Holy Spirit, the Apostles became wise: simple fishermen turned into missionaries.

Blessed are you, O Christ our God, who have shown forth the fishermen as supremely wise by sending down upon them the Holy Spirit, and through them did draw the world into your net. O Befriender of man, glory be to you.[119]

The Holy Spirit supplies all things: He causes prophecies to spring up; he sanctifies priests; to the uninitiated he taught wisdom; the fishermen he turned into theologians. He holds in unity the whole structure of the Church.[120]

In the same vein, St. Ephraim the Syrian—a most unique figure in that he was only an Easter *deacon* and yet is regarded by the hierarchy in the Latin church as one of only thirty-three "Doctors"—proposes an insightful comparison between the apostles and the mute people that Jesus healed by giving both the gift in speaking in languages that they did not have previously:

Now the Prophets performed all [other] signs; but on no occasion supplied the deficiency of members. But the deficiency of the body was reserved, that it should be supplied through our Lord; that souls might perceive that it is through Him that every deficiency must be supplied. It is meet, then, that the prudent should perceive that He Who supplies the deficiencies of the creatures, is Master of the formative power of the Creator. But when He was upon Earth, our Lord gave to the

118. Vespers, The Second Canon, Katavasia, Grave Tone.
119. Pentecost Sunday, Troparion.
120. Pentecost, Hymn.

deaf [and dumb], [the power] of hearing and of speaking tongues which they had not learned; that after He had ascended, [men] might understand that He gave to His disciples [the power] of speaking in every tongue.

From Disunity to Unity

Once, when he descended and confounded the tongues, the Most High divided the nations; and when he divided the tongues of fire, he called all men into unity; and with one accord we glorify the All-holy Spirit.[121]

121. Liturgy, Kontakion.

CHAPTER 3

Acts 7 and the Stoning of Stephen

Matthew Levering (Catholic)

Acts 7 depicts the death of Stephen, one of the seven deacons appointed by the apostles after they received complaints that the widows of the "Hellenists" were not receiving equal treatment in the daily distribution of food. Like his fellow deacon Philip, Stephen ended up doing far more than serving tables. In fact, he seems to have exceeded many of the apostles in doing "great wonders and signs among the people" (Acts 6:8) as well as in teaching the gospel publicly.[1] Certainly, he attracted the attention of those who did not accept the gospel, since they had him seized and brought before the Sanhedrin. There he encountered "false witnesses" (Acts 6:8)—whose testimony is nonetheless true at a certain level—who accused him of attacking the Torah and the temple: "This man never ceases to speak words against this holy place and the law; for we have heard him say that this Jesus of Nazareth will destroy this place, and will change the customs which Moses delivered to us" (Acts 6:13–14).

This accusation provides the context for Stephen's death by ritual stoning, in accord with the Torah's punishment for blasphemy. When the high priest asks Stephen to defend himself against the charge brought by those who accuse him, Stephen delivers a lengthy speech that, in fact, confirms the charge in the minds of his hearers, but is intended for Christian readers as a strong defense of the reasons why the Messiah came to die and of the meaning of death within the messianic community.

The present chapter explores Stephen's speech and its aftermath, with the goal of reflecting upon Christian dying. I argue that the way in which Stephen, in his dying, looks backward and looks forward should instruct all Christians in their dying (as in their living). In the speech, Stephen is

1. All Scripture quotations are from the RSV Catholic Edition.

speaking as a Jew who has accepted the Messiah of Israel. When he looks backward, then, he describes not only his own life but also the life of his people Israel; and when he looks forward in faith and hope, he describes not only his own victory but also that of Jesus and of all whom Jesus gathers to himself. It follows that Stephen's speech teaches us that in dying as Christians, we do not die as isolated individuals; rather our dying belongs to the history of God's people, so that the history of Israel and of the church is *our* history.[2]

When we look at this history—our own past, the past of God's people—we find it to be gravely distorted by sin. In my reading, the martyr Stephen teaches us that the answer to the burden of our sinful history consists specifically in Jesus, the Messiah who was crucified for our sins and has redeemed the history of his people. To look forward in a hope grounded in union with the crucified and risen Jesus, we must forgive others as he has forgiven us, repent of our sinful history, and embrace Jesus as the one who has redeemed our history.

Since Stephen's speech can seem to be merely an anti-Jewish polemic—indeed many have heard it precisely in that fashion—I seek first to contextualize it in its Jewish context in two ways. First, I compare it with the Lord's words in Ezekiel 20, where the Lord looks backward upon Israel's history in a strongly negative fashion and then looks forward in hope to his own redemptive work. I propose that Stephen's rhetoric echoes Ezekiel's and thus belongs within the Jewish context. Second, I point out that while Stephen looks backward to Israel's history negatively, Hebrews 11 looks backward to the same history positively.

Given the two ways that Israel's history can be remembered,[3] I suggest that our history—the (communal and personal) past that we look back upon when we are dying—should be remembered with *gratitude* marked by deep *repentance* for sin. Importantly, each of us dies not merely as an isolated individual but as a member of a people of the Messiah; and in hope we should take heart that "God has not rejected his people" (Rom 11:2).

2. Craig S. Keener shows that "Jewish thought included categories of corporate personality foreign to modern Western individualism. Thus Jewish people confessed the sins of their ancestors and pleaded that God not hold these against them. They recognized that they could suffer for the sins of their own ancestors and could seek atonement for their ancestors' sins as well as their own. Greeks could also appeal to a sense of solidarity with one's ancestors" (Keener, *Acts: An Exegetical Commentary*, vol. 2, *3:1–14:28* [Grand Rapids: Baker Academic, 2013], 1426).

3. See also such texts as Pss 78, 105, and 106.

Remembering our history with gratitude and repentance, dying Christians should reach forward in hope toward the Redeemer of history.

Ezekiel 20 as a Context for Stephen's History of Israel

Ezekiel 20 derives from the tumultuous period in which some Israelites had already been exiled to Babylon and others would soon be.[4] Elders of Israel come to Ezekiel to inquire of the Lord as to what will happen and what should be done. The Lord responds that they do not deserve any response other than condemnation. Through the prophet Ezekiel, the Lord recalls all the times that the people of Israel have sinned and he has had mercy on them. The emphasis of this history is to condemn the people and explain to them why they no longer will receive mercy from the Lord.

In the background to this history is death, not only the death of an individual but also the dying of the people of Israel. This death is spiritual, without thereby lacking a physical dimension, since Ezekiel sees the two as connected. In Ezekiel 18, God tells the people through Ezekiel that "if a wicked man turns away from all his sins which he has committed and keeps all my statutes and does what is lawful and right, he shall surely live; he shall not die" (Ezek 18:21).[5] Repentance and embracing the Torah is the path of life; one's sinful past need not be the final word. God emphasizes in this regard that he is not pleased by the death of a wicked person, because he would wish instead that the wicked person would repent: "Have I any pleasure in

4. Joseph Blenkinsopp suggests that we read Ezekiel 20 in light of Israel's "increasing need to seek explanation of the current crisis in the past" (Blenkinsopp, *Ezekiel*, Interpretation: A Bible Commentary for Teaching and Preaching [Louisville: John Knox Press, 1990], 86). He dates Ezekiel 20 to 591 BC, a few years prior to the Babylonian siege of Jerusalem in 588 and the Babylonian exile in 586. The basic idea of Ezekiel 20, according to Blenkinsopp, is that the judgments of God against his people's infidelities have finally reached the boiling point, so that the infidelity of the present generation will unleash the long-deserved punishment of exile. Blenkinsopp states that "Ezekiel is presenting present and future disasters as the climax of a history of estrangement but a climax that also entails an unanticipated new beginning (vs. 33–44). And this remains true even if, as seems plausible, much of this last section was added after the judgment had become unmistakably clear with the Babylonian conquest and ensuing exile" (*Ezekiel*, 87).

5. For the point to which Ezekiel is responding, see Ex 34:7, where the Lord describes himself as "visiting the iniquity of the fathers upon the children and the children's children, to the third and the fourth generation." See also the contrary legal teaching in Dt 24:16: "The fathers shall not be put to death for the children, nor shall the children be put to death for the fathers; every man shall be put to death for his own sin." Blenkinsopp comments that "Ezekiel's teaching on moral accountability in chapter 18 served to forestall an objection arising out of his theology of history. By choosing freely to replicate the conduct of their forebears, they, unlike the son who sees the sins of his father yet does not do likewise (18:14), place themselves within that historical pattern and so perpetuate it" (*Ezekiel*, 87).

the death of the wicked, says the Lord God, and not rather that he should turn from his way and live?" (Ezek 18:23).[6] It then becomes apparent that in speaking about the wicked individual, God is speaking also about the whole people (since the individual is not separated from the whole people, and the whole people is implicated in the individual's sin). God urges that Israel repent of its sins and turn to God before it is too late. As God asks, "Why will you die, O house of Israel? For I have no pleasure in the death of any one, says the Lord God; so turn, and live" (Ezek 18:31–32).

Two chapters later, it becomes clear that Israel—individuals and the whole people—is going to die. Looking back on its past, dying Israel must accept that it deserves death; it has repeatedly sinned. The history of our sins is never pretty, and Israel's is no prettier than a reader of the Bible to this point would expect. Even though God has chosen and blessed Israel, Israel did not respond as it should have. In dying, Israel now has to face this fact.

The Lord begins the history not with Abraham, but with the chosen people in Egypt. As the Lord recalls, "On the day when I chose Israel, I swore to the seed of the house of Jacob, making myself known to them in the land of Egypt" (Ezek 20:5).[7] God swore to them by his name that he would rescue them from slavery in Egypt and bring them into the land he had appointed for them, "a land flowing with milk and honey, the most glorious of all lands" (Ezek 20:6). When he made this promise, he asked simply that they worship him rather than worshiping the false gods of Egypt. But the people rebelled against God and remained attached to their Egyptian idolatry.[8] Therefore, even when the people were still in Egypt, God

6. Here Blenkinsopp reflects upon what "life" entails: "This assurance of life, in the context, means rather more than a promise of survival in the coming holocaust (which would then demand a date before the fall of Jerusalem). It also implies rather less than eternal life in the usual sense of postmortem existence—though that dimension cannot be absolutely excluded at least at the implicit level. Life here has the broader and less precise connotation of association with God, some sense and intimation of which is available for the person who desires it in the act of worship. Here ... a reading of those psalms which speak of the divine presence as life-giving and joy-conferring would be appropriate. The death which is the absence of that association is the lot of the son who chooses evil" (*Ezekiel*, 83–84).

7. Blenkinsopp notes that "Ezekiel follows priestly tradition according to which the divine name is first revealed in Egypt (Exod. 6:2–3, 28–29). This is quite different not only from other traditions about the origin of the divine name (see Gen. 4:26; Exod. 3:13–15) but from the alternative account according to which Moses had to retreat into the wilderness of Midian to encounter Yahweh" (*Ezekiel*, 88).

8. Blenkinsopp points out that "nowhere else [in the Bible] is the history of apostasy traced back to these Egyptian beginnings. Worship of Egyptian gods may have been suggested by the—for Ezekiel—baleful influence of Egypt on Judah during the last decades of its independent existence.... It is, nevertheless, a bold move which goes significantly beyond previous historical reinterpretations, as, for example, that of Hosea, for whom Israel's deviation began with settlement in the land and the establishment of the monarchy" (*Ezekiel*, 88).

thought to obliterate them in his wrath. But because of what God owed to his name, he chose not to obliterate them and, as he had promised, he brought "them out of the land of Egypt" in the sight of the nations (Ezek 20:9).

Having freed them from Egyptian slavery and brought them to the wilderness (Mount Sinai), God gave them the law and Sabbath, so that they would be able to flourish and to be sanctified by the living God. But they rejected the commandments of the law and neglected the Sabbath. Again God thought to obliterate them then and there, but again God "acted for the sake of my name, that it should not be profaned in the sight of the nations" (Ezek 20:14).[9] In sparing them, however, God ensured that the generation that rejected the law and Sabbath and continued in idolatry would not attain to "the most glorious of all lands" (Ezek 20:15).

Ezekiel's history so far has not been positive in its presentation of the people of Israel. But Ezekiel's history gets even worse, and goes so far as to seem (in the words of Stephen's accusers) to "speak blasphemous words against Moses and God" (Acts 6:11). Having twice thought to obliterate the people he had chosen from out of all nations, God spoke to the children of the exodus generation, and he urged these children to remember that "I the LORD am your God" (Ezek 20:19) and to obey the law, observe the Sabbath, and not commit idolatry. But still the people did not worship God, rejecting him despite his efforts to be their God. Again God thought to obliterate them, and again he spared them for the sake of his name. But, while this new generation was still in the wilderness, he willed to punish them in two ways. First, he promised to "scatter them among the nations and disperse them through the countries" (Ezek 20:23): because of their disobedience, exile would be their destiny. Second, he "gave them statutes that were not good and ordinances by which they could not have life," and he even made them offer their firstborn in horrific human sacrifice to him (Ezek 20:25–26).[10]

9. With respect to God acting for the sake of his name, Blenkinsopp observes that this is a "way of expressing the intense reciprocal involvement of Israel and its God. To speak of the name in this context is to say that Israel exists not for itself but to fulfill the divine purpose in history" (*Ezekiel*, 88). Blenkinsopp also contrasts Hosea's "idyllic" portrait of the wilderness period with Ezekiel's view of it "as a time of infidelity and judgment" (*Ezekiel*, 89).

10. Attempting to understand this claim (or at least to understand how Ezekiel could have justified it), Blenkinsopp reasons that "the story of the 'binding of Isaac' in Genesis 22 could be read as recommending the substitution of an animal [for the Israelite firstborn], and this could be taken to imply that the practice was not unknown in early Israel" (*Ezekiel*, 89–90). See also Jon D. Levenson, *The Death and Resurrection of the Beloved Son: The Transformation of Child Sacrifice in Judaism and Christianity* (New Haven: Yale University Press, 1993). Commenting on Ezek 20:25–26, Levenson argues that God gives

These punishments sound worse than obliterating the people of Israel, because if God literally means what he says, then God deliberately causes his beloved people to commit terrible sins, which would imply that God can hardly be infinitely good and innocent of all wrongdoing. It is therefore worth pointing out that earlier in the book of Ezekiel, the Lord condemned the Israelites precisely for the sin of sacrificing their firstborn children: "And you took your sons and your daughters, whom you had borne to me, and these you sacrificed to them [idols] to be devoured" (Ezek 16:20). As the Lord asks in this context, "Were your harlotries so small a matter that you slaughtered my children and delivered them up as an offering by fire to them [idols]?" (Ezek 16:21). Given that Ezekiel 16:21 and Ezekiel 20:31 condemn in the strongest possible terms the ritual sacrifice of children, I consider it likely that Ezekiel 20:25–26 should be interpreted along lines that affirm that God did not literally make Israel "offer by fire all their first-born" (Ezek 20:26), just as in Ezekiel 16:3 God condemns idolatrous Israel by metaphorically—*not* literally—asserting that "your father was an Amorite, and your mother a Hittite."[11]

bad laws as *just* punishment which the people deserved: "because the people in their rebellion refused to obey YHWH's life-promoting laws (especially those governing the Sabbath [vv. 21–24]), he, in turn, saddled them with bad laws that would, nonetheless, ultimately serve his sovereign purpose. The product of his punishment is . . . *the laws themselves*" (*Death and Resurrection*, 7). Thus Levenson holds that "there is no reason to think that he [Ezekiel] regards the practice of the sacrifice of the first-born as contrary to God's will in the time for which God ordained it," since the law commanding the offering of the first-born was "YHWH's retaliation for idolatry" without being in itself idolatrous (*Death and Resurrection*, 7). For Levenson, there was probably an "older normative tradition" according to which "YHWH once commanded the sacrifice of the first-born," in order to punish Israel for its idolatry (*Death and Resurrection*, 8). In obeying this law that YHWH commanded as a punishment of its idolatry, Israel was punished; the law served as "a means to bring about the death of those who had turned away from the means to abundant life" (*Death and Resurrection*, 8). On these grounds, Levenson advocates a literal interpretation of Ex 22:29, "The first-born of your sons you shall give to me." See further the position of the Lutheran exegete Horace D. Hummel, which distinguishes God's "positive will" from his "punitive will": "The 'not good' statutes were 'independent of Yahweh's positive will' but yet were 'enclosed within the purview of his punitive will' and were indeed given by God. Impervious to positive attempts to teach them to know and recognize God (Ezek 20:5, 7, 12, 19), the people finally had to encounter God in a life-negating judgment 'so that they might know that I am Yahweh' (20:26)" (Hummel, *Ezekiel 1–20* [Saint Louis: Concordia Publishing House, 2005], 599). In my view, it is crucial to maintain that God is infinite goodness and pure innocence: God does not deliberately lead his people astray, even as an act of punishment. See Matthew J. Ramage, *Dark Passages of the Bible: Engaging Scripture with Benedict XVI and Thomas Aquinas* (Washington, D.C.: The Catholic University of America Press, 2013), 181–95, for a helpful discussion of biblical texts in which "God himself is the cause of apparently evil actions" (182), including Ezek 20:23–26 (although Ramage focuses on other texts).

11. Literally, these words contradict the origin of Israel from Abraham and Sarah, who were neither Amorites nor Hittites. Arguably, therefore, Ezek 16:3 puts in the mouth of the Lord something that was not considered to be literally true—namely, that Israel descended from the conquered, despised, and idolatrous Amorites and Hittites—as a way of conveying what Israel would have been like without God's

For my purposes here, however, it is not necessary to settle upon the correct interpretation of Ezekiel 20:25–26. After all, Ezekiel 20's scathing recounting of Israel's history does not end with the description of the punishment that consists in receiving bad statutes and ordinances. Having spared the generation of the children in the wilderness, God "brought them into the land which I swore to give them" (Ezek 20:28). But once in the land, Israel proceeded to offer sacrifices not prescribed by the Torah in all the idols' shrines—"any high hill or any leafy tree" (Ezek 20:28). Again, God condemns the Israelites for sacrificing their own children as idolatrous nations do. God states, "Will you defile yourselves after the manner of your fathers and go astray after their detestable things [idols]? When you offer your gifts and sacrifice your sons by fire, you defile yourselves with all your idols to this day" (Ezek 20:31). The point is that Israel has no standing to judge God for abandoning Israel; it is solely God, innocent of any evil, who has been abandoned and who can stand as judge: "And shall I be inquired of by you, O house of Israel? As I live, says the Lord GOD, I will not be inquired of by you" (Ezek 20:31).

The purpose of God punishing Israel through the destruction of Jerusalem and exile, then, is to make clear to Israel that he is precisely not an idol of the kind that they have been worshiping, the kind that commands people to offer children in sacrifice. The prophetic judgment contained in Ezekiel 20's highly negative narrative of the history of Israel concludes with God insisting that Israel's efforts to deny God and to worship idols will not in fact succeed. As God says, Israel wants to "be like the nations, like the tribes of the countries, and worship wood and stone" (Ezek 20:32). But God promises that Israel will never succeed in definitively making itself into a mere idolatrous nation among all the other idolatrous nations—no matter how idolatrous Israel's history has been. God promises that the purpose of his deadly and destructive wrath is Israel's salvation. The end result of the deadly punishment that God inflicts will be that "I [God] will be king over you" (Ezek 20:33) and

covenantal election and thus also what Israel *will now become* if Israel continues to turn away from God. In accord with the genre of prophetic judgment, God's statement that Israel descended from Amorites and Hittites has a metaphorical truth. If so, then Ezek 20:25–26 need not be read as contradicting Ezek 16:21, since the metaphorical truth is that Israel now worships a god who gives evil precepts and demands child sacrifice. The real God does precisely the opposite, just as in fact Israel descends from Abraham and Sarah. But in the prophetic judgment, God paints things as it were from Israel's perspective: if their idolatry means that they descend from Amorites and Hittites, then their god must be an idol who gives evil precepts and requires that they kill their children to appease him. The gods of the Amorites and Hittites required child sacrifice.

that Israel will worship the living God. God will judge Israel in order to purge and purify it, not in order to destroy it (see Ezek 20:34–38).

Indeed, God promises a restoration far exceeding anything that was ever present to be "restored." God states that for his name's sake, he will accomplish the fulfillment of all he has covenantally bound himself to be and do for his people Israel. This utterly unmerited consummation will include the restoration of Jerusalem, perfect worship, the return of all exiles, and Israel's repentance. Ezekiel depicts this consummation: "For on my holy mountain, the mountain height of Israel, says the Lord God, there all the house of Israel, all of them, shall serve me in the land; there I will accept them, and there I will require your contributions and the choicest of your gifts, with all your sacred offerings. As a pleasing odor I will accept you, when I bring you out from the peoples" (Ezek 20:40–41). This promise befits the God who says, "Why will you die, O house of Israel? For I have no pleasure in the death of any one . . . ; so turn, and live" (Ezek 18:31–32). After Israel does in fact die by undergoing the judgment that God will administer "with a mighty hand and an outstretched arm, and with wrath poured out" (Ezek 20:33), Israel will be restored and far more than restored, with the result that Israel will finally "know that I [God] am the Lord" (Ezek 20:44). No wonder that God later leads Ezekiel in prophetic vision to a valley of dry bones, where God speaks to Ezekiel: "Prophesy to these bones, and say to them, O dry bones, hear the word of the Lord. Thus says the Lord God to these bones: Behold, I will cause breath to enter you, and you shall live" (Ezek 37:4–5). In fact, the prophet witnesses their restoration to life: "So I prophesied as he commanded me, and the breath came into them, and they lived, and stood upon their feet, an exceedingly great host" (Ezek 37:10).[12]

Thus Ezekiel's prophetic narrative of Israel's sins, sins that distort Israel by enchaining it to a false god who is the embodiment of all the evil that God is not, shows that the wrathful punishment that God brings—the

12. Blenkinsopp sums up contemporary scholarship on this text: "Ezekiel does not rule out the possibility of resuscitation, of a reversal of the natural life-death sequence. He does not affirm it either, since belief in the postmortem survival of the individual was not part of Israelite faith at that time; even considerably later the author of Job raises it as a possible solution only to dismiss it (Jb 7:9–10, 21; 14:7–12). He leaves it up to God—'Lord Yahweh, thou knowest'—who is the living God, the source of life, he who kills and restores to life (Deut. 32:39). That death was not an insuperable obstacle to the life-bestowing power of God was also illustrated by well-known stories of restoration of the dead to life through the intercession of Elijah and Elisha (I Kings 17:17–24; II Kings 4:18–37). . . . While, therefore, Ezekiel's vision certainly deals with the restoration of Israel—as the explanation in vs. 11–14 makes abundantly clear—it would probably be mistaken to exclude systematically any hint of the postmortem destiny of the individual" (Blenkinsopp, *Ezekiel*, 172–73).

seeming death of the people—will be transformed, entirely due to God's love and faithfulness, into the superabundant fulfillment of all the good things that God has promised. Through Ezekiel, God shows that his condemnation of Israel is total; there is nothing in Israel's covenantal history that God (in Ezek 20) identifies as good. Yet God loves his people and without doubt he "will be king" (Ezek 20:33) over his people. Condemnation and death are not the final word; God's love and royal power will be the final word, and will change Israel's death into perfect life for "all the house of Israel" (Ezek 20:40).

Further Context: Hebrews 11

Ezekiel 20 represents Israel's history as perceived in light of Israel's failures and God's righteous punishment. Israel's history, however, can also be represented in the opposite way, as found in Hebrews 11. The evident tension between Hebrews 11 and Acts 7 need not be smoothed over; rather, these two perspectives correspond to looking backward at our past in repentance (Acts 7) and looking backward at our past in gratitude for the gifts God has given us (Heb 11). Both perspectives are valid, and both are needed in preparation for death—even while, as in Ezekiel 20, we should trust God to overcome death for us in a way that is unmerited by us, that will reveal God's kingship, and that will enable us to worship God as his people in a perfect way. In this section, I will survey Hebrews 11 for what it teaches about looking back at our (communal) past in gratitude for what God has accomplished our lives (broadly understood).

Hebrews 11 is best known for its opening verse: "Now faith is the assurance of things hoped for, the conviction of things not seen" (Heb 11:1). The context of this passage is unjustly neglected. The author of Hebrews recalls to his congregation that after their conversion to Christ, they "endured a hard struggle with sufferings, sometimes being publicly exposed to abuse and affliction, and sometimes being partners with those so treated" (Heb 10:32–33).[13] They were able to endure this "hard struggle" due to their confidence in Christ and in the "great reward" (Heb 10:35) promised

13. Harold W. Attridge observes (in words that also apply to biblical Israel in the Old Testament period): "The summons to 'remember' (ἀναμιμνῄσκεσθε) is a regular feature of early Christian homiletics. Here, however, the memory is not to be of the words of scripture or of Christ, but of the experience of the community itself, its own 'former days'" (Attridge, *The Epistle to the Hebrews*, Hermeneia [Minneapolis: Fortress, 1989], 298). In Heb 11:3, it is admittedly unclear whether the text is referring to what aspects of faith Christians share with those who lived prior to Christ.

to those who have faith in him. Although in danger of death, they looked forward to eternal life. The lesson that the author of Hebrews wishes to inculcate is that in face of deadly danger, "you have need of endurance, so that you may do the will of God and receive what is promised" (Heb 10:36).

This lesson about deadly danger and the need to look forward in faith and hope to eternal life propels the way in which Hebrews 11 looks back upon the representative figures of the people of Israel. Obviously, therefore, this telling of Israel's history focuses not on sin and failure (as in Ezekiel 20), but on courage and victory made possible by God. Faith prior to the coming of Christ involved looking forward to the Messiah, but it also involved affirming "that the world was created by the word of God" (Heb 11:3) and most importantly affirming that God "exists and that he rewards those who seek him" (Heb 11:6).[14]

A central part of the lesson conveyed by Hebrews 11 consists in the fact that the great Israelite heroes of faith "died in faith, not having received what was promised" (Heb 11:13). In dying, Christians likewise await in faith the fulfillment of God's promise of eternal life. Yet Hebrews 11 makes clear that Christians should have even stronger faith than did the Israelites, since we have received what was promised, namely, the Messiah, who conquered sin and death by his Pasch. Christian faith, however, is the same faith as that of the Israelites, and therefore we can learn much from how the great figures of Israel (as well as though who preceded Israel) faced suffering and death.

The first representative model of faith named by Hebrews 11 is Abel. Abel exemplifies righteous worship: he offered a pleasing sacrifice to God "through which he [Abel] received approval as righteous, God bearing witness by accepting his gifts" (Heb 11:4). It might seem that Cain had the greater impact, since Cain lived to see children who founded cities and devised notable inventions. But Hebrews 11 presents the one who died, Abel, as the one who had the greater impact: "he died, but through his faith he is still speaking" (Heb 11:4). He can only be "still speaking" in a way that

14. Attridge notes that "Hebrews' understanding of faith obviously stands in continuity with Jewish tradition or, more precisely, with a certain type of Jewish tradition. This continuity is underscored by the lack of any explicit christological referent in the notion of faith" (*Hebrews*, 313). Regarding Heb 11:3, Luke Timothy Johnson comments: "The author clearly alludes to the creation account in Genesis 1, where God creates by a word alone (see also Ps 32:6; Wis 9:1; Sir 42:15; 2 Pet 3:5; Philo, *God's Immutability* 57)" (Johnson, *Hebrews: A Commentary*, New Testament Library [Louisville: Westminster John Knox, 2006], 280). On Heb 11:6 Attridge explains that the "articles of faith mentioned here, God's existence and providence, were widely presumed, both by pagans and by Jews, to be fundamental conditions sine qua non for a proper understanding of and hence relationship to God" (Attridge, *Hebrews*, 318).

is worth hearing if his path—namely, dying as a righteous man in God's sight—is the better path. In faith, Abel knew that holiness in God's sight was worth dying for; and Christ proves him right, since the reward of faith (see Heb 11:6) becomes fully manifest in the risen Christ. The next hero of faith is Enoch, who avoided death altogether due to his faith and to the fact that he pleased God. Next is Noah, who trusted in God to prepare for "events as yet unseen" (Heb 11:7); he too became "an heir of the righteousness which comes by faith" (Heb 11:7). The pattern of risking one's life out of trust in God's promise continues in Abraham, who braved great dangers because "he looked forward to the city which has foundations, whose builder and maker is God" (Heb 11:10). In the context of Hebrews, this "city" or land is eternal life: "Therefore let us go forth to him [Jesus] outside the camp, bearing abuse for him. For here we have no lasting city, but we seek the city which is to come" (Heb 13:13–14).

Sarah too appears as a hero of faith, because she trusted God that she would conceive the son promised by God. Indeed, Abraham ended up having a huge number of descendants despite being "as good as dead" (Heb 11:12) at the time of Isaac's conception. Trusting God, then, overcomes fear of death and its power for these representative figures of Israel. They "all died," but their death was not like that of those who lack faith, because they had seen what was promised "and greeted it from afar, . . . having acknowledged that they were strangers and exiles on the earth" (Heb 11:13).[15] A crucial dimension of faith in God is that we not fear to die, because faith shows us that God created us for eternal life rather than merely for an earthly home. The mark of the faithful people of Israel is that in living, "they are seeking a homeland" (Heb 11:14)—they do not act as though earthly life and comfort were the goal, but instead "they desire a better country, that is, a heavenly one" (Heb 11:16). It is precisely for this reason that they are able to overcome fear of death and live in faith and trust; and the result is that "God is not ashamed to be called their God, for he has prepared for them a city" (Heb 11:16). In living and in dying, the faithful people of Israel look forward to dwelling with God.

Isaac has a role among the heroes of faith, although his role is derivative upon Abraham's, since Isaac's pivotal moment comes when God tests

15. Attridge provides context here: "In the Hellenistic Judaism represented by Philo this understanding of the imagery of the alien is used extensively to interpret the biblical motif of the patriarchs as resident aliens" (*Hebrews*, 330).

Abraham to see whether Abraham trusts God's promises enough to offer up to God the son of the covenant. Hebrews makes clear that God is testing Abraham rather than actually desiring child sacrifice. But Hebrews also suggests that Abraham's willingness to relinquish his son shows Abraham's faith in the resurrection of the dead. Isaac thereby becomes a symbol of the resurrection to come, since God returned Isaac to Abraham. Isaac, Jacob, and Joseph are also portrayed by Hebrews as heroes of faith because, in dying, they looked forward in faith to "future blessings" (Heb 11:20) and trusted in God's work.

According to the rendition of Israel's history in Hebrews, the next hero of faith is Moses, as we would expect. Hebrews presents Moses as great because his faith leads him to spurn earthly goods and instead, fearless of dying, to seek divine reward. Thus Moses chose "rather to share ill-treatment with the people of God than to enjoy the fleeting pleasures of sin. He considered abuse suffered for the Christ greater wealth than the treasures of Egypt, for he looked to the reward" (Heb 11:25–26).[16] Risking death, he despised the privileges of Pharaoh's court and opposed Pharaoh to his face. He celebrated the first Passover with its sprinkling of sacrificial blood, so as to preserve the people from the deadly plague. In so doing, he exhibited faith in the Christ who was to come—since it is Christ's blood that conquers death and gives eternal life.

The whole people of Israel, and not solely their representatives, receive praise for their faith during the exodus from Egypt (quite a strong contrast to Ezekiel 20!). Hebrews 11 observes that it was by faith that the people managed to cross the Red Sea on dry land, and likewise the victory over Jericho took place by the power of faith rather than military might. Rahab, though a prostitute and not an Israelite, earns a place among the heroes of faith due to the assistance she gave to the Israelite spies. Hebrews goes on to emphasize that faith enabled God's people not only to risk death and to look forward to their heavenly country (eternal life) but also to perform many consequential acts during their earthly lives. Even Jephthah obtains credit for faith, despite the fact that he sacrificed his own daughter during a lawless

16. Johnson states with regard to Heb 11:26, "The phrase *oneidismon tou Christou* ('reproach of the Messiah') is difficult, and almost impossible to translate adequately, but two points can confidently be made. First, in the honor-shame world of the author, *oneidismos* falls emphatically on the side of shame (see Jos 5:8; 1 Sm 17:26; Neh 5:9; Hos 12:18; Jl 2:19; Jer 6:10; 23:40; *T. Reu.* 4.7; *T. Jud.* 23.3). Second, just as the hearers were reminded that in earlier days they had been exposed to afflictions and *oneidismoi* and were partners of people who lived that way (Heb 10:33), so Moses here serves as a model of identifying with the shame of those who are being shamed" (Johnson, *Hebrews*, 300).

period of Israel's history. So positive is Hebrews about Israel's history that even the wild and reckless avenger Samson receives praise for faith, alongside Gideon, Barak, David, Samuel, and the prophets.[17] The representatives of God's people Israel "through faith conquered kingdoms, enforced justice, received promises, stopped the mouths of lions, quenched raging fire, escaped the edge of the sword, won strength out of weakness, became mighty in war, put foreign armies to flight" (Heb 11:33–34).

This positive history of Israel, with its emphasis on spiritual and even earthly triumphs, does not minimize the suffering of the people of Israel. Holy Israelites, living by faith in God and the promised reward of eternal life, "were tortured" and "suffered mocking and scourging, and even chains and imprisonment" (Heb 11:35–36). The Israelites were so impressive that the current suffering of Christians, at least as related by Hebrews, seems to pale in comparison. Since the Israelites suffered in faith, they looked forward to the coming kingdom of the Christ, who redeems Israel by his suffering and death. Hebrews reports the extent of the Israelites' noble, faith-filled suffering for their witness to the true God: "They were stoned, they were sawn in two, they were killed with the sword; they went about in skins of sheep and goats, destitute, afflicted, ill-treated ... wandering over deserts and mountains, and in dens and caves of the earth" (Heb 11:37–38).[18] These Israelites were so praiseworthy, so "well attested by their faith" (Heb 11:39), that Hebrews says that "the world was not worthy" of them (Heb 11:38).

Hebrews concludes that followers of Christ should look backward to the history of Israel and, with grateful admiration, should imitate the Israelites: "Therefore, since we are surrounded by so great a cloud of witnesses, let us also lay aside every weight, and sin which clings so closely, and let us run with perseverance the race that is set before us" (Heb 12:1). In imitating the Israelites, after all, we are imitating their faith in God's ability to conquer

17. As Attridge remarks, "Why these figures should be singled out is not immediately clear. Jephthah, remembered for his tragic vow, seems to be particularly inappropriate. Our author may have relied on a traditional summary of the period of the Judges at this point. Whatever his sources and rationale, the naming of these six figures serves primarily as a transition from the preceding pericope with its attention to individuals of the patriarchal and exodus periods to the generically depicted later history of Israel" (Attridge, *Hebrews*, 348).

18. Attridge comments: "That some were 'stoned' ... refers either to Zechariah, son of Jehoida, or to Jeremiah, who, according to legend, met this fate in Egypt. That some were 'sawed asunder' ... applies primarily to Isaiah, who, again according to legend, met his end in this fashion. Only one case of 'death by the sword' ... is recorded of an Old Testament prophet, that of the obscure Uriah. The phrase used here is, however, a common biblical expression, and that prophets were regularly persecuted and slain was a commonplace" (*Hebrews*, 350).

death and to reward the just. Ultimately, the Israelite "cloud of witnesses" bears witness to Christ, who had been promised but was not yet given to them. The greatness of Israel's history depends upon Christ's coming for its completion, and thus it also depends upon followers of Christ today. In this regard, Hebrews states that "God had foreseen something better for us, that apart from us they [the Israelite heroes of faith] should not be made perfect" (Heb 11:40).[19]

Looking backward to Israel's noble past, then, does not compete with "looking to Jesus the pioneer and perfecter of our faith" (Heb 12:2). Jesus Christ is at the center both of our looking backward to our (Israel's) past and of our looking forward to eternal life with Christ, because he has conquered death by dying and rising. He has achieved that which Israel's heroes of faith trusted God would accomplish. He is the perfect model of a faith that despises death and trusts in the saving power of God, since "for the joy that was set before him [Jesus] endured the cross, despising the shame, and is seated at the right hand of the throne of God" (Heb 12:2). Thus Jesus is the greatest of Israel's heroes of faith, and indeed he is far more than the greatest. When we look backward to Israel's heroes of faith, we learn to look preeminently to Jesus and to cleave to his dying so that we might share in his glorious reward.

Stephen's Speech: Looking Backward and Looking Forward

Ezekiel 20 and Hebrews 11 help us to see that in dying, we must look backward with gratitude at God's work (Hebrews 11) and with deep repentance for our sins (Ezekiel 20). These texts also remind us that we die as members of God's people, and therefore, in dying, we should remember not only our own lives but also the whole history of God's people, whose center is the crucified and risen Christ. In light of these texts about Israel's past (and ours), let me now turn to Stephen's historical remembrance in Acts 7.

Stephen's speech in Acts 7 precedes his death, but in fact the whole speech belongs to his dying.[20] When he remembers his past, he remembers

19. In this regard Attridge explains that for Hebrews, "perfection, which involves cleansing of conscience, sanctification, and ultimate glorification, is made possible by Christ's sacrifice. Hence the perfection of the Old Testament figures mentioned here cannot take place 'apart from us'" (*Hebrews*, 352).

20. Thus, commenting on Acts 6:10–15, where Stephen is accused and arrested (and where the members of the Sanhedrin see "that his face was like the face of an angel" [Acts 6:15]), Luke Timothy

the history of Israel, and he speaks to his "brethren and fathers" (Acts 7:2). Although he expresses deep gratitude at the beginning of his speech, he goes on to speak largely in the mode of one remembering in order to repent.[21] We must keep in view that Stephen is speaking in prophetic judgment to his own people (whose past is his own), and also that Stephen confesses his own need for Jesus as Redeemer, thus including himself among those who must repent. Furthermore, Stephen forgives those who stone him; despite the harshness of his prophetic judgment, he concludes on a note of mercy.

Johnson draws a parallel to the scenes pertaining to Jesus's passion: "The succession of events leading to Stephen's speech imitates the sequence of Jesus' passion: the open confrontation, the suborning of spies, the agitation of the populace, the arrest, and the delivery to the council (6:10–12).... Luke has shifted to Stephen's 'passion' elements that the other Synoptists made part of Jesus' passion: not Jesus but Stephen has 'false witnesses' stand against him and accuse him; not Jesus but Stephen has the charge of 'blasphemy' laid against him; not Jesus but Stephen is accused of speaking against the temple" (Johnson, *The Acts of the Apostles*, Sacra Pagina [Collegeville, Minn.: Liturgical Press, 1992], 112). As Johnson goes on to say, "Stephen is deliberately portrayed by Luke in terms that insistently evoke the passion and death of Jesus. As did Jesus, so does Stephen have grace and power, and works wonders and signs among the people (6:8); he enters into dispute with those who challenge him (6:9; see Luke 20:1–7), including those who are sent as spies (6:11; see Luke 20:20). He is arrested (6:12; see Luke 22:54), and brought to trial before the Sanhedrin (6:12–15; see Luke 22: 66–71). Stephen has false witnesses accuse him (6:13), an element left out of Luke's passion narrative, though found in the Synoptic parallels of Mark 14:56 and Mt 26:59. Stephen is taken out of the city to be executed (7:58) as was Jesus (23:32). At his death, there is the disposition of clothing (7:58), though not of his own as it was for Jesus (Luke 23:34). Stephen prays that his spirit be accepted (7:59) as did Jesus (Luke 23:46). Stephen asks forgiveness for his murderers (7:60) as did Jesus (23:34). Stephen is buried by pious people (8:2) as was Jesus (Luke 23:50–55). The major contrast between the death of Jesus and of his witness Stephen (apart from the mode of execution) is the fact that Jesus was portrayed as keeping silence in the face of his accusers, whereas Stephen's speech is precisely the sort of response to an accusation a sage would be expected to make (7:1–53). But even this is in fulfillment of Jesus' prophecy: 'I will give you speech and wisdom such that all those opposing you will not be able to resist or contradict' (Luke 21:15)" (*Acts of the Apostles*, 143). For my purposes, the key point is that Stephen's speech is framed entirely by his dying, even if his speech can be read in other ways as well.

21. In response to scholars who argue against the historicity of the Acts account of Stephen on the grounds that "it portrays Jewish murderous behavior and hence is an example of Luke's rhetorical violence against Jewish people," Craig Keener shows in detail that "an anti-Jewish reading of the Stephen narrative runs counter to Luke's narrative as a whole" (Keener, *3:1–14:28*, 1295). As Keener observes, Stephen's speech should be read within the context of Hellenistic forensic rhetoric and of the use of historical retrospectives. Keener points out: "Historical retrospectives and lists of heroes of the faith were a common literary device.... Moses recites God's past deliverances (Adam, Noah, Abraham, and Joseph) to encourage Israel (Jos *Ant.* 3.87); Josephus recounts history to address his own day in a speech as well as in his writings (*War* 5.379–411).... Minority groups within Judaism could recount these historical retrospectives in different ways. Most such voices, whether the Qumran sectarians, or Hellenistic Jewish philosophers such as Philo, or authors of apocalypses recounting history with a view to the future, reread the biblical narratives from their own perspectives and with their own agendas" (*3:1–14:28*, 1334). Keener remarks, with what to me seems like understatement, that "given Stephen's execution immediately after his speech, it might also be relevant that such historical retrospectives could provide exhortation in testaments, a dying father's final instructions to his successors (e.g., 1 Macc 2:51–60 in 2:49–69)" (*3:1–14:28*, 1335). I consider it appropriate to read Stephen's speech within the context of his dying, though admittedly I have taken this approach partly due to my interest in Christian dying.

In his speech, Stephen first remembers his (Israel's) past with gratitude. Stephen recalls that God came to Abraham and commanded him to go first to Haran and then to the promised land.[22] Abraham obeyed, but God did not give him an inheritance in the promised land; instead God promised him that his descendants would inherit the land. In addition, God told Abraham that his descendants would be slaves in a foreign country for four hundred years, prior to inheriting the promised land. Stephen observes that Abraham received "the covenant of circumcision" (Acts 7:8) and also received a son, Isaac, whom he circumcised on the eighth day. When combined with the symbolism of circumcision on the eighth day (a new relationship with God that goes beyond the seven days of creation), the promise that Abraham's descendants would undergo a lengthy enslavement before inheriting the promised land already suggests the pattern of dying followed by rising to life with God.[23]

Stephen then recalls with gratitude God's care for Jacob and his sons, especially Joseph. Although through envy his brothers sold Joseph into slavery in Egypt, God "rescued him out of all his afflictions" (Acts 7:10) and enabled him to rescue the entire family of Jacob from a deadly famine. Stephen tells this story in a manner that prepares for a rejected Savior. He then describes the multiplication of the people of Israel and their enslavement in Egypt, as well as Pharaoh's command that their children be killed. With deep gratitude, he observes, "At this time Moses was born, and was beautiful before God" (Acts 7:20).[24] In Stephen's rendering, Moses's first encounter with his own people—in which Moses defended an Israelite against an Egyptian but was misunderstood by his own people—becomes another symbolic reference to Jesus, who came to save Israel but was misunderstood.[25] Moses sought to reconcile his people to each other, but they rejected him.

The next scene Stephen details belongs again to grateful remembering:

22. Keener notes that Stephen's (or Luke's) account differs somewhat from that of Genesis: "Terah died in Gen 11:32, in Haran (also in Jos. *Ant.* 1.152); then Abram's call to the promised land came explicitly in Gen 12:1–3 (also Jos. *Ant.* 1.154), but Luke approaches the chronology differently. Because the family had already started en route to Canaan when they settled in Haran (Gen 11:31), Luke reports the calling (Acts 7:2–3) not only before the migration to Canaan but also before the migration to Haran" (*3:1–14:28*, 1357).

23. Certainly, as Luke Timothy Johnson says, "for Luke the story of Abraham reaches its true fulfillment only now in the messianic realization of the promise" (Johnson, *Acts of the Apostles*, 121). Johnson rightly remarks that "Luke seeks to legitimize the messianic appropriation of Torah by showing how Torah itself demanded such an appropriation" (*Acts of the Apostles*, 120).

24. For background to the phrase "beautiful before God," see Johnson, *Acts of the Apostles*, 125.

25. On this reference to Jesus, see Johnson, *Acts of the Apostles*, 126.

Moses's trembling in awe at the manifestation of God "in the wilderness of Mount Sinai, in a flame of fire in a bush" (Acts 7:30). The Lord here appears as Israel's deliverer: "I [the Lord] have come down to deliver them" (Acts 7:34). Since the Lord wills to deliver the people through Moses, Stephen draws a clear (though still implicit) connection to Jesus, the deliverer who was rejected but who now is exalted at the Father's right hand as the deliverer of his people: "This Moses whom they refused, saying, 'Who made you a ruler and a judge?' God sent as both ruler and deliverer" (Acts 7:35).[26] Gratefully, Stephen recalls that Moses led the people out of Egypt; and Stephen also remembers Moses's prophecy that "God will raise up for you [the Israelites] a prophet from your brethren as he raised me up" (Acts 7:37; cf. Dt 18:15). Indeed, the Lord promised through Moses that "I will put my words in his mouth, and he shall speak to them all that I command him. And whoever will not give heed to my words which he shall speak in my name, I myself will require it of him" (Dt 18:18–19). In Stephen's view, though he does not say so yet, this prophet who has authority like that of Moses is clearly Jesus.

Having recalled with gratitude God's covenantal works in the past (Stephen's *and* Israel's past), Stephen now approaches Israel's past with repentance, in a tone of prophetic condemnation. Stephen's accusation is that the people of Israel rejected God's gifts. This point can be clearly seen in the history of Moses. Although God appointed Moses as deliverer and Moses "received living oracles [the law] to give to us" (Acts 7:38), the people turned away from Moses. Stephen recalls, "Our fathers refused to obey him, but thrust him aside, and in their hearts they turned to Egypt" (Acts 7:39). The preeminent example of their rebellion is their making and worshiping a golden calf while Moses was with God on Mount Sinai.[27] Their idolatry did not stop after Moses came down the mountain, but only intensified, with the result that God "gave them over" to their chosen path (Acts 7:42). They worshiped God, but they also equally worshiped many other gods. In this respect Stephen cites the prophetic condemnation expressed by God through Amos:

26. For discussion of the connection here between Moses and Jesus, see Keener, *3:1–14:28*, 1401–3.

27. For Jewish condemnations of the golden calf from the same broad time period of the book of Acts, see Keener, *3:1–14:28*, 1407. Keener notes that Jewish sources, in criticizing the people of Israel for the golden calf, "could be quite harsh (e.g., R. Simeon ben Yohai in *Exod. Rab.* 42:7). For the sin of the golden calf, R. Eliezer ben Jacob lamented, God could justly punish Israel until the resurrection of the dead (ʾ*Abot R. Nat.* 34A)" (Keener, *3:1–14:28*, 1407).

Did you offer to me slain beasts and sacrifices,
forty years in the wilderness, O house of Israel?
And you took up the tent of Moloch,
and the star of the god Rephan,
the figures which you made to worship;
and I will remove you beyond Babylon. (Acts 7:42–43;
cf. Am 5:25–27)[28]

Stephen nonetheless still has gratitude for Israel's (and his) past, because God did not stop caring for Israel. On Mount Sinai, God showed Moses the pattern for the "tent of witness" (Acts 7:44), and Moses constructed the tent so that the people would be able to worship God. God enabled Israel to dispossess the nations that dwelt in the promised land. God loved David, and David's son Solomon built the temple in Jerusalem for the worship of God. But these gifts too did not lead Israel to obey God, in part because "the Most High does not dwell in houses made with hands" (Acts 7:48; cf. Is 66:1–2, quoted by Stephen).[29] An implied contrast with the church of Christ, in which God dwells fully, seems to be observable here.[30]

After this point about the ultimate failure of the temple to bring about true worship on the part of Israel, Stephen moves completely into prophetic condemnation. Echoing Moses's condemnation of Israel as a "rebellious and stubborn" people (Dt 31:27)—a passage in which Moses prophesies that Israel will continue to be rebellious—and also echoing the Lord's description of Israel as "a stiff-necked people" (Ex 33:3 and elsewhere), Stephen calls Israel a "stiff-necked people, uncircumcised in heart and ears" (Acts 7:51).[31] He intensifies this condemnation and his corresponding call

28. As Keener points out, "Stephen's speech follows the LXX, which speaks not of 'Sikkuth' or 'Kiyyun' but of 'Moloch' (Μόλοχ) and 'Raiphan' (Ῥαιφάν).... Rabbis and other ancient interpreters who had access to various readings usually selected the reading, translation, or interpretation that best fit their point. Even had Stephen known the Hebrew *Sikkun*, his use of the LXX interpretation σκηνή (tent; shared in Hebrew by CD VII) plays into his midrashic application. Israel's singular 'tent' in its wilderness wanderings (the quoted context in Am 5:25; Acts 7:42) could be only the tabernacle, but Amos called this 'tent' (Heb. *Sikkun*) an idolatrous image (Amos 5:26; Acts 7:43). Thus, with this reading, Israel made an idol even of the holy tabernacle!" (*3:1–14:28*, 1410–11).

29. Keener notes here: "In the context of answering the charge that he denounces the temple (6:11–14), Stephen prepares to respond that his accusers have made an idol of it" (*3:1–14:28*, 1411).

30. See Keener's discussion in *3:1–14:28*, 1417–18.

31. Keener provides helpful context: "'Stiff-necked and uncircumcised in heart and ears' was familiar Jewish language, though not, of course, normally directed against one's judges.... Israelite prayers of penitence recalled the stubbornness of the ancestors in the wilderness (Neh 9:16–17).... Qumran scrolls condemned those walking in the 'stubbornness' of their 'hearts.' Some later rabbis claimed that Jews in the Diaspora were stiff-necked.... Scripture complains about uncircumcised hearts (Lv 26:41), which made Israel's people like spiritual pagans (Jer 9:26; cf. Ezek 44:7, 9). Some later Jewish thinkers continued this

for repentance by noting that Israel has always resisted the Holy Spirit and that the current generation is no different from their fathers. Echoing Jesus's words with regard to the persecutions endured by the prophets, Stephen says that the Israelites persecuted and killed the prophets and failed to keep the law. It is not surprising, he concludes, that the present generation has "now betrayed and murdered" the Messiah, whom Stephen describes as "the Righteous One" (Acts 7:52).[32]

My focus is on the looking backward and looking forward that a dying person inevitably does, unless death comes suddenly. Stephen looks backward with both gratitude and repentance, a repentance that conforms with Israel's tradition of prophetic judgment. At the same time, Stephen looks backward always with Jesus Christ in view. Thus his looking backward is *already* a looking forward, in the sense that Israel's past, for Stephen, contains manifold prefigurings and prophetic announcements of Jesus Christ. Again, since Stephen sees his life primarily as located in the story of Israel/church, he is looking back on his *own* past when he remembers Israel's past. When Stephen looks backward with gratitude and repentance, he sees Jesus—the deliverer authorized by God who was rejected by his people, the prophet like Moses that God will raise up, the true sacrifice who constitutes the true temple.

Likewise, when Stephen finishes his looking backward, he looks for-

emphasis; God would circumcise Israel's heart (*Jub.* 1:23); God's servants must circumcise their desire (or inclination; lit., *yetzer*) and remove what was hard (1 QS V, 5); the wicked leader failed to circumcise his heart (1 QpHab XI, 12–13, esp. XI, 13). Rabbi Samuel later prayed that God would circumcise the heart of his people to fear him (*b. Ber.* 29a)" (Keener, *3:1–14:28*, 1423–24).

32. With respect to the troubling intensification of Stephen's rhetoric, Keener notes: "Returning charges against one's accusers was standard rhetorical practice in all periods of Greek and Roman forensic rhetoric" (*3:1–14:28*, 1419). Stephen engages in this turning of the tables: "Had Stephen's accusers charged him with opposition to the law (Acts 6:11–14)? Stephen now returns the charge with interest (7:51–53). It was in fact his accusers who were the law's violators—spiritually uncircumcised (7:51), murderers of the prophets (7:52), and general disobeyers of the law (7:53)" (*3:1–14:28*, 1419). Keener rightly comments that in saying that his hearers killed the prophets, "Stephen apparently essentially invites them (and certainly at least expects them) to kill him, thereby confirming his message and prophetic status" (*3:1–14:28*, 1423). Crucially, Keener makes clear that Stephen is not simply blaming the Jewish people as though he were not a Jew. As Keener says, "Some scholars contrast later rabbis' explanation of the temple's destruction with Luke's explanation as the difference between confessing 'our sins' and pointing out 'your sins.' Although this was undoubtedly the historical trajectory that Christian polemic followed (when it moved from intra-Jewish to interreligious polemic), it overlooks the frequency of 'our fathers' in Stephen's speech. This is instead part of the polemical turn in the closing argument. '*Your* fathers' rhetorically emphasizes moral continuity among those in all generations who break God's covenant, but it does not repudiate Stephen's ethnic continuity with Israel or hope for Israel. 'Your fathers' is not negative in Acts 3:25 or 7:32 (though it is equivalent toward Acts' conclusion in 28:25), and 'our fathers' is far more common (3:13; 5:30; 13:17; 15:10; 22:3, 14; 24:14; 26:6; also at the conclusion in 28:17), including in this speech (7:11–12, 15, 19, 38–39, 44–45)" (*3:1–14:28*, 1425).

ward and sees Jesus in an astounding way. We read that Stephen, "full of the Holy Spirit, gazed into heaven and saw the glory of God, and Jesus standing at the right hand of God" (Acts 7:55).[33] This statement, while it can be interpreted in various ways, involves the fulfillment of the messianic prophecy of Daniel 7:13,

> I saw in the night visions,
> and behold, with the clouds of heaven
> there came one like a son of man,
> and he came to the Ancient of Days
> and was presented before him.
> And to him was given dominion
> and glory and kingdom,
> that all peoples, nations, and languages
> should serve him.

Thus in Matthew 26:64, Jesus's statement to the high priest that "hereafter you will see the Son of man seated at the right hand of Power, and coming on the clouds of heaven" causes the high priest to tear his robes and accuse Jesus of blasphemy.

When Stephen looks forward, then, he gazes upon the living King, the one who stands "at the right hand of God" and shares in some way in the divine glory. He looks forward to his own full entrance into the kingdom of the Son. In looking backward at his past, Stephen emphasizes Moses and the promised land; in looking forward he sees the Christ and the eschatological kingdom (cf. Acts 8:12).[34] As he is being stoned, Stephen commends

33. Johnson identifies the important place of the "glory of God" in this passage: "Three separate connections are established by Stephen's vision of the *doxa tou kyriou*: a) he is connected to the story of the people, which began with the appearance of the 'God of glory' to Abraham (Acts 7:2); Stephen is therefore a legitimate spokesperson for the people; b) *doxa* is associated with Jesus, especially with his resurrection (Luke 9:31–32; 24:26; Acts 3:13); thus, Stephen is a witness (*martys*) to the resurrection, a status explicitly affirmed by Paul in Acts 22:20; c) *doxa* is also associated with the coming of the Son of Man (Luke 9:26; 21:27), which sets up the content of Stephen's vision" (Johnson, *Acts of the Apostles*, 139). Johnson also notes that the report of a vision during a martyr's death was common at the time, and Johnson also reflects helpfully upon why Stephen sees Jesus "standing" rather than sitting (as in Ps 110:1 and Lk 22:69).

34. See Costantino Antonio Ziccardi, *The Relationship of Jesus and the Kingdom of God according to Luke-Acts* (Rome: Gregorian University Press, 2008). Rather surprisingly, Stephen's claim that his hearers had killed the Messiah, just as their (and his) fathers had killed the prophets, did not cause his hearers to attack him violently. Although the charge of killing the Messiah certainly caused his hearers to become "enraged" (Acts 7:54), it was not until Stephen proclaimed that he saw "the Son of man standing at the right hand of God" that his hearers "cried out with a loud voice and stopped their ears and rushed together upon him" (Acts 7:57). This fact suggests that his remembering of Israel's history corresponded well enough to the accepted genre of prophetic condemnation that his hearers were willing to listen to it,

his spirit to the "Lord Jesus" (Acts 7:59), which I take as evidence of his awareness that he is among the sinful people who need the Messiah as their Savior. Imitating Christ's merciful dying, the dying Stephen kneels down and prays for those who are stoning him: "Lord, do not hold this sin against them" (Acts 7:60).[35] These are his last words.

Conclusion

I have construed the entirety of Stephen's words and deeds in Acts 7 as an exemplification of Christian dying. In dying, we should look backward with deep gratitude and deep repentance, and we should remember always that we are not dying as isolated individuals but as members of the body of Christ, the church. The primary history for which we are to give thanks and offer repentance is the history of the church, to which our lives have contributed both positively (through our good acts) and negatively (through our sins). Rather than focusing on ourselves in our dying, we should focus on Christ and on our relationship to Christ in his church. In this way, our looking backward takes on its proper dimensions, which otherwise would be far too narrowed by a focus upon our own earthly achievements and failures. In looking forward, we should prayerfully confess our utter dependence upon Christ for salvation and our joyful hope to be united to him forever. Such unity will only be possible if we are like him, and to be like him is to forgive those who wrong us. In dying, we must forgive as Christ forgives: this is the path of the cross, the path that bridges death and leads to resurrection and the kingdom of God. Prophetic judgment must also be part of our dying, insofar as our remembering of our past (or even of the church's past) cannot be a time for self-congratulation: it must be a time for gratitude to God, certainly, but also for deep repentance and begging for mercy caused by a real attunement to what we have done and failed to do, despite God's great gifts to us.

For the Christian, then, Christ must be central not only to the looking

---

even while becoming angry. By contrast, they were not willing to hear his proclamation of the fulfillment of Daniel's prophecy, since they deemed this proclamation to be blasphemous against the Lord rather than simply insulting toward themselves.

35. Note that the parallel text in the Gospel of Luke, Lk 23:34 ("Father, forgive them; for they know not what they do"), belongs to canonical Scripture but not necessarily to the original text. For discussion of the manuscript evidence, in which Lk 23:34 is "omitted in very early and important mss. from diverse geographical areas," see Joseph A. Fitzmyer, SJ, *The Gospel according to Luke (X–XXIV)* (Garden City, N.Y.: Doubleday, 1985), 1503.

forward but also to the looking backward: In remembering our lives, we must discern gratefully the presence and work of Christ, and we must repent for our sins (for which he died) and imitate his mercy. We must not measure our lives in terms of transient worldly accomplishments and mutually beneficial friendships (or the lack of such things). Rather, the true measure of our lives is Christ. A life for which we can be grateful, as we die, is a life in which the love and mercy of Christ can be discerned and identified, even in hidden ways known only to God. Furthermore, we must not envision our dying (or our living) only or even primarily in terms of our personal, familial, and/or professional relationships. When we die, we die primarily as a member of Christ's body, just as when Jacob (for example) dies, he dies primarily as the patriarch of Israel. As Paul emphasizes, "If one member suffers, all suffer together; if one member is honored, all rejoice together" (1 Cor 12:26); and "it is no longer I who live, but Christ who lives in me; and the life I now live in the flesh I live by faith in the Son of God, who loved me and gave himself for me" (Gal 2:20). Even more to the point is Romans 14:7–8: "None of us lives to himself, and none of us dies to himself. If we live, we live to the Lord, and if we die, we die to the Lord; so then, whether we live or whether we die, we are the Lord's."

Yet there seems to be a major problem with my way of framing the dying of Stephen. To repeat an earlier question: Is he not dying with a rather self-righteous spirit? Certainly his words, when linked with other New Testament words, have been used over the centuries to persecute Jews as Christ-killers. Should he not have put his prophetic message into terms better suited to his audience, or at least should not Acts, as inspired Scripture, have presented them in a way that avoided the accusation that the Jewish people "murdered" Jesus Christ, who after all was killed by Roman soldiers and betrayed by his own disciples?

The answer to this question ultimately depends upon whether one thinks Stephen has received a prophetic vocation from God. If he has received such a vocation, then his prophetic judgment of the people of Israel (to which he belongs) is not an act of pride, since Stephen recognizes that he himself needs the salvation brought by the crucified Messiah, who came to take away the sins of Israel. The assessment of the validity of Stephen's prophetic vocation depends upon whether one affirms that Jesus is the Christ who died on the cross, was raised from the dead, and now reigns at the right hand of the Father.

To accept Jesus as the Christ does not mean, however, that one would then be compelled to interpret Stephen's statement that his Jewish brethren "betrayed and murdered" the Messiah as an indictment of the Jewish people more than other peoples (though Stephen's prophetic judgment, of course, is directed toward his own people). The Jewish *disciples* of Jesus—not only Judas but also Peter and the others—betrayed and abandoned Jesus, thereby causing him to be killed at the hands of the Romans. Paul himself, who (as Saul) consented to the stoning of Stephen (Acts 7:58; 8:1), states that "none of the rulers of this age understood this [wisdom of God]; for if they had, they would not have crucified the Lord of glory" (1 Cor 2:8). In making this statement, Paul has both Roman and Jewish leaders in view, and he could also have in view Jesus's own disciples who betrayed and abandoned their master. Far from condemning the Jewish people as being more responsible than others for the killing of Jesus, Paul argues that the rejection of Jesus as Messiah by many Jews belongs to God's plan to ensure "that by the mercy shown to you [Gentiles] they [Jews] also may receive mercy. For God has consigned all men to disobedience, that he may have mercy upon all" (Rom 11:31–32). Stephen indicates his own emphasis on mercy by his final words of forgiveness.

In taking the form of prophetic judgment, then, Stephen's speech should not confuse us about the nature of his dying. It is because he identifies so deeply with his people that his remembering focuses on the history of Israel. He sees Christ throughout this history, and therefore he is both deeply grateful and deeply repentant. He looks forward in faith (which becomes vision in Acts 7:56) to the consummated kingdom of Christ, but he does not forget his utter dependence upon the Lord in the passage from death to life. In dying, he testifies to Christ's mercy and he calls for mercy toward the people of Israel (and thus toward himself)—and in so doing, he concurs fully with Moses and the prophets. He dies in gratitude, repentance, faith, hope, and mercy as a member of the people of Israel and the people of the Messiah. In his imitation of Christ, he shows us how to look backward and look forward on the journey of dying.

Since we are all loath to remember anything with repentance—thereby depriving ourselves of the mercy that sinners such as ourselves (however much we may deny it) need and require in order to have life with God—Israel's prophets remembered Israel's past in ways that emphasized the sins of Israel. A prime example of such prophetic judgment comes in Ezekiel 20, in which the Lord looks backward in judgment and then looks forward with promise and hope. At the same time, since judgment of Israel's past is not the only true way of remembering Israel's past according to the New Testament, I explored Hebrews 11 with its descriptions of the heroes of faith. This element of gratitude must be present, in our dying, as we remember our life.

In this context, Stephen's speech in Acts 7 is rightly understood not as a bitter rendition of Israel's past, let alone an act of self-righteous condemnation of others, but rather as an exemplar of the prophetic mode of remembering one's past with deep repentance in order to render oneself open to receiving and sharing God's mercy. Mercy is the way of Christ; as such, mercy is the bridge from death to life. In her *Dialogue*, Catherine of Siena depicts God as saying that those "who travel by the way beneath the bridge.... never turn back to admit their sins or to ask for my mercy."[36] Just as in his prophetic judgment Stephen had in view his own people (Israel, the Jewish people), in the equally forceful prophetic judgment contained in her *Dialogue* Catherine has in view her own people (the church, clerical and lay Christians).

If we are to avoid dying (and living) "beneath the bridge," we need to learn how to appreciate Acts 7 on Stephen's dying. In looking backward upon our lives as members of the church and looking forward to resurrection life, we need to perceive the presence of Christ with deep gratitude and deep hope. But the note of deep repentance that Stephen also sounds is crucial for the dying (and living) Christian, as it was for the prophets of Israel. By repenting, we open ourselves to divine mercy.

According to his friend and biographer Possidius, Augustine always counseled that even "exemplary Christians and priests ought not to depart from this life without fitting and appropriate repentance"—a counsel that Augustine put into practice in his own dying, during which he continually prayed the penitential psalms with tears.[37] We have all "betrayed" the Lord's gifts and have thereby been responsible for his dying for our sins. But as his messianic suffering shows, the Lord is infinitely merciful and has "no pleasure in the death of any one" (Ezek 18:32). In dying, then, let us be filled with gratitude and hope in the Lord's gifts, and let us follow the Lord's urgent command through the prophet Ezekiel: "Repent and turn from all your transgressions, lest iniquity be your ruin" (Ezek 18:30).

36. Catherine of Siena, *The Dialogue*, trans. Suzanne Noffke, OP (New York: Paulist Press, 1980), 87.

37. Possidius, *The Life of Saint Augustine*, trans. Herbert T. Weiskotten (Merchantville, N.J.: Evolution Publishing, 2008), 56.

RESPONSE

Stephen, the Spirit, and Bearing Witness

Dale M. Coulter (Evangelical)

In his ecclesiological reading of Stephen's martyrdom, Matthew Levering has turned Luke's narrative into a proto–*ars moriendi* for the Christian church. Stephen's speech evinces a deep identification with the people of God embodied in the history of God's acts, which frames Stephen's prophetic call to repentance as well as his gratitude for God's mercy in Christ and expectation of God's embrace. To borrow from Elie Wiesel, Stephen has entered the kingdom of memory as a form of protest and solidarity because "to forget is, for a Jew, to deny his people—and all that it symbolizes—and also to deny himself."[38] This communal memory of God, passed along in the sacred accounts of the people of God, roots Stephen, not only by supplying the language of prophetic critique, but also by forming an identity and freedom that transcends death. One dies as one lives, in Abraham's bosom—the history and identity of that people God has called into existence through concrete acts of deliverance that culminate in the Messiah's life, death, and resurrection.

In this response, I wish to reflect further on the role of memory in the formation of the people of God while also underscoring the Spirit's operations that take us up into that people. It is the latter proposition, in particular, that is missing from Levering's theological appropriation of Stephen's speech. Levering rightly points toward the role of memory in forming our identity as persons in community, but needs to ground this claim in the Spirit's graciously taking us up in to the new community God has called into existence.

38. Elie Wiesel, *From the Kingdom of Memory: Reminiscences* (New York: Summit, 1990), 9.

Memory and the Formation of the People of God

The primary purpose of Levering's theological analysis is the call to remember the history of the people of God with gratitude and in repentance. Hovering between Stephen's speech in its historical context and Luke's literary reworking of that speech, Levering argues that living and dying occur in the context of the history of the people to which Christians belong, which comes to each believer through the narratives that form the collective memory of the church. Memory shapes identity, reminding Christians that they are always persons-in-communion who together form a new society. Let me respond to this insight with two additional points.

First, Luke-Acts is narrative catechesis designed to transmit the memory of the first generation for the purpose of spiritually forming the second and third generations of early Christianity.[39] While Luke-Acts was most likely written between AD 70 and 90, Luke writes about what Paul would describe in Ephesians as the "household of God, having been built on the foundation of the apostles and prophets" (Eph 2:19–20).[40] This judgment assumes that Ephesians was written in the 60s by Paul or a close associate in order to describe the foundational period of early Christianity.[41] Both Luke-Acts and Ephesians define this period in terms of the first thirty years of the movement in which the charismatic life flowed in and through apostles, prophets, evangelists, and local teachers with shepherding roles. Taken together, they look back on the foundational period with a view to articulating the nature of the church as the new community God has called into existence at Pentecost (Acts 2; Eph 4:1–17).

With respect to the stoning of Stephen, the reader of Acts must move between the historical event in the 30s and Luke's literary account of it.

39. See John T. Carroll, *Luke: A Commentary*, New Testament Library (Louisville: Westminster John Knox, 2012), 1–6.

40. Despite recent challenges, the range of AD 70–85 remains the scholarly consensus. See Craig S. Keener, *Acts: An Exegetical Commentary*, vol. 1, *Introduction and 1:1–2:47* (Grand Rapids: Baker Academic, 2012), 383–401; Richard P. Thompson, "Luke-Acts: The Gospel of Luke and the Acts of the Apostles," in *The Blackwell Companion to the New Testament*, ed. David Aune (Oxford: Wiley-Blackwell, 2010), 330–31.

41. Whether one attributes sole authorship to Paul or to Paul and a companion, the relevant point is that the letter was written within Paul's lifetime. Luke Timothy Johnson, *The Writings of the New Testament: An Interpretation* (Philadelphia: Fortress, 1986), 367–80; Stephen E. Fowl, *Ephesians: A Commentary*, New Testament Library (Louisville: Westminster John Knox, 2012), 6–15. For an argument that Paul wrote Ephesians between 60 and 61, see Harold W. Hoehner, *Ephesians: An Exegetical Commentary* (Grand Rapids: Baker Academic, 2002), 1–61.

Keeping these two perspectives to Acts distinct helps underscore Luke's narrative agenda of preserving the memory of the "foundational" period of the church in the postapostolic context within which he was writing. Part of Luke's task is to bear witness to the early witness of the church in order to transmit this memory to Christians of the 70s and 80s concerned with the transition away from apostolic leadership. He makes this purpose clear in the prologue to the Gospel when Luke asserts that his task is to compose an orderly narrative account of the tradition he received from the "eyewitnesses and servants of the word" (Lk 1:2 NIV). The importance of witness is born out in Acts not simply through the Pentecostal outpouring but also in the "we" passages, in which Luke claims his status as eyewitness (Acts 16:10–17; 20:5–15; 21:1–18; 27:1–28:16).[42] Luke-Acts embodies the memory of the church by weaving together in the narrative the task of bearing witness, eyewitness accounts, and acts of witnessing (of which Stephen's is one). As a Spirit-empowered activity, bearing witness stands behind Luke's use of ancient biography and historiography as the way to shape the character of Christian communities.[43] Thus Luke-Acts itself is catechetical—"an identity-forming, legitimacy-providing" historical narrative designed to construct Christian character within the postapostolic house-church communities after the destruction of the temple.[44]

Second, Luke's Spirit-empowered witnesses become models for the Christian life who transmit the life of Christ to others. Although this includes turning persons like Stephen into exemplars of Christian existence, Luke also employs a layering effect in which he shows how the witness of Jesus continues in the witnesses of the early church. He patterns witnessing in Acts on the ministry of Jesus in the Gospel to show how the former participates in and extends the latter. This is apparent at the end of Acts 7, in which Stephen's martyrdom echoes Jesus's death on the cross. In imitation of Jesus, Stephen cries aloud for forgiveness to his accusers and asks the Lord to receive his spirit (Acts 7:59–60). Stephen's witness takes a christological shape even as it occurs in the power of the same Spirit who anointed the Messiah.

42. On the "we" passages and Luke as a companion of Paul, see Keener, *Introduction and 1:1–2:47*, 407–14; Ben Witherington III, *The Acts of the Apostles: A Socio-rhetorical Commentary* (Grand Rapids: Eerdmans, 1998), 480–84.

43. Luke may see himself as akin to Peter and John who "cannot but speak of what we have seen and heard" (Acts 4:20).

44. Carroll, *Luke*, 5.

On the literary level of catechesis, the reader begins to see the story of Luke-Acts as a single plot that moves from Jesus as the divine, eschatological prophet and Davidic Messiah to the new community of messengers reconfigured around him. Acts flows from the Pentecost story, with its echoes of Sinai, to Stephen's declaration that Israel was the ἐκκλησία in the wilderness (Acts 7:38). As David Seccombe suggests, Luke is claiming a unity between the fledgling house-church communities and the congregation in Israel.[45] The ultimate aim is to convince readers in the postapostolic context that they are part of a larger plot, a salvation history. The figure of Stephen serves as one point of connection between Jesus of Nazareth and the community the risen Lord has called into existence.

Luke's use of mimesis as a literary convention to insert Stephen into the story of Jesus speaks to a deeper mimetic fellowship with the risen Lord. Stephen participates in the death of Christ and so becomes an image bearer of Christ, which the statement of the risen Lord to Saul underscores ("I am Jesus, whom you are persecuting," Acts 9:5).[46] Saul's consent to the stoning of Stephen is an act of persecution against Christ because Stephen's life exemplifies, participates in, and extends the life of the risen Lord through the Holy Spirit. In this sense, mimesis moves beyond the literary world of the text to the union between Christ and his people.

Stephen is a model for Christian existence as he imitates Christ and becomes what Ignatius of Antioch called an "image bearer" (θεόφορος) of Christ. It is through this layering effect in which Stephen imitates and extends the life of Christ while those in the postapostolic community are called to imitate Stephen that discipleship occurs. As Paul had written, "Be imitators of me, as I am of Christ" (1 Cor 11:1). Christians imitate the great cloud of witnesses that surrounds them and through such models find their way back to Christ. Such ethical imitation, however, presupposed a real participation in and thus extension of the life of the risen Lord made possible through the Holy Spirit.

To press the thought even further, Augustine argues that such imitation is grounded in creation itself. He states that when some thing turns "in the way suited to its kind, to that which truly and always is, to the creator that is to say of its own being, that it really imitates the form of the Word which al-

45. David P. Seccombe, "The New People of God," in *Witness to the Gospel: The Theology of Acts*, ed. I. Howard Marshall and David Peterson (Grand Rapids: Eerdmans, 1998), 358, 371.

46. Unless otherwise noted, Scripture quotations are from the ESV.

ways and unchangeably adheres to the Father, and receives its own form, and becomes a perfect, complete creature."[47] Created being receives not simply its form of being from the Word but also its form of beauty, goodness, and truth. Imitation concerns the contemplative participation in the form of our lives as found in the eternal reasons, which are themselves embedded in the eternal discourse that is the second person of the Trinity. Augustine picks up where Luke's thought ends. While participation in the life of Christ comes concretely through the models of Christian witness that transmit this life to us, it concludes at its highest level by returning to the Word in whom the form of human existence resides. At this level, mimesis is participation in life of the Word through the reception of the likeness particularized to human existence. Both Luke and Augustine think that this occurs through the Spirit who graciously catches believers up into story of God and his people.

The Spirit, Ecstasy, and the People of God

As has often been noted, the Spirit is a central theme of Luke-Acts. The same Spirit that the Gospel portrays as essential to Jesus's mission Acts portrays as central to the mission of the church. What connects the "foundation of the apostles and prophets" Luke describes to the house churches he addresses is the Spirit's ongoing charismatic and missionary activity. As Bonaventure suggests, the reference to the promise of the Father at the end of the Gospel (Lk 24:49) points toward the distribution of spiritual χαρίσματα without which the church cannot discharge her call to bear witness.[48] Spirit baptism caught the disciples up into the story of Jesus and thrust them out into the world in the power of Jesus.

One way of moving beyond the impasse over various ways to interpret Luke's understanding of "baptism in the Spirit" is to see the phrase as shorthand for the full manifestation of the grace of God in the life of the new community.[49] Luke closely associates the term *grace* with divine power and

47. Augustine, *The Literal Meaning of Genesis* 1.4.9, in Augustine, *On Genesis*, trans. Edmund Hill, The Works of Saint Augustine: A Translation for the 21st Century (Hyde Park, N.Y.: New City Press, 2002), 171.

48. Bonaventure, *Commentary on the Gospel of Luke*, ed. Robert J. Karris, OFM, Works of St. Bonaventure 8 part 3 (St. Bonaventure, N.Y.: Franciscan Institute Publications, 2004), 2243.

49. The literature surrounding the debate between Pentecostals and non-Pentecostals over the issue of subsequence is quite large. For starters, see James D. G. Dunn, *Baptism in the Holy Spirit: A Reexamination of the New Testament Teaching on the Gift of the Spirit in Relation to Pentecostalism Today*, 2nd ed. (London: SCM, 2010).

presence. The angel's declaration that Mary is full of grace (Lk 1:28) anticipates his pronouncement that "the Holy Spirit will come upon you ... the power of the Most High will overshadow you" (Lk 1:35). Stephen is "full of grace and power" because signs and wonders flow from him (Acts 6:8). It is also clear that Spirit baptism results in inspired speech, inspired interpretation of Scripture, the miraculous, ecstatic speech, visions, and other forms of charismatic activity.

The best way to accommodate Luke's rich understanding of the Spirit-filled life is to see it as composed of various modes of grace or power at work within persons. The Spirit flows into the life of the person in a number of different ways, making it difficult to demarcate initial reception from subsequent outpourings. For Luke, the baptism of the Spirit and fire is part of conversion-initiation insofar as it unleashes sanctifying and charismatic graces, giving rise to inspired speech, visions, dreams, and miracles, all of which advance the *missio Dei*. It is clear that many of these inspired actions are subsequent to initial conversion and that most of them center upon inspired forms of speech. Nevertheless, they are all the outflow of grace as divine presence and power at work within the person.

Against this backdrop, Stephen's speech and his vision are Spirit-induced events. Luke peppers his narrative with phrases like "full of grace and power," "full of faith and the Holy Spirit," "wisdom and the Spirit," and "full of the Holy Spirit," to reinforce the connection between grace, power, wisdom, and the Spirit (Acts 6:3, 5, 8, 10; 7:55). In several places throughout Acts 6 and 7, Luke links Spirit and wisdom, making it clear that the former produces the latter (Acts 6:3, 10). There is an echo of Jesus's declaration to the disciples that "I will give you a mouth and wisdom, which none of your adversaries will be able to withstand or contradict" (Lk 21:15).[50] The risen Lord remains operative in the church to fulfill his promises. Moreover, references to "wisdom" most likely allude to the Isaianic list in which the Spirit is poured out on the messianic figure. Max Turner suggests that Luke had already connected Isaiah 11 to the young Jesus's growth in wisdom because the outpouring the Spirit upon the Christ child results in his becoming holy (Lk 1:35).[51] In the broader context of Luke's narrative, the Spirit flows into Jesus the Messiah to lead a new exodus, which continues in and through the

50. So Witherington, *Acts of the Apostles*, 257.

51. Max Turner, *Power from on High: The Spirit in Israel's Restoration and Witness in Luke-Acts* (Sheffield: Sheffield Academic, 2000), 158–61.

mission of the church. The wisdom Stephen possess is a result of the Spirit's endowing him with the same gifts that flowed into Christ.

Stephen flows in the sanctifying and charismatic graces of the Spirit, which culminate in a vision that catches him up into the presence of the risen Lord so that the one who had the face of an angel now perceives the glory of God. Luke uses the same verb to refer to the council's "gazing" into the angelic face of Stephen and Stephen's "gazing" into the heavens at the Son of Man. One glimpses in these passages how the power and presence of the Spirit cause Stephen to radiate with divine glory. This is the deifying activity of God at work. The sanctifying graces of the Spirit further give rise to charismatic vision, moving Stephen from one degree of glory to another.

Luke provides clues in the narrative as to how the Spirit induces prophetic acts, inspired forms of speech, dreams, and visions. His description of the event at Pentecost employs the language of inebriation to point toward the term ἔκστασις that he would later use to describe Peter's vision on the roof and Paul's vision in the temple (Acts 10:10; 11:5; 22:17). As John Levison argues, the fiery presence of the Spirit, tongues speech, and visual intoxication cradle Pentecost in the language of ecstasy.[52] Ἔκστασις was employed by Philo of Alexandria and Plutarch to refer to a mental rupture and temporary loss of conscious awareness of oneself and one's surroundings as divine inspiration took hold. Luke draws upon this notion of ecstasy, employing it to describe how charismatic grace unfolds. Having been caught up in tongues speech, prophetic activity, or visionary encounters, Peter and Paul momentarily lose awareness of others as they are overwhelmed with the divine embrace.

Something similar could be said of Stephen's vision. The Spirit elevates Stephen above his circumstances even as he is rushed by the men who surround him. There is an implicit contrast between the inspired ecstasy of Stephen and the frenzied or manic state of the crowd. The former is Spirit-induced, while the latter is more akin to Dionysian frenzy in which adherents would whip themselves into a manic state or an alcohol-induced rage.

To be caught up into God's story passed along in the church's memory is itself an ecstatic event, a momentary break from one's own surroundings in the encounter with the Spirit. The true meaning of human existence is refracted through the prism of divine glory. As the tradition has put it, knowledge of God and knowledge of self remain intertwined. The true meaning

52. John R. Levison, *Filled with the Spirit* (Grand Rapids: Eerdmans, 2009), 325.

of the human person becomes known in relation to the tripersonal God. Yet the knowledge of God comes through the history of the people of God and the Spirit, who ecstatically catches us up in to that history through the graces he dispenses.

While Luke reserved the term ἔκστασις for Peter's and Paul's visionary experiences, the language of Pentecost suggests that he envisioned the Spirit's charismatic presence as simultaneously ecstatic. Within patristic writers, the connection between ecstasy and the Christian life was preserved and extended. Following Jerome, Augustine understood ecstasy as an *excessus mentis* or an *alienatio mentis*. Both terms speak of a mental loss (*excessus*) or rupture (*alienatio*) in the sense that the mind's energies are redirected away from the visible world of sensation to the invisible world of God and the self. There is a connection between dreams, visions, and moments of rapture because they all denote being "asleep" to the world and "awake" unto God. Hence Augustine could define a form of Spirit inspiration as "when the mind is alienated from the body's senses so that a person's spirit, having been caught up by the divine Spirit, might be open to receiving and contemplating images, as when what Daniel did not understand was manifested to him and that vessel was lowered on four lines from heaven to Peter."[53] Augustine postulates an ascent to God from the visible world into the self and up into a vision of God.

It is through this ecstatic ascent that the affections begin to be turned toward God and concupiscence is overcome as the soul becomes enraptured in the delights of wisdom and truth. In describing his mystical ascent with Monica, Augustine notes that it was their mutual longing that kept moving them higher until they touched "that land of never-failing plenty where you pasture Israel for ever with the food of truth."[54] Later in the *Confessions* Augustine suggests that it is the Spirit who is the gift of divine charity that sets the heart ablaze, turning the movement of cupidity that drags the soul down to the earth into the movement of charity.[55] Augustine weaves the notion of ecstasy into his understanding of the person's ongoing conversion to God.

The interaction between faith, hope, and love in Augustine's under-

53. Augustine, *Miscellany of Questions in Response to Simplician* 2.1.1, in Augustine, *Responses to Miscellaneous Questions*, trans. Boniface Ramsey, The Works of Saint Augustine: A Translation for the 21st Century (Hyde Park, N.Y.: New City Press, 2008), 209.

54. Augustine, *Confessions* 9.10.24, in Augustine, *Confessions* trans. Maria Boulding, OSA, The Works of Saint Augustine: A Translation for the 21st Century (Hyde Park, N.Y.: New City Press, 1997), 227.

55. Augustine, *Confessions* 13.6.7–13.9.10.

standing of salvation is undergirded by the pneumatological turning of the affections toward God in ecstatic embrace. In the *Enchiridion,* Augustine defines faith in relationship to sight on the basis of Hebrews 11:1.[56] Faith is a kind of knowledge of invisible realities made available to the mind through the images contained in the memory. Regardless of whether it concerns the past, present, or future, faith remains a vision brought before the mind. This is why faith needs love. Whereas faith concerns the cognitive dimension, love relates to emotion and desire. Perceiving the truth is not the same as delighting in the truth. Saving faith is the faith that works through love, which moves the person from faith to understanding or from the cognitive vision of the mind to beatific vision of God. Given the absence of the full beatific vision, hope's desire for future goods fuels the process even as the ecstatic glimpses of God offer a foretaste of the final vision.

There is one final point to Augustine's understanding of faith. Grounded in Scripture, the church's common confession supplies the content of the vision of faith. In the same way that the narrative of Luke-Acts offers the story of salvation and invites believers to be caught up in this narrative, the church's ongoing confession of faith narrates the truths that form faith's sight. The church's teaching mimics Luke's narrative catechesis by reminding believers of the foundational period of the church's existence and the foundational truths. This is ultimately what is meant by tradition as a living witness being formed from the living witnesses who together constitute the communion of the saints in the Spirit. Like Stephen, Augustine was caught up into this communion and continues to be caught up as the Spirit ecstatically turns his cupidity into charity.

Indeed, this is how early Protestants understood faith as entailing the simultaneous illumination of the mind and igniting of the heart. Faith flows, molten hot from the ecstatic embrace with the bridegroom as the Spirit breaks in upon the consciousness of the person. In his work on Luther, Heiko Oberman suggests that faith concerned a movement situated between *gemitus et raptus,* the sighs of a terror-stricken conscience and the raptures of the Word's consolation received through the church's witness to the promises of forgiveness. He suggests that Luther relates the *excessus mentis* of Christian mystical streams to faith and tribulation, that is, to the transition from a sinful person to a spiritual one. Ecstasy is then a term indicating faith and struggle because it is premised upon a person stuck by

56. Augustine, *Enchiridion,* prologue.

compunction who then must depend solely on God.[57] Faith breaks forth from the movement between the bitter sighing (*gemitus*) that comes from divine judgment and shatters confidence in one's own conscience and the joyful consolation of being lifted up (*raptus, exstasis*) into the promises of the Word. One sighs over one's sins and judgment while also being caught up in the gospel of Christ's saving righteousness.[58]

The confidence of faith one finds among early Protestants was directly related to defining faith in terms of *fiducia*. In the 1521 *Loci communes*, Philip Melanchthon defines faith simply as "a heartfelt reliance [*fiducia*] of the mercy promised because of Christ."[59] In later editions of the *Loci communes*, Melanchthon will define *fiducia* as a movement in the will whereby it necessarily looks at Christ with agreement and rests in Christ. Moreover, this kind of agreement and rest or reliance cannot occur apart from the Holy Spirit.[60] Likewise, Martin Bucer closely connects *fiducia* to faith as a "firm persuasion." Yet Bucer defines *fiducia* and *dilectio* as "affections of the mind" that stem from the will.[61] For Melanchthon and Bucer, *sola fide* denoted that faith was the first affective movement or form of delight in the promises of God. This occurred as the soul was caught up in God's presence through an encounter driven by the Word and the Spirit. The interior confidence was a result of the "rest" when one began to delight in the things of God in which rest denoted both an interior state and the initial right ordering of the affections.

We have now come full circle to Luke's narrative catechesis. Luke intends to pass along the memory of the people of God through his narrative reworking of the foundational events of early Christianity. By retelling the stories of Peter, Paul, and Stephen and connecting those stories to the history of Israel, he places the reader within the framework of salvation history. Moreover, there is a mimetic participation in these stories as Luke frames Stephen's martyrdom in terms of Christ's death, thereby setting the pattern

57. Heiko Oberman, *The Dawn of the Reformation* (Grand Rapids: Eerdmans, 1992), 145–49.

58. Berndt Hamm, *The Early Luther: Stages in a Reformation Reorientation*, Lutheran Quarterly Books (Grand Rapids: Eerdmans, 2014), 54.

59. Philip Melanchthon, *Loci communes*, ed. C. G. Bretschneider and H. E. Bindseil, Corpus Reformatorum 21 (Brunswick, 1854), 163. All editions of Melanchthon's *Loci communes* are in this volume.

60. Melanchthon, *Loci communes*, 744: "For *fiducia* is a motion necessarily responding with assent or by which the will rests in Christ, which … is kindled by the Holy Spirit and the new light" (Nam fiducia est motus in voluntate necessario respondens assessioni, seu quo voluntas in Christo acquiescit, quod … accenditur spiritu sancto et nova luce).

61. Martin Bucer, *On the True Reconciliation and Composition of the Churches* (Strasbourg: Wendelin Rihel, 1542), 146.

for how Christians should approach life. This is the tradition of the church as Luke understands it.

By the time one reaches Augustine, the creed has become the basis for narrative catechesis. This common confession of faith supplies the content upon which the believer must rest. For early Protestants, the basic content was less contained within the creed and more within the promises of God as they came through Scripture. Yet the full understanding of these promises occurred in the context of the church's ongoing witness to the Scriptures through her preaching. There could be no *nuda Scriptura* in the early Protestant slogan of *sola Scriptura*. The point is to shape *memoria* as the person becomes conformed to Christ in the midst of the people of God.

Giving form to the person is not simply related to the stories and the theological interpretation of those stories. For Luke, narrative catechesis only occurs through the Spirit poured out by the risen Lord at Pentecost. It was this Spirit who dispensed sanctifying and charismatic graces by which Stephen was ecstatically caught up and transformed into glory. Augustine took this insight and wove it into his approach to faith in general. The journey from faith to understanding remains punctuated with ecstatic moments that offer a foretaste of the glory to come. This is how the Spirit forms the disordered desire of cupidity into the ordered passion of charity. Early Protestants understood this movement in terms of *fiducia*, an affective moment the Spirit generated in which the individual comes to rest in the promises of God. Following Luther, such a movement was yet another form of ecstasy. The memory of the church comes alive in the power and presence of the Spirit, who bestows graces upon believers over the course of their lives.

To return to Levering's proto–*ars moriendi*, Stephen's movement backward and forward through the story of Israel, which has become the story of the church, is made possible by the Spirit's catching him up ecstatically into the great cloud of witnesses. He beholds the risen Lord and tastes the sweetness of the Lord to whom he cries out "receive my spirit." The assent of faith requires illumination and intoxication, *notitia* and *fiducia*. From the vantage point of faith, hope's desire and love's union bubble up as the Spirit transforms Stephen into the image through which he beholds his Lord. He has crossed over into Abraham's bosom—the bosom of the Father, from whom the Son descends and to whom the Son ushers Stephen into on the wings of the Spirit.

RESPONSE

A Response to Professor Levering

Marcus Plested (Orthodox)

Let me begin by paying tribute to Professor Levering's profound and perceptive paper. The art of dying is something of a lost art within our contemporary culture. We live in a world that avoids confronting death wherever possible, that treats abortion as a surgical procedure yet prolongs life almost at all costs, that drugs the dying so that they end their days not in repentance but in opiate-fueled hallucination, that sends off its loved ones in closed coffins in a mood of stimulated pseudo-celebration. Our age, as St. Nikolai Velimirovich puts it, is one of "life without aim and death without hope." Professor Levering sketches out a profoundly Christian antidote to all this, taking the gratitude and repentance (personal and communal) of Stephen as a paradigm for the way in which we should approach and prepare for our own deaths. Professor Levering's paper is salutary in the fullest possible sense of the term.

But I shall in the remainder of this paper focus on the Orthodox understanding and appropriation of the narrative of Stephen's martyrdom in the book of Acts. Stephen is, in the first instance, remembered as protomartyr and protodeacon. It goes without saying that Stephen's witness unto death has remained an inspiration and exemplar for the untold numbers of Christian martyrs from the apostolic era down to our own. Stephen is also remembered for his being numbered among the first seven deacons appointed by the apostles. It is as a deacon that he is invariably depicted within the iconographic tradition.

The patristic tradition contains a good deal of reflection on Stephen. A place of honor in this respect belongs to St. Augustine, who writes at length of the glories and miracles attendant upon the translation of the relics of St. Stephen to North Africa. These astonishing scenes prompt Augustine to reflect weightily on the puzzling relationship between death and life. Augustine takes the miracles of healing and conversion worked by the relics of St. Stephen as a powerful testimony to the power of life over death: "He would not be visiting us as dead if in death he were not alive."[62] St. Maximus the Confessor, like Professor Levering, takes Stephen as a paradigm of Christina repentance: "A man who has been assiduous in acquiring the fruits of love will not cease loving even if he suffers a thousand calamities. Let Stephen, the disciple of Christ, and others like him persuade you of the truth of this."[63]

But the most distinctive current of reflection on Stephen within the Orthodox Christian tradition pertains to his role as a paradigm and exemplar of mystical experience. Here I refer to his angelic countenance (Acts 6:15) and his heavenly vision: "But he, full of the Holy Spirit, gazed into heaven and saw the glory of God, and Jesus standing at the right hand of God; and he (Acts 6:55–56 RSV).

The first great Eastern Christian theologian to center his account of mystical experience on the vision of God as light is Macarius (pseudo-Macarius/Macarius-Symeon). For this fourth-century ascetic and mystic, the vision of God as light is *the* defining characteristic of the Christian life:

> The blessed Apostle Paul, the architect of the Church, forever anxious for the truth and not wishing that those who hear the word should be impeded by ignorance, indicated with great exactitude and clarity the goal of the truth and made known the perfect mystery of Christianity in every believing soul, this being to receive through a divine operation the experience of the effulgence of the heavenly light in holy souls in the revelation and power of the Spirit.[64]

This experience, Macarius insists, "is not a revelation of knowledge and concepts but the eternal illumination of the hypostatic light."[65] This unambiguous teaching on the uncreated character of the divine light witnessed in prayer was to be of incalculable import for the development of Orthodox mystical theology. For Macarius, as for the Byzantine tradition as a whole, St. Paul is chiefly reverenced as an apostle of mystical experience. His blinding vision of God as light on the road to Damascus and his rapture

62. Augustine, *Sermo* 317.1, quoted in Robert A. Marcus, *The End of Ancient Christianity* (Cambridge: Cambridge University Press, 1990), 94.

63. Maximus the Confessor, *Centuries on Love* 1.37, in G. E. H. Palmer et al., trans., *The Philokalia* (London: Faber and Faber, 1981), 2:56.

64. Macarius, *Logos* I 58.1.1. Note on references to Macarius: I = Heinz Berthold, ed., *Makarios/Symeon, Reden und Briefe: Die Sammlung I des Vaticanus Graecus 694 (B)*, 2 vols., GCS 55–56 (Berlin: Akademie-Verlag, 1973); II = Hermann Dörries, Erich Klostermann, and Matthias Kroeger, eds., *Die 50 Geistlichen Homilien des Makarios*, PTS 4 (Berlin: de Gruyter, 1964).

65. Macarius, *Logos* I 58.1.1, 58.2.1.

into heaven loom larger in the Byzantine mindset than his teaching on faith and works or his approach to Jews unable or unwilling to accept Jesus as the Christ. Macarius routinely associates Paul with Stephen as prime examples of the possibility of the vision of God by the saints in this life.[66] Elsewhere he makes a further connection with Moses and the light that shone from his face on his descent from Sinai (Ex 34:29–35). These three, Moses, Paul, and Stephen, serve for Macarius as a demonstration of the fact that the vision of God as light is not merely a matter of conceptual illumination but represents the "real and substantial shining of the divine light of the Holy Spirit in the worthy and faithful."[67] This comes in the context on a meditation on the nature of scriptural exegesis. While Macarius finds it plausible to interpret such a passages on the level of concepts and knowledge, he is adamant that they must first and foremost be interpreted as calls to each and every Christian to seek out and experience this same divine light. The title of the first English translation of the *Macarian Homilies* sums up the nature of this call rather nicely, if not exactly in accordance with the pithier titles demanded by publishers today:

Primitive Morality or the Spiritual Homilies of St Macarius the Egyptian; Full of very profitable instructions concerning that Perfection which is Expected from Christians and which it is their Duty to Endeavour after. Done out of Greek with several considerable emendations and some enlargements from a Bodleian MS, never before printed.[68]

Elsewhere, Macarius makes a further connection between the vision of God as light and the light of the Transfiguration.

As the body of the Lord, when he went up onto the mountain, was glorified and transfigured into the divine glory and infinite light, so also are the bodies of the saints glorified and resplendent. For just as the inner glory of Christ covered his body and shone forth, so in the same way, on that day, the power of Christ which the saints [now] have within, will be poured out upon their bodies.[69]

This connection was to be of incalculable importance for the later Byzantine mystical tradition and in particular for the Hesychasts of the fourteenth century.

But before we turn to the fourteenth century, let me stop awhile in the

66. Macarius, *Logos* I 5.3.2.

67. Macarius, *Logos* I 17.1.2

68. *Primitive Morality or the Spiritual Homilies of St Macarius the Egyptian . . .*, trans. Thomas Haywood (London, 1721).

69. Macarius, *Homily* II 15.38.

eleventh. St. Symeon the New Theologian stands very much in the tradition of light mysticism inaugurated by Macarius. Symeon, like Macarius, characterizes the vision of God as light as something to which all Christians must aspire. Indeed he comes perilously close to suggesting that those who do not experience God in this way are not really true Christians—a depressing admonition to those of us whose mystical experiences fall somewhat short of those described in such spectacular style by Symeon.

Symeon also shares with Macarius a singular lack of reluctance to speak about his own mystical experiences. Symeon goes so far as to claim a direct affinity with both Paul and Stephen as a co-witnesses to the possibility of the vision of God in this life. Of Stephen, Symeon notes that he was stoned principally on account of his claim to see the heavens opened and the "Son of man standing at the right hand of the glory of the Father":

> And as if he were speaking blasphemy,
> he was stoned by the teachers of the law.
> He died by the law of nature and lives forever.
> Although he was an apostle, he was also sanctified
> and completely full of the All-Holy Spirit.
> But it was the beginning of the proclamation and there was a crowd
> of unbelievers
> who by trusting in Christ through the apostles
> received the grace which is a gift of faith.
> Now then, what does this strange thing mean,
> this thing happening in me? What would this frightening terror
> that is now accomplished signify?[70]

Note that for Symeon the vision of Stephen is "the beginning of the proclamation." As protomystic, Stephen announces to all the possibility of the vision of God in this life—and indeed the necessity for all Christians to seek out that vision. Symeon claims that that which Stephen saw, he also saw:

> I see Christ frightfully opening the heavens for me,
> himself stooping to look and to be seen by me
> at the same time with the Father and the Spirit, the thrice holy light,
> alight that is one and three and three in one.
> By all means they are the light, and the one light is the three

70. *Divine Eros: Hymns of St Symeon the New Theologian*, trans. Daniel K. Griggs, Popular Patristics Series (Crestwood, N.Y.: St. Vladimir's Seminary Press, 2011), 64–65.

which also enlightens my soul more than the sun,
and illuminates my darkened mind.[71]

All this is both terrifying and dizzying. Symeon is in no doubt that he sees but a fragment of God's self-revelation "as the whole of water is displayed in a drop"—but even this glimpse is wholly overpowering, causing Symeon to fear that he might be subsumed into God:

> I have passed my time with my mind engaged in these things,
> and as though, it seemed, I gazed into heaven,
> and I tremble lest I received more and he should absorb me.
> I have found him who I saw from afar,
> Whom Stephen saw when the heavens opened,
> and whom again Paul saw afterward when he was blinded,
> truly and entire like a fire in the middle of my heart.

Symeon, it should be acknowledged, is in no doubt as to his absolute unworthiness for such a life-giving and deifying vision:

> But I the living corpse, under the earth, covered by a stone (Rev. 1:18),
> I have found life, the one who gives life.[72]

Symeon was most scornful and dismissive of anyone who claimed such visions as were vouchsafed to Stephen or Paul were not in principle open to and incumbent upon all Christians to pursue in every age. Indeed he regarded any skepticism as to the possibility of the vision of God as light as the sin against the Holy Spirit (Mk 3:28–30). Symeon's unsettling and unusual evangelical fervor in this matter goes some way to explaining the sobriquet "new theologian," a descriptor initially intended as a slur but later adopted as a badge of honor. Controversy surrounding the vision of God as light did not disappear with Symeon's rapid canonization. Indeed, the controversy was to erupt spectacularly in the Hesychast controversy of the fourteenth century.

The Macarian tradition of light mysticism was a direct source of inspiration for the Hesychasts of the fourteenth century. By this time, it had become standard in the Christian East to use Paul and Stephen as witnesses to the possibility of the vision of God as light. In figures such as St. Theoleptos of Philadelphia and St. Gregory of Sinai such visions are taken to be visions

71. Symeon, *Divine Eros*, 64–65.
72. Symeon, *Divine Eros*, 68.

of the same light that shone from Christ on Tabor. Pursuit of such defying visions invariably revolved around the practice of the Jesus Prayer: "Lord Jesus Christ, Son of God, have mercy upon me, the sinner." Concentrated repetition of this prayer often involved particular bodily postures (e.g., crouching on a small stool) and, sometimes, control of breathing. Many Byzantine monks of the Hesychast tradition claimed that such practices prepared them for the experience of the vision of God as light. All this became especially contentious with the eruption of the polemic between St. Gregory Palamas and Barlaam the Calabrian. Barlaam had served as the Orthodox spokesperson in series of debates with two Latin papal legates held in Constantinople in 1334. In these debates, Barlaam had poured scorn on the rationalist excesses of Latin theology and cast doubt on the possibility of any sort of demonstrative or apodictic argumentation in the realm of theology. Gregory Palamas, writing from Athos, objected that such agnosticism was wholly unacceptable and wrote a pair of *Apodictic Treatises* (1335) to prove the point. Seeking to know more about the origin and immediate context of such impertinent critiques, Barlaam took himself to Mount Athos and was appalled by what he found: uneducated and ignorant monks claiming to see God as light. Barlaam attacked such rustics as *omphalopsychoi* (those who have their soul in their navels) and Messalians—an ancient heresy believed to have dispensed with the sacraments of the church and to have taught that prayer alone brings about the vision of God with the physical eyes. The best sort of illumination we can hope for, argued Barlaam, was the kind of epistemological illumination vouchsafed to the classical philosophers of old. Even the Transfiguration is to be understood as a created symbol or sign of Christ's divinity and as such to stand at a lower level than philosophical enlightenment. The monks found a champion in Palamas, who vigorously defended the role of the body in prayer and the possibility of the experience of God as light. Palamas specified that this is an experience operative in the first instance on the level of the spiritual senses but extended by virtue of the psychosomatic unity of the human person also to the body. He went on to affirm that when we speak of the vision of God as light we are not speaking of the divine essence (which remains forever hidden to human sight) but the divine operation or action or energy.

The vision of Stephen was quite literally a God-send for Palamas in his efforts to demonstrate the biblical basis of all that he had to say in defense of Hesychast practices of prayer. It is a passage to which he returns time and time again. For Palamas, the narrative of Stephen's vision neatly conveyed three things: (1) the possibility of the vision of God; (2) the role of the body in that vision through the intermediary of the spiritual senses; and (3) the principle that the vision of God as light is a vision of the energy and not the essence of God. I give just a few examples in what follows.

The first mention in Palamas's *Triads in Defense of Holy Hesychasts* emphasizes that Stephen's vision was "not sensible, nor was it intellectual, nor did it take place by abstraction, but in some ineffable manner."[73] It was a spiritual illumination apprehended by the spiritual or intellectual senses and communicated to the body. Sometimes—as in the case of Moses and of Stephen—this inner illumination can even be physically manifested upon the body. This is why Moses's face shone as he came down from Sinai and why Stephen's face shone like that of an angel—being in both cases the result of an inward participation in the divine light.[74] Elsewhere, Palamas affirms that the vision of Stephen was not a vision of God in glory but a vision of the glory of God—that is to say a vision of God himself in his divine glory or energy. This is in essence the same glory as was revealed to the disciples as light on Tabor and indeed to Paul on the road to Damascus. These visions are to be understood as unifying and deifying in accordance with the declaration of the psalmist: "In thy light shall we see light" (Ps 36:9).[75] Time and time again, argues Gregory, Scripture witnesses to the fact that the vision of God as light is indeed a vision of God himself if, to be sure, a vision of God's energy and not of his essence.[76] The essence will remain forever hidden to us even as God manifests himself in his self-giving revelation or energy.

For St. Gregory Palamas, the vision of the apostle Stephen becomes a central reference point in his ultimately successful effort to establish the reality of the possibility of the vision of God as light, the role of the body in that vision (if only in a secondary sense), and the principle that God is seen and experienced not according to essence, or indeed hypostasis, but according to energy. The apostle Stephen is in this once again not only protomartyr and protodeacon but also protomystic—a herald and witness to the reality of salvation understood as deification, or *theosis*. And while Gregory's efforts yielded some decisive achievements in the realm of dogmatic theology (most notably the essence-energies distinction), his treatment of the

73. Palamas, *Triads* 1.3.30–31.

74. Palamas, *Triads* 1.3.30–31; cf. *Triads* 2.2.12–13.

75. Palamas, *Triads* 2.3.27.

76. See also Palamas, *Triads* 2.3.66; 3.3.4–5.

vision of Stephen also serves to express and recapitulate the long-standing emphasis on mystical experience characteristic of the Orthodox Christian tradition and consistently evident in its treatment of narrative of the martyrdom of St. Stephen.

None of this is to condone any sort of world-denying mysticism or indeed to detract from Stephen's place as perennial inspiration of martyrs (and indeed deacons). Nor does it detract from the value of the narrative of his martyrdom as a practice of Christian dying as so eloquently expressed by Professor Levering. Nor, certainly, is it to shirk Christian responsibility for the propagation of the gospel. On the contrary, the long tradition of Orthodox reflection on Stephen as protomystic (and indeed its analogous reflection on Paul) serves as a sign of its belief that direct experience of God in the fullness of the Holy Spirit must lie at the heart of any properly apostolic effort.

CHAPTER 4

Divine Action and Human Response

Four Theological and Visual Interpretations of Paul's Conversion in Acts 9

Ralph C. Wood (Evangelical)

All reading of Scripture is contextual—no matter whether it stands under the authority of the Roman Catholic magisterium, the Orthodox understanding of tradition, or the priesthood of believers that characterizes free-church Protestantism. There is no view from nowhere, to repeat a commonplace. All seeing is lensed and located. This is not a disabling limit, I believe, not a condemnation to a hopeless historicism. On the contrary, our spectacles can be polished, our hearing sharpened, our fingers and feet made nimbler as we traverse the various ways whereby the narrative of Paul's conversion in Acts 9 has been interpreted. Like Paul himself, we may even be converted from one tradition-laden account to another, even to one that contradicts our original stance. Accordingly, I shall examine Acts 9:1–9 through four differing lenses. We shall also be asking whether any of these four interpretations of Acts 9 might constitute a distinctively Christian call to *metanoia* in our own time? Amid our increasingly post-Christian age, wherein there is widespread doubt that God acts at all if indeed God exists at all, how might we better interpret and envision divine action and the human response to it—especially in relation to one of the most miraculous events in Christian history: the conversion of Paul?

According to Acts 9, Saul/Paul was ordered by the high priest of Jerusalem to arrest Jews who had been converted to the gospel and to bring them in chains back to the temple city. There, presumably, they would be subjected to the same cruel treatment that had led to the execution of Stephen. The story of Paul's conversion outside Damascus is narrated three times in Acts and then repeated again in Galatians. Suffice it here to concentrate only on the famous scene from the first nine verses of Acts 9, namely, Paul's being struck by a bright light, thrown to the ground, queried by Jesus about tormenting Christians, then answering Christ by calling him "Lord," and finally remaining blind for three days even though his eyes were opened. To read this encounter for its rightful impingement on our time requires us to read it in conversation with other interpreters, both theological and artistic, from previous ages: patristic, medieval, Renaissance, and modern.

Patristic

Already the early iconographers were demonstrating their refusal to be bound by the limits of linear time, except insofar as the narrative moves from left to right—from the Jerusalem plotting to the prostration of Paul and then onto his being led to the house of Ananias—with Christ gesturing down on the whole episode. Icons often depict such events as occurring simultaneously because God himself dwells beyond chronicity: He is the Eternal Now, the one in whom there is "no shadow of turning," the God who has neither future nor past, neither anticipation nor remembrance, dwelling rather in the timeless present of *totus simul*. The iconic form, in its two-dimensionality, is able to render such simultaneity as art in the Christian West is rarely able to do. The Western notion of perspective, rather than transforming the natural, often seeks to imitate it. The vanishing point of a Western realistic painting is thus situated in the center and *behind* the picture, as our eyes are drawn forward, in panoptic fashion, so as to master the whole scene. An icon, by contrast, has no disappearing point. The focus usually moves out and away from the icon toward the beholder, as the image comes forth to engage the viewer. Rather than our *looking at* an icon, it *looks at and beckons us*; it seeks to transform us into our own likeness to Christ. "The power of an icon," writes Paul Evdokimov, "is maximal by reason of its opening upon the transcendent that has no image. The gaze thus purified and made attentive can descend, scrutinize and reveal the interior of the soul"[1]

The aim of icons, it follows, is to reveal, to our earthly, unspiritual eyes, the invisible spiritual reality of the eternal world that everywhere envelops us. This desire to spiritualize the human world means that realistic proportions are abandoned. The size of figures in an icon is usually determined

1. Paul Evdokimov, *Ages of the Spiritual Life* (Crestwood, N.Y.: St. Vladimir's Seminary Press, 1998), 194.

by their importance and significance. A person standing in the background can thus be larger than a person in the foreground. Heads and haloes often overlap, for depth has no overriding importance. The incarnation has overthrown all ordinary dimensions and perspectives. Indeed, nearly everything in the icon takes place in the forefront. Rarely are there shadows in icons, for the *illumination* of darkness is their essential aim; the light radiates from them rather than upon them.

These conventions are at work in the icon of Paul's conversion shown in figure 4-1. The high priest is instructing an all-too-willing Paul to continue ravaging Jewish converts to Christ, dragging them in bonds to Jerusalem. There is no overt reference to the city, though the large rock may suggest the Place of the Skull, since the story of Paul's execution (albeit in Rome) would have already been known. Yet the figure presiding over the whole scene is Christ himself. The nimbus surrounding his head indicates that, at least here, he alone is crowned with the uncreated light. Far from being one saint among others, he is the Lord's own anointed. The burning twin rays of the divine energies plunge directly onto the stricken Paul, who has been brought to his knees. A lesser ray points downward to Ananias as he leads the blinded Paul to his home, as does another aimed at the city of Damascus, whose turrets and walls are figured behind, perhaps a sign of the hospitality the new Christians had received there as not in Jerusalem.

The open-eyed but blinded Paul gazes uncertainly upward, whether toward the Jesus who is speaking to him, or else backward at the Jerusalem scene, perhaps as he guiltily remembers his collusion in the stoning of Stephen.[2] The key feature of the icon is surely Jesus's mild-featured face. It has no menacing quality. Christ grasps what may be the scroll of the new law that Paul will soon proclaim, and he gestures with a hand of blessing rather than rebuke. The shape of Jesus's kind hand is repeated in the hands of both Saul and Ananias. Such repetition may indicate that Ananias himself is being more fully converted, for he had feared and dreaded Paul, at first failing to recognize him as Christ's new apostle. This most decisive of all conversions—it has been called the greatest miracle apart from the resurrection itself—is depicted almost calmly, as if to indicate that the total turnabout of the church's most terrible enemy happens without fanfare or acclaim, but quietly along a road and within a house located in the Herodian city of Damascus.

2. "Though his eyes were open, he could see nothing" (Acts 9:8 NRSV).

FIGURE 4-1. Greco-Serbian Group of Masters, *The Conversion of Saul* (c. 1340)

Certain features of the ancient icon appear in St. John Chrysostom's two sermons devoted to the conversion of Paul. The golden-mouthed preacher is concerned principally with the transformation Paul undergoes, which he treats as more remarkable than the blinding blast of light that throws Paul to the ground. Jesus addresses the stricken Paul, Chrysostom notes, not by claiming to be the true Messiah and Son of God, but rather by identifying himself as the one whose disciples Paul has persecuted, making clear the strong identification between the Lord and his church: to oppress the church is to oppress Christ himself. Chrysostom does not pause to ask how Saul could have addressed Jesus as Lord, when this is precisely the title that, as an unbelieving Pharisee, he had refused to accord Christ. Neither does Chrysostom seize upon the rich allegorical possibilities inherent in the paradox that, though his eyes remained open, Paul was blinded. Imagine what allegorical enticements Origen must have found in such a splendid paradox! What chiefly interests Chrysostom is that both Paul and Ananias are given visions that demand their total *obedience*—the blinded Paul seeing that he must seek healing at the hands of Ananias in Damascus, and the fearful Ananias discerning that the nefarious Paul has been turned into a man of prayer, a fellow disciple who is not to be dreaded but to be healed and baptized and set apart for his special mission. "[Paul] was no longer a wild beast," Chrysostom notes, "but a man mild and gentle!"[3]

As in the icon, so in Chrysostom: Christ's forgiveness of Paul is the heart of the matter; indeed, this early church father calls such mercy "the very goal of Christianity." The gospel of divine mercy that Paul began so courageously and fearlessly to preach is the summons of every Christian, Chrysostom iterates. We make a fool of God, he says, if we do not persuade others to become Christians. "Nothing is more frigid than a Christian," he writes, "who cares not for the salvation of others.... Do not insult God. To say, that the sun cannot shine, is to insult God, and call him a liar. For it is easier for the sun not to give heat, nor to shine, than for the Christian not to send forth light: it is easier for the light to be darkness, than for this to be so. Tell me not that it is impossible: the contrary is the impossible. Do not insult God."[4]

3. John Chrysostom, "In Praise of St. Paul," in *Chrysostom and His Message: A Selection from the Sermons of St. John Chrysostom of Antioch and Constantinople*, ed. and trans. Stephen Neill (New York: Association Press, 1962), 74–75. This is one of seven panegyrics that Chrysostom delivered in honor of Paul. He also preached sermons on all of the Pauline Epistles.

4. St. John Chrysostom, *Homilies on the Acts of the Apostles* 20, in *NPNF*[1] 11:133–34, http://www.newadvent.org/fathers/210120.htm.

Fully imbued with the doctrine of *theosis*, Chrysostom summons his hearers to live a virtuous life by bringing their malleable *likeness* to God into full accord with the damaged but indestructible *image* of God in which they are made. Paul realizes such deification by his character as much as his message, Chrysostom claims:

> Knowing therefore these things, let us hold fast to virtue, as knowing that it is not possible to be saved otherwise, than by passing through this present life in doing good works, that we may also obtain the good things which are to come, through the grace and mercy of our Lord Jesus Christ, with Whom to the Father together with the Holy Spirit be glory, might, honor, now and ever, world without end. Amen.[5]

There is nothing anodyne about this summons to go forth in the light of Christ, to imitate Paul as he imitated Christ (Rom 2:11). Christians thus kindled with the flame of the gospel are meant to set the world ablaze, even if they are themselves consumed by it:

> So this Paul, who was more passionate than fire, did not remain a single day in idleness; but the moment he came forth from the sacred fount of waters, he kindled a great flame of fire about himself. He took no account of dangers, or of the mockery or contempt of the Jews, or of the distrust in which he was held by them, or anything else. He had now received new eyes, the eyes of love, and another mind; and, charging down with the force of a mountain torrent, he swept away all the defences of the Jews, proving from Scripture that Jesus is the Christ.... He was all on fire; his every action showed that in his heart of hearts he was ready even to die; he did all this as though he was trying to make up for what he had done in time past, and he contrived to throw himself into that place where the battle was hottest and most full of perils and terrors.[6]

Chrysostom is not much concerned with the question of Paul's freedom in responding to Jesus's summons. With wonderful brevity, he declares that Paul came to be the greatest of the apostles "partly through his own natural gifts, and partly by the gift of God; and the gift of God was given because of what [Paul] was through his natural gifts."[7] Lest such circularity seem suspect, it needs to be remembered that, in the Orthodox tradition, such perfect reciprocity between divine and human action entails no burdensome choice. In true freedom, Christians participate in the life of God so fully as to need no recourse to anxious deliberation. Vladimir Lossky

5. Chrysostom, *Homilies on the Acts of the Apostles* 20.
6. Chrysostom, "In Praise of St. Paul," 74–75.
7. Chrysostom, "In Praise of St. Paul," 72.

quotes St. Maximus in this regard: "Freedom of choice is already a sign of imperfection, a limitation of our true freedom. A perfect nature has no need of choice, for it knows what is naturally good. Its freedom is based on this knowledge. Our free choice (*gnomé*) indicates the imperfection of fallen human nature, the loss of the divine likeness."[8]

Medieval

St. Thomas Aquinas's comment on the conversion of Paul is brief but telling. It comes in a section of the *Summa* asking whether conversion to Christ requires any prior human disposition. Since Paul's immediate conversion seems to have left no time for preparatory grace, Aquinas's first objector asks, why speak of grace at all? Aquinas admits the severity of the problem: Paul received converting grace while he was still "breathing out threatenings and slaughter against the disciples of the Lord" (Acts 9:1).[9]

Aquinas replies with the exquisitely paradoxical insistence that God enables every good movement of the human will, while at the same time leaving it utterly free; indeed, our freedom lies precisely within such enabling grace.

> Even the good movement of the free-will, whereby anyone is prepared for receiving the gift of grace is an act of the free-will moved by God. And thus man is said to prepare himself, according to Prov. 16:1: "It is the part of man to prepare the soul"; yet it is principally from God, Who moves the free-will. Hence it is said that man's will is prepared by God, and that man's steps are guided by God.[10]

Thomas concedes that God works such perfect preparation of the human will in two ways—either gradually, step by step, or else instantaneously. In Paul's case, it is the latter. Though Aquinas doesn't use the word *miracle*, an event whose sole efficient cause is God, this seems to be what he has in mind. Miracles are not invasions of the natural so much as the right fulfillment of it. If so, then the speed of Paul's Damascus-road conversion becomes an earthly form of the divine simultaneity. What matters here, however, is that Aquinas differs quite markedly from Chrysostom. In Paul's instant conversion, Aquinas emphasizes the prevenient divine enablement

8. Vladimir Lossky, *The Mystical Theology of the Eastern Church* (Crestwood, N.Y.: St. Vladimir's Seminary Press, 1976), 125.

9. Thomas Aquinas, *Summa theologiae* II-I, q. 112, obj. 2, http://www.newadvent.org/summa/2112.htm.

10. Aquinas, *Summa theologiae* II-I, q. 112, obj. 2.

FIGURE 4-2. Pieter Bruegel the Elder, *Conversion of Paul* (1567)

(operative grace) over the human response to it (cooperative grace). All glory and honor belong to God, therefore, not to Paul.

A similar emphasis can be found in Pieter Bruegel the Elder (1525–1569), though he can hardly be regarded as a medieval artist in the chronological sense. Michelangelo and Leonardo da Vinci had already finished their masterpieces during the Italian High Renaissance; indeed, Martin Luther had posted his Ninety-Five Theses roughly eight years before Bruegel was born. Yet a medieval spirit imbues his work. Perhaps because he lived in a humanistic age that exalted personal heroism, whether religious or secular, over divine deliverance, Bruegel painted often against the grain of his contemporaries. His work is filled with landscapes taken directly from the Flemish scene; he elevates the peasantry to a dignity rarely witnessed in high art; and he casts almost all of his subjects within his own century so as to make their contemporary relevance clear. This is true also of his *Conversion of Paul* (figure 4-2).

Bruegel transfers the conversion of Paul to his own time. The changes are both major and multiple. Most notably, Bruegel supplies Paul with an entire army. Painting this work in 1567, Bruegel intentionally likens the Pauline militia to the troops of the Duke of Alba as they marched across the precipitous Alps, also in 1567. They were making their way through Piedmont and Savoy in order to crush the Protestant disturbances that were rife in the Low Countries, so as to reclaim them for the duke's monarch, Philip II of Spain. It is not difficult to discern the link between this much-hated invasion of Flanders with the throwing of Paul to the ground in Acts 9: both the Jewish persecutor and the Spanish militia are guilty of overweening hubris. Yet here the analogy seems to collapse. If Paul is leading the charge, why is he so difficult to locate? Unlike the horse's rump that dominates the foreground, Paul himself is exceedingly hard to find (see figure 4-3). Bruegel does not depict the dazzling light of Christ that strikes Paul supine. At last, with our eyes straining, we discern a balding Paul to be the figure in blue lying awkwardly on the ground, beside his virtually kneeling horse, his head lifted slightly, as if to acknowledge that he has been confronted by a Lord who commands an army totally unlike the one surrounding him.

What does Bruegel the Elder intend by this strange rendering of Paul's volte-face? As a painter imbued with a medieval vision of the virtues and vices, he may be suggesting that Paul has been properly humbled by the Lord, who has wrenched him back from his persecutory mission. If so, why isn't this drastic shaming made the dominant focus of the painting, rather than being rendered obscurely, almost invisibly? Bruegel seems almost to reverse the pattern of icons, since the viewer must search for the central figure rather than his reaching out to confront us, in icon fashion. Quite apart from his hatred of Spanish rule over Flanders, Bruegel may be reminding those imbued with preening self-confidence of the High Renaissance that the world turns not on the axis of mighty human works, but on the humble spindle of God's miraculous deeds as they turn the world in ways that remain insensible to the great and the powerful.

Better than most theologians, Bruegel understands that divine action often occurs on the smallest stages, in the oddest places, amid the least earthly notice. This keen theological reversal is no mere Mannerist convention; it is the searing insight of Bruegel himself.[11] W. H. Auden catches a

11. Michael Francis Gibson compares Bruegel's *Conversion of St. Paul* with Caravaggio's *Conversion on the Road to Damascus*. Whereas Bruegel's viewpoint is mostly from above, Caravaggio's is from below.

FIGURE 4-3. Detail from Pieter Bruegel the Elder, *Conversion of Paul* (1567)

kindred kind of divine irony in "Musée des Beaux Arts," a poem written in response to another Bruegel painting, *The Fall of Icarus*, where the focal event is reduced to virtual triviality. Auden's first stanza applies equally

As we shall see, this represents a shift from the divine, as it were, to the human. Gibson regards Bruegel's "unusual philosophy of history" as "a Christian theme par excellence," though he puts the matter in humanist terms: "Bruegel conveys this momentous [significance] by means of the composition itself: a truly new idea will inevitably go unnoticed by those who possess the wisdom of former times. It does so to the extent that it does not fit into their mental categories and is foreign to their system of values. How could things be otherwise, considering that it establishes an entirely *new* category and a *new* order of values. The great turning point, the event which contains in germ a general mutation of the world, is inevitably concealed from the field" (Gibson, *The Mill and the Cross: Peter Bruegel's "Way to Calvary"* [Lausanne: Acatos, 2000], 124).

well to Bruegel's *Conversion of St. Paul,* especially if we substitute the phrase "life-converting revelation" for the word "suffering":

> About suffering they were never wrong,
> The Old Masters: how well they understood
> Its human position; how it takes place
> While someone else is eating or opening a window or just walking
> dully along;
> How, when the aged are reverently, passionately waiting
> For the miraculous birth, there always must be
> Children who did not specially want it to happen, skating
> On a pond at the edge of a wood:
> They never forgot
> That even the dreadful martyrdom must run its course
> Anyhow in a corner, some untidy spot
> Where the dogs go on with their doggy life and the torturer's horse
> Scratches its innocent behind on a tree.[12]

Renaissance

For a High Renaissance commentary on the conversion of Paul, there is none better than the paraphrase of it by Desiderius Erasmus (1456–1536).[13] Though younger than Bruegel, Erasmus is saturated with the spirit of the new learning as a means of making Scripture readily accessible to Christians who were literate but not scholarly. As a humanist Christian who shared little of Luther's dark concern with our inveterate propensity for evil, Erasmus declares that Paul's persecution of Christians, though savage, was but his well-intended means of combating heresy. Paul was a Jew, declares Erasmus,

12. W. H. Auden, *Collected Shorter Poems 1927–1957* (New York: Random House, 1966), 123–24.

13. Because Martin Luther looks back toward the early church more than forward to the newborn age of self-confident humanism, and perhaps because he himself has grievously suffered from his own opposition to the Roman Catholic Church, he emphasizes Christ's mercy on disciples who are afflicted by Paul-like persecutions: "Christ Himself testifies when He says in Acts 9:4: 'Saul, Saul, why do you persecute Me?' Saul had not done any violence to Christ, but only to His church. But whoever touches this, touches the apple of His eye (Zech. 2:8). The head is more sensitive and responsive in its feeling than the other parts of the body, as experience teaches. When the small toe or some other tiny part of the body is hurt, the face immediately shows that it feels this; the nose contracts, the eyes flash, etc. In the same way Christ, our Head, makes our afflictions His own, so that when we, who are His body, suffer, He is affected as though the evils were His own" (Luther, *Commentary on Galatians* [Grand Rapids: Fleming H. Revell, 1988], 407–8). I owe this reference to my colleague Mikeal Parsons, who assisted in other helpful ways in the shaping of this essay.

who had such "zeal for the ancestral law" that he "thought he was doing a service pleasing to God."[14]

For Erasmus, the marauding Paul had acted not with malicious intent but from religious ignorance. Rather than requiring the total transformation of Paul's will and desires in conformity to Christ, therefore, the one thing needed is a proper illumination of Paul's mind. Jesus threw him to the ground not in censure, Erasmus insists, so much as to startle him and thus to make him "teachable." Having confessed that a paraphrase is a commentary, an interpretation no less than a transmission of the text, Erasmus has Jesus speak to Erasmus's readers as if he were living in the sixteenth century and facing an oppressive Catholic hierarchy! "By erring simply in judgment [Paul] has given evidence of the sort of champion he will be for my gospel. Thus far armed with the bulls of pontiffs, with threats and chains, he has fought against those who profess my name."[15] Erasmus assures his audience that Paul would become a champion of virtue, as his arising from the ground has already indicated. "The first step to virtue," Erasmus observes in rare recourse to allegory, "is to stand erect." The converted Paul thus proved himself to be a true ἄνθρωπος, an upward-reaching man of truth. As Erasmus declares, he "had been changed from a restless troublemaker into a teacher of moderation and peace."[16]

Where, in High Renaissance art, might we locate paintings depicting such a valiant Paul who needs instructing more than transforming—that is, a heroic more than a humbled Paul? I suggest that Michelangelo Merisi da Caravaggio (1571–1610) supplies our need. Caravaggio depicted Paul's conversion not once but twice. His first version, titled *The Conversion of St. Paul* (1600; figure 4-4), was rejected, whether because his patron thought it too vulgar or else because Caravaggio himself was dissatisfied with its jumble of incoherent parts—"the tangle of shields, spears, helmets, plumes, branches, rumpled garments and harness."[17]

Caravaggio's tenebrist use of chiaroscuro makes the scene so dark that our gaze is focused almost entirely on the three fully illumined faces: the elderly soldier who has accompanied Paul, the youthful angel who restrains

14. *Collected Works of Erasmus*, vol. 50., *New Testament Scholarship: Paraphrase on Acts*, ed. John J. Bateman (Toronto: University of Toronto Press, 1995): 65, 63.

15. Erasmus, *New Testament Scholarship*, 65.

16. This is the same mild-mannered "teacher of peace" who cries out, "Wretched man that I am! Who will deliver me from this body of death?" (Rom 7:24); "O foolish Galatians! Who has bewitched you?" (Gal 3:1); and "Woe to me if I do not preach the gospel" (1 Cor 9:16; all from RSV).

17. Michael Kitson, *The Complete Paintings of Caravaggio* (New York: Harry N. Abrams, 1967), 94.

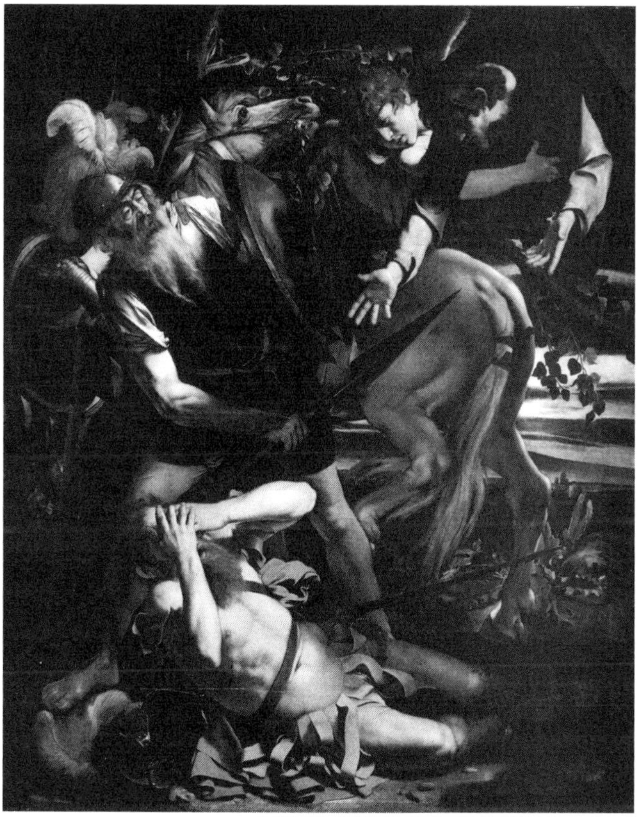

FIGURE 4-4. Caravaggio, *The Conversion of St. Paul* (1600/1601)

Christ from reaching out to his persecutor, as well as the bearded and supine Paul shielding his eyes from the piercing light. Caravaggio wants his viewers to be caught up in the inner struggle of Paul no less than his outward display of agony. As in our ancient icon, so does Caravaggio's dimly depicted Jesus seem to be surging forward in solicitude for Paul.

Yet there is something disturbingly ambiguous about the entire painting. Why are there no markers to identify the almost totally obscured Christ, who is barely visible at all? What are we to make of the boyish face of the angel? Why the emphasis on the almost nude torso of an elderly Paul, including even a disfiguring growth or scar on his chest? A vaguely erotic quality suffuses the whole scene, from the decadent bagged eyes of the soldier to the saliva-foaming mouth of the horse. Why is the Adonis-like angel focused on Paul rather than the Christ whom he restrains? And from what passion—spiritual, moral, physical—would a rescuing Christ need to be restrained? In comparison with Bruegel, is this less a Christian than a pagan rendering of the miracle of Acts 9? Perhaps Caravaggio's second painting of this same event, *The Conversion on the Road to Damascus,* from just a year later, will yield an answer (see figure 4-5).

This second version, displayed in the Cerasi Chapel of the church of Santa Maria del Popolo in Rome, was commissioned as a pair of paintings: one showing the agony of Peter as he is crucified head downward, and the other depicting the desperation of Paul as he lies sprawled on the Damascus road. Unlike the previous version, Paul is now turned away from the viewers, almost erupting into our own space. The diagonals and counter-diagonals are masterly. The horse's shod foot lifted delicately so as not to crush Paul, the bald pate of the companion who holds the bit of the bridle, with the veins protruding from the man's leg, the richly clothed Paul indicating his once-proud position as a Pharisee, now reduced to a desperate creature on his back with his hands beckoning upward—these are Caravaggio's superbly managed means for showing that Jesus has literally capsized Paul's world, as Madeleine Stebbins has observed:

> In an instant his world had been turned upside down. All he had lived for and was zealous for turned not only to ashes, but was seen in its truth as wicked. Conversion is depicted here as a total inversion, as a reverse, at antipodes with [his] perspective worldview.
>
> A miracle of grace happens here, one of vast consequence for the history of Christianity. A shaft of "light from heaven" (Acts 9:3) causes instant blindness. Caravaggio gives this powerful sense of light in darkness, a glowing light that is mysterious, unfathomable and beautiful, like the light of eternity. He focuses with intense concentration on this intimate moment to the exclusion of all else.[18]

"In the guise of naturalism," Karen Wilkin adds, "Caravaggio has created a stunning visual metaphor for transfiguration. Miraculous enlightenment is embodied by apparently everyday experience, so subtly that only if we spent a long time with this sublime painting do we begin to unlock its secrets."[19]

18. Madeleine F. Stebbins, "Looking at a Masterpiece: St. Paul's Conversion on the Way to Damascus," *Catholics United for the Faith,* May/June 2009, http://www.cuf.org/2009/05/looking-at-a-masterpiece-st-pauls-conversion-on-the-way-to-damascus/.

19. Karen Wilkin, "A Transfiguring Moment: Caravaggio's Potent, Astonishing 'Conversion of Saul,'" *Wall Street Journal,* March 6, 2010, http://tinyurl.com/jc9e9k8.

FIGURE 4-5. Caravaggio, *The Conversion on the Way to Damascus* (1601)

No wonder that Robert Hughes once said of Caravaggio: "There was art before him and art after him, and they were not the same."

Yet can we be sure that this acknowledged masterpiece has such singular significance for Caravaggio the artist—and thus for us the viewers? Troubling ambiguities abound. When asked why the light falls mainly on the horse, Caravaggio is supposed to have snapped back, "Because the light is from God!" Even so, why is the horse's presence so dominating? Is it the beautiful animal meant to display its bestial virility, unlike Bruegel's rear-viewed horse indicating military might? Why is Christ no longer present at all? Why might Paul's recumbent position indicate a state of orgasmic ecstasy no less than a desperate plea? Why, in both paintings, does the emphasis fall more on the human than the divine, more on the converted Paul than the converting Christ? And if the painting resounds with homoerotic overtones, is its religious significance nullified? Perhaps more so than Bernini's rendering of Teresa in ecstasy is made sub-Christian for also having an unmistakably erotic quality.

Such exquisite union of opposites was the very stuff of Baroque art, as we can also witness in the poetry of John Donne, especially in the sestet of Holy Sonnet XIV, "Batter my heart, three person'd God":

> Yet dearely I love you, and would be lov'd faine,
> But am betroth'd unto your enemie:
> Divorce mee, untie, or breake that knot againe,
> Take mee to you, imprison mee, for I
> Except you enthrall mee, never shall be free,
> Nor ever chast, except you ravish mee.[20]

One needs not be a prude to acknowledge the patent risks inherent in erotic spirituality. The positive revelation of God that comes by desire is no less dangerous than the negative disclosure via renunciation. The two are not opposites so much as complements, as the great mystics of the Western church have understood: Bernard of Clairvaux, Teresa of Ávila, John of the Cross are the obvious example. Yet Donne's poem manifests the perils inherent in this delicate balance. To "enthrall," for example, is not only to captivate or charm; it is also to hold or to be held in bondage for the sake of sexual stimulation. So does "ravish" mean more than "enrapture." It's from the Old French *raviss-*, the lengthened stem of *ravir,* which in turn derives from an alteration of the Latin *rapere* (to seize). Thus does "ravish" also indicate "rape," the forcing of

20. *The Complete Poetry of John Donne*, ed. John T. Shawcross (Garden City, N.Y.: Anchor, 1967), 344.

another into unwilling sexual intercourse. In what way, if any, does Acts 9 indicate that Paul is enthralled or ravished by Christ in Donne's sense?[21] Given the choice between Erasmus's paraphrase and Caravaggio's paintings, which is more faithful and edifying? Is it possible that both the humanist scholar and the humanist painter may have missed the heart of the matter?

Modern

It may seem that I have offered a story of declension, a jeremiad lamenting, if not the death of God, then something akin to a divine eclipse. Charles Taylor has famously described ours as a secular age. Though generally true, such a claim cannot account for the emergence of a latter-day church father in the midst of such a divine eclipse: Karl Barth. Against all auguries to the contrary, Barth became the utterly unanticipated legatee of his nineteenth-century forebears. In a time when Christian theology, whether from the left or the right, was seeking accommodations to modernity, Barth offered massive resistance against all attempts to base Christian thinking on anything other than God's self-disclosure in Jesus Christ. His christological reading of Paul's conversion, it follows, is quite unlike anything preceding it. Instead of treating the Lord who blinds Paul as the one *for whom* we are meant to make witness, Barth insists that Paul's conversion reveals Jesus Christ *himself* as the first and final witness to God's action in the world. Like Erasmus, Barth regards Saul of Tarsus as a man who dwelt in darkness, yet he is ignorant in way unfathomed by Erasmus:

> What he did not know was the necessity of radical conversion thus laid upon Israel, its obligation to accept this divine decision [i.e., God's giving of Jesus to be Israel to be Israel's Messiah] which actually precludes all seeking of its own righteousness. What he did not know was the urgency of the command ... to recognise in this decision of God His helping action and binding Word, and to give to it all the faith and obedience required of Israel. This is what Saul of Tarsus did not know. What it all amounts to is that he did not know Jesus.[22]

21. At least Caravaggio hasn't reduced Paul's conversion to the submiraculous quality that John Stuart Mill found there: "St. Paul, the only known exception to the ignorance and want of education of the first generation of Christians, attests to no miracle but that of his conversion, which of all the miracles of the New Testament is the one which admits of the easiest explanation from natural causes" ("Theism," pt. 4 in *Three Essays on Religion*, quoted in *A Dictionary of Biblical Tradition in English Literature*, ed. David Lyle Jeffrey [Grand Rapids: Eerdmans, 1992], 592).

22. Karl Barth, *Church Dogmatics*, IV/3.1, *The Doctrine of Revelation*, trans. Geoffrey W. Bromiley, ed. Geoffrey W. Bromiley and T. F. Torrance (Edinburgh: T&T Clark, 1961), 200.

Unlike Erasmus, Barth claims that Saul's ignorance was not complete. Citing 1 Timothy 1:13, Acts 22:14, Acts 26:14, 2 Corinthians 5:16, and Romans 1:19–20, he describes Saul as having a paradoxical "ignorant knowledge." In persecuting Christ and his church, Saul was not attacking a caricatured version of the covenant made with Israel (i.e., persecuting the followers of a pseudo-messiah); he was making an onslaught against the real, the true, the factual, the objective thing—namely, the righteousness of God as it had become flesh in the person of Jesus as "the *telos* of the Law, fulfilling the Abrahamic, Sinaitic, and Davidic covenant (Rom 10:4)."[23]

The gravamen of Barth's case is that Paul lacks the agency to move from partial but damning ignorance to complete and saving knowledge. Only as Jesus "gave Himself to be perceived 'objectively' as a distinct Other," declares Barth, could Saul be converted. Jesus thus presented him to Paul on the road to Damascus.

> For He encountered Saul as Himself the Subject acting on [Saul], thus giving Himself to be known in the biblical sense of the term [i.e., personally, intimately].... There is an encroachment by [Jesus] upon the human existence of Saul. Saul in his subjectivity can no longer maintain his distance in relation to the existence of this Other, this acting Subject.[24]

Gnosis and *metanoia*, Barth insists, are inseparably and simultaneously linked.

Thus far Barth sounds much like Aquinas: there is no faith without knowledge, even if such faith and knowledge are delivered instantaneously. Yet whereas Aquinas stresses Paul's Christ-enabled freedom, Barth makes clear that the man of Tarsus could have done no other than obey his summons, precisely because he has met with the one who is like none other. Saul sees Christ, according to Barth, in

> His *doxa* [i.e., his glory, brilliance, honor], in the strange and even frightening irresistibility of His majesty, in a way which could only annihilate all his previous vision and call in question all his earlier existence, so that when He gave himself to be seen Saul was first reduced to impotence and totally routed from the field.[25]

23. Barth, *Church Dogmatics*, IV/3.1:201.
24. Barth, *Church Dogmatics*, IV/3.1:201.
25. Barth, *Church Dogmatics*, IV/3.1:204.

Knowing well that the word κύριε could also be translated "Sir,"[26] since it is a formal noun of address, Barth claims that the exclamation heard by Saul is at once anonymous and imperious, a voice "clothed with supreme authority and acting with supreme power" (204). Yet Saul cannot name this speaker: Jesus must name himself. Without a second salvific moment, therefore, Saul would simply have been crushed. Jesus not only knocks Saul to his knees with blinding light; he also identifies himself as the one whom Saul, in attacking Jewish converts to the gospel, has been attacking Jesus himself. Like Chrysostom, Barth discerns the inseparable link between Christ and his community. Only by means of Christ's self-identification can Paul trust and obey this true Κύριος. Unlike Aquinas, Barth does not speak of Paul's cooperative agency acting dependently on God's operative grace. For Barth, the movement from Christ to Saul is in no way bilateral; it is entirely unilateral.

> With overwhelming and irresistible force, [Jesus's] light has burst into the darkness of the opposition and contradiction which dominated [Saul]. A total and effective No is said to this man.... No future has been left to him. Jesus, who has done this, has made himself known as his superior Antagonist.... Hence [Saul] does not merely know the *kuriótes*, the superiority, of this Other as such. Suffering defeat at His hands, [Saul] knows [Christ's] name.... [Saul] knows Him, not merely objectively as he did before, but subjectively.[27]

In response to such a complete miracle, there is but a single answer—not Yes *or* No, but Yes alone. Paul the persecutor now has "no option," says Barth, "but to be an apostle." Only in the house of Ananias, after his vision is restored, his three-day fast is broken and he is baptized, does Paul receive his mission. Paul is able to preach the gospel immediately, Barth declares, just as he was converted immediately—by "Jesus Himself through the mediation of His community." Hence Barth's summation that sets his reading of Paul's conversion apart from the others we have thus far encountered.

> Saul might have lain blinded where he was, or have been swept aside as the wreckage which he was at the end of the first act. A second act—this second act—did not have to follow the first. What we have here is history in which both the presupposition and the consequence, both the passing of the ignorance of Saul and the rise

26. C. Kavin Rowe convincingly argues that, without exception, Luke intended his variants of the word κύριος to refer to Jesus (Rowe, *Early Narrative Christology: The Lord in the Gospel of Luke* [Berlin: de Gruyter, 2006], 147–48).

27. Barth, *Church Dogmatics*, IV/3.1:205.

of the knowledge of Paul, are the work of the free act of the all-dominating Subject, of the Kyrios Jesus.[28]

It is doubtful that any visual artist—patristic, medieval, Renaissance, or modern—could render Paul's conversion in such uncompromising terms as Barth's. In fact, Barth was chary not only of images but even analogies of the gospel found outside Scripture itself. He was so suspicious of attempts to link it with worldly similitudes that he notoriously declared that the little conjunctive *and* is the chief enemy of Christ. All human questions derive from the Answer he has already incarnated. Yet toward the end of his career Barth mollified this adamantine insistence that the gospel is self-validating, having no necessary linkage to things outside it. With due diligence, he confessed, Christians must seek secular parables of the kingdom *extra muros ecclesiae*. Not to honor these echoes of the kingdom from beyond the walls of the church is to be unfaithful:

> In so doing [i.e., denying such parables], would it really be obedient to Scripture, which in both Testaments often introduces witnesses to the truth from the darkness of the nations and therefore from outside the community of the elect and called, giving them a serious message to deliver and thus displaying that which is old and familiar in a new guise? Does it not necessarily lead to ossification if the community rejects in advance the existence and word of these alien witnesses to the truth? It must test them by the witness of Scripture. But it must really hear them, although without prejudice to its own mission to preach the one Word of God in its own tongue and manner as grounded in and directed by the biblical witness.[29]

At considerable risk, I maintain that William Blake's *The Conversion of Saul* provides a distant reflection of Barth's uncompromising christological account of the Damascus road event (figure 4-6). How so, given Blake's notorious heterodoxy, if indeed he is Christian at all? Every quasi- orthodox moment in Blake's poetry and painting can be offset with another that seems to cancel it. Yet we approach Blake aright only if we discern that he was not opposed to Christ or the gospel themselves, but rather to their enemies, as Curtis Freeman convincingly argues.[30] Nor was Blake so naive as to believe that the religious hegemony of the established Church of England, the ra-

28. Barth, *Church Dogmatics*, IV/3.1:208.

29. Barth, *Church Dogmatics*, IV/3.1:110.

30. Freeman argues that Blake belongs with Daniel Defoe and John Bunyan as three prophetic Protestant voices offering radical Christian alternatives to the religious and cultural tyrannies of their day. See Curtis Freeman, *Undomesticated Dissent* (Waco: Baylor University Press, 2017).

FIGURE 4-6. William Blake, *The Conversion of Saul* (c. 1800)

cial chauvinism of the imperial British state, and the commercial industrialism of Manchester and Birmingham were anything other than outward and visible signs of an inward and invisible rot. The "dark Satanic mills" that were grinding the bodies and souls of rich and poor alike, he insisted, were turned by the "Loom of Locke," the "wheels of Newton," the gears of Bacon.

Like few others, Blake was early to discern that the Cartesian/Kantian "turn to the subject" as it was embodied in such English thinkers had not been personally liberating, as they intended, but massively oppressive instead. They were silencing the resounding mystery of God and man alike.

They were "unweaving the rainbow," as Keats said. Not only did Blake set his face like flint against these God-denying and dehumanizing forces; he also resolved to remedy them. Hence Rowan Williams's claim that "there's no more moral poet in the English language than William Blake."[31] "Some aspects of Blake's understanding of the divine image," the former archbishop of Canterbury says elsewhere, "are more closely connected than might initially appear with the classical theological picture of [the] self-dispossessing God.... The God who is ... neither conditioned by the world nor imaginable apart from divine engagement with it."[32] The real wonder of Blake's artistic witness is that he accomplished so much despite the theological thinness of an age characterized by the two Josephs—Butler and Priestley.

Unlike the unmystical Barth, Blake dreamed dreams and saw visions. He conversed with angels, had concourse with friends in heaven, and believed that Milton, appearing to him in a dream, had entered his left foot, so that Blake could continue his journey from Felpham to London. Mrs. Blake tartly complained that William was seldom at home, since he spent most of his time in Paradise. Such visionary eccentricities are often attributed to a putative mental illness, perhaps schizophrenia. Against such a trite etiology of the terrors and wonders that Blake encountered, G. K. Chesterton offers this penetrating critique:

> I differ from the common or sceptical critics of a man like Blake. Such critics say that his visions were false because he was mad. I say he was mad because his visions were true. It was exactly because *he was unnaturally exposed to a hail of forces that were more than natural* that some breaches were made in his mental continuity, some damage was done to his mind. He was, in a far more awful sense than Goldsmith, "an inspired idiot." He was an idiot because he was inspired.[33]

I maintain that Blake depicted the chief of those wonders that were also terrors in his painting titled *The Conversion of Saul*.

Blake's blond, balding, and lightly bearded Jesus may seem to be a thoroughly human figure. As the second Adam, he very much resembles Blake's several depictions of the first Adam. Yet Blake's Christ is clearly more than

31. "Rowan Williams on Poetry," *Dr Rowan Williams 104th Archbishop of Canterbury*, January 20, 2009, http://rowanwilliams.archbishopofcanterbury.org/articles.php/1752/rowan-williams-on-poetry.

32. Rowan Williams, "'The Human Form Divine': Revelation and Orthodoxy in William Blake," in *Radical Christians Voices and Practice: Essays in Honour of Christopher Rowland*, ed. Zoë Bennett and David B. Gowler (Oxford: Oxford University Press, 2012), 147.

33. G. K. Chesterton, *William Blake* (London: Duckworth, 1909; Project Gutenberg Australia, 2012), http://tinyurl.com/zmpetu9 (emphasis added).

human, as the swirling energy of his transcendent power sweeps downward no less than upward, so as to make his legs seem but an extension of his torso. Light emanates from him in all directions, not only toward Paul. It carries two angel-like figures in its train, yet further evidence that Jesus possesses divine authority. Set against the brilliant yellow are dark clouds that menace from left and right alike, as the Light of the World overcomes them. There is also the contrasting whiteness of the horse, whose arched neck suggests a startled response to the light, so that its bucking has caused the feet of the red-haired, curly-bearded Paul to slip their stirrups. Unlike the nearly naked Paul of Caravaggio's first depiction, the nudity of Blake's Paul does not draw our attention. His mantle is not intended to cover his nakedness so much as to indicate the prophetic gospel he is commanded to preach. The eyes of Christ and Paul are firmly locked onto each other, perhaps to indicate that Lord and apostle are inseparably bound.

That Paul is not faced with an agonizing either/or decision is indicated most clearly by his being drawn *out of* the white sphere of the horse *into* the yellow radiance of Christ. The imperious command of Jesus, signaled by his outstretched right arm and pointing index finger, suggests no possibility of disobedience. And Paul's splayed arms, neither recoiling nor embracing, declare sheer astonishment instead, as if to confess: "How can I do aught else but *obey*?"[34] In many Blake paintings, there is a subversive subtext at work, an ironic undermining of what might appear as straightforward statement or affirmation.[35] I can detect none here. On the contrary, by depicting the Saul of Tarsus as claimed and commissioned irrevocably by Christ, William Blake's *The Conversion of Saul* is a painting worthy of Karl Barth's theology.

Conclusion

I have traced four stages of theology and art as they bear upon the account of Paul's conversion in Acts 9. Their trajectory leads to two major conclusions, though neither can be worthily explored here. The first is that the Holy Spirit often broods over the waters of each successive age, reveal-

34. Surely this is the sentiment conveyed in the infamous sentence, "It is hard for thee to kick against the pricks" (Acts 26:14 KJV). The ox that recoils against the steely goad of the master drives the sharp point in further and more painfully. It is better, in lower and higher things alike, to obey than to resist.

35. For example, *The Ancient of Days* depicts God as the omnipotent Fabricator, as with his gigantic compass he creates the circles of the world. Yet Blake depicts Isaac Newton, ever so scornfully, in virtually the same pose, thus subverting the apparent praise for the Great Geometer in the other painting.

ing the nature of divine action at work in the conversion of Paul as fundamentally congruous with the spirit of the time. Chrysostom's sermons and the early icon of Paul's conversion are not primarily concerned with the miraculous character of the event, for they inhabited a world in which miracles were the rule rather than the exception; instead, they both emphasize the mercy of Christ as it prompts total obedience. The real wonder of Paul's conversion lies in his transformed life. Aquinas and Bruegel, by contrast, are more concerned with what is humanly unaccountable—that is, what is virtually imperceptible in the event that reversed the course of Paul's life. The God-saturated world of theologian and painter alike prompted them to stress the congruence of divine and human freedom, lest the world look for these things in the wrong places. In a humanistic age such as the High Renaissance, by contrast, God's converting grace must be envisioned in human terms, lest it seem something utterly inhuman. Erasmus's paraphrase, alongside Caravaggio's quasi-erotic depictions of the Damascus road event, thus mark the ways in which human knowledge and desire become this-worldly sites of divine action, even at the risk of its threatened diminishment.

In comparison to our other six figures, Blake and Barth were most thoroughly out of step with their age. While no human happenings are completely without historical origin and cause, it hardly needs to be said, this artist and theologian were nonetheless atypical products of their time. As such, they require us to ask how we should beseech the Holy Spirit to break forth with new light in "the present evil age" (Gal 1:4), as Paul himself called his own era. I believe that we should pray for another strike of the blinding light that will knock an unlikely Paul to the ground, so as rescue not only him but us as well. If the Spirit were so to move, I suggest that the second greatest convert to the church would be none other than a figure akin to Friedrich Nietzsche.

Like Paul, Nietzsche had an ignorant knowledge of Jesus. He was a despiser of Christians, and he called himself the Antichrist. Though he knew not the real Christ, he knew all too well the pseudo-Christ who had converted many Christians of his time into the unwitting nihilists whom Nietzsche called the Last Men. Such men live not in obedience to the Christ who transvalues all values, who overcomes all ressentiment, who lays down the will to power, whose genealogy lies beyond good and evil. Refusing this true Christ, these Last Men turn themselves into small-souled creatures who take no risks, who lack all courage, who are such spiritual ciphers that their vacuity is quickly filled by openly nihilistic terrorists. Hence Nietzsche's terrifying prophecy from 1883:

> Alas, the time is coming when man will no longer shoot the arrow of his longing beyond man.... "We have invented happiness," say the last men, and they blink.... No shepherd and one herd! Everybody wants the same, everybody is the same: whoever feels differently goes into a madhouse. "Formerly, all the world was mad," say the most refined [of these Last Men], and they blink.[36]

Nietzsche did not blink, not even when he seems to have discerned that his Overman was but the mirror image of these Last Men. The decisive moment—the real break, if not the true conversion—came in Turin on January 3, 1889, when Nietzsche caused a disturbance in the Piazza Carlo Alberto. The story quickly circulated that Nietzsche had seen a horse being mercilessly whipped by a drayman. Outraged, the philosopher who had ridiculed pity as the chief vice of Christians threw his arms around the horse's neck, collapsing in sheer mercy on the helpless beast, never again to regain what is commonly regarded as sanity.[37] Thereafter Nietzsche no longer signed himself as the Antichrist but often as *der Gekreuzigte,* the Crucified. It was not a sentimental term of self-pity; it was Nietzsche's trumpeted call, however muffled and distorted, to the madhouse of radical conversion, whether instantaneous or gradual. As we have heard Chesterton declare, to receive and to follow such a summons is to be "unnaturally exposed to a hail of forces that [are] more than natural." The conversion of Paul in Acts 9 is its paradigm case, as we there encounter the irresistible unveiling and self-naming of the Christ who calls not only the great-souled Paul but also all sorts and conditions of pusillanimous Last Men.

36. Friedrich Nietzsche, *Thus Spoke Zarathustra,* in *The Portable Nietzsche,* ed. and trans. Walter Kaufmann (New York: Viking, 1954), 129–30.

37. "Christianity is called the religion of *pity.* Pity stands opposed to the tonic emotions which heighten our vitality: it has a depressing effect. We are deprived of strength when we feel pity. That loss of strength which suffering as such inflicts on life is still further increased and multiplied by pity. Pity makes suffering contagious" (Friedrich Nietzsche, *The Antichrist,* in *The Portable Nietzsche,* 572–73).

From Death to Life, from Madness to Logic

St. Paul's Conversion and St. Friedrich of Basle

Gary W. Jenkins (Orthodox)

In the summer of 1881, at a rock on the shores of Lake Silvaplana, in the Grisons, the heavens opened and the universe spoke to Friedrich Nietzsche:

> Something suddenly, with unspeakable certainty and subtlety, becomes *visible*, audible, something that shakes and overturns one to the depths.... One hears, one does not seek; one takes, one does not ask who gives; a thought flashes up like lightning, with necessity, unfaltering formed—I never had any choice. It is an ecstasy whose tremendous tension sometimes discharges itself in a flood of tears.... You are enraptured, taken outside of yourself, and you maintain a clear consciousness of infinity.... A profundity of blessedness such that sorrow and sadness no longer have the effect of a contrast but seem rather a required condition, a shade of meaning called forth in all necessity by the profusion of light.... Accompanied by a tumultuous feeling of liberty, of independence, of divinity ... there you have my experience of inspiration.[38]

Conversion is a perennial theme in St. Paul, central to both his life and doctrine. And in keeping with Professor Wood's conclusion, it lives large in the opera and life of Friedrich Nietzsche as well. The above recollection was not Nietzsche's only brush with the transcendently sublime, for in the autumn of the next year near Portofino, a second vision occurred, one he put into verse:

> Here I sat waiting—not for anything—
> Beyond good and evil, fancying
> Now light, now shadows, all a game,

38. Friedrich Nietzsche, *Ecce Homo*, trans. R. J. Hollingdale (New York: Penguin, 1979), 102–3, and in Henri de Lubac, *Drama of Atheist Humanism*, trans. Edith M. Riley (London: Sheed & Ward, 1949), 469–85.

All lake, all noon, all time without all aim.
Then suddenly, friend one turned into two,
And Zarathustra walked into my view.[39]

Nietzsche elaborates the content of his mysticalia in both *Ecce Homo* and *Also Sprach Zarathustra*, namely, the eternal return as the destroyer of history, and the Zarathustra theme its salvation through conversion and metamorphosis. Nietzsche's answer to insignificance, the search for purpose in the face of the impersonal, calls forth a new human, seen in his "Three Metamorphoses of the Spirit." This new human with its new morality aims to transcend the nihilism of his present culture by valorizing the Übermensch, whose herald Nietzsche the Antichrist is. In the Übermensch he seeks to end any thought of the old notions of the good, the beautiful, and the true having any relationship to ethics and reality, let alone the holy. One finds the seeming opposite to Nietzsche and his Übermensch, both as to purpose and manner of conversion, in Tolkien and his simple hobbits, those inhabitants of a world where nurture, observance, contentment, and the patient cultivation of mushrooms, barley, and hops shrieks against Nietzsche's enthusiasm and conversionism. The theological substance of Tolkien's vision is in his little-known appendix to the *Silmarillion* that Christopher Tolkien had only published some sixteen years afterward in volume 10 of *The History of Middle-Earth*, titled *Athrabeth Finrod ah Andreth*, the dialogue between Finrod and Andreth.[40] This dialogue between an Elvish prince and what Tolkien termed a human "wise woman," redolent of St. Anselm's *Cur Deus homo*, addressed the questions of how and why death arises among mortals, and how Iluvatar will remedy the problem of human death. That is, how do we overcome the all-too-human? Tolkien's text engages far more than St. Anselm, for it poses a question the answer to which I find often separates Orthodox from Latin visions, namely: Is our biggest problem sin, or is it death?

Both Nietzsche and Tolkien came to mind while pondering Professor Wood's paper, and contemplating what St. Paul's conversion fully entailed, what it says about the human condition, and not just about Saul of Tarsus. I accept, mutatis mutandis, Professor Wood's conclusion about St. Friedrich Nietzsche, but do query his Barthian prism for understanding Acts 9, that

39. Friedrich Nietzsche, *The Gay Science*, trans. Walter Kaufmann (New York: Vintage, 1974), 371.

40. J. R. R. Tolkien, *The History of Middle-Earth*, vol. 10, *Morgoth's Ring: The Later Silmarillion, Part One*, ed. Christopher Tolkien (London: HarperCollins, 1993), 307–26.

what confronted St. Paul made him radically other than what he had been, for he encounters in his faith event "Christ the Other." This ultimate existential crisis could only be remedied by an irresistible grace, and by a radical alteration in Saul of Tarsus. So how would one keep Professor Wood's St. Friedrich Nietzsche and at the same time slight his embrace of Barth's version of the road to Damascus?

Barth, informed by *Deus absconditus*, propelled by the existential otherness of God the "Other," an otherness only heightened by sin, is propelled as well by a revulsion of the liberalism that dominated so much of Protestant theology. Liberalism had made a god so immanent as to tie him to creation and human sentiment, and hardly in need of special revelation. As with Kierkegaard as regards Hegel before him, this drove Barth to save God from the system, and preserve revelation as something wholly other than could be comprehended in human experience, for theology could only be encountered in the absurd.[41] For Barth, as for his philosopher brother Heinrich, the Word of God exists before all human experience or it is not the Word of God.[42] Reading Barth had never been as enjoyable as reading Kierkegaard, who also came to mind while reading Professor Wood's paper; and in particular, Kierkegaard's *Fear and Trembling*, his extended sermon on Genesis 22 and Abraham's near sacrifice of Isaac.[43] The third problem Kierkegaard posed about Abraham, is whether Abraham could have spoken to someone about his experience, his felt confrontation with Christ. Kierkegaard sought a theology of experience, what he would call the "subjective truth," not in a relativist way, but in that God's dealings were always first personal, and not bound to systems. Both points, the existential loneliness of the believer and the approach of God separate from system and "theology," touches Barth's St. Paul.[44] For Kierkegaard, Abraham could not have discussed his dilemma with Sarah or Eleazer, or even Isaac, as this would have compromised

41. Jaroslav Pelikan, *Fools for Christ: Essays on the True, the Good, and the Beautiful; Impressions of Kierkegaard, Paul, Dostoevsky, Luther, Nietzsche, Bach* (Philadelphia: Muhlenberg, 1955), 20–21.

42. Karl Barth, *Church Dogmatics*, vol. I/1, *The Word of God*, trans. Geoffrey W. Bromiley, ed. Geoffrey W. Bromiley and T. F. Torrance (Edinburgh: T&T Clark, 1975). See section 6, that the Word of God is grounded only in itself.

43. Barth certainly has greater affection for the community of the church than Kierkegaard would often present, but this can be deceiving, as Walter Lowrie, in his introduction to *Attack on Christendom* notes that Kierkegaard stood on the verge of converting to Roman Catholicism at life's end. See Lowrie, introduction to *Attack upon "Christendom"* by Søren Kierkegaard, trans. Walter Lowrie (Princeton: Princeton University Press, 1944), xvi–xvii.

44. Søren Kierkegaard, *Fear and Trembling*, in *"Fear and Trembling: A Dialectical Lyric" and "The Sickness unto Death,"* trans. Walter Lowrie (Princeton: Princeton University Press, 1941), 91–129.

his unique experience of the confrontation with Christ. This sense of solitary Barth echoes in *Evangelical Theology*, where he speaks on the task of the theologian, and how God stands in contradiction to a theologian: "God more clearly opposes the theologian, who is *ex professo* concerned with the communion between God and man, and between man and God, than he opposes the work of the doctor, engineer, or artist.... The mystery of the special threat to theology is precisely its special hope. Precisely for the sake of this hope, the theologian is made to suffer from solitude, doubt, and temptation more noticeably than other men.... With Abraham he believes in hope, where there is nothing to be hoped for (*contra spem in spem*)."[45]

Kierkegaard's division of revelation from rational system, from "the True," is as well awake in Barth, as we have seen that he quarantined revelation from prior human experience. Putting this into the context of Professor Wood's paper, where the radically other Christ strips Saul of any willing, leaving him with no alternatives but to follow that Christ who comes as the overwhelming Revelation of all revelations and the Contradiction of all contradictions, we can see a Christ opposed to Saul's vendetta, remaking him into a peculiar instrument of grace. And it is from here that I take the bulk of my dissent, for Christ comes to Saul not as Other, but as the truly human, the true *anthropos* showing Saul what the truly human is, what St. Irenaeus captured in his "Gloria Dei est vivens homo."[46] But my dissent comes with an affirmations, as will be seen.

Both dissent and affirmation begin with the human telos, inextricably bound for the Orthodox—and as will be seen in the Anglican divine Richard Hooker—to our material, formal, and efficient causes. In *On the Incarnation of the Word* St. Athanasius states that "Man is by nature mortal, since he was made out of that which has no existence; but because of his likeness to Him that is (and if he preserved still this likeness by contemplation of him), he would thwart this natural decay and remain in incorruption.... For God not only made us from nothing, but by the grace of the Word freely given bestowed on us a life commensurate with the divine."[47] Our composition is not merely that of the dualists, that is, flesh and spirit; but rather, made from nothing, we tend to nonbeing. Yet at the same time, having been both fashioned and likened to the Word, made after the image of life, we as

45. Karl Barth, *Evangelical Theology*, trans. Grover Foley (Grand Rapids: Eerdmans, 1980), 150–51.
46. Irenaeus, *Haer.* 4.20. Unless quoted from English translations, all translations are the author's.
47. Athanasius, *De incarnatione* 1.4, PG 25:104.

well naturally tend to life, toward our telos, namely, the Word. Thus, marked by the express image of the invisible God, an image and existence we once enjoyed by contemplation, St. Athanasius explains that this union with the Word is why repentance alone cannot obtain life, for "repentance does not recall men from what they are naturally, as it only hinders them from sinfulness."[48] What Adam had naturally as made after the image of God is not lost by sin, but the corruption of human nature is a declension from its true telos and a declension from the creative Word of God. St. Maximus the Confessor in his disputation with Pyrrhus further clarifies St. Athanasius's teaching: "For what exists came to be out of nothing, and has therefore a power that impels them [humans] to hold fast to existence, and not to non-existence, which power at the same time inclines them towards that which naturally maintains them in existence, declining them from annihilation."[49]

What this has to do with St. Paul's conversion can be seen in what St. Maximus concludes from this, that the two natures of Christ do not have a synthetic union. St. Maximus's interlocutor, the former patriarch Pyrrhus had hinted that the will in Christ was not natural but composite. St. Maximus immediately notes that this cannot be, for the union is only accomplished in the single hypostasis of the Word, that this alone effects the union of create and uncreate, since the Word alone is the basis, the *logos*, of created natures. The hypostasis of the Logos, since not synthetic, acts humanly in the human will, and in Christ the human will wills its own good of existence, the basis of the struggle in the Garden of Gethsemane. For Maximus, Christ shrank from death as an evil, seeing a will to life as the good, but submitting to the Father knowing that death would bring life.

As regards Barth, later in the disputation, when Maximus comments on Christ's desire for life that naturally resides in humans, it provokes a protest from Pyrrhus, seemingly from an Aristotelian vantage, that if Maximus's doctrine were true, then virtues would be natural things, to which St. Maximus replies that indeed, virtues are natural things. Thus Christ's desire in the garden for life, willing a good and proper human telos, existed naturally in his human nature, propelling him to his natural end.[50] This is all consonant with St. Athanasius, who wrote that God "did not merely create humans, as he did the world's brutes, but made humans in his own image, giving them a portion even of the virtue of his own Word [τοῦ ἰδίου λόγου

48. Athanasius, *De incarnatione* 2.7, PG 25:107.

49. Maximus, *Disputatio cum Pyrrho*, PG 91:297.

50. Maximus the Confessor, *Disputatio*, col. 309.

δυάωμεως], that possessing as it were a reflection of the Word and being made rational [γενόμενοι λογικοὶ], they should obtain eternal beatitude."[51] As this is so, humans are themselves revelatory and revelations of God, possessing within themselves the seed of the Word, as Justin Martyr put it, and reflect even the divine acts, for as Pope Benedict XVI noted, quoting the emperor-scholar Manuel II Palaeologos, that God acts "according to logic/reason (συν λόγω)."[52] And so, Paul's conversion was a natural realization of his created nature, for he came to Christ, not as Other, but as to the fullness of what it meant to be human.

Orthodox are quite happy to agree with Henri de Lubac that among the Greeks there had never obtained that doctrine that he perceived in the West of a division between nature and the supernatural.[53] St. Augustine, at the very beginning of his *Confessions*, sums up the patristic sense of the matter when he writes, "Fecisti nos ad te et inquietum est cor nostrum donec requiescat in te."[54] This same notion about our hearts naturally disposed to God is repeated by St. Maximus the Confessor in *Ambiguam* 7, that

> what is more desirable to God's precious ones than to be divinized, that is for God to be united with those who have become gods and by his goodness to make everything his own. Hence the state that comes from contemplating God and enjoying the gladness it gives is rightly called pleasure, rapture and joy. It is called pleasure because the term means that for which we naturally strive; rapture, because it is an active receptivity by which what has received power from without becomes itself capable of generating power that is effective beyond itself, as in the previous examples of light permeating air and fire suffusing iron. For God's precious ones are persuaded that in truth human nature is given no loftier telos.[55]

St. Athanasius, in *On the Incarnation*, writes

> God had made man thus (that is, as an embodied spirit), and had willed that he should remain in incorruption. But men, having turned from the contemplation of

51. Athanasius, *De incarnatione* 1.3, PG 25:101.

52. Benedict XVI (Joseph Ratzinger), "The Regensburg Lecture," in James V. Schall, *The Regensburg Lecture* (South Bend, Ind.: St. Augustine's Press, 2007), 133–34.

53. When beginning his discussion of the whole matter anew in *The Mystery of the Supernatural*, de Lubac asserts that the concept of pure nature's dominance "appears short in the context of twenty centuries of Catholic tradition. We may also note that it is a theory that has never penetrated the theology of the East." And whom does de Lubac reference as witness to this, but that bête noire of twentieth-century ecumenism Vladimir Lossky (he cites Lossky's *Essai sur la théologie mystique de l'Eglise d'Orient*). De Lubac, *The Mystery of the Supernatural*, trans. Rosemary Sheed (New York: Crossroad, 1998), 5.

54. Augustine, *Confessiones* 1.1.1, PL 32:661.

55. St. Maximus the Confessor, *On the Cosmic Mystery of Jesus Christ*, trans. Paul M. Blowers and Robert Louis Wilken (Crestwood, N.Y.: St. Vladimir's Seminary Press, 2003), 63–64.

God to evil of their own devising, had come inevitably under the law of death. Instead of remaining in the state in which God had created them, they were in process of becoming corrupted entirely, and death had them completely under its dominion. For the transgression of the commandment was making them turn back again [to nonexistence] according to their nature; and as they had at the beginning come into being out of non-existence, so were they now on the way to returning, through corruption, to non-existence again.[56]

In short, the natural state of nonexistence requires contemplation in the created state for the preservation of a life oriented toward God. Earlier in his seventh *Ambigua*, St. Maximus had stated that "no creature has ever ceased using the inherent power that directs it towards its end, nor has it ceased the natural activity that impels it towards its end, nor harvested what it had anticipated. I am referring of course to being impassible and unmoved. For it belongs to God alone to be the end and the completion and the impassable."[57] Humans have a natural, constitutional end in God, and with that a natural movement toward God. Again from St. Maximus's *Ambigua* 7: "Surely then, if someone is moved according to the *Logos*, he will come to be in God, in whom the *logos* of his being pre-exists as his beginning and cause." Maximus cited St. Gregory of Nazianzus, that "'we shall in time to come, *know even as we are known*,' which, he says, 'will take place when the Godlike divine thing, I mean our intellect and reason, mingles with its kin, when the image ascents to the archetype it now longs after.'"[58] St. Maximus distinguishes in humans between the natural will and each human's hypostatic "mode of willing," specifically in regard to the will as a natural part of every human. Humans, however, in their personal mode of willing, that is, with respect to the discrete ends or aims for which they will, are each hypostatically distinct. Again St. Maximus:

The mode of willing, like the mode of seeing, i.e., to will to walk or not, or to look right or left . . . or to see out of concupiscence or in order to understand the logoi of beings, is a mode of the use of willing and seeing and belongs only to him who uses it. . . . To will to eat or not; or to will to walk or not is not a negation of the natural will, but of the mode of willing, viz., the coming to being and passing out of existence of the objects of willing.[59]

56. Athanasius, *On the Incarnation*, trans. a religious of CSMV (Crestwood, N.Y.: St. Vladimir's Seminary Press, 1993), 29–30.

57. Maximus, *Cosmic Mystery*, 51.

58. Maximus the Confessor, *On Difficulties in the Church Fathers*, vol. 1, *The Ambigua*, trans. Nicholas Constas, Dumbarton Oaks Medieval Library (Cambridge, Mass.: Harvard University Press, 2014), 93.

59. Maximus the Confessor, *Disputatio*, col. 293.

This mode of personal willing St. Maximus termed the gnomic will, which only pertains to the fallen individual mode of willing.[60] In each human this gnomic will, according to St. Maximus, wavers between options, a dialectic of indeterminate ends that are often themselves abuses of thus sinful uses of created things. This is what Maximus means about looking either with concupiscence or to inner essences. Here I question Professor Wood's use of Vladimir Lossky, for choice in the context that Lossky used Maximus had to do with the gnomic will. In Christ, in the saints in the eschaton, there are still choices, but now not between the wrong uses of things, but between goods rightly perceived and employed. Christ's choice in the garden was not between an evil and a good, but between goods.

Conversion as a turning of our souls to the proper ends and true functions was not merely a patristic affectation, for the Anglican divine Richard Hooker reflects the patristic material, namely, that the telos of our creation to which we are naturally suited is union with and contemplation of God: "Then are we happie therefore when fully we injoy God, as an object wherein the powers of our soules are satisfied even with everlasting delight; so that although we be men, yet by being unto God united we live as it were the life of God."[61]

In keeping with de Lubac's clear assertions that we are created "for the supernatural," even while admitting our affinities with the brutes, Hooker also notes that "whatsoever externall perfection they [the brutes] tende unto, it is not better than them selves, as ours is. How just occasion have we therefore even in this respect with the Prophet to admire the goodness of God! 'Lorde what is man, that thou shouldest exalte him above the workes of thy hands,' so far as to make thy selfe the inheritance of his rest and the substance of his felicitie?"[62]

Natural human beatitude distinguishes humans from brutes, but more importantly leads them to an end greater than the race possessed by mere createdness. This fits hand-in-glove with St. Athanasius: by nature, having been created from nonexistence, we can "naturally" tend back to that state; but at the same time having been created as the image of God, we can obtain immortality by the contemplation of God, through intellection, that is,

60. This is why the incarnate Christ cannot sin, for his personal mode of willing is that of the second person of the Trinity, the Logos who lacks the gnomic will.

61. Richard Hooker, *Of the Lawes of Ecclesiastical Polity* 1.11.2. All quotations of Hooker are from *The Works of Richard Hooker*, ed. Georges Edelen et al., 4 vols., Folger Library Edition (Cambridge, Mass.: Belknap Press of Harvard University Press, 1977–1990). None of Hooker's spellings has been modernized.

62. Hooker, *Lawes* 1.11.3.

through theoria. Once again from Hooker: "Now if men had not naturally this desire to be happie, how were it possible that all men shoulde have it? All men have. Therefore this desire in man is naturall.... It is an axiome of nature that naturall desire cannot utterly be frustrate. This desire of ours being natural should be frustrate, if that which may satisfie the same were a thing impossible for man to aspire unto."[63] Here we see St. Augustine's "fecisti nos ad te et inquietum est cor nostrum donec requiescat in te." This desire in us for God is not something that can be removed without altering the nature and making it other than what it is. Yet even this desire and will to God, had it been exercised by Adam, could not have obtained felicity merely by virtue of its exercise: "Wherein I confesse notwithstanding with the wittiest of the Schoole-divines, that if we speak of strict justice God could no way have beene bounde to requite mans labors in so large and ample manner as humaine felicitie doth import; in as much as the dignitie of this exceedeth so far the other's value."[64] How then comes beatitude for the Christian?

Hooker cites the Pseudo-Dionysus that prelapsarian reason or natural law was the medium through which created natures communed with God, and that divine, special revelation became the medium in the postlapsarian world. The divine law was the pattern of creation, the Dionysian *exitus* of our life, and special revelation and the work of the incarnation the divine act that grants to us the *reditus*, the way back to God.[65] While Hooker never claims that the incarnation was necessary were the fall never to have occurred, he does maintain that the institution and restitution of the world have the same source in Christ: "It became therefore him by whome all things are to be the waie of salvation to all, that the institution and restitution of the world might be both wrought by one hand."[66] St. Athanasius expresses this same thought: "Even so was it with the All-holy Son of God. He, the Image of the Father, came and dwelt in our midst, in order that He might renew mankind made after Himself."[67] That the created and the redeemed therefore flow from the same source bespeaks the unity of creation with the gospel, and thus of natural and the supernatural. Hooker declines

63. Hooker, *Lawes* 1.11.4.

64. Hooker, *Lawes* 1.11.5.

65. W. J. Torrance Kirby, "Grace and Hierarchy: Hooker's Two Christian Platonisms," in *Hooker: Reformer and Platonist* (Aldershot: Ashgate, 2013), 29–44.

66. Hooker, *Lawes* 5.51.3.

67. St. Athanasius, *On the Incarnation*, 41–42.

from this where his clearly Reformed eucharistic thought collides with these patristic notions, as seen in *Lawes* 5.53–54, especially his embrace of Peter Martyr Vermigli's eucharistic thought. Hooker is far more precise than Vermigli in avoiding Nestorianizing tendencies in his Christology,[68] but he fails to see that for the Fathers, the person of the Son as mediator does not mediate some substance or qualities, whether grace, or righteousness, and so on, but that the person of the Son is mediating the divine and the human. The distinction and division of created and uncreated is bridged in the hypostatic union, a bridge that Hooker on the one hand embraces: "Finally, sith God has deified our nature, though not by turning it into himself, yet by making it his own inseparable habitation, we cannot now conceive, how God should without man, either exercise Divine power, or receive the glory of Divine praise. For man is in both an associate of Deitie."[69] But on the other hand within his eucharistic thought he eschews it: "For albeit the properties of ech nature doe cleave onlie to that nature whereof they are properties, and therefore Christ cannot naturallie be as God the same which he naturallie is as man; yeat both natures may verie well concurre unto one effect, and Christ in that respect be trulie said to worke both as God and as man one and the selfe same thinge."[70]

This same bridge-and-chasm dilemma arises in looking at Hooker's accounts of inherent righteousness in the *Discourse of Justification* and his discussion on aptness and ableness in *The Dublin Fragments*. In the *Discourse* he notes that "there is a glorifying rightuousness of men in the world to come: and there is a justifying and a sanctifying rightuousness here. The rightuousness, wherewith we shall be clothed in the world to come, is both perfecte and inherent. That whereby here we are justified is perfect, but not inherent. That whereby we are sanctified, inherent, but not perfect."[71] In the *Dublin Fragments* he writes, "You peradventure think aptness and ableness all one: whereas the truth is, that had we kept our first ableness, grace should not need; and had aptness been also lost, it is not grace that could work in us more than it doth in brute creatures."[72] Hooker will, a few

68. Vermigli kept at more than arm's length a hypostatic union in which "the Lord of Glory was crucified" or "One of the holy Trinity suffered"; the *communio idiomatum* was merely a verbal affirmation. See Gary W. Jenkins, "Dinner with Raphael: The Prolegomena of Peter Martyr Vermigli's Eucharistic Intellections," *Zwingliana* 36 (2009): 103–13.

69. Hooker, *Lawes* 5.54.5.

70. Hooker, *Lawes* 5.53.3.

71. Richard Hooker, *A Learned Discourse of Justification* 3.

72. Richard Hooker, *Dublin Fragments* 1.

paragraphs on, make a telling assertion about the grace that precludes sin's having been given neither to the angels nor to Adam, but will be given in the age to come. Hooker, like Athanasius, formulates salvation in terms of contemplation, and a perfect contemplation, which alone can free from sin: "God bestoweth not in this present life grace so nearly illustrating goodness, that the will should have noe power to decline from it. Grace is not therefore here given in that measure which taketh away possibilitie of sinning, and soe effectuallie mooveth the will, as that it cannot."[73] Thus the aptitude to see God, to partake of the beatific vision, is always present via aptness, but in this life the grace of faith is insufficient to reveal the full truth that "sight" or "theoria" will give in the world to come. For Hooker, to see the truth in all its glory binds the will so as not to decline from the truth, and this leads back to the earlier passage about righteousness in the world to come being both inherent and perfect. Aptitude enables the intellect and reason, being natural, though corrupt, the potency to see God, though they need healing. Thus for Hooker, as for the Fathers, theoria and contemplation are tied to the natural will.

Maximus the Confessor sets out that each human has their own mode of willing that because of the corruption of death brought about by Adam's turning from theoria, we have become subject to a dialect in which we do not choose only the good and fulfill the purpose of the *logos* of our existence, but now treat the ends of our own personal willing as ends in themselves and not ends ordered toward the kingdom of heaven, seeing by concupiscence as opposed to investigating the inner essence or *logoi* of created things. In looking at Hooker we see that these elements are explicit in Maximus, which Maximus admits come from other fathers (the substance of his *Ambigua*), appear in Hooker as terms that Hooker does not draw directly from St. Maximus, but from a common source, namely, Pseudo-Dionysus.

For Hooker the divine law of creation is still active in us, even though it is now powerless to move us to the good, and our ability has itself been turned to that which is not good, namely, sin. Apart from the gift of illumination and the virtue of faith, latent in us, but also a gift of the Holy Spirit, we cannot obtain to glorification.[74] Reason in Hooker, that primal, Dionysian law

73. Hooker, *Dublin Fragments* 4.

74. Consequently, Corneliu Simut's notion that Hooker divides the natural from the spiritual and redeemed lacks precision, since the natural is the basis and foundation of the latter. By making faith a superior epistemic virtue in opposition to reason he undercuts the beatific vision, for how can one account for *theoria* in the world to come being perfect? Corneliu Simut, "Richard Hooker's Epistemology of Faith

that constituted our natures, corresponds, if not wholly univocally, at least formally, with Maximus's teachings on the one Logos being the many *logoi*, which we could rightly translate as many *rationes*. Consequently, Hooker slights the term common grace, since the desire for the divine exists naturally in each human, and despite our present want of righteousness or true theoria, we nonetheless have a natural desire for felicity, and thus a bent to virtue.

When St. Paul said to the Galatians that "it pleased God to reveal his Son in me," and when he speaks of "being found in Christ," and that "Christ in you [is] the hope of glory," he does not speak as a post-Abelardian thinker, let alone a Cartesian one, who inhabits a world of things and meanings, but instead in the world of what F. Edward Cranz has called "the extensive self."[75] This world, one whose epistemology at once posited the soul as a microcosm of the cosmos, and the cosmos as the soul writ large, saw agent intellect, that immortal part of the soul, as knowing "things," *res* and *pragmata*, not as mere external objects, items to be studied and discovered, but rather realities already resident in the soul as forms. As such intellection is union: "The intellect is somehow potentially the intelligibles, but it is none of them actually until it intellects," says Aristotle in *De anima*.[76] With this in mind, our reading of St. Paul and his use of μεταμόρφωσις in 2 Corinthians 3 assumes a new meaning, for as we all behold the glory of God as in a mirror, to which glory we are being metamorphosed, transfigured and transformed, now shows that beatific vision is ultimately christological, and that the vision of God has to do with the glorified Christ.[77] St. Augustine writes in *De Trinitate* 14.17.23–14.18.24, reflecting both 1 John 3:2 and 2 Corinthians 3:18 that perfect vision brings about perfect likeness.[78] The revelation of Christ to St. Paul was not of Christ the Other, but of Christ Saul of Tarsus's true purpose, that for whom he was created, his true telos, the logos of Saul's

in the 'A Learned and Comfortable Sermon of the Certaintie and Perpetuitie of Faith in the Elect' (1585)," *Annales Philosophici* 2 (2011): 88–89.

75. F. Edward Cranz, *Reorientations of Western Thought from Antiquity to the Renaissance*, ed. Nancy Struever (Aldershot: Ashgate, 2006), essays 4 and 5 (each individually paginated).

76. Aristotle, *De anima* 3.4 (429b30), in Aristotle, *De anima*, ed. W. D. Ross (Oxford: Oxford University Press, 1956).

77. Vladimir Lossky, *Vision of God*, trans. Ashleigh Moorehouse (Crestwood, N.Y.: St. Vladimir's Seminary Press, 1983), 134.

78. PL 42:1055: "In hac quippe imagine tunc perfecta erit dei similitudo quando dei perfecta erit uisio. De qua dicit apostolus Paulus: Videmus nunc per speculum in aenigmate, tunc autem facie ad faciem. Item dicit: Nos autem reuelata facie gloriam domini speculantes in eandem imaginem transformamur de gloria in gloriam tamquam a domini spiritu; hoc est quod fit de die in diem bene proficientibus. Apostolus autem Iohannes: Dilectissimi, inquit, nunc filii dei sumus, et nondum apparuit quod erimus. Scimus quia cum apparuerit similes ei erimus quoniam uidebimus eum sicuti est."

existence. This simple truth stands behind Joseph Pieper's paradoxical "We are not yet what we already are."[79]

Metanoia and *conversio* therefore are not the response of the faith event that is a confrontation with Christ the Other, but the culmination of what we are, a realignment of our existence, and the healing of salvation, bringing the subject from a movement to death to a movement to life, and a restoration of the portrait marred by sin and death. It is radical, even a crisis, but not in the way Barth has painted it. And this brings back St. Friedrich Nietzsche.

Nietzsche had his breakdown in early January 1889. Upon recovering some of his senses, he shot off some twenty-four short letters, including to his friends Peter Gast, the then-well-known historian of theology Franz Overbeck, and the celebrated historian Jacob Burckhardt. The letters show the remarkable deterioration of Nietzsche's hold on reality. The longest, to Burckhardt, had raving marginalia, while the one to Overbeck was just pure raving, as were the others. He ended the one to Gast in a peculiar way, for while he had signed his name for Burckhardt "your Nietzsche," and to Overbeck as Dionysus, he signed himself to Gast "the Crucified." With the exception of the letter to Burckhardt, all the others were signed either Dionysus or "the Crucified." It is Burckhardt who convinced Overbeck to go to Turin to collect their friend. The opposition of Dionysus to the Crucified exists throughout Nietzsche's writings, but the tension they represent comes out clearest in Zarathustra. Nietzsche's affection for Zarathustra (Zoroaster) played into his theme of life as struggle, life as contest, good and evil versus good and bad. Over the last eight years of his sanity, the contest for Nietzsche had been between Dionysus—the spirit of tragedy, of the dithyramb—and the Crucified, the spirit of priestly asceticism and aesthetics, the wretched revolt of the masses against the strong, the Jewish revolt of morality over their conquerors. Perhaps an allegory could be pulled out of Nietzsche's final act: on that January morning he had come upon a man beating his mule, which had simply lain down in the street and refused to pull its load any further. A sobbing Nietzsche threw himself on the beast, protecting it from its master whereby he showed that compassion has a greater place than strength, mercy over an unslaked will to power. Nietzsche like St. Paul had also preached a conversion, a transformation, using the same word as St. Paul, metamorphosis, in his well-known "The

79. Josef Pieper, *An Anthology*, trans. Margareta Svjagintsev et al. (San Francisco: Ignatius, 1989), 4.

Three Metamorphoses of the Spirit" from book 1 of *Also Sprach Zarathustra*. The spirit changes into a camel, a beast of burden carrying its load into the desert to face the great dragon "Thou Shalt." Here the camel becomes a lion, to dispose of the dragon with a violent "No," which leads to the last metamorphosis, of the lion into a child, for the child alone can speak the "Yes" of the new morality. Nietzschean conversion entails the antithesis of Christian conversion. His conversions existed to overcome the insignificance to which eternal return had consigned history, a salvation realized by the breakthrough of the Übermensch's will into existence, transfiguring the all-too-human into the greater-than-human. Thus Nietzsche's own personal conversion left him wavering between Dionysus and the Crucified, identifying with one, then the other, his sanctity (one can only hope) arising from the realization that the more-than-human would treat the merely human the way the owner had treated his horse; and in opposition to his Übermensch Nietzsche casts his fortune with the botched and bungled, with the all-too-human. Knowing that the holy had to be eliminated in order for the Übermensch to live, the holy that demanded humans repent of what they were, repent of their aspirations to be more than human,[80] Nietzsche's compassionate breakdown stands as an indictment of all his thought.

In opposition to this sits Tolkien. Whether by an act of rebellion, or by the curse of Morgoth, human existence now sits as tragedy, one that befuddles the Elves. Finrod cannot comprehend the general human despair in the face of death, which he has always taken as a gift from Iluvatar. He contradicts this despair by the assertion of a deep hope born of faith: "But there is another [hope] which is founded deeper. *Estel* we call it, that is 'trust.' It is not defeated by the ways of the world, for it does not come from experience, but from our nature and first being. If we are indeed the *Eruhin*, the Children of the One, then He will not suffer Himself to be deprived of His own, not by any Enemy, not even by ourselves."[81] A few lines later, Andreth confesses, that a rumored hope exists among humans: "They say that the One will himself enter into Arda, and heal Men and all the Marring from the beginning to the end.... Can the singer enter into his tale or the designer into the picture?... But they speak of Eru Himself *entering into Arda*, and that is a thing wholly different. How could He the greater do this? Would it not shatter Arda, and indeed all Eä?"[82]

80. Pelikan, *Fools for Christ*, 139–40.
81. Tolkien, *Morgoth's Ring*, 320.
82. Tolkien, *Morgoth's Ring*, 321–22.

And so we see in Tolkien as we have seen in Athanasius, Maximus, and Hooker the Christian hope that we are suited for God, purposed beyond "the human, all too human," for it is God himself who effects this by transfiguring us into what we were meant to be. Thus with Professor Wood and Barth I see something radical has happened, a momentous turn that indeed makes conversion a christological event, but one whereby Saul of Tarsus "puts on Christ" at the hands of Ananias, and as we see in St. Augustine who turns his back on "chambering and wantonness" to "put on the Lord Jesus Christ." Thus, "in becoming man he was not subjugated to nature, but on the contrary, he elevated nature to himself, making nature itself another mystery."[83] It is in light of this mystery that I think we should read the conversion of Saul of Tarsus.

83. Maximus, *Ambigua* 5.5.

RESPONSE

Paul's Conversion in His Own Words

Fr. Thomas G. Weinandy, OFM, Cap. (Catholic)

Professor Ralph Wood has provided a very creative and insightful presentation on the conversion of St. Paul. He did so by interpreting visual artistic renderings of Paul's conversion taken from artists of the patristic, medieval, Renaissance, and modern periods. His desire was to make their past visual theological interpretations present to our time—that what they saw in Paul's conversion and attempted to express visually in their icons and canvases relevant to us today. In response to Professor Wood's essay it would be appropriate, and clever on my part, to paint my own theological interpretation of Paul's conversion. However, I am reduced to mere words for I am devoid of almost any aptitude when it comes to practicing the visual arts though I am probably not much better as a wordsmith than I am as an artist. Nonetheless, in my words I do want to portray the theological content of Paul's conversion, but I want my words to be the words of Paul himself. How did Paul theologically interpret and express his own conversion? In a real sense, what did Paul, the artist, *see* within his conversion experience on the road to Damascus? In this essay I will examine the three accounts of Paul's conversion within the Acts of the Apostles—the first being Luke's narrative account (Acts 9:1–22) and the following two being Paul's own verbal accounts (Acts 22:1–21 and 26:1–23). I also want to examine Paul's account of his conversion in his Letter to the Galatians (Gal 1:11–17). Through theologically examining these various accounts of Paul's conversion, I want to disclose that what was revealed to Paul in his conversion experience lies at the heart of his gospel as expressed in his letters. Actually, Paul's conversion experience can be used as a hermeneutical key for understanding much of his later theology found within his letters.[84] I will not be able to address

84. While I have not read his book, Frank Matera has employed Paul's conversion as one of the hermeneutical principles for interpreting his theology. See Matera, *God's Saving Grace: A Pauline Theology* (Grand Rapids: Eerdmans, 2012), 10.

all of the various theological points that reside within and flow from Paul's conversion experience nor develop them fully, yet I hope to highlight what I consider some of the most salient ones. In doing so I hope to allow Paul to paint verbally his own theological interpretation of his conversion experience, an interpretation that is still relevant today.

Paul's Religious Observance Prior to His Conversion

Even for himself, who Paul was prior to his conversion experience is theologically significant for properly interpreting his conversion experience. Introducing the story of Paul's conversion, Luke narrates that Saul was "breathing threats and murder against the disciples of the Lord" (Acts 9:1).[85] His latest endeavor was to obtain from the high priests in Jerusalem authorization to ferret out Christians in Damascus and bring them back to Jerusalem for prosecution. Paul himself provides the motivation for his own zealous actions. He tells his fellow Jews that he himself is a Jew from Tarsus who ardently studied under the famous rabbi Gamaliel and so was educated in the strict observance of the law. Being zealous "for God," he persecuted "this Way to the death, binding and delivering to prison both men and women" (Acts 22:3–5). In his defense before King Agrippa, Paul is even more effusive about his Jewish lineage and practice. "My manner of life from my youth, spent from the beginning among my own nation and at Jerusalem, is known by all the Jews." What they know is that Paul belonged "to the strictest party of our religion" for he was a Pharisee, and because of this he was convinced that it was right and proper for him to oppose "the name of Jesus of Nazareth," casting votes against his disciples and "in raging fury against them, I persecuted them even to foreign cities" (Acts 26:4–11). Paul knew that the Galatians were aware of his former way of life in Judaism: "I persecuted the church of God violently and tried to destroy it; and I advanced in Judaism beyond many of my own age among my people, so extremely zealous was I for the traditions of my fathers" (Gal 1:13–14). Paul, it would seem, never let slip the opportunity to brag about his former religious life as a practicing fervent Jew. To the Corinthians he boasts: "Are they Hebrews? So am I. Are they Israelites? So am I. Are they descendants of Abraham? So am I" (2 Cor 11:22). Paul tells the Philippians that he has more

85. All quotations of Scripture are from the RSV.

confidence in the flesh than any other person. He was "circumcised on the eighth day, of the people of Israel, of the tribe of Benjamin, a Hebrew born of Hebrews; as to the law a Pharisee, as to zeal a persecutor of the church, as to righteousness under the law blameless" (Phil 3:4–6). In his own estimate, Paul was the perfect Jew. Yet he could confess: "But whatever gain I had, I counted as loss for the sake of Christ. Indeed I count everything as loss because of the surpassing worth of knowing Christ Jesus my Lord" (Phil 3:7–8). If Paul must boast, he will no longer boast of his circumcision, but he will only glory "in the cross of our Lord Jesus Christ" (Gal 6:13–14). This incredible change within Paul occurred within his conversion experience. What did Paul experience and so learn from that experience that so radically changed his life and the way he perceived himself and what was now, for him, the gospel of his Lord and Savior Jesus Christ?

The Gracious Liberality of Salvation and the Priority of Faith

Prior to examining the theological content of Paul's conversion experience, it is essential to grasp that the fact that he even had such an experience was itself foundational for Paul. Given Paul's preconversion commitment to his Jewish faith and practice, and his zealous persecution and hatred of Christianity, the mere reality of Jesus appearing to him demonstrated above all else the gracious and merciful liberality of God. Even though he "formerly blasphemed and persecuted and insulted" Jesus, yet he received "mercy because I had acted ignorantly in unbelief." Paul's very sinfulness manifests the unreserved mercy of God. "I am the foremost of sinners; but I received mercy for this reason, that in me, as the foremost, Jesus Christ might display his perfect patience for an example to those who were to believe in him for eternal life" (1 Tm 1:13–16). Jesus appeared to many immediately after his resurrection, but what is even more extraordinary for Paul is that he appeared to him last of all, "as to one untimely born" and because of this "I am the least of the apostles, unfit to be called an apostle, because I persecuted the church of God. But by the grace of God I am what I am" (1 Cor 15:5–10). From the mere event of Jesus's appearing to him, Paul immediately grasped that salvation is not something that one earns by keeping the law and being zealous for the traditions of his Jewish ancestors, but a free gift of God given to him and everyone else in Christ Jesus. Thus Paul could later write that both Jews and Greeks are condemned sinners, "for God has consigned all men to disobedience, that he may have mercy upon all" (Rom 11:32; see also Rom 3:9). For Paul, the free merciful love of God shown to him in the event of his conversion is but a singular example of the free, universal, and all-embracing benevolence of God for all. Paul realized that not only he but all of humankind was helpless at the time "Christ died for the ungodly." God proved his love for all not by sending his Son to die for the good but for sinners. While Paul and all of humankind were God's enemy, God reconciled all "by the death of his Son" and so provided the assurance of eternal life (Rom 5:6–11). If Paul thought himself righteous prior to his conversion experience, he does so no longer for the very experience demonstrated to him that righteousness is a free gift of God freely given to him in Christ Jesus.

If salvation is a free gift of God freely given in Christ Jesus, as he learned from Jesus's undeserved gratis appearance to him, then Paul immediately perceived that the response to such a free gift can be nothing other than laying hold of it in faith. The gift is free and not earned, and therefore it must be freely accepted through faith. After Ananias healed Paul's blindness, he exhorts him: "And now why do you wait? Rise and be baptized, and wash away your sins, calling on his name" (Acts 22:16). Calling on the name of Jesus *in faith* and being "filled with the Holy Spirit" within the baptismal act obtains the free gift salvation (Acts 9:17).[86] Paul's entire later theology of the foundational priority of faith is founded upon his conversion experience, an experience of God's mercy. In writing to the Ephesians, he is merely telling his story on a universal scale. "But God, who is rich in mercy, out of the great love with which he loved us, even when we were dead through our trespasses, made us alive together with Christ (by grace you have been saved), and raised us up with him, and made us sit with him in the heavenly places in Christ Jesus.... For by grace you have been saved through faith; and this is not your own doing, it is the gift of God—not because of works, lest any man should boast" (Eph 2:8–10). If Jesus freely revealed himself to Paul, then Paul could only respond in faith—for that of which he could boast previously, his being a Jew who faithfully kept the law, was now rendered of no account. Paul now counts all else that he considered of salvific value mere dung "in order that I may gain Christ and be found in him, not having a righteousness of my own, based on law, but that which is through faith in

86. Paul would later declare: "No one can say 'Jesus is Lord' except by the Holy Spirit'" (1 Cor 12:3). Only within a Spirit-engendered faith can one profess Jesus as Lord.

Christ, the righteousness from God that depends on faith" (Phil 3:8–9). His own conversion has taught him that man is "not justified by works of the law but through faith in Jesus Christ" (Gal 2:16). From his own experience Paul could rhetorically ask the Galatians: "Did you receive the Spirit by works of the law, or by hearing with faith?" (Gal 3:2). The whole of Paul's theology of "faith," as found within his Letters to the Romans and Galatians, is simply the mature expression of what the conversion event itself revealed to him—God graciously and freely has saved all through Jesus Christ, and one is righteously reconciled to God through faith. "Since all have sinned and fall short of the glory of God, they are justified by his grace as a gift, through the redemption which is in Christ Jesus, whom God put forward as an expiation by his blood, to be received by faith" (Rom 3:23–25).

The Revelational Content of Paul's Conversion Experience

While the event of Paul's conversion experience cannot be completely separated from the revelation contained in that event, I have attempted in the above to focus primarily on what Paul learned from the mere event itself—the gratuity of Jesus appearing to him and the thus free gift of salvation with the corresponding response of faith to that free gift. That revelation alone forced Paul to acknowledge that he could no longer find righteousness in his Jewish observance, but in Jesus Christ through faith. That being said, Paul's conversion experience contains revelation, that is, revealed truth. Using Luke's narrative account as the template, I want now to examine what Paul knew to be revealed to him, both within his own narrations of the event as well as in his later letters.

Luke states: "Now as he [Paul] journeyed he approached Damascus, and suddenly a light from heaven flashed about him" (Acts 9:3). Paul himself later speaks of a "great light from heaven" that "suddenly shone about me" (Acts 22:6), "brighter than the sun" (Acts 26:13). This heavenly light signals for Paul a theophany—what is taking place is of the divine and not some earthly phenomenon. Upon beholding the light, Paul "fell to the ground and heard a voice saying to him, 'Saul, Saul, why do you persecute me?'" (Acts 9:4). Paul's falling to the ground upon beholding the divine light is reminiscent of God calling Moses at the burning bush: "Moses, Moses!" Moreover, God tells Moses to take off his shoes, "for the place on which you are standing is holy ground" (Ex 3:4–5). The ground upon which Paul now lies is holy ground, for Jesus, the Lord, has appeared to him. Jesus does not reveal who he is, but pointedly asks Paul as to why he is persecuting him. Jesus, then, has personally identified himself with those whom Paul is persecuting. Paul is purposely on his way to persecute Christians, and thus he realizes that whoever is appearing to him is someone whom he is persecuting. However, in response, Paul significantly asks: "Who are you, Lord?" (Acts 9:5). Some translations here translate κύριε as "sir" rather than "Lord."[87] They do so thinking that, at this initial point in the conversation, Paul does not know that he is speaking to the Lord Jesus and so is merely responding to an anonymous person, whom he is respectfully addressing as "sir." However, I believe this is a false interpretative translation. Because of the heavenly brilliant light that surrounds him, Paul perceives that he is in the presence of God, the Lord, but he does not know who this God, the Lord, might be whom he is persecuting, for he, up until this point, firmly believes he is zealously doing the Lord God's will by persecuting Christians. Paul is mentally utterly disordered and emotionally wholly distraught! His question—"Who are you, Lord?"—is his befuddled attempt to sort things out. Jesus replies: "I am Jesus, whom you are persecuting; but rise and enter the city, and you will be told what you are to do" (Acts 9:5–6).[88] There are at least three significant, interrelated truths revealed within Jesus and Paul's dialogue.

Jesus Is God

First, Jesus is God. Paul asks: "Who are you, Lord?" Like Moses, Paul wants to know God's name. God revealed to Moses that he is YHWH, "I AM WHO I AM," and when Moses returns to the people of Israel, he should tell them that "I AM has sent me to you" (Ex 3:14). Jesus does not contest Paul's addressing him as Lord, as if it were inappropriate. Rather, in revealing himself to Paul, Jesus accentuates that he is indeed the Lord in its fullest divine

87. It is well known that the divine name YHWH, because it was so sacred, was not spoken. The Hebrew word *Adonai* (Lord) was used in its place. When the Hebrew Scriptures were translated into Greek, the Septuagint employed the word κύριος (Lord). Besides being used to designate YHWH/God, it could also be used as a title of address—sir. For a translation that renders κύριε as "sir," see the New American Bible: Revised Edition.

88. The dialogue between Jesus and Paul is substantially the same in all three accounts within the Acts of the Apostles. However, in Paul's second account before King Agrippa, he has Jesus also saying: "It hurts you to kick against the goads" (Acts 26:14). This common Greek proverb indicates that Paul is only hurting himself in fighting against Christianity and the gospel.

sense—that he is the Lord God YHWH—for in the Greek he says: ἐγώ εἰμι Ἰησοῦς. While God revealed to Moses that he is I AM (ἐγώ εἰμι), Jesus, by employing the emphatic ἐγώ εἰμι, is commandeering that very same divine title, and so placing himself within the one Lord God YHWH, He Who Is. Jesus has emphatically subsumed the "I AM" into his very name, Jesus. To be Jesus is to be YHWH! This is his very identity. Being Jesus, he is simply "I AM."[89] For Paul, the Jew, to know who Jesus is is to know, as did Moses, "the LORD, the God of your fathers, the God of Abraham, the God of Isaac, and the God of Jacob" (Ex 3:15).[90] Because of this revelation, Paul grasps that the one God of Israel now comprises two subjects. After subsequently being baptized in Damascus, Luke tells us that "in the synagogues immediately he proclaimed Jesus, saying, 'He is the Son of God'" (Acts 9:20). Paul informs the Galatians that "when he [God] who had set me apart before I was born, and had called me through his grace, was pleased to reveal his Son to me" (Gal 1:15–16). Thus, in his greeting to the Corinthians he can declare: "Grace to you and peace from God our Father and the Lord Jesus Christ" (2 Cor 1:3; see also Eph 1:1 and Col 1:1). He exclaims in Ephesians: "Blessed be the God and Father of our Lord Jesus Christ" (Eph 1:3). In the

89. This is in keeping with Jesus's very name—"YHWH-Saves." Significantly, within the Gospel of John, when Jesus approaches those who have come to arrest him, he asks: "Whom do you seek?" They respond: "Jesus of Nazareth." Jesus, in turn, replies: "I am he" (ἐγώ εἰμι). As in Paul's conversion, Jesus identifies himself as ἐγώ εἰμι and so subsumes within his very identity the name of YHWH. Moreover, within both events those who are in his presence fall to the ground, for they are afore Jesus, the all-holy Lord God (Jn 18:4–6).

90. In revealing himself to Moses, the Lord God sent him back to the Israelites in order to set them free from slavery in Egypt and lead them into the freedom of the promised land. Jesus, in appearing to Paul and revealing himself to him, also gives to him a mission. Jesus tells Paul: "Rise and enter the city, and you will be told what you are to do" (Acts 9:6). At Damascus the Lord tells the reluctant Ananias to go to Paul "for he is a chosen instrument of mine to carry my name before the Gentiles and kings and the sons of Israel; for I will show him how much he must suffer for the sake of my name" (Acts 9:15–16). In his first account, Paul asks Jesus what he is to do "and the Lord said to me, 'Rise, and go into Damascus, and there you will be told all that is appointed for you to do'" (Acts 22:10, see also Acts 22:21). In his second account before King Agrippa, Paul has Jesus giving him rather detailed instructions: "But rise and stand upon your feet; for I have appeared to you for this purpose, to appoint you to serve and bear witness to the things in which you have seen me and to those in which I will appear to you, delivering you from the people and from the Gentiles—to whom I send you to open their eyes, that they may turn from darkness to light and from the power of Satan to God, that they may receive forgiveness of sins and a place among those who are sanctified by faith in me" (Acts 26:16–18). Paul tells the Galatians that God revealed his Son to him "in order that I might preach him among the Gentiles" (Gal.1:16). If God revealed himself to Moses in order to bring salvation to the Israelites, so now God revealed to Paul his Son, the Lord Jesus Christ, in order to send him as the apostle to the gentiles (see Rom 11:13; Gal 2:8; Eph 3:1–2). Jesus's giving to Paul the commission to preach to the gentiles was formally enacted in Antioch when the Christian community, at the verbal command of the Holy Spirit, laid hands on Paul and Barnabas "and sent them" to the gentiles (Acts 13:1–3). In Jesus, then, true freedom from sin is achieved and universal salvation and eternal life is offered to all nations and peoples, Jews and gentiles alike.

light of what Jesus revealed to him at his conversion, Paul can, without in any way impugning God's oneness, declare both the divinity of the Father and of Jesus, for God is the Father of Jesus who, as the Father's Son, is the Lord. From that moment on Paul addressed Jesus, as he unknowingly did from the onset, as Lord—though now not in fear and confusion but in faith and love. The Lordship of Jesus was so impressed upon Paul's heart and mind that within his letters he would refer to Jesus as "Lord" 252 times, with 164 of those times referring to him simply as "the Lord." This title is only exceeded by his referring to Jesus as "Christ" (376 times), many of which are used by Paul as Jesus's proper name—"Jesus Christ" or "Christ Jesus."[91] That Paul recognized the Lord Jesus as "the Christ" leads us to another revelation contained with his conversion experience.

The Incarnation: Jesus as the Risen Christ and Savior

Inherent within the dialogue between Jesus and Paul is the revelation of the mystery of the incarnation. Since the Lord, whom he addresses, identifies himself as Jesus, Paul would have grasped that, for this to be the case, the Lord, the preexistent Son of God, would have become man. Within his defense to the Jews in Jerusalem, Paul actually accentuates the historicity of the incarnation by narrating that Jesus informed him that he is "Jesus *of Nazareth*" (Acts 22:8). The Lord, as man, historically grew up in a specific town in Galilee called Nazareth. Thus the incarnation is not some ethereal mythological tale but is embedded within human history.

Moreover, in the incarnation, Paul recognizes that Jesus assumed Adam's sinful flesh. "For God has done what the law, weakened by the flesh, could not do: sending his own Son in the likeness of sinful flesh" (Rom 8:3). On the cross he became "a curse for us" so as to free humankind from the curse of the law and providing for all "the promise of the Spirit through faith" (Gal 3:13–14). Thus God made Jesus "to be sin who knew no sin, so that in him we might become the righteousness of God" (2 Cor 5:21). As one of Adam's sinful and disobedient race, Jesus on the cross obediently offered his holy and innocent life to his Father and in so doing put to death our sinful humanity, our "old self," so that we might no longer be enslaved to sin. Simultaneously, what is immediately obvious to Paul in the appearance of Jesus is that the man Jesus is alive. He is the risen and ascended

91. See Gordon Fee's excellent book *Pauline Christology: An Exegetical-Theological Study* (Peabody, Mass.: Hendrickson, 2007), 558.

Lord. Therefore, for Paul, in rising from the dead, Jesus assumed a new and glorious humanity, a humanity freed from sin and death, and so became the new Adam, the father of new and holy human race. In baptism Christians share in Jesus's death, the putting to death of the old humanity, and rise so as to share in his new and glorious humanity (see Rom 5:12–22; 6:3–11; 1 Cor 15:45).[92]

Moreover, if Jesus of Nazareth is the Son of God now existing as a risen man, then he must be the promised Spirit-anointed Messiah, the Christ. When Paul immediately preaches in Damascus, Luke narrates that he "increased all the more in strength, and confounded the Jews ... proving that Jesus was the Christ" (Acts 9:22). Likewise, then, since Jesus, as the Son of God incarnate, is the expectant Christ, he is equally the expectant Savior. Upon this logical conclusion, Paul was confronted with the great mystery of humankind's salvation—the mystery of the cross. Whatever expectation of the Messiah Paul may have previously contemplated, he would not have envisaged him as one who would die as a condemned criminal upon the cross. For Paul, the cross shattered all of his preconceived notions of salvation and all of his previous reading and understanding of the Hebrew Scriptures. However, his conversion experience itself provided Paul with the hermeneutical key for interpreting the cross—he who appeared to him in heavenly light was the glorious risen Jesus. The very humiliation of the cross gave rise to the glory of the resurrection, and so the cross itself assumes its own splendor. Within those conjoined acts, that of Jesus, the Son, dying on the cross and that of God, his Father, raising him from the dead, humankind's salvation was achieved. Paul could testify before King Agrippa that from the time of the Lord's appearance to him "to this day I have had the help that comes from God, and so I stand here testifying both to small and great, saying nothing but what the prophets and Moses said would come to pass: that the Christ must suffer, and that, by being the first to rise from the dead, he would proclaim light both to the people and to the Gentiles" (Acts 26:22–23). When Paul came to Thessalonica, Luke narrates

92. For a fuller treatment of Paul's theology of the Son of God assuming a humanity from the fallen race of Adam see, Thomas Weinandy, *In the Likeness of Sinful Flesh: An Essay on the Humanity of Christ* (Edinburgh: T&T Clark, 1993), 73–90. For Paul, the incarnation exemplifies the saving humility of Jesus. He became poor in becoming man that we, who are poor, might become rich in his divinity (see 2 Cor 8:9). The Philippians hymn heralds the humility of God's Son, who did not cling to his divinity but humbled himself in becoming a servant-man even to suffering death on the cross, and in so doing the Father exalted him above all others. The name of Jesus, YHWH-saves, reigns supreme (see Phil 2:6–11 and also Col 1:15–20).

that Paul went into the synagogue and argued with the Jews, "explaining and proving that it was necessary for the Christ to suffer and to rise from the dead, and saying, 'This Jesus, whom I proclaim to you, is the Christ'" (Acts 17:3). This was revealed to him, "the least of the apostles" when the risen Jesus appeared to him (1 Cor 15:3–4, 9). To the Jews in Perga, Paul narrates their whole salvific history, beginning with their fathers, the judges, prophets, and kings. From David's posterity "God has brought to Israel a Savior, Jesus, as he promised." Because the Jews in Jerusalem did not understand the prophets, they had Jesus killed, and so "fulfilled all that was written of him.... But God raised him from the dead," and this is "the good news" that Paul brings to them (Acts 13:11–33). Paul reminds the Corinthians what he first preached to them: "I delivered to you as of first importance what I also received, that Christ died for our sins in accordance with the scriptures, that he was buried, that he was raised on the third day in accordance with the scriptures" (1 Cor 15:3). While the Jews demand signs and the Greeks search for wisdom, Paul preaches "Christ crucified, a stumbling block to the Jews and folly to Gentiles." For God is "the source of your life in Christ Jesus, whom God made our wisdom, our righteousness and sanctification and redemption; therefore, as it is written, 'Let him who boasts, boast in the Lord'" (1 Cor 1:22–31). Paul summarizes the very heart of his gospel, the gospel that was revealed to him within his conversion, in his opening declaration to the Romans: "Paul, a servant of Jesus Christ, called to be an apostle, set apart for the gospel of God which he promised beforehand through his prophets in the holy scriptures, the gospel concerning his Son, who was descended from David according to the flesh and designated Son of God in power according to the Spirit of holiness by his resurrection from the dead, Jesus Christ our Lord" (Rom 1:1–4). As the above demonstrates, Paul grew in his depth of understanding of who Jesus is and in the saving significance of his salvific work, yet the light that Paul would proclaim to Jew and gentile alike is the same heavenly light that first shown about him at his conversion, the light of his Lord, Jesus Christ, in whom shines the light of the gospel of salvation. As Paul declared to the Corinthians: "And we all, with unveiled face, beholding the glory of the Lord, are being changed into his likeness from one degree of glory to another; for this comes from the Lord who is the Spirit" (2 Cor 3:18).[93]

93. Those Jews who do not believe in Christ are like Paul before his conversion—they have not seen the heavenly light of Christ the Lord, and so their faces, like Moses, remain veiled (see 2 Cor 3:12–14).

Third, as has often been remarked, Paul's theology of the body of Christ springs directly from his conversion experience. As we saw, in retelling of his conversion, Paul always prefaces the event by relating his ardent and violent persecution of Christians and then immediately proceeds to Jesus's opening questioning rebuke: "Saul, Saul, why do you persecute me?" This is significant for Paul, for he learned that in persecuting his followers he was persecuting Jesus himself. There is a living identity between Jesus and those who abide in him. Thus there is a living relationship, a living unity, between Christ the Lord and his followers. Unsurprisingly, then, Paul proclaims to the Corinthians: "You are the body of Christ and individually members of it" (1 Cor. 12:27; see also 1 Cor 6:15–17). The reason being: "For just as the body is one and has many members, and all the members of the body, though many, are one body, so it is with Christ. For by one Spirit we were all baptized into one body—Jews or Greeks, slaves or free—and all were made to drink of one Spirit" (1 Cor 12:12–13). For Paul, by sharing in the Holy Spirit, Christians live in the Spirit-anointed Christ and so form one living body with him—they constitute and comprise one living reality. The Holy Spirit is the everlasting fount of life that unites Christ and his body. Thus, for Paul, to live in communion with Christ the head, "the whole body, nourished and knit together through its joints and ligaments, grows with a growth that is from God" (Col 2:19; see also Eph 1:23; 5:23; Col 1:24). The body of Christ, the church, is to "grow up in every way into him who is the head, into Christ, from whom the whole body, joined and knit together by every joint with which it is supplied, when each part is working properly, makes bodily growth and upbuilds itself in love" (Eph 4:15–16; see also Eph 4:12). The singular and universal significance of the church, the body of Christ, lies precisely in her Spirit-enlivened communion with Christ, her head from whom she is nourished and finds her growth in holiness and love (see 1 Cor 12:28–13:13). Jesus wanted to "create in himself one new man" (Eph 2:15). All gifts and ministries of the Spirit are "for building up the body of Christ, until we all attain to the unity of the faith and of the knowledge of the Son of God, to mature manhood, to the measure of the stature of the fulness of Christ" (Eph 4:12–13). For Paul, this was God's plan from before

However, Paul and all Christians have been given "the light of the knowledge of the glory of God in the face of Christ" (2 Cor 4:6).

the foundation of the world, for which all human beings were predestined, the mystery that has now been revealed: "To unite all things in him, things in heaven and things on earth" (Eph 1:3–10). This, for Paul, is the eschatological end—an end he first began to perceive at his conversion, when Jesus revealed to him that he and all who believe in him form one living body in the unity of the Holy Spirit.

In the process of examining the three truths that resided within his conversion experience, though there are undoubtedly more, we perceive that Paul experienced the one God as a trinity of persons. The Father in his mercy revealed to Paul his Son, the Lord and Savior Jesus Christ through the heavenly light of the Holy Spirit. Thus Jesus, as Son, possessed the fullness of the Holy Spirit, and as the definitive risen Lord and universal Savior he is empowered to pour out his Holy Spirit upon his church and its members, thus constituting himself as head of his body. As stated above, the Father achieves his salvific goal by uniting all things in Christ through the communion of the Holy Spirit. Thus Paul could confer the fullness of God's blessing upon the Corinthians: "The grace of the Lord Jesus Christ and the love of God and the fellowship of the Holy Spirit be with you all" (2 Cor 13:14).

Conclusion: It Came through a Revelation of Jesus Christ

I want to conclude this brief exposition of Paul's conversion by emphasizing that he perceived his conversion experience as the revelation of the gospel that he subsequently lived and preached. He unapologetically, though somewhat defensively, declared to the Galatians: "For I would have you know, brethren, that the Gospel which was preached by me is not man's gospel. For I did not receive it from man, nor was I taught it, but it came through a revelation of Jesus Christ" (Gal 1:11–12). He insisted that what he preached was "the mystery … made known to me by revelation" (Eph 3:3; see also Col 1:25). This revelation was the appearance of Jesus. Jesus himself tells Paul that he has appeared to him (see Acts 26:16). Ananias confirmed that it was Jesus who appeared to him on the road (see Acts 9:17), and that "the God of our fathers appointed you to know his will, to see the Just One and to hear a voice from his mouth" (Acts 22:14). This appearance and revelation is what makes Paul no less inferior to the super-apostles (see 2 Cor 11:4–6). Thus for Paul himself, the gospel he preached was founded upon what he learned when Jesus appeared to him in a heavenly light and revealed to him that he is Jesus, the Father's Son, Christ the Lord and Savior.

Professor Wood demonstrated how the artistic renditions of Paul's conversion have, throughout history, made relevant the mystery that was revealed to Paul. We have seen, in this brief essay, how difficult this task was and is, for it is impossible to render in paint and even in words all that was revealed in those few moments as Paul journeyed on the road to Damascus. Nonetheless, Paul attempted to do so in his own words, words anointed by the Holy Spirit, and in so doing he freely bent his knee to the ground before him and with his tongue lovingly and knowingly confessed all the remaining days of his life what he had learned—that Jesus Christ is Lord to the glory of God the Father (see Phil 2:11).

CHAPTER 5

Acts of the Apostles 15

Robert Louis Wilken (Catholic)

Christianity came into the world as a corporate body with distinct offices (apostles), rituals (baptism and the breaking of bread), reverence for tradition ("For I delivered to you.... what I also received" [1 Cor 15:3]), and simple formulas of belief ("We ... have one God the Father from whom are all things ... and one Lord Jesus Christ ... through whom are all things" [1 Cor 8:6]). Early Christianity was not an aggregate of individuals, but the "church" (ἐκκλησία; Acts 5:11; 8:1), the "household of God" (Eph 2:19), descended from Israel according to the flesh. The famous passage in 1 Peter, "a royal priesthood," refers not to individual priests, but to the body of Christians, a "chosen race" and a "holy nation."

As an ordered society, the church's leaders met together regularly to decide what is good for the Christian body as a whole, and to act on behalf of the community of Christians. By my reckoning the account in Acts 15 of the so called apostolic council was the third time the leaders met to weigh matters of consequence for the future.

The first gathering took place shortly after Christ's ascension, when the apostles met in the "upper room" to decide on a replacement for Judas. His "habitation" had become "desolate" (Ps 69:25), they said, "Let another one take his office" (Ps 109:8). This was not an open election; the apostles had clear criteria as to whom was eligible. His successor had to come from those who had "accompanied us during all the time that the Lord Jesus went in and out among us" (Acts 1:21). Only such a person, one who had known Christ in the flesh and beheld with his own eyes his death and resurrection, could succeed to the office of apostle. When the eleven apostles had cast their flat stones, the lot fell on Matthias and he was enrolled with the others (1:20–26).

The second council, if you will, took place because widows were being neglected in the daily distribution of food among Christians. The company of apostles, again numbering twelve, "summoned the body of the disciples" (6:2) to propose candidates to serve tables so the apostles could devote themselves to preaching the Word of God. Seven men "of good repute full of the Spirit" were chosen for this new ministry (6:3). Here as in the election of Matthias those chosen were not a nameless lot; the names of all seven, beginning with Stephen, are recorded in the Acts of the Apostles chapter 6. In the Gospels, in Acts, and in the Letters of Paul named persons are the markers by which the community could be identified. This company of seven was set before the assembly, "and they prayed and laid their hands upon them" (6:6).

The apostles met for the third time in Jerusalem, probably in the late 40s, because some had come from Judea to Antioch and were teaching the "brethren" that gentile Christians cannot be saved unless circumcised according to the custom of Moses. A reasonable expectation because most Christians at this time were Jews and hence circumcised. The Judean embassy caused great consternation in Antioch because there gentiles had been admitted as full members in the church without circumcision. So Paul and Barnabas had "no small discussion and debate" with the Judeans (Acts 15:2).

Antioch was not Jerusalem; it was the home of a mixed community of Christians living in the midst of a large Hellenistic city, second only to Rome and Alexandria. As some stepped outside familiar environs to speak of Christ to Greeks, not just to Jews, conflict with Jerusalem was inevitable and had been building for some time. A few years earlier Peter had spoken to Cornelius, a Roman centurion stationed in Caesarea, about Christ, and the Holy Spirit had come upon those who heard him. When "believers from among the circumcised" saw this they were amazed that "the gift of the Holy Spirit had been poured out even on the Gentiles." Peter boldly decided without consulting anyone—no doubt because he was Peter—to baptize those who believed (Acts 10:44–48).[1]

About the same time some Christians from "Cyprus and Cyrene," that is, far out of the Jerusalem orbit, showed up in Antioch and began to speak to Greeks about Christ. This news traveled swiftly and soon reached the church in Jerusalem (Acts 11:20). Not surprisingly when this intelligence

1. Peter's vision of the sheet let down from heaven with "unclean" food is a continuation of the account of Cornelius (Acts 11:1–18).

was received its leaders dispatched a delegation to Antioch to find out what was going on. Wisely they chose Barnabas, a Jew from Cyprus, who could have been expected to have an understanding of this surprising development. High marks then for the leaders in Jerusalem.

When Barnabas arrived in Antioch and met the new converts he was "glad"—a happy choice of the KJV translators followed by the RSV; the tone-deaf NRSV translators have the more prosaic "he rejoiced" for ἐχάρη (Acts 11:23). The sins of the NRSV translators are also literary not only ideological. To the astonishment of the Antiochene Christians—so we can imagine—a great number turned to the Lord. This was revolutionary, for people who had been "alienated from the commonwealth of Israel" and "strangers to the covenants of promise" (Eph 2:12) were now brought near. Barnabas knew it was his responsibility to instruct them in the faith, so he set out at once for Tarsus to recruit Paul to help him. Paul agreed and the two returned to Antioch, and for a "whole year" they labored there among the new Christians (Acts 11:25–26).

Several things to note. First, no one raised any question about whether Greeks could become members of the church. The precedent had already been set by Peter when he baptized Cornelius. Second, it was here in Antioch that the term "Christian" was used for the first time (Acts 11:26). Up to that time the followers of Christ formed a "way" (ὁδός) within Judaism (Acts 9:2). Only when outsiders come on the scene was the term "Christian" used. At a very early stage in its history Christian self-understanding was being shaped by the perceptions of non-Christians. It is a tribute to the faithfulness of these first Christians that what outsiders heard from them was the name "Christ," that is, "Christ's people," not simply that they were followers of Jesus. As Athanasius put it: "From Christ we are named Christians."[2] They sensed what escapes some biblical scholars, that there was more here than a Jesus movement.

The most significant detail in the account is that a "large company was added to the Lord" (Acts 11:24). No doubt this simple demographical fact made a deep impression on the pillars in Jerusalem. The scale of gentile converts was without precedent, and the leaders in Jerusalem feared that welcoming so many gentile believers would bring about a weakening of Christian moral standards and a dilution of Jewish identity. They were still thinking of Christianity as a "way" within Judaism. But numbers counted.

2. Athanasius, *Contra Arianos* 1.2.

Nor must it be forgotten that the church in Jerusalem was poor and the Antiochene Christians provided relief for Christians in Judea (Acts 11:29–30).

During the next year Paul and Barnabas headed off on another missionary journey to Greek-speaking cities on Cyprus and in Asia Minor, addressing Jews in their synagogues, but welcoming Greeks, most likely "God-fearers," who heard their message (Acts 14:1). On return to Antioch the "church" in the city gathered together and Paul and Barnabas told all that God had done and "how he had opened a door of faith to the Gentiles" (14:28).

And so we come to the account of the council in Jerusalem in Acts 15. Soon after Paul and Barnabas had returned to Antioch an embassy from Jerusalem arrived putting Paul and Barnabas on the defensive (Acts 15:1). The word from Jerusalem—almost an ultimatum—undercut their work in the Greek-speaking cities and in Antioch. Without circumcision according to the custom of Moses, Jerusalem instructed them, one could not be saved. Paul and Barnabas protested but without success. So the two of them and "some others" went up to Jerusalem to the "apostles and the elders about this question" (15:2). When they arrived they made the case for accepting gentiles without circumcision and apparently won the support of the worthies in Jerusalem. But some, Christians who were aligned with the Pharisees—an interesting historical detail—were displeased and invoked the principle: "It is necessary to circumcise them, and to charge them to keep the law of Moses" (15:5). This division was the occasion for the council.

At this point the story becomes complicated, because it seems that Peter was in Antioch at the time the embassy from Judea arrived. In Acts Peter comes on stage only at Jerusalem, but in Galatians, probably written about the same time as the council in Jerusalem, Paul says that Peter was in Antioch when "certain men came from James" (Gal 2:12).[3] If this is a reference to Acts 15, "some men came down from Judea," as it seems to be, then the matter of table fellowship and the debate over circumcision are part of the same dispute. They Judeans came to protest receiving Greeks without circumcision, but were offended that some Jewish Christians, including Peter, were not keeping the food laws. Not a small matter if you have ever entertained observant Jews in your home.

When the Judeans arrived, Peter, according to Paul, "drew back and separated himself, fearing the circumcision party" (Gal 2:12). Outraged at Pe-

3. On the interpretation of Gal 2 and Acts 15 see James D. G. Dunn, "The Incident at Antioch (Gal 2:11–18)," in *The Galatians Debate,* ed. Mark D. Nanos (Peabody, Mass.: Hendrickson, 2002), 199–234.

ter's reversal Paul rebukes his deception. Here the KJV does better than the RSV. It translates the Greek (ὑποκρίνομαι) with "dissimulation"; RSV has the weaker "insincerity." NRSV has "hypocrisy," which is I think too strong. Dissimulation is just right. As Mark Twain once said: "The difference between the almost right word and the right word is really a large matter. 'Tis the difference between the lightning bug and the lightning." Barnabas as well as other Jewish Christians were also taken in and broke off fellowship with the Greek Christians.

The dispute between Peter and Paul was a great embarrassment to early Christian commentators. Porphyry had exploited the clash of the two apostles, charging Paul with impudence and Peter with backsliding, to discredit Christianity. A string of Greek commentators, beginning with Origen, took the position that Paul had only pretended to criticize Peter, and Peter only pretended to keep the Jewish food laws. Jerome adopts this interpretation and explains that it was a tactical strategy to win Jews over to Christ.[4] Augustine was irked at Jerome's opinion and wrote to say that his view left him "in more than a little pain," especially because he would not expect "a fine a man as you" to defend a lie.[5] After all in Galatians Paul wrote, "Look, what I write to you before God I do not lie."[6] Jerome is wrong because his interpretation casts doubt on the veracity of the Scriptures. But Jerome could not accept that the two great apostles had a fundamental disagreement. For Augustine, however, the truthfulness of the Scripture was more sacred than the reputation of an apostle. Jerome, knowing that Augustine could not read Greek, condescendingly says that he has no business taking a position on the matter without reading Origen and John Chrysostom.[7]

But there was more at issue between Jerome and Augustine than whether the two apostles had disagreed or the Scriptures had erred. The exchange between Jerome and Augustine puts before us the chief issue raised by the council: how should Christians view the Jewish law?

4. Jerome, *Ep.* 112.7–8 (*Ep.* 75.7–8 in Augustine's correspondence).

5. Augustine, *Ep.* 28.3.3.

6. Augustine, *Ep.* 40.3.3, citing Gal 1:20.

7. Jerome, *Ep.* 112.6 (*Ep.* 75.6 Augustine). On the patristic interpretation of Gal 2:11–14, see J. B. Lightfoot, *St. Paul's Epistle to the Galatians* (London: Macmillan, 1880), 128–32; Karlfried Froelich, "Fallibility Instead of Infallibility? A Brief History of the Interpretation of Galatians 2:11–14," in *Teaching Authority and Infallibility in the Church*, ed. Paul C. Empire, T. Austin Murphy, and Joseph A. Burgess, Lutherans and Catholics in Dialogue 6 (Minneapolis: Augsburg, 1980), 259–69, 351–57. For the medieval interpretation of Gal 2 see selections of commentators, e.g., Peter Lombard, as well as discussion of Jerome and Augustine, in Ian Christopher Levy, ed., *The Letter to the Galatians*, The Bible in Medieval Tradition (Grand Rapids: Eerdmans, 2011), 22–35, 193–201.

Before turning to that, a few more details of what transpired in Jerusalem. When James, Peter, Paul, and Barnabas gathered in the same room the great consultation began. Peter speaks first and reminds the assembly that this matter had been settled years ago when the Spirit had come to the household of Cornelius. Peter was certain and unambiguous, and his speech silenced the assembly.[8] Then Paul and Barnabas told what God had done among the gentiles. Finally James, the acknowledged leader of the Jerusalem church, stands up and gathers the sense of the assembly in a short speech quoting Peter and the prophet Amos that the tabernacle of David will be rebuilt and the "Gentiles who are called by name will seek the Lord" (Am 9:11–12 LXX; Acts 15:16–18).

Then comes James's peroration. "In my judgment we should stop troubling the Gentiles who turn to God" (Acts 15:19). Strong language. We have no right to impose on the gentiles what God has left free. But his speech ends with the big except: they are to "abstain from the pollutions of idols and from unchastity and from what is strangled and from blood" (15:20). To which he adds a puzzling explanation: "For from early generations Moses has had in every city those who preach him, for he is read every Sabbath in the synagogues" (15:21).

On the central issue, circumcision of gentiles, the decision was unequivocal: circumcision cannot be a condition for membership in the Christian community. Yet Christianity was a form of Judaism, and the first Christians were pious and observant Jews, not renegades. For them the law was a good and holy thing, a gift from God that gave grace and beauty to their lives and lifted their hearts to the praise and adoration of God. Their faithfulness to the Jewish law was a sign of a living faith, and they were unwilling to jettison the ancient ways of their people. So they proposed a solution in Jewish terms that dealt with veneration of idols, marriage practices, and meat improperly slaughtered. The aim, as the letter sent to Antioch explains, was to put "no greater *burden* than these necessary things" on the gentiles (15:28), and not sever ties to Jewish tradition.[9] The wished to hold fast to the unity of the church yet not break all ties with Judaism.

The recommendation about hearing the law read in the synagogues was

8. Some biblical scholars have charged Peter with "Judaizing," but Kirsopp Lake observed: "The figure of a Judaizing St. Peter is a figment of the Tuebingen critics with no basis in history" (Lake, *Earlier Epistles of St. Paul: Their Motive and Origin* [London: Rivingtons, 1914], 116).

9. The strictures are those the Old Testament places on "strangers among the Jews" (Lv 17:8, 10–13; 18:26).

apparently addressed to the gentiles. Jewish Christians were assured that gentile Christians would not abandon Israel and could learn more about the law by attending the synagogue. The proposal assumed good relations between Christians and Jews in Antioch.

On what authority did James and the other apostles rule on this issue? Were they acknowledging the right of the law to legislate certain Christian practices? That seems unlikely, as John Chrysostom saw clearly in his commentary on Acts. James spoke on his own authority, writes John. For he says: "I judge" (ἐγὼ κρίνω). He draws on what had been taught by Moses in the law so that the decision does not make the law of "no authority." Nevertheless he acted not on the basis of the law "but *from himself*." Or better, says John: "We have judged. The decree is made in common."[10] James acted on behalf of the community as a whole.

The legislation of the Jerusalem council was a decision of the church, not an imposition of the law of Moses on Christians. It was similar to later "canons" of church councils, that is, regulations agreed upon by the bishops that dealt with moral, administrative, or liturgical matters distinct from doctrinal decrees. Significantly the Western text of Acts transmits the decree as follows: "that they abstain from idolatry, from fornication and from bloodshed." By omitting "strangled," it subtly transformed the decree into a straightforward moral exhortation.[11]

Nevertheless the Jewishness of the decree as well as Peter's accommodation to Jewish food laws were problems for later gentile Christians. Jerome mounts a vigorous critique of Augustine by showing that Paul, contrary to what he says about law in Galatians, himself did what he criticized Peter for doing.

Jerome gives three examples from Acts. (1) When Paul was in Derbe and Lystra he took on a disciple named Timothy, son of a Jewish woman and a gentile father, and circumcised him "on account of the Jews who were in those places" (Acts 15:41–16:3). (2) When Paul was at Cenchreae, the port near Corinth, "he cut his hair, for he had made a vow" (Acts 18:18). This was apparently a temporary Nazirite vow (Nm 6:1–21). (3) When James and the elders in Jerusalem heard of Paul's success among the gentiles, they glorified God. But some said that he was teaching Jews not to

10. John Chrysostom, *Commentary on the Acts of the Apostles,* homily 33.1, PG 60:239.

11. See F. F. Bruce, *Commentary on the Book of Acts* (London: Marshall, Morgan and Scott, 1968), 312–13.

circumcise their children nor observe Jewish customs (Acts 21:21).[12] To avoid offense James tells—really commands—Paul to give proof that he still respects Jewish tradition and that he lives "in observance of the law" (21:24). Paul complies and agrees to go into the temple to purify himself according to the Law of Moses and to offer sacrifices (21:26). Jerome takes these three actions as proof that Paul did precisely what Peter did: when observant Jews objected, he conformed to Jewish ways.

Jerome held that no matter what the circumstances, observing the Mosaic law is contrary to the gospel, and he has the cheek to accuse Augustine of Ebionitism.[13] Augustine, however, sees nothing wrong in Jewish Christians in those early years observing the law. Paul was faithful to what he had received from his parents. As long as Christians do not place their hope of salvation in Jewish observance there was no harm in keeping the law. Paul, after all was a "Jew by birth" and corrected Peter because "he was *forcing* the Gentiles to live like Jews." It is one thing to observe the old sacraments in faithfulness to tradition and custom, that is, out of "habit," another because they are necessary for salvation. He acted out of "merciful compassion not out of false pretense."[14]

But Jerome will not let him off that easily. He zeroes in on Augustine's repeated statement that it was acceptable for a Jewish Christian to observe the law as long as "it was not thought necessary for salvation." If they are not necessary for salvation, he asks, why are they observed? Observing the law "cannot be something indifferent." It is either "good or bad." And he trots out a number of biblical texts in support: "Christ is the end of the law for the justification of every believer" (Rom 10:40). "The law and the prophets existed up to John the Baptist" (Lk 16:16). "The law was given through Moses, but grace and truth came through Jesus Christ." (Jn 1:16–17). "If you have yourselves circumcised, Christ does you no good" (Gal 5:2).[15]

At the end of a letter brandishing his rhetorical sword Jerome makes a sarcastic thrust at the great bishop. Don't tell me I am a "teacher of lies," for "I follow Christ, who said, 'I am the way, the truth, and the life'" (Jn 14:6). As a

12. James's mention of the particulars of the decree of the Jerusalem council suggested to some commentators that this is the first Paul hears of the decree. But, as F. F. Bruce observes: "The repetition of these terms is perfectly natural in the present context.... We are glad to know, they say in effect, that you do not teach Jewish believers to abandon the law, and we should like you to make this quite clear to the Jewish believers here" (Bruce, *Acts*, 431).

13. Jerome, *Ep.* 112.13 (*Ep.* 75.13 Augustine).

14. Augustine, *Ep.* 40.6.

15. Jerome, *Ep.* 75.16.

“worshiper of truth I do not bend my neck to a lie.” “Do not,” he admonishes Augustine, “stir up against me a crowd of the ignorant who reverence you as a bishop and welcome you with the honor due to the priesthood as you preach in church, but who look down on me as someone at the end of his years [early fifties] and decrepit, a man who pursues the privacy of the monastery and the countryside. Seek for yourself people to teach or to criticize.”[16]

Augustine will not be cowed by Jerome’s derision. He says he was pleased to receive Jerome’s letter, but it was “a much shorter one than I would have liked to receive from you. For you are such a man that from you no amount of words is too long, no matter how much time it takes.” But there is no need to press the argument, he assures Jerome. Enough has been said for someone as wise as you. “I would never claim that I am trying to enrich with a few coins your fine mind, which by God’s gift is solid gold, nor is anyone better suited than you to correct your work.”[17]

Augustine took the position that in the early years of the church’s history there was no harm in Jewish Christians observing aspects of the Jewish law. In that spirit he interprets the apostolic council. The ruling on food and on sexual matters did not touch on matters essential to the faith, and what the apostles proscribed was not “burdensome.” It was “easy for that time.” It showed that gentile Christians had “something in common with the Jews” based on “that cornerstone which unites in itself the two walls [of Ephesians 2:14–16].”

Though Paul had written that there was a single wall dividing Jews and Christians, Augustine takes his statement to signify two walls intersecting at the cornerstone that is Christ, “one coming from the circumcised, the other from the uncircumcised.” In the early years of the church’s history, Jewish and gentile Christians “still stood out as quite distinct with their own characteristics.” But when the church of the gentiles became such that “no Israelite was found in it in a fleshly sense, what Christian would observe this commandment by not touching thrushes or small birds unless their blood was drained or by not eating a rabbit if it was killed by being struck by hand on the neck without shedding blood?” Today people would be laughed at if they were afraid of such things. For Jesus says, “It is not what enters your mouth that defiles you” (Mt 15:11).[18]

16. Jerome, *Ep.* 75.18.

17. Augustine, *Ep.* 40.3.3.

18. Augustine, *Contra Faustum Manichaeum* 32.13.

Augustine resolves the matter with a historical explanation. Decisions taken in the early years were shaped by the unique character of the early Christian communities. Most Christians were Jews, but the number of gentiles admitted to membership was growing. Their presence was a challenge to Christian identity and self-understanding. To maintain unity and cohesion within the churches the apostles rendered a decision that was not burdensome for Christians yet respected Jewish tradition. Significantly, though circumcision was the occasion for the dispute, the decree makes no mention of circumcision. It was a nonstarter; circumcision could have no place in Christian life. The earliest Christians were willing to tolerate diversity of practice—up to a point. Recall that in Philippians Paul says that the mature Christian is able to respect those who "think otherwise," and adds "let us hold true to what we have come to hold" (Phil 3:16).

I do not think, however, that toleration of differences is what should be taken from this early Christian controversy. Surely that is true, but there is a deeper wisdom that holds long after the give-and-take of the first century. And that is the abiding significance of Judaism for Christians. At the end of the Epistle to the Romans Paul uses the metaphor of the olive tree to explain the relation between Christians and Jews. You, he says to the gentile Christians, are a "wild olive shoot" that was grafted into the domestic tree that you may share its riches. The engrafted wild branch has no life if it is not united with the domestic tree. Remember, he says, that "it is not you that support the root, but the root that supports you" (Rom 11:17–18).

Note that the term Paul uses for "support" (βαστάζεις) is in the present tense. The "root supports you." Paul does not say that the root, Israel, *supported* the church, or that the church comes from Israel, or that the church was born from Israel. No, he says that the domestic root *nurtures* the wild olive shoot. It is of great significance that at Vatican Council II, in the decree *Nostra Aetate,* dealing with the Jews, the council fathers paraphrased Romans 11 and kept the present tense: "The Church cannot forget that through that people with whom God out of his ineffable mercy deigned to enter into an ancient covenant, it received the revelation of the Old Testament and *is nourished* from the root of the good olive tree, onto which the branches of the wild olive tree of the Gentiles have been grafted."[19]

The domestic olive can give life to the wild olive only if it is alive and

19. Vatican Council II, *Nostra Aetate,* par. 4, in *Decrees of the Ecumenical Councils,* ed. Norman P. Tanner, SJ (Washington, D.C.: Georgetown University Press, 1990), 2:970.

flourishing. Which means that the church continues to be dependent on the witness of Israel. As Christians we should give thanks to God that twenty centuries after the coming of Christ Moses is still read in the synagogue. But we must also learn, what earlier generations did not, that as Christians we have a stake in the fortunes of the Jewish people. The relation of Christianity to Judaism is unique, because only Christians are able to understand and cherish the eternal covenant God made with Israel. In centuries past Christians have had difficulty seeing and grasping this biblical truth (see Ps 89: 30–37). Revisiting the council of Jerusalem can help to open our eyes. Just as Christians many centuries ago could not define who they are without reference to Jewish tradition, so today the church, the wild olive twig, cannot present itself to the world without honoring Israel according to the flesh.

RESPONSE

The Gospel in Acts 15 and the Ecumenical Councils

Bradley Nassif (Orthodox)

My first task, an easy and pleasant one, is to express my gratitude to the organizers and hosts of this second consultation of Catholic, Orthodox, and Evangelical representatives sponsored by the Paradosis Center. Thank you for the honor given to me to address this distinguished group of scholars who have convened to explore the book of Acts from the perspective of our respective ecclesial traditions. As a student of the New Testament and patristics who nurtures deep interests in questions of continuity and change, and as an Orthodox theologian from the church of Antioch, "where the disciples were first called Christians" (Acts 11:26), I welcome the opportunity to share an ecclesial perspective on Acts 15.

Let me begin by sharing two goals that I hope to achieve in this essay. First, I would like to briefly respond to the interpretation that has been offered by Dr. Wilken on the Jerusalem council of Acts 15, along with an assessment of where things stand today in Orthodox-Jewish relations. The second and lengthiest part of my essay, however, will seek to expand on the Jerusalem council of Acts 15 as it relates to the "authority" and "ecclesiology" of the subsequent ecumenical councils that were held in the Byzantine Empire from 325 to 787. By illuminating the historical and sacramental realities that surrounded the ecumenical councils, my Catholic and Evangelical dialogue partners may understand some of the reasons *why* the Eastern Orthodox Church sees itself as faithfully preserving that tradition in an unbroken succession of truth. Though Roman primacy will remain an unresolved area in Orthodox relations with Catholicism, the history and theology I will describe here is substantially shared by Rome. The ecclesial realities presented will, however, challenge Evangelicals in particular to reassess the consistency of their commitment to and continuity with historic orthodoxy. Rather than putting a period after the Council of Chalcedon (451) as the end of classical orthodoxy, as Evangelicals often do, they may discover that orthodoxy does not end with a date in the history books, but lives on in the "catholicity" of the church's ongoing tradition—in what Fr. George Florovsky called "the mind of the Church" or as Frs. John Meyendorff and Alexander Schmemann described as the church's "living tradition." Evangelicals may come to realize that the theology of the Great *Tradition* they wish to embrace is also inseparably tied to the Great *Church* that bears witness to it—namely, the historic Orthodox communities of the Middle East, Greece, Russia, Eastern Europe, and their various children here in the West. Evangelicals may come to embrace not only the classical faith of the early church but also the church itself.

If I may use an analogy: the church is like a flower. The stem and the bud belong together. One without the other destroys the very nature of a flower. The stem may represent the church's doctrine, and that doctrinal stem is intended to feed the flowery bud. The beautiful bud is the church's spirituality, worship, and sacramental life. It is the outworking of the stem's nourishment. The stem and bud are inseparably united. Yet Evangelicals often cut off the stem from the flower and want only the doctrinal purity without the church and bud to which it belongs. My hope is that this essay will show at least in part why the two must be kept together, and that such unity is a gift of the Orthodox Church. If this conference is to bear any lasting fruit, we must love each other enough to "speak the truth in love."

The Jerusalem Council: Jews and Gentiles in Christian Perspective

Dr. Wilken has done a very fine job explaining the nature of the problem that occasioned the church's gathering in Acts 15, so I have no significant suggestions to offer along those lines. His work is characteristically solid, irenic, and relevant. Dr. Wilken's answer to the validity of messianic Judaism from the second to third centuries, and in modern times within the Evangelical movement, is noteworthy. He explained that messianic Judaism continued to exist throughout the second and third centuries simply because of the fact that it took the church two centuries to slowly understand and assimilate the New Testament's teaching on how Christ fulfilled the law, thus ending many of the Jewish practices that continued in the church up to the time of Emperor Constantine. That is a very practical and reasonable explanation that accounts for the historical persistence of Jewish practices in certain quadrants of early Christianity in the first two centuries of church history.

When looking at contemporary relations between the Eastern Orthodox Church and Judaism, relatively little progress has been made beyond surface recognition of similarities held by both faith communities. Although the ecumenical patriarchate has conducted a bilateral dialogue with Jewish scholars over the past two decades, the engagement has been on the general level of understanding Judaism and Christianity as being from the same spiritual family based on Scripture, but decisively separate regarding the Trinity, Christ, the church (who are the true people of God?), and salvation.[20]

So we Orthodox must move forward in this important dialogue with the Jewish community today. I would like to do that, in part, by responding to Dr. Wilken's assertion that speaks to the general Christian concern that Jews and gentiles are of the same spiritual family. He states: "The domestic olive [Israel] can give life to the wild olive [gentiles] only if it is alive and flourishing. Which means that the church continues to be dependent on the witness of Israel." These sentences, however, exemplify Wilken's analysis, which seems to mix and use only part of the respective testimonies of Acts and Paul. He does not seem to really reconcile the two, but moves on to a vision, hopefully to be embraced by Christians, that the church can receive energy and life "only if it [the domestic olive tree, Israel] is alive and flourishing"—a view missing even in Paul, who has the most positive witness concerning Israel in the New Testament.

Acts 15 no doubt presupposes the rightness of Jewish Christians to hold on to their Jewish traditions, and presents freedom from the law as somewhat of a concession to the gentiles based on the ultimate and universal criterion of the gospel. Luke, the author of Acts, accepts apostolic Jewish Christianity, but such acceptance does not apply to nonbelieving Jews, who

20. As from that, contemporary Orthodox scholarship has had almost no constructive engagement with defining the continuing role of Israel in God's plan of salvation in the church age. That task will require substantial knowledge of the New Testament and unusual courage by patristic scholars to critique the church fathers on the subject, recognizing the New Testament has both negative and positive views on the Jews' heritage. The truths arrived at from such study would be not only Orthodox (since the Bible is the church's Bible), but can also be employed to illuminate and critique the church fathers as necessary. For the importance of Judaism in late antiquity and the church, see Robert Wilken's *John Chrysostom and the Jews: Rhetoric and Reality in the Late 4th Century* (1983; repr., Eugene, Ore.: Wipf and Stock, 2004).

are portrayed as the first persecutors and ongoing opponents of Christians. For Luke, the apostolic faith is that only Christ is the Savior and that in no other name can salvation be attained. Paul, of course, has deep and genuine love for the unbelieving Jews, fully recognizing the revelatory character of the wealth of the Jewish heritage, which only sharpens the paradox of Jewish unbelief.

In Romans 9–11, which is an integral and essential part of Paul's exposition of the gospel as a revelation of God's righteousness, the "why" of Jewish unbelief is treated under the theme of God's faithfulness: How can God be still viewed as a faithful God (promising all those blessings to Israel) in view of the new situation of Christ, the church (as Christ's people, largely assumed in Romans 9–11), and the fact of unbelief by the majority of Jews? In brief, Paul's answers are that God is still faithful, but that in his faithfulness as sovereign God he has distinguished historically between a "spiritual" and "carnal" Israel. The spiritual Israel is the believing remnant who have embraced Christ, and the carnal Israel is unbelieving Israel. Why the unbelief? Because they have stumbled over the cornerstone, Christ, sticking with the law and its righteousness, which law for Paul has been fulfilled and terminated by Christ (Rom 10:4). Only in invoking the name of the risen Christ as Lord is salvation to be found. Christ is now preached to all, including unbelieving Israel, which is being blinded according to God's plan, yet only for a time. Paul has a fervent hope, conviction, and teaching that in God's due time (which for Paul was no doubt a fairly short time, perhaps Paul's lifetime or so) all Israel would believe and be saved by God's mysterious action. Paul states unequivocally that God remains as faithful as ever and that his promises to Israel are irrevocable and will be fulfilled. Rudolf Bultmann thought this to be Paul's pipe dream, but others would disagree, invoking Paul's inspiration and authority. That all Israel will be saved does not mean both many Jews and gentiles combined and thus constituted the new and true Israel (so N. T. Wright), nor every single unbelieving Jew at any given generation, but the bulk of unbelieving Jews.

Thus Paul can serve as a strong witness for the continuing value of the Old Testament heritage as revelation, and the law as holy, good, and God's gift (though never intended to have the power to quicken and save, but only to guard the Jews until the time of Christ and to provide a thorough knowledge of sin). Even today, by Paul's principles, faithful Jews are the elect people of God—but yet they are also the disobedient elect, waiting for God's mysterious actions to be converted to Christ, the only Savior.[21] That is why Orthodox witness to Jewish people remains as a missionary mandate today. In the simplest of terms we may say that the preaching of the gospel to Jewish people today is no less demanded by Christ than is the preaching of the gospel to the gentiles. That perspective seemed to be lacking in Dr. Wilken's presentation.

The Gospel in Acts 15 and the Ecumenical Councils (325–787)

What has Acts 15 to do with the ongoing need to confess the gospel in the postapostolic age of the ecumenical councils? The word given by the Jerusalem council to gentile believers in Acts 15:28 was: "It has seemed good to the Holy Spirit and to us." Commenting on this text, Jaroslav Pelikan described the relationship between the Jerusalem council and the later ecumenical councils of the church in the Roman Empire:

> This entire chapter has served throughout Christian history as a model for decision-making in the church and as a charter both for authority *at* church councils and for the authority *of* church councils. Therefore these very words, "it has seemed good to the Holy Spirit and to us," identifying the voice of a council with the voice and will of the Holy Spirit and not "something human," were quoted by later councils and confessions, including some Protestant ones.... Historically, a council has become necessary in the life and teaching of the church when there arose "no small dissension and debate" (15:2).[22]

It is along these lines that I would like to enlarge our perspective of Wilken's illuminating presentation of the Jerusalem council of Acts 15. Aside from what I have said above, there is very little to take issue with in his presentation. So I would like to expand the implications of Acts 15 for the ongoing life of the church by focusing on three questions that are tied to the preservation of the gospel in the ecumenical councils, which took their inspiration, in

21. Credit belongs to Fr. Theodore Stylianopoulos for much of the above material. See his essay titled "Faithfulness to the Roots and Commitment toward the Future: An Orthodox View," *Orthodox Christians and Jews on Continuity and Renewal: The Third Academic Meeting between Orthodoxy and Judaism*, ed. Malcolm Lowe, *Emmanuel* 26/27 (1994): 142–59; "The Churches and the Jewish People: Toward a New Understanding—The Sigtuna Statement," *Jewish-Christian Relations* (winter 1988): 43–48; and "A Brief Statement on the Status of Jewish-Christian Relations in the Orthodox Church," in *Consultation on the Church and the Jewish People* (Geneva: World Council of Churches, 1992), 36–37.

22. Jaroslav Pelikan, *Acts*, Brazos Theological Commentary on Scripture (Grand Rapids: Brazos, 2005), 175.

part, from the Jerusalem council. Those questions are: (1) How do we know if a church council is genuinely voicing the will of God? (2) How is the gospel linked to the ecclesiology of the churches that produced the decisions of the ecumenical councils? (3) What is the relationship between the dogmas that are confessed by the ecumenical councils and the saving realities of the gospel?

How Do We Know If a Church Council Is Genuinely Voicing the Will of God?

The authority of the seven ecumenical councils is affirmed by both Eastern Orthodox and Roman Catholics, as well as many classical Protestants (at least up to the Council of Chalcedon in 451). Pelikan notes that each council had one main "dissention and debate" that was of no small consequence:

1. At the First Council of Nicaea (325), it was the doctrine that the Son of God is identical in being (*homoousios*) with the Father.
2. At the First Council of Constantinople (381), it was the relation of the Holy Spirit to the Father and the Son, and therefore the dogma of the Holy Trinity.
3. At the Council of Ephesus (431), it was the inseparability of the man Jesus from the Logos, and therefore the propriety of calling the Blessed Virgin Mary *Theotokos*, Mother of God.
4. At the Council of Chalcedon (451), it was the relation in the person of Jesus Christ of the two natures, "which undergo no confusion, no change, no division, no separation."
5. At the Second Council of Constantinople (553), it was the distinction between the two wills of the one incarnate Logos.
6. At the Third Council of Constantinople (680–681), it was the attribution to each nature in Christ of its own "center of action" in opposition to the idea that there was a single center of action in Christ that was divine and human at the same time.
7. At the Second Council of Nicaea (787), it was the long and bitter "dissension and debate" over the use of images in the church.

Pelikan further observes that, following the example of Acts 15, the authority of "the apostles and the elders, with the whole church" (v. 22) became the basis for the later theological doctrine that a church council's authority must take into account its "reception" by the faithful. While this is true, the authority of the ecumenical councils as a voice of the Holy Spirit is more complex than it appears. The question, How do we know if a given council is genuinely voicing the will of God or not? involves several external *signs* that we can observe, though none can be a *guarantee* or taken in isolation.[23] That is not an easy reality to embrace for those whose theology rests on an objective religious authority, be it the papacy or *sola Scriptura*. Here are some of the major signs of authenticity surrounding an ecumenical council along with the insufficiencies of each:

The number of bishops in attendance. The number of bishops who attended a council is no proof of ecumenicity, since some councils were more numerous than others.

Geographical distribution of the bishops. The geographical distribution of the bishops and their representative character requires, in principle, that they represent all local expressions of the catholic church. This does not mean that the bishops must be from every location in the world, but simply that those who are in attendance are to be in communion with the other bishops who themselves may not have been able to attend. But this representative character, while being indispensable, is hardly in itself a sufficient criterion for authentic ecumenicity in the deepest sense. Externally, the Councils of Rimini-Seleucia (358) and Ferrara-Florence (1438–1439) were as representative as each of the seven ecumenical councils, but neither the one nor the other has been recognized as ecumenical by the Orthodox Church because they have not reflected the teachings of Scripture and the church's Great Tradition.

The conviction of a council itself. The conviction of a council itself is also no guarantee of its ecumenicity. Many councils explicitly proclaimed themselves ecumenical that were not, however, recognized as such by the church (the notorious Robber Synod of 449, and the iconoclast Council of Hieria in 754 are two examples). So this criteria is not by itself determinant. On the other hand, a council may in fact be ecumenical even though it did not proclaim itself as such. For example, it is not certain that the Council of Constantinople in 381 even considered itself as ecumenical, yet it was

23. Bradley Nassif, "'Authority' in the Eastern Orthodox Tradition," in *By What Authority? The Vital Questions of Religious Authority in Christianity*, ed. Robert Millett (Macon, Ga.: Mercer University Press, 2010), 45–50.

subsequently recognized as such by the church. The self-proclamation of a council, therefore, is not needed or itself reliable.

Recognition or ratification by a later ecumenical council. Recognition by a later ecumenical council is theologically important, but again it is not sufficient by itself. One of the first tasks done by each ecumenical council was to ratify the decisions of the previous ones. This is an important step in the process of the "reception" of a council by the wider church, but once again this is not a sufficient criterion in itself. For as long as additional ecumenical councils might be needed in the future, there will necessarily be a future council in the series that has not as yet been confirmed by a later synod. Consequently, if we rest on the sole criterion of the approval of a later council, the validity of the entire series is diminished.

Acknowledgment by the Christian emperor. Acknowledgment by the emperor was important in Christian antiquity, but it was not sufficient in the past nor will it be required for any future council that may be held in our day. To be sure, emperors tried to manipulate the outcome of ecumenical councils, ratified their decisions and enforced them as law; but they could not impose their beliefs upon the church. The reception of a council by the emperor was of great importance in the process of "reception," but it did not constitute final and decisive criteria. John Chrysostom and Maximus the Confessor demonstrated with their lives that the state had no right interfering with the faith of the church, and that the church had a mind and a will of its own. The absence of a Christian emperor in the modern world does not render a modern ecumenical council impossible because truth is not determined by a particular time period or a specific political system.

Acknowledgment by the pope. Acknowledgment by the pope of Rome is critical so long as the pope is not isolated or exalted above his episcopal brethren. It was of great importance that the bishop of Rome accept an ecumenical council simply because he had so often functioned as a theological referee in theological disputes, not to mention the authority of his purported double-apostolic succession and prestigious geographical location in the capital of the Roman Empire. But the Orthodox cannot regard the ratification by the pope as decisive by itself, for Orthodox ecclesiology does not wish to isolate the pope from his brothers in the episcopate and from other members of the body of Christ. For example, the Eastern Orthodox churches do not regard the Council of Ferrara-Florence as ecumenical, even though it received the affirmation of both the emperor and of the pope.

"Reception" by the church. In the final analysis, there is but one decisive indicator of ecumenicity, and it is retrospective, namely, "reception." The key question to answer is, Has a given assembly been accepted by the general conscience of the church? In practice, the one way to determine if a given assembly is or is not authentically ecumenical, and thereby infallible insofar as it accords with apostolic truth, is to discern if the council in question has been later accepted as ecumenical by all the church. No conciliar decision carries binding force until the communities of faith and their bishops in communion with each other receive that decision.

But even here, "reception by the faithful" cannot provide automatic proof. One need only to study the complicated developments that followed the Council of Chalcedon to see how this is so. To what extent can it be said that this council was in fact "accepted by the faithful"? It was rejected by the majority of Christians in the patriarchate of Alexandria and by about half of those of the patriarchate of Antioch. So these facts merely confirm the point already made, namely, that the truth cannot be established by a mechanical application of formal criteria.

Still, the reception of councils by the church is a historically vital part of the theological authority of an ecumenical council. How, then, does reception take place? There are no rules to follow in which this process is concretely carried out, much to the embarrassment of systematic theologians who are fond of clearly structured answers. As one studies the reception history of the ecumenical councils, we find that no precise number of people are required, nor a precise time limit in which the process of recognition must necessarily be finished. Historically, the process of recognition took place in various and sundry times and ways. The "reception" of Nicaea as "ecumenical" was more or less an accomplished fact during the conclusions of the Council of Constantinople. But the council of 381 does not seem to have been counted by Rome among the number of ecumenical councils before 517. And the seventh ecumenical council was not generally received in the West before the eleventh century. The process of reception is thus not subjected to an external law or referendum. It is simply a historical fact that took place under the guidance of the Holy Spirit. At a true ecumenical council the bishops witnessed to the truth, and that witness was then welcomed by the assent of the whole people of God, including laypeople, who, by virtue of their baptism, were to be responsible guardians of the faith. That verification by the church was expressed not formally or explicitly, but simply *lived* in the worshiping community and individual lives of the saints. The decrees of an ecumenical council are "authoritative" and "infallible" because they bear witness to the apostolic faith given in Scripture and lived out in the ongoing life of the church. But at the same time this later consent by the church is the visible manifestation by which we know by faith that a council has in fact been guided by the Holy Spirit.

Conciliar decisions, therefore, are not true because they have been accepted by the church, but they have been accepted by the church because they are true. The definitive authority is the authority of the Living Truth who is Jesus Christ, the Lord of the church, acting among us and in us by the Holy Spirit. From an Orthodox point of view, there exists no criterion or collection of criteria that would automatically guarantee the ecumenicity of a council, but rather an organic, Spirit-illumined witness to the truth that was accepted by the faithful. The ecumenical councils were not legal institutions but Spirit-inspired witnesses to the unity of the faith accepted by the people of God in communion with their local bishops. In an illuminating essay on this subject, Georges Florovsky states that Christ himself is the ultimate criterion of truth, not councils per se:

> The teaching *authority* of the Ecumenical Councils is grounded in the *infallibility* of the Church. The ultimate "authority" is vested in the Church which is for ever the Pillar and the Foundation of Truth. It is not primarily a canonical authority, in the formal and specific sense of the term, although canonical strictures or sanctions may be appended to conciliar decisions on matters of faith. It is a *charismatic* authority, grounded in the assistance of the Spirit: *for it seemed good to the Holy Spirit, and to us.*[24]

How Is the Gospel Linked to the Ecclesiology of the Churches That Produced the Decisions of the Ecumenical Councils?

The ecclesiology of the Jerusalem council in Acts 15 is not highly developed at this time, so we should guard against anachronistic descriptions of the evolved model of the episcopate by Ignatius of Antioch at the beginning

24. Georges Florovsky, "The Authority of the Ancient Councils and the Tradition of the Fathers," in *Bible, Church, Tradition: An Eastern Orthodox View* (Belmont, Mass.: Norland, 1987), 93, 103. Florovsky says more in this one chapter on the authority of the ancient councils than what it takes others an entire book to write.

of the second century. This is not to say, however, that the evolved Ignatian model is incompatible with the form of leadership we find governing the earlier Jerusalem council ("It has seemed good to the Holy Spirit and to us," Acts 15:28).[25] The eucharistic ecclesiology that we find in Ignatius appears to be already present, at least in incipient form, in the earliest history of the church over which James and the apostles presided.

Without going further into this complex subject, there are at least two points to make concerning how early Christian ecclesiology played out in the ecumenical councils. It is especially relevant for Evangelical Protestants today because many seemed to have overlooked the church's ecclesiology when claiming their allegiance to the Councils of Nicaea and Chalcedon.

The first point is the recognition that the churches that gathered at the ecumenical councils were already in eucharistic communion with each other before they gathered (unless, of course, the bishop of a given church was the subject of heresy). The ecclesiological principles of Ignatius of Antioch continued to shape the life of the communities who gathered at the ecumenical councils. The bishops present came from local communities of believers who were in communion with their local bishops who gathered with their flock around the celebration of the Eucharist. Those bishops, in turn, were in communion with other local communities. This eucharistic ecclesiology and its structures of communion existed before an ecumenical council gathered and continued to exist during and after the councils' proceedings. It is important for Evangelicals to see this because those who have congregational forms of government do not share the same ecclesiology, which is vitally connected to the theological orthodoxy of the ecumenical councils.

Second, Irenaeus of Lyons (mid-second century) emphasized the importance of "apostolic succession" against the Gnostics by affirming that true bishops were (and are) those whose ordination stand in historic succession with the original Twelve and the authority of Jesus. Historic succession by itself, however, was no guarantee of truth for Irenaeus. No less important is a succession of apostolic truth within each local community headed by its local bishop. Both successions (historical and theological) were necessary preconditions for every bishop's participation in the ecumenical councils.

These ecclesiological realities are as relevant today for Christianity as they were in the age of the ecumenical councils. They underscore the con-

25. Thomas Robinson, *Ignatius of Antioch and the Parting of the Ways: Early Jewish-Christian Relations* (Peabody, Mass.: Hendrickson, 2009), 99–102.

viction that Christian truth is a communal, not individual matter. Scripture, tradition, authority, and the "mind of the church" worked together symbiotically in the decision-making process of the ecumenical councils.[26] The conclusions that were reached by the fathers of the councils are the faith of "the one, holy, catholic, and apostolic church" to which the Nicene Creed refers. This leads us to the final question I would like to raise.

What Is the Relationship between the Dogmas That Are Confessed by the Ecumenical Councils and the Saving Realities of the Gospel?

The Nicene Creed and Chalcedonian Definition constitute the foundation of Orthodox soteriology and thus express the very content of the gospel. The incarnate Son of the Father, in his trinitarian relations, lies at the heart of Nicaea and Chalcedon (in tandem, of course, with the other five ecumenical councils, which surrounded them). For example, the Nicene Creed declares the saving significance of the incarnation when affirming

> Jesus Christ . . . of one essence [*homoousion*] with the Father. . . . Who for us humans and for our salvation, came down from heaven and was incarnate of the Holy Spirit and the Virgin Mary, and became human.

Likewise, the crucial negative adverbs of the famous Chalcedonian Definition use apophatic language[27] to set the boundaries around the mystery of the union of the two natures of Christ ("without confusion, change, separation or division").

Chalcedon, however, was not the final word on the christological debates in the Christian East. Against the heresy of monothelitism (the belief that Christ had only one divine-human will), the sixth ecumenical council (680/681) formally attested to the complete integrity of, and cooperation between, the human and divine wills of Christ:

26. Bradley Nassif, "Tradition, 'Catholicity,' and the Mind of the Church," in *The Mission of God: Studies in Orthodox and Evangelical Mission*, ed. Mark Oxbrow and Tim Grass (Eugene, Ore.: Wipf and Stock, 2016), 215–23. See also Alexander Schmemann, "Towards a Theology of Councils," in *Church, World, Mission* (Crestwood, N.Y.: St. Vladimir's Seminary Press, 1979), 159–78.

27. The church's use of apophatic (negative) and kataphatic (affirmative) language as paths to the knowledge of God are explained by Andrew Louth, "Apophatic and Cataphatic Theology," in *The Cambridge Companion to Christian Mysticism*, ed. Amy Hollywood and Patricia Z. Beckman (Cambridge: Cambridge University Press, 2012), 137–46. The Chalcedonian Definition condemned Apollinarianism, Nestorianism, and Eutychianism, which, in their own ways, undermined either the full humanity of Christ or the unity of humanity with divinity.

We also proclaim two natural willings or wills in him and two natural operations [modes of action], without separation, without change, without partition, without confusion, according to the teaching of the holy Fathers—and two natural wills not contrary [to each other], God forbid, as the impious heretics have said [they would be], but his human will follows, and does not resist or opposes, but rather is subject to his divine and all-powerful will.[28]

The Christology of St. Maximus the Confessor lies behind this conciliar statement. Maximus advanced the work of Chalcedon by distinguishing between the "natural" and "gnomic" (deliberative) wills. He maintained that Christ has a natural will that followed its created instincts toward union with God, but he did not have a gnomic will, which is characterized by hesitation and deliberation between two or more options. Christ never deliberated between doing the will of the Father or not. He sinlessly followed the natural will of his fallen, but now healed, humanity. In his incarnate life, Christ did for humans what we could never do for ourselves. His obedience to the Father through the natural operations of his human will, in synergy with the divine will, makes it possible for humans to obey God when we become united with his redeemed humanity.

Notice well that the soteriological significance of these saving truths are not just about getting a correct formula for christological chemistry. Rather, they are *affirmations about the good news of the gospel*. In becoming human, the Son of God assumed a human body, a human soul, a human mind, and a human will. In taking up our full humanity, the hypostatic (personal) union of the divine and human natures in Christ brought about a reconciling, atoning union in the very being of the Savior. As "the only mediator between God and humans" (1 Tm 2:5), the Son of the Father took our full humanity into the very life of God, destroying the separation between God and humanity within his own divine being. The incarnation re-created and reoriented our fallen humanity back into a proper relation to God that Adam and Eve had lost in the garden of Eden.

Nicaea and Chalcedon are not the last words on the content of the

28. Deno John Genakoplos, *Byzantium: Church, Society, and Civilization Seen through Contemporary Eyes* (Chicago: University of Chicago Press, 1984), 152. The heresy of aphthartodocetism (the belief that Christ's body was incapable of death and corruption) explained such passages as Lk 2:52 ("Jesus grew in wisdom and stature" etc.) as divine pedagogy and not real growth from ignorance to knowledge. The church's opposition to aphthartodocetism indicates a biblical and Chalcedonian perception ("the preservation of the properties of each nature") that Christ's humanity was identical to ours in every way except sin. See John Meyendorff, *Christ in Eastern Christian Thought* (Crestwood, N.Y.: St. Vladimir's Seminary Press, 1975), 86–89.

gospel that was so important to those present at the Jerusalem council in Acts 15. The last of the ecumenical councils confessed a *visualized* gospel through iconographic depictions of Christ made possible by the Word made flesh (Jn 1:14). Icons, in other words, are the church's "visual gospel." The church's ultimate theological justification for the use of images in liturgy and devotion is the incarnation. Icons bear witness to the saving realities of the God who became human. To reject the icons, therefore, is to implicitly deny salvation itself. John of Damascus sums up the Orthodox position with brilliant christological insight:

> In former times God, who is without form or body, could never be depicted. But now when God is seen in the flesh conversing with men, I make an image of the God whom I see. I do not worship matter; I worship the Creator of matter who became matter for my sake, who willed to take His abode in matter; who worked out my salvation through matter. Never will I cease honoring the matter which wrought my salvation! I honor it, but not as God.[29]

Jesus Christ: The Defining Center of the Gospel

In responding to Robert Wilken's presentation, I have tried to bring out some important connections between the Jerusalem council in Acts 15 and the later ecumenical councils of the Christian church, as viewed from an Orthodox perspective. The common concerns of both—in different times, ways, and contexts—focused on the good news of salvation that was accomplished through Jesus Christ. The relationship between Acts 15 and the ecumenical councils can be summarized: Whereas Peter declared to the council in Jerusalem that the message of the gospel is *for all who believe* in the Lord Jesus Christ (Acts 15:6–11), the ecumenical councils bore witness to *who* the Lord Jesus Christ *is* in whom they have believed.

29. St. John of Damascus, *Three Treatises on the Divine Images*, trans. Andrew Louth (Crestwood, N.Y.: St. Vladimir's Seminary Press, 2003), 29.

RESPONSE

What about Jewish Followers of Jesus?

Gerald R. McDermott (Evangelical)

Robert Wilken is one of the church's great historians in our time. I remember how reading his *The Land Called Holy* helped open up for me, years ago, new ways of looking at the significance of Judaism and the land of Israel in the first millennium of Christianity. I appreciate the intent and overall conclusion of his paper insofar as he calls Christians to recognize the abiding significance of Judaism for Christians. They should remember, as Wilken rightly points out, that Paul says in Romans 11 that the olive tree of Israel still supports (present tense) the grafted-in gentile branches.

But I want to challenge what I take to be Professor Wilken's penultimate conclusion—that the council of Jerusalem ruled that circumcision was no longer required of any disciples of Jesus, and that Jew-gentile distinctions were forever ended by the coming of the Messiah. Of course, both of these interpretations have been mainstream since the time of Augustine, except for Pietist and Puritan traditions starting in the sixteenth century, and now in the last half century for a growing number of New Testament scholars, such as James Dunn, Richard Bauckham, Markus Bockmuehl, Mark Nanos, David Rudolph, and Mark Kinzer, building on the earlier work of W. D. Davies, Krister Stendahl, and E. P. Sanders.

Let's start with the Jerusalem council decision, where James and the other leaders in Jerusalem concluded that gentiles do not have to keep kosher or circumcise their sons. They were to abstain (see Acts 15:29) from food sacrificed to idols and from blood, and from what is strangled and sexual sin (πορνεία), which probably meant the well-known list of sexual sins in Leviticus 18 and 20. But contrary to what a certain "sect of the Pharisees" had claimed (notice that not all Pharisees were the same; this was probably the rigorist school of Shammai, not the more lenient Pharisaic school of Hillel), it was not necessary for gentiles "to be circumcised and to keep the law of Moses" (15:5). These Pharisees who had recognized Yeshua (the

Hebrew name for Jesus) as Messiah said the gentiles must become Jews and submit to Mosaic law if they were to be first-class Jesus followers.

The Jerusalem council unanimously decided that these Jesus-accepting Pharisees were wrong: gentiles who received the Spirit did *not* have to become Jews or keep kosher to be full-fledged members of Yeshua's kingdom. Most scholars agree that kosher rules were *among* the practices meant by "keep[ing] the law of Moses" (15:5).

Consider this: If these Jewish leaders were debating whether gentile converts had to keep kosher and circumcision, they must have been practicing these things too. Otherwise, if they had already concluded that kosher and circumcision had been dispensed with by Jesus, why would they keep observing these practices? And if they as Jews were no longer bound by kosher, because of Jesus's teaching, then why in the world would they waste their time debating whether gentiles should keep these rules? That would be a no-brainer—that gentiles don't have to observe Jewish rules that Jesus had already declared irrelevant, even for Jews!

Now if this Jerusalem council took place in the late 40s, about fifteen years after Jesus's supposed teaching that circumcision and kosher were now defunct even for his Jewish followers, we have a problem. For one would guess plausibly that his Jewish followers, especially the apostles who lived with him for three years, would have known this. The word would have spread like wildfire because circumcision and kosher were two of the "boundary markers" distinguishing Jews from gentiles in the first century. All scholars agree on that. His teaching on this would have been revolutionary and well-known—precisely because it was so shocking. But if it was well-known—and surely the Jewish leaders of the early church would have taken it to heart—why were they now asking fifteen years later if these Jewish rules, now supposedly defunct for Jewish followers of Jesus, had to be imposed on *gentile* followers of Jesus?

It makes no sense. That is, the traditional interpretation of this council does not make sense. But consider what we do know: The rabbis had already been teaching for centuries that kosher and circumcision were *never* intended for gentiles. They were always God's special rules for his special people, the Jews. And for at least a century before the time of Jesus and the apostles, the rabbis had been teaching that gentiles could have a share in the world to come if they would obey what were later called the Noachide commandments, roughly equivalent to the Ten Commandments. They were expected to come to synagogue on Saturday mornings to "listen to

Moses" and participate in worship of the God of Israel, and Philo tells us that multiplied thousands of gentiles around the empire were doing this. But they were never expected to circumcise themselves or their sons, or to keep kosher. Just as men and women had different ways to be righteous, so did Jews and gentiles. These "righteous gentiles" were the "God-fearers" whom Luke describes in Acts who sat alongside the Jews in the synagogues in Asia Minor and Greece when Paul came to persuade them that the Messiah had finally come, a certain Jesus.

In other words, what James and the other Jewish leaders decided at Jerusalem was precisely what the rabbis had been teaching for a good long time—that God never expected them to become Jews in order to have a share in the world to come, as long as they worshiped the God of Israel and kept the commandments of the covenant with Noah. The messianic Jews from Jerusalem who had come from the school of Shammai insisted, contrary to the teaching of most of the rabbis, that gentiles did indeed have to become Jews first if they wanted to be first-class followers of Jesus. This was not shocking, for Jews in the first century were divided into many different sects, and the Pharisees themselves were divided, as we have seen.

Of course the new twist at Jerusalem, different from what the rabbis had taught, was that the Messiah had recently come. And now the question was whether his coming, and his Spirit's dispersion to gentiles, meant that gentiles had to become Jews in order to be fully united to the Messiah. After all, the Messiah was Jewish!

As on most questions, Jews were divided, even among the Pharisees. And just as before the coming of the Messiah when the majority of rabbis permitted a different way for gentiles, so too now the new rabbis of the messianic group decided on a different way for gentiles.

The behavior of both Peter and Paul confirms this interpretation. Professor Wilken says that Peter was "not keeping the food laws," and cites for evidence Galatians 2, where we read that "before certain men came from James, he was *eating with the Gentiles*; but when they came he drew back and separated himself, fearing the circumcision party" (v. 12 ESV). Paul rebuked him publicly: "If you, though a Jew, live like a Gentile and not like a Jew, how can you force the Gentiles to live like Jews?" (v. 14)

There is no clear evidence here that Peter was breaking kosher, only that he was "eating with the Gentiles." We know that Jews were divided between the rigorists, who said Jews should never sit at table with gentiles, and the more lenient Jews, who taught commensality as long as Jews kept kosher.[30] (By the way, Torah never forbids Jews to eat with gentiles; it merely forbids them eating nonkosher foods.) Peter was afraid of the rigorist party who taught the extra-Torah rule of not eating with gentiles, even though he knew Jesus had clearly set the opposite example. There is no sign that Jesus ever broke kosher, but clear proof that he broke with the rigorists and shared his table with all sorts of people considered unclean. In other words, the problem was not the menu but the men, not the food but the company.

But what about Paul's accusation that Peter was living like a gentile? James Dunn says this is Jewish hyperbole, a common thing in intra-Jewish polemics, where Torah-observant Jews accuse less rigorous cohorts of not being "true Jews" or of being "like gentiles."[31] David Rudolph suggests that Paul is echoing the stricter Pharisees from Jerusalem (probably from the Shammai school) who accused Peter of living like a gentile because he ate *with gentiles*.[32] James Crossley goes further: "Paul is not urging Peter to join him again in a 'non-Jewish way of life' but rather he urges 'for a Jewish life which does not force gentiles to Judaize.'"[33]

We have good evidence that Peter did not break kosher laws in the very story that is usually taken as proof that he did indeed break them: his vision of the unclean animals being lowered on a sheet where he was told to "get up, kill, and eat" (Acts 10:9–16). You may recall that Peter's response, repeated twice in Acts 10–11, was, "By no means, Lord! I have never eaten anything that is profane or unclean" (10:14). Peter of course was referring to the laws of *kashrut*, prescribed for all Jews by Torah.

Note the problem here for the traditional interpretation. Here Peter was protesting—some years *after* Jesus had supposedly dispensed with kosher law—that he would never set aside kosher rules. If Jesus had invalidated kosher rules, why was Peter still saying some years later that he would never break any kosher rules? It is because of this and other problems for the traditional interpretation that such distinguished scholars as Dunn, Bauckham, and Bockmuehl have challenged the traditional interpretation that Jesus and the early church threw out Jewish law for Jews.[34]

30. For evidence that Jews ate with gentiles, see David Rudolph, *A Jew to the Jews: Jewish Contours of Pauline Flexibility in 1 Corinthians 9:19–23* (Tübingen: Mohr Siebeck, 2011), 127–30.

31. James D. G. Dunn, *The Epistle to the Galatians*, Black's New Testament Commentary (Peabody, Mass.: Hendrickson, 1993), 127–28.

32. Rudolph, *A Jew to the Jews*, 51.

33. James Crossley, *The Date of Mark's Gospel: Insights from the Law in Earliest Christianity* (London: T&T Clark, 2004), 152.

34. James D. G. Dunn, *Jesus, Paul, and the Law* (Louisville: Westminster John Knox, 1990), 51;

What about Paul? Professor Wilken informs us that Jerome criticized Paul for being inconsistent, that is, declaring in some venues that the law, especially concerning circumcision, was no longer applicable to Jesus followers, while observing that very law in other venues. As Professor Wilken records, Paul circumcised Timothy (his mother was Jewish), took a temporary Nazirite vow defined by Torah, and followed James's advice in Acts 21 to prove that he was still teaching Jews out on the mission field in Asia Minor to circumcise their children.

Now, if Jerome and many interpreters are right—that Paul didn't believe in these things but did them in order to satisfy certain Jews—then we have another problem. Paul was being disingenuous. But is that consistent with everything else we know about the apostle? The apostle who insisted to the Corinthians that he behaved in the world "with simplicity and godly sincerity, not by earthly wisdom," and who asked rhetorically, "Was I vacillating ... ready to say 'Yes, yes' and 'No, no' at the same time?" (2 Cor 1:12, 17). To the Thessalonians he averred that his "appeal does not spring from deceit or trickery" (1 Thes 2:13). Was this double behavior—appearing to be one thing with Jews and something else with gentiles—not deceitful? Was this in character with everything else we know about Paul? And were Jews so clueless as not to recognize this deceit?

The reason that most traditional interpreters like Jerome have thought Paul was inconsistent has been his vituperative language to the Galatians: "Every man who accepts circumcision ... [is] severed from Christ!" (Gal 5:3–4). John G. Gager has contended that Galatians has been misunderstood because its audience has been misunderstood. In reality, he says, Paul was addressing only gentiles in this letter, and his purpose was to explain the relation of law to gentiles—which for Paul means not at all. "The Gentiles [in Galatia were] ... being pressured by other apostles, within the Jesus-movement, to take on circumcision and a selective observance of the law." So Paul explained that "the law was never the intended path for Gentiles." Gager reasons that Galatians is addressed only to gentiles because "the descriptions of the circumstances of the Galatians before Christ can only apply to Gentiles: 'we were slaves to the elemental spirits of the universe' [4:3]; 'you did not know God' (v. 8); and 'you were in bondage to beings that by nature are no gods' (v. 8)." Even the phrase "those who were under the law"

Richard Bauckham, *The Book of Acts in Its Palestinian Setting* (Grand Rapids: Eerdmans, 1995), 464–75; Markus Bockmuehl, *Jewish Law in Gentile Churches* (Edinburgh: T&T Clark, 2000), 3–15.

refers to gentiles who had been pressured by the Judaizers to take on the yoke of the law. But this phrase "is not a characteristic phrase in Jewish texts for describing the relationship of the law and Jews." So the Paul of Galatians can be reconciled with the Paul of Romans. Galatians tells gentiles that the law is not for them, while Romans insists that the law for Jews is "holy and righteous and good" (7:12). The two are compatible because the legal and ceremonial rules of the Pentateuch (Torah) are for Jews, not gentiles.[35]

Gager might go too far. Paul's words in Galatians 2 ("We ourselves are Jews by birth"; 2:15) suggest that there were *some* Jews in his audience at Galatia. Besides, the idea of angelic mediation of the law can be found in at least one Jewish source (Testament of Dan 6.2), and the notion that Jews could be under the elemental spirits of the universe has been found in Jewish apocalyptic literature.

But it does seem that gentiles were in the majority at Galatia. No Jew would say to his fellow Jews in the first century that before they knew the Messiah, "You did not know God" (4:8). Nor would they question if the law (which in Galatians probably means the legal parts of Torah as opposed to other parts such as Genesis) was opposed to God's promises, as Paul does in Galatians 3:21. Observant Jews believed there was perfect harmony between the legal and nonlegal parts of Torah. They might not have been able to explain that harmony, but they would refuse to countenance the possibility that God was incoherent in his revelation. Furthermore, if the church in Galatia was primarily Jewish, Paul would never have to say, "If you belong to messiah, then you are the seed of Abraham" (3:29). Jews *knew* they were the seed of Abraham already.

So even if there were Jews at Galatia too, it seems that gentiles were Paul's primary addressees. This lends supports to the thesis that when Paul says in Galatians that circumcision is no longer required (5:2–6; 6:12–15), he is reminding gentiles of what Torah and Judaism had always said.

Thus Paul was not dispensing with Torah (the law). Neither was he starting a new religion that would reject the law. As Pauline specialist Frank Thielman has put it, "Paul's talk of his 'former manner of life in Judaism' in Gal. 1:13–14 (cf. Phil. 3:4–11) should no longer be regarded as a statement about Paul's flight from Judaism to a new religion, but as an indication of a switch, in light of his experience with Christ, from one Jewish way of looking at the law to another."[36]

35. John G. Gager, *Reinventing Paul* (New York: Oxford University Press, 2000), 86, 89, 91.

36. Frank Thielman, *From Plight to Solution: A Jewish Framework for Understanding Paul's View of the*

There are many other signs that Paul respected the law: he circumcised Timothy, made and kept a Nazirite vow, and participated in another Nazirite vow (Acts 16:1–3; 18:18; 21:21–24). In the last vow Paul proved to "James, and all the elders" of the Jerusalem church, who seemed pleased that "thousands … among the Jews … who have believed" were "zealous for the law," that he himself was "liv[ing] in observance of the law" (Acts 21:18, 20, 24). Luke goes out of his way in Acts to show that Paul was *not* "teach[ing] all the Jews who are among the Gentiles to forsake Moses, telling them not to circumcise their children or walk according to *our customs*" (Acts 21:21). By "our customs" James surely meant kosher laws, Sabbath keeping, and circumcision—and probably other Jewish-specific customs. In Romans, Paul claims that God's purpose in sending Jesus was for "the righteous requirement of the law" to be fulfilled in Jesus's disciples (Rom 8:4).

In one respect, Paul was even more Jewish than Jesus: he took a more positive approach to Pharisees than we see in the Gospels. He proudly presented himself as a Pharisee (Acts 23:6), and Luke reports that Pharisees came to Paul's defense (Acts 23:9). Throughout Acts 21–26, Paul "affirms his identity as a Torah-observant Jew, indeed, a Pharisee, and one not guilty of breaching the Torah or desecrating the Temple."[37] The great Catholic Bible scholar Raymond Brown speculated that if Paul had had a son, he would have circumcised him. Michael Wyschogrod wondered, "Could it be that Paul was, after all, an Orthodox Jew?"[38]

We have looked at Peter and Paul, and argued that they accepted the continuing applicability of the legal aspects of Torah for Jewish disciples of Yeshua, but not for gentile disciples. But did Augustine, as Professor Wilken points out, pull out the trump card by citing Jesus's teaching that what enters one's mouth can never make a person unclean? Did that not mean that Jesus himself dispensed with Mosaic law as represented by the food laws

Law in Galatians and Romans (Eugene, Ore.: Wipf and Stock, 2007), 119. Thielman does not distinguish as I do between Jews and gentiles in Paul's thinking about the applicability of the law, but he agrees that "Paul did not regard Christ and Torah as mutually exclusive but as complementary."

37. Mark Nanos, "The Myth of the 'Law-Free' Paul Standing between Christians and Jews," Mark Nanos personal website, December 10, 2008, http://www.marknanos.com/Myth-Lawfree-12-3-08.pdf (p. 6 on the paginated PDF). See also Nanos, "Paul and the Jewish Tradition: The Ideology of the Shema," in *Celebrating Paul: Festschrift in Honor of J. A. Fitzmyer and J. Murphy-O'Connor*, ed. Peter Spitaler (Washington, D.C.: Catholic Biblical Association of America, 2009), 62–80; Nanos, "Rethinking the 'Paul *and* Judaism' Paradigm: Why Not 'Paul's *Judaism*'?" Mark Nanos personal website, May 28, 2008, http://www.marknanos.com/Paul%27sJudaism-5-28-08.pdf.

38. Michael Wyschogrod, "The Impact of Dialogue with Christianity on My Self-Understanding as a Jew," in *Abraham's Promise: Judaism and Jewish-Christian Relations*, ed. R. Kendall Soulen (Grand Rapids: Eerdmans, 2004), 232–34.

in kosher? Is that what Jesus meant when Mark says in his version of this pericope, "Thus [Jesus] declared that all foods are clean" (7:19)?

Let's go to the actual text of Mk 7 to get a full sense of what precedes this declaration in verse 19. I will render the Greek in wooden fashion, word by word, to get us closer to the actual text.

And the Pharisees and some of the scribes came to him from Jerusalem. And having seen some of his disciples that with defiled [lit. "common"] hands, that is unwashed, they ate their loaves of bread—for the Pharisees and all the Judeans [this is usually translated "Jews" but here the word clearly means those who came from Jerusalem, the capital of Judea; the word literally *is* Ἰουδαῖοι] unless they with a fist wash their hands do not eat—holding fast to the tradition of the elders, and from the market unless they baptize themselves they do not eat, and there are many other things that they have received [from their tradition] to hold fast to, [such as] baptizing cups and pots and copper vessels. (Mk 7:1–4)

It is important to note that Mark places his focus not on Torah but on "the tradition of the elders" about handwashing and washing cups and pots. These elders and Pharisees came from Jerusalem in Judea. They have come to Galilee, where Jesus and his disciples are. The Galileans had been suspicious of the Judeans for centuries by this time, in fact since the Babylonian exile in the sixth century BC, when the exiles returned to Jerusalem and surrounding Judea with new traditions they had developed in Babylon. The Galileans rejected these new traditions as innovations unwarranted by the text of Torah.[39]

Notice too that the focus is *not* on kosher, which is clearly commanded by Torah in Leviticus 11 and Deuteronomy 14. The issue is not eating kosher food but eating with unwashed hands. The first *is* commanded by Torah, and the second is not.

By the way, the word πυγμῇ, or "fist," indicates that Mark was thoroughly familiar with Pharisaic tradition. For this school of Pharisees in fact poured water over a loose *fist*. Talmudic scholar Daniel Boyarin observes, "This suggests strongly that [Mark's] perspective (as well as that of Jesus) is firmly from within the Jewish world—nearly the opposite of what has been usually said of Mark."[40]

39. Daniel Boyarin, *The Jewish Gospels: The Story of the Jewish Christ* (New York: New Press, 2012), 117.
40. Boyarin, *Jewish Gospels*, 117.

And the Pharisees and the scribes asked him, "Why do your disciples not walk according to the tradition of the elders, but with defiled hands eat the bread?" He said to them, "Well did Isaiah prophesy about you hypocrites, as it is written that 'This people with their lips honors me, but with their heart they hold off from me far away. In vain do they worship me, teaching as teachings commandments of men.' Laying aside the commandment of God, you hold fast the tradition of men." (Mk 7:5–8)

There are several other interesting things: In verse 6, Jesus contrasts lips to heart, and in verses 7–8 he contrasts the commandments of men to the commandment of God. In the first contrast, he is emphasizing something in the *inner* man rather than outward action, and in the second contrast he distinguishes precepts of *men* from precepts of God.

What does Jesus mean here by "the commandments of men"? He makes it very clear: not kosher rules but handwashing and "baptisms" (washing) cups and pots and bronze vessels.

And he said to them, "Well do you set aside the commandment of God, so that your own tradition you can keep. For Moses said, 'Honor your father and your mother,' and, 'He who [continually] reviles his father and mother shall be put to death.' But you say, 'If a man says to his father or to his mother, Korban [a Hebrew word for "offering"], that is, Gift, whatever you would have gotten from me,' you no longer permit him to do anything for his father or mother, rendering void the word of God for your tradition which you have delivered. And many similar things you do. (Mk 7:9–13)

We might notice some other intriguing things at odds with the traditional interpretation. Jesus speaks approvingly of Moses and quotes from Mosaic law. The issue for Jesus here is not food but (1) obeying Mosaic law, (2) honoring one's parents, and (3) keeping to Torah ("the word of God") rather than these Pharisaic traditions. The contrast is not between "mere" ritual and "moral" commandments, but between what is in Torah—explicitly said here to be Moses's law—and what is newly delivered by the traditions of men (Pharisees).

My penultimate conclusions are that (1) the focus of this text is handwashing not food and (2) the contrast is between the law of Moses on the one hand and traditions of men that depart from Mosaic law on the other.

But there is still more in this critical passage, and it too supports this new interpretation that is gathering support from scholars.

And calling to himself again the crowd, he said to them, Listen to me, all, and understand. There is nothing from the outside of the person that going into him is able to defile him. But things going out of a person are what defile the person. (Mk 7:14–15)

Some ancient texts include a verse here: "If someone has ears to hear, let him hear" (v. 16).

And when he entered the house, away from the crowd, his disciples were asking him about the parable. And he said to them, "Are you also without understanding?" Don't you realize that everything from the outside going into the person is not able to defile him? That it does not go into him, into the heart but into the stomach, and then goes out into the latrine? *Cleansing all foods*?" (Mk 7:17–19)

There are several things to notice here. First, Jesus makes two distinctions: outside versus inside, and stomach versus heart. He is concerned with what defiles a person on the inside, in his heart. It is clear that Jesus does not think food defiles a person in his heart. His focus in the whole passage is on handwashing, and here he does not refer to kosher rules that were about permitted and unpermitted foods. In fact, his defense of Mosaic law just a few sentences before suggests that he would never abrogate Moses. His only point here is that no food, presumably even that which is not permitted by kosher laws, can defile a person in his heart.

That suggestion—that food itself can defile a person in his heart or in an inner spiritual way—is what the Pharisees presumed by their innovation of handwashing. Jesus is not saying that unpermitted foods are suddenly permitted for Jews, merely that foods in and of themselves do not make a person unclean in his heart. In other words, there is a difference between ritual impurity and spiritual impurity. The kosher laws are about the former and not the latter. Jesus knew this, most Jews knew it then, and most all observant Jews know it today. That is what Torah already presumed. So Jesus is not overturning Torah, which clearly forbids certain foods to Jews, but merely defending it against a new rule with an implication about food itself that is foreign to Torah.

Besides, Mark's audience was undoubtedly gentile, and the last words from Jesus's mouth above, which I emphasized, were meant for gentiles: all foods are cleansed for gentiles because Torah's food laws are not meant for gentiles anyway.

How do we know Mark's audience was largely gentile? He translates seven Aramaic words into Greek to help his Greek (gentile) audience. A

Jewish audience would have understood the Aramaic, which is very close to Hebrew.[41] So, as David Rudolph has argued, the meaning of Jesus's cryptic words in Mk 7:19 is that all foods are clean for gentiles. Rudolph thinks Mark quoted Jesus in 7:19 because the early church was still wondering by this time (between AD 64 and 75) if it was true that gentiles did not have to keep kosher. The Jerusalem council (about 49) never quoted Jesus for support. So perhaps both Jews and gentiles wondered if it was right, and if Paul was right when he wrote in Romans (probably written 55–57) nearly the same words in Greek in Rom 14:14: πάντα βρώματα μὲν καθαρά (all foods are clean). Paul was addressing the same issue—differences in eating between Jews and gentiles.[42]

Rudolph argues that Mark recalled Jesus's using nearly these same words in order to reassure gentiles that kosher commandments did not apply to them—even if they were still required of all Jews, even Jesus-believing Jews.[43]

Whether or not Rudolph gets the context and rationale quite right, there is another interpretation of those last words ("cleansing all foods") that would also support this newish interpretation. (I say newish because a growing number of scholars are rejecting the traditional view.) First of all, notice that the Greek text does not contain the words that most translations use, "Thus Jesus declared." These words are added by translators in order to bring out what they consider to be the meaning. The absence of these words in the Greek, and the presence of the simple phrase "cleansing all foods," might mean that what Jesus is saying is this: "The fact that all food goes into the stomach and not the heart and then gets digested and travels out of the body into the toilet and sewer proves that food itself does not change the person in any permanent way." For food comes in and then goes out, and the person remains the same spiritually. Perhaps Jesus is saying, "Look at the biological facts: the person is not changed in his heart by the food. Only sins can change the *heart,* which apart from grace means permanent defilement." He goes on to say in verses 20–23 exactly what sins *can* change the heart, and thus permanently change the person, apart from the forgiveness and spiritual cleansing of God.

Hence we see, once again, further evidence that for the early church

41. David Rudolph pointed this out in his groundbreaking article, "Jesus and the Food Laws," *Evangelical Quarterly* 74, no. 4 (2002): 291–311.

42. Rudolph, "Jesus and the Food Laws."

43. Rudolph, "Jesus and the Food Laws."

kosher laws were still applicable to Jesus-believing Jews but not to gentiles. They are about what is permitted and not permitted for Jews to eat. They are about ritual impurity not spiritual impurity. Food passes in and out of the body and so does not change the person permanently. Only sin can do that. Jesus was not overturning Mosaic law on foods for Jews. He was simply drawing a distinction between Jews and gentiles, and between ritual impurity and spiritual impurity.

The great Jewish scholar of Jesus at the Hebrew University in Jerusalem, David Flusser, once wrote: "What Jesus said [in Mk 7:19], thus, has nothing to do with a supposed abrogation of Judaic law, but is part of a criticism directed at the Pharisees. . . . Jesus had no desire to oppose the law of Moses. He only wanted to expose the rigidity of the bigots."[44]

So what does all this matter? It has large implications. One of the most important is the light it sheds on the character and meaning of the Jesus movement of the first century. If all this is true, it means that Jesus and the early church were even more Jewish in background and orientation than most of us thought. The connections between the church and Judaism persist today in ways that have escaped most of us in the church. It also means that Jesus and Paul and the other movement leaders were not starting a new religion that broke in fundamental ways with Judaism. It also meant that Jewish-gentile differences remained in the church, and this was not considered a bad thing. On the contrary, it pointed to the fundamental unity that Messiah brought, a unity that did not eliminate differences.

It will be objected immediately that this suggestion of persisting Jew-gentile differences violates the unity of the church so powerfully proclaimed by Paul in Ephesians 2 ("The Messiah himself is our peace, who has made one both Jew and gentile, and has broken down in his flesh the dividing wall of hostility," v. 14) and in Galatians 3:28 ("There is neither Jew nor Greek, there is neither slave nor free, neither male nor female, for you are all one in messiah Jesus"). But continuing distinctions between Jews and gentiles need violate that unity in Messiah no more than do continuing distinctions between men and women, which Paul clearly articulates for both home and church. And what about the distinctions he articulates between marrieds and singles in 1 Corinthians 7? They are all one in Christ—men and women, marrieds and singles, Jews and gentiles—and that oneness is not broken but instead made more impressive by their distinctive ways of

44. David Flusser, *Jesus* (Jerusalem: Magnes Press, 2001), 60, 62.

following Jesus. There is diversity in unity, just as in the Trinity. Unity in God, diversity in persons and roles.

This is not the place to discuss how this works practically. It is enough to recognize that for Jesus and the apostles, Jews and gentiles were to *continue* to worship and serve the God of Israel through his Messiah by the Spirit in different ways.

CHAPTER 6

Acts 17 and Mars Hill

Fr. Andrew Louth (Orthodox)

Patristic Interpretation

The first stage in discussing the reception and interpretation of this passage would normally be to survey its reception in the Fathers. This, however, is difficult in the case of Acts, as it seems to have been overlooked by most of the early Christian writers.[1] There is an extant series of homilies by John Chrysostom and a commentary by the beacon of the so-called Northumbrian enlightenment of the seventh/eighth century, Bede of Jarrow, but these are not very enlightening for this passage; otherwise there are occasional references, not least to this passage, in Clement of Alexandria. The story of the apostle Paul's sermon to the Athenian judges of the Areopagos on Mars Hill is fairly straightforward. Paul is in Athens, waiting for the arrival of Silas and Timothy. He is provoked by the multitude of gods worshiped there by the pagans. His initial discussion of this takes place in the synagogue among the Jews, but he meets Greek philosophers, Epicureans and Stoics, who wonder about the novelty of his teaching, which they take to be the preaching of Jesus and the resurrection, *Anastasia*, a feminine word that could well be the name of a goddess: this is how Chrysostom took their assertion that Paul is a "preacher of foreign gods, or δαίμονες." In the speech in his defense before the court of the Areopagos, Paul takes as his starting point an altar inscribed Ἀγνώστῳ Θεῷ, "to an unknown god." Again, Chrysostom confirms what this has been generally taken to mean for the Athenians themselves: in a passage of Chrysostom's preserved in the catena it is said, "They erected an altar and inscribed it with the words,

1. For the patristic discussion of this passage I have relied, shamelessly, on the relevant volume, *Acts*, in the Ancient Christian Commentary on Scripture: New Testament 5, ed. Francis Martin in collaboration with Evan Smith (Downers Grove, Ill.: InterVarsity Press, 2006), 214–22.

'to an unknown god' in order to signify through the inscription: If by any chance there is another god who is still unknown to us, we will worship him too." Clement, discussing this passage in *Stromateis* 5, advances a more interesting interpretation, which we shall come back to later. Paul himself takes the inscription as a cue to proclaim to the Athenians the God whom they do not know, God the creator of the world, a transcendent God who does not live in temples made by human hands, nor does he need anything from human beings, but is rather the source of "life and breath and everything." The whole human race has been constituted by him from a single source (ἐξ ἑνὸς), ruled by his providence, in order to seek God that they might "feel after him and find him": Something made possible for this transcendent creator God is immanent, "not far from each of us," something Paul confirms by quoting two pagan sources: Ps.-Epimenides, "for in him we live and move and are," and the poet Aratus, "for we are indeed his offspring." Taking off from this second citation, Paul affirms that if we are indeed God's offspring, then we cannot demean him by treating him as our offspring, depicting him by using our art and imagination (τέχνης καὶ ἐνθυμήσεως ἀνθρώπου), using gold or silver or stone, which Ammonios, in a passage preserved in the catena, interprets to mean that God is beyond any human conception. From this Paul moves on to saying that the times of ignorance are past, and that all are now called to repentance, before we are judged by the appointed one whom God has raised from the dead. At the mention of resurrection, there is mocking, though others speak of hearing him again. There are then mentioned a few who believed, including Dionysios the Areopagite and a woman called Damaris.

As it stands, it is an episode presented as an interlude in Paul's travels, preaching the gospel, mostly in synagogues, between leaving Silas and Timothy and going on to Corinth, where he meets up with a Jew, Aquila, and his wife, Priscilla, lately come from Rome, after the Emperor Claudius's expulsion of the Jews from the city. As it stands, not much attention is drawn to it by the author of Acts. Nevertheless, there are aspects of the story that beg for closer attention, though, again, we have the impression from its patristic reception that these aspects are scarcely noticed. For the conception of God presented by the apostle Paul is *philosophically* interesting: this "unknown God" is the transcendent Creator who is also immanent within the cosmos he has created; furthermore there are hints, taken up by one or other of the Fathers, that this God is beyond any human conception—Ammonios puts it by saying that Paul "teaches that the human mind cannot comprehend God as he is by nature," still less depict him by human art or imagination.

In *Stromateis* 5, already referred to, Clement develops this hint of God's ineffability, suggested by the inscription on the altar, ἀγνώστῳ θεῷ, which he takes to mean not a god, unknown because overlooked, but God, unknown by nature. *Stromateis* 5.12 begins with two well-known quotations from the "truth-loving Plato" run together: the first from the *Timaeus*, "To find the father and maker of this universe is a task indeed and, having discovered him, to declare it to all impossible";[2] the second from the seventh letter, "for in no way is there utterance [of it] as in other branches of learning," a sentence that goes on to say that "as a result of being greatly occupied with it and living with it, of a sudden [ἐξαίφνης] it comes upon the soul, as it were like light kindled from a leaping spark, and thereafter it nourishes itself."[3] These two citations, both favorites of Clement, are perhaps the strongest assertions of the hiddenness and unknowability of God, for, by Clement's time, Platonists would have regarded these passages as referring to God, whatever Plato himself thought (for him, ostensibly at least, the fashioner of the universe in the *Timaeus*, the δημιουργός, is a mythical figure, and what qualifies for Plato as divine is a matter for discussion). Clement continues by evoking other seekers after God, who discover that he is beyond human comprehension. First, Moses ascending Mount Sinai and entering into the "darkness, where God was," indicating that God is invisible and ineffable. Then Orpheus, who says "clearly" that "he sees him not." Then Paul, caught up to the third heaven, where "he heard ineffable words, of which it is not permitted for man to speak." Then back to Plato. Then on to Clement of Rome, who speaks of an "ocean illimitable by humans." Our Alexandrian Clement continues with example after example, drawn from the Old and New Testaments, including the Savior's speaking to his apostles ἐν μυστηρίῳ, and in parables. There follow quotations from Solon and Empedocles (the "Agrigentan") and the apostle John: "No one has seen God at any time; the only-begotten God, who is in the bosom of the Father, has made him known" (Jn 1:18). So Clement continues, piling citation upon citation denying knowledge of God, and closing with: "It is left to divine grace and the word alone that comes from him to know the unknowable, as Luke records Paul saying in the Acts of the Apostles," and then goes on

2. Plato, *Tim.* 28C.
3. Plato, *Ep.* 7.341C.

to quote the passage we have already discussed about the altar to the unknown God, concluding, "the one whom you worship in ignorance, this one I proclaim to you." Clement is often claimed to be the father, or at least the Christian godfather, of apophatic theology, the theology of negation; this passage is central to such a claim. According to such a theology, God is unknowable, beyond any human affirmation, better characterized by confessions of human ignorance, by denial of any attributes applied to him, but also one who is revealed in a way beyond human devising, of a sudden—ἐξαίφνης, conveying, I think, immediacy in both senses, not only temporal (that is, sudden) but also without intermediary, that is, by presence, which could suggest, as Clement expressly puts it, the immediacy of divine grace.

Dionysios's Interpretation

The most striking, and vastly influential, interpretation of this passage from the Acts of the Apostles is, however, much more than a matter of exegesis, but involved an author finding his whole being in this passage, and expressing his whole vision of the Christian faith from this perspective. I mean, of course, the author of the *Corpus Dionysiacum*, the collection of treatises that purported to be the work of the Dionysios the Areopagite mentioned at the end of the account of Paul's speech on Mars Hill. I want to suggest, in the rest of this paper, that this is something we have only now been able to realize with full seriousness.

The bare outlines of what I am suggesting can be stated quite easily and are relatively uncontroversial. Dionysios (as I shall call him) takes his cue from Clement (in whose writings he was most likely deeply read) and his understanding of ἄγνωστος θεός as the God beyond any knowing or understanding. Like Clement, he sees this as something affirmed by both the Bible and the best of the classical tradition. This latter means especially, though not exclusively, Plato, or more to the point the developments of the Platonic tradition that we find in the later Platonists, whom modern scholars call Neoplatonists. It is Dionysios's dependence on this later tradition, especially as manifest in Proklos, the fifth-century *diadochos,* or successor of Plato at the Academy in Athens, that has made clear to scholars, beyond a cavil, that the Dionysios of the *Corpus* cannot be Dionysios the convert of St. Paul. In trying to divine what Dionysios was doing in assuming the identity of Paul's convert as he composed the Dionysian *Corpus*—four fairly short treatises and ten letters—we have to bear in mind both Dionysios's own understanding of his relationship to the first century, where he seeks to place himself, and our understanding of what was happening in the early church as it found its feet within the world of late antiquity. These different perspectives operate in different ways. Historical consciousness, as we know it, was not shared by Dionysios or any of his contemporaries: they had a foreshortened sense of the past—it was still very close, whereas we presuppose a succession of different eras, all very different from each other; as we say, in L. P. Hartley's words, "The past is a foreign country; they do things differently there." There is perhaps something unusual about Dionysios in the care with which he constructed his first-century alibi; it is as if he *had* some sense of historical distance. For Dionysios went to some care in constructing his first-century identity, and used as his guide Eusebius's *Church History*.[4] From our perspective, the emergence on the scene of history of Dionysios's corpus of writings seems uncannily providential. The first certain reference to his works occurred at the colloquy the emperor Justinian had called between the supporters of Chalcedon and its opponents in 532. Those opposed to Chalcedon cited a passage from Dionysios's fourth epistle about Christ's "theandric activity," θεανδρικὴ ἐνέργεια. Here we are not concerned with the detail of this citation, just with its date: 532, only a few years after the suppression, by Justinian, of the Platonic Academy in 529. Just as Platonism, in its institutional and religious form, was suppressed, Dionysios emerges speaking for the convergence of Christian theology and Platonic philosophy. Dionysios himself cannot have been aware of his curious timeliness, for him the convergence of Christianity and Platonism had to belong to apostolic times (a foreshortened notion of history has no space for development), so it was in the time of the apostles, the time recorded in the Acts of the Apostles, that Dionysios inserted himself: more precisely, he found this union of the Christian and Platonic visions in Paul's encounter with the philosophers of Athens at the Areopagos on Mars Hill. There he found his place in history as Paul's convert, Dionysios the Areopagite.

4. See my article "Constructing the Apostolic Past: The Case of Dionysius the Areopagite," in *The Church on Its Past*, ed. Peter D. Clarke and Charlotte Methuen, Studies in Church History 49 (Woodbridge: Boydell Press, 2013), 42–51.

I think we should see in his adoption of the Dionysios's identity a mode of interpretation of the episode from Acts 17 that goes well beyond what we normally regard as interpretation. For what the author of the *Corpus Dionysiacum* is doing is making the apostle Paul's teaching in his speech to the court of the Areopagos absolutely central to his understanding of the nature of the Christian faith: in that speech, Paul proclaimed the true God as ἄγνωστος θεός, which Dionysios takes to mean not simply an unknown, or even overlooked, god, but a God beyond any understanding or knowing, a God who is essentially *unknowable*. He does this, however, by losing himself, as it were, in Dionysios, one of the judges of Areopagitical Court who heard Paul and was converted according to the account in Acts (17:34). The author of the *Corpus Areopagiticum*, who calls himself Dionysios, *becomes* the historical Dionysios the Areopagite, one of a group of the apostle Paul's disciples, including Titus, Timothy, and Bartholomew, and also the apostle John (Dionysios is surprisingly contemporary with us, in finding a profound coinherence between the two great theologian-apostles; a sense of opposition between the two having been the ruling opinion in the last century), as well as seemingly familiar figures from the early decades of Christianity, associated with the circles around these two apostles—Gaios, Ignatios, Polycarp: these are his fellow disciples, with whom he is in correspondence, addressing to them his treatises and his letters—as well as his mentor, Hierotheos, regarded, like Dionysios, as an early bishop of Athens. The *way* Dionysios the author loses himself in Dionysios the Areopagite is not just a matter of imaginative sympathy, but something much more serious: the identity he finds with the Athenian judge is a corollary of the identity his master Paul, finds with Christ "For I live, but no longer I, but Christ lives in me" (Gal 2:20). For this is not an exclusive identity, distinguishing him from his fellow Christians, but an inclusive identity, since it is through the communion of those who are "in Christ," that we discover our true selves.

It seems to me, too, that this understanding of Dionysios as someone who exegetes himself into the apostolic age is one that has only now become open to us. It was closed to those who first encountered the *Corpus Areopagiticum*, for they quickly seem to have accepted the authenticity of these writings, ranking them with the apostolic writings, treating them as next to Scripture; the alternative, then, would have been to reject them altogether. Once Dionysios was unmasked as an impostor—something that took centuries, from Lorenzo Valla in the fifteenth century to the German scholars Hugo Koch and Josef Stiglmayr, who finally laid any doubts to rest at the end of the nineteenth—scholarship occupied itself largely with the pursuit of the "real" author, a pursuit that has led nowhere, all possible candidates satisfying hardly anyone than their proposer.[5] Alongside this pursuit, Dionysios was treated as a second-rate Neoplatonist, slavishly dependent on Proklos (or more recently on Damaskios), his theology being of only historical interest, owed to its influence. Only recently has Dionysios been taken as a Christian theologian, whose identity as the Areopagite should be regarded as a clue to where he saw the source of his vision. Perhaps the most important example of this latest turn in Dionysian studies is Charles Stang's *Apophasis and Pseudonymity in Dionysius the Areopagite: "No longer I,"*[6] which takes the pseudonym, together with the claim to be Paul's disciple, as the key to understanding the Areopagite. The pseudonym accomplishes the death of the author—"no longer I"—and the author clothes himself in Scripture, inserting himself in Acts 17, and reading his theology out of a profound grasp of the theology of the apostle Paul.

In his book, Stang develops his insight into the way Dionysios's theology is to be seen as developing out of his reading of the apostle Paul by considering the Dionysian notion of hierarchy, the idea of mystical union with an unknown, and unknowable, God, and what he calls, the "apophatic anthropology" of the Areopagite. I want to do something rather different (though I fully acknowledge the debt I owe to Stang's book) and, given the theme of this conference, reflect more generally on the implication of Dionysios's endeavor for our own attempt to understand the meaning of Scripture. First, if understanding Scripture has a central role in Christian discipleship, then it must be affected by the conviction that God is utterly unknowable: so, the first area of discussion will be concerned with grasping what is meant by understanding the revelation of the unknown God. Second, it seems to me that Dionysios's doctrine of hierarchy is, in essence, about the essentially communal nature of the Christian church, the way it is

5. Twenty-two by the time of Hathaway's monograph in 1969; since then the search has looked to people less well-known, or even completely unknown: see Beate Suchla, *Dionysius Areopagite: Leben—Werk—Wirkung* (Freiburg im Breisgau: Herder, 2008), 24–25.

6. Charles M. Stang, *Apophasis and Pseudonymity in Dionysius the Areopagite: "No longer I"* (Oxford: Oxford University Press, 2012). Christian Schäfer, in his book, *The Philosophy of Dionysius the Areopagite: An Introduction to the Structure and the Content of the Treatise "On the Divine Names"* (Leiden: Brill, 2006), also sees Dionysios's pseudonymity as the key to understanding him.

rooted in κοινωνία, a term with both profound resonances in the New Testament and in the Platonism contemporary with Dionysios. But it seems to me that beyond these lines of inquiry, there lies another, which is concerned with the role of the liturgical, which takes off from the symbolism provided by the Scriptures, understood less as a quarry for arguments to support our theological notions (something, we shall see, heavily called into question by Dionysios's sense of the centrality of the unknowability but more as a treasury of imagery and symbolism to lift our hearts to union with God—"non plus seulement comme un arsenal, mais comme un trésor," no longer simply as an arsenal, but as a treasury).[7]

Dionysios and the Unknown God

Dionysios makes the apostle Paul's preaching of the "unknown God" to the judges of the court of the Areopagos central to his understanding of Paul, and therefore of the Christian gospel. According to the criteria of current New Testament scholarship, this would certainly be regarded as methodologically unusual, or even improper: Paul is to be interpreted primarily from his own writings and not from the picture of Paul provided by St. Luke in his Acts of the apostles. From an older perspective, there is nothing strange about Dionysios's approach here: For the New Testament writings are regarded as inspired, so that Luke's perspective on Paul cannot be regarded as a purely human one, but inspired by the same Holy Spirit who inspired the apostle. Furthermore, Stang has shown how Dionysios's reading of St. Paul, though privileging his speech on the Areopagos, can be seen as arising from Dionysios's (admittedly Neoplatonic) reading of the writings of the apostle. Indeed, the Pauline corpus seems shot through with a profound conviction of God's unknowability and ineffability. Paul's discussion of the relationship of Israel and the church in Romans 9–11 closes with his exclamation: "O the depth of the riches of both the wisdom and knowledge of God! How unsearchable his judgments and his ways past finding out!" (Rom 11:33). Ἀνεξερεύνητος and ἀνεξιχνίαστος are both words that occur several times in the *Corpus Areopagiticum*. Paul's hymn to love in 1 Corinthians closes with his saying, "For now we see through a mirror in puzzling fashion, then we shall see face to face. Now I know in part, then

7. Paul Claudel, "Du sens figuré de l'Écriture," in *Œuvres Complètes de Paul Claudel*, vol. 21, *Commentaires et exegeses* (Paris: Gallimard, 1963), 11. The whole page, indeed the whole article, is worth pondering.

I shall know even as I am known" (1 Cor 13:12); again we find here themes that Dionysios is to pick up as he reflects on our knowledge of God. Paul's account of his own (though presented indirectly: "I know a man in Christ") mystical rapture in 2 Corinthians 12 very much preoccupied the Fathers, not least Dionysios. There are many other passages where Paul gestures toward the overwhelming richness and mystery of God: For example, the exordia of Ephesians (Eph 1:3–14) and Colossians (1:3–23), the latter of which is epitomized a few verses later in the words, "the mystery, hidden from the ages and generations, now made manifest to his saints, to whom God willed to make known what is the richness of the glory of this mystery among the nations, which is God in us, the hope of glory" (Col 1:26–27). In Dionysios's grasp of the Pauline gospel, starting from his proclamation of the ἄγνωστος θεός of his Athenian speech, passages like these assume a central significance. There seem to me to be two points worth dwelling on: first, Dionysios's understanding of the revelation of the unknown God, and second, closely related, his understanding of the notion of mystery.

In the past it has not been sufficiently noticed how central Scripture is to Dionysios's understanding of, in particular, his signature doctrine of apophatic and kataphatic theology. It has been too often presented as simply a logical doctrine, or procedure, concerning the attribution of qualities to God—a logical doctrine of simply universal application. It may well be that the principles Dionysios develops seem to be principles that could be applied to any discourse whatever about God, but for Dionysios it applies explicitly to the names of God revealed in Scripture. It is certainly true that the lists of names of God owes something—a good deal—to the categories of Neoplatonic metaphysics, but according to Dionysios's explicit intention these names are revealed in the Scriptures. It is worth commenting that in more recent scholarship on the Areopagite the scriptural basis of Dionysios's doctrine of the divine names has been taken more seriously.[8] For Dionysios, Scripture is God's revelation, at the center of which is God's revelation in the incarnation. It is, however, a revelation of the unknowable God, so that God remains unknowable, even as he makes himself known. Dionysios discusses this in his short *Epistula* 3, where he explains to the monk Gaios the meaning of the word ἐξαίφνης ("sudden," "immediate," see above). The word is used by Dionysios in *Celestial Hierarchy* 15.2 in his ac-

8. See Schäfer, *Philosophy*, 89–111, esp. 100–111, and Rorem's comment in his foreword to Schäfer's book: xv–xvi.

count of the significance of the fiery nature of the seraphim.[9] Dionysios's explanation of the term refers it to the incarnation, which supports Alexander Golitzin's insistence that Dionysios is referring to Malachi 3:1 ("the Lord whom you seek will suddenly come to his temple"), though that does not exclude a further reference to Plato's *Epistula* 7:[10]

> "Sudden" is that which, against hope, is brought out of the unmanifest into the manifest. Concerning [God's] love for human kind according to Christ, I think this way of speaking of God suggests the procession from the hidden of that which is beyond being in his manifestation among us by assuming being in human form. It is hidden however after the manifestation or, to speak more divinely, in the manifestation. For this of Jesus has been hidden, and the mystery concerning him can be expressed neither rationally nor intellectually, but even when spoken remains ineffable and when understood unknown.[11]

So, even in the incarnation of the Word of God, Christ is hidden in his manifestation; what is revealed cannot be expressed: the mystery "when spoken remains ineffable and when understood unknown."

What then is meant by revelation and how do we come to understand it? Dionysios's doctrine of apophatic and kataphatic theology is intended to take us beyond anything we might make of revelation through concepts and ideas. To speak of "revealed truths," as is customary, is to misunderstand the nature of revelation. It is not as if the Scriptures reveal a collection of truths that can form, as it were, premises for our developing a supposedly objective understanding of God's nature and his relationship to the world. Any "revealed truths" are quite provisional, and intended as stepping stones to take us more deeply in the mystery of God revealed in Christ, or, more commonly, to prevent us from imposing on the mystery of God our own misconceptions, which thereby prevent us from engaging truly with the mystery of God in Christ. The whole history of doctrinal formulation is to be considered not as adumbrating some kind of Christian metaphysic

9. *Corpus Dionysiacum*, vol. 2, *De coelesti hierarchia, De ecclesiastica hierarchia, De mystica theologia, Epistulae*, ed. Günter Heil and Adolf Martin Ritter, Patristische Texte und Studien 67 (Berlin: de Gruyter, 2012), 53.1.

10. See Alexander Golitzin, "Revisiting the 'Sudden': Epistle III in the Corpus Dionysiacum," *Studia Patristica* 37 (2001): 482–91; Golitzin also discusses this in his *Et Introibo ad Altare Dei: The Mystagogy of Dionysius Areopagita, with Special Reference to Its Predecessors in the Eastern Christian Tradition*, Analekta Vlatadon 59 (Thessaloniki: Patriarchal Foundation of Patristic Studies, 1994), 222–29, and his reworking of this in his *Mystagogy: A Monastic Reading of Dionysius Areopagita*, Cistercian Studies 250 (Collegeville, Minn.: Liturgical Press, 2013), 298–99.

11. Plato, *Ep.* 341C, Heil and Ritter, 159.3–10.

that enshrines a true understanding of God and his nature, but rather as pointing out various errors that hinder our engagement with the mystery of God in Christ. The term "mystery" is central. One might recall the distinction made by Gabriel Marcel and other thinkers of the last century between mystery and problem:

> A problem is something met with that bars my passage. It is before me in its entirety. A mystery, on the other hand, is something in which I find myself caught up, and whose essence is therefore not to be before me in its entirety. It is as though in this province the distinction between *in me* and *before me* loses its meaning.[12]

A problem is something that we solve, and thereby it ceases to be a problem: a mystery is something into which we enter; it engages us; we do not pass beyond it. For Dionysios, revelation is the manifestation of a mystery, not the solution of problems, however deep they may be. Christian revelation in Scripture is the manifestation of the mystery of Christ; there is no resolution, only the continuing engagement with Christ, the way of discipleship.

Dionysios and Hierarchy

The second point I want to explore concerns Dionysios's doctrine of hierarchy, which I shall argue is rooted in the notion of κοινωνία, communion, as fundamental to the nature of the church. Dionysios's notion of hierarchy is persistently misunderstood. A good example of how to misunderstand the Dionysian notion of hierarchy is to be found in what I suspect is one of the earliest attempts in English to give a balanced account of the Dionysian vision: an essay by Bishop B. F. Westcott, first published in the *Contemporary Review* in 1883, and republished in his collection *Essays in the History of Religious Thought in the West,* in 1903, by which time he was bishop of Durham.[13] Westcott was primarily a New Testament scholar, though in an older mold when biblical scholars were expected to draw on the Fathers in their interpretation of the Scriptures. Westcott's approach to Dionysios is ambivalent: he is not altogether negative in his assessment of him, though he is clearly not attracted to him. He characterizes Dionysios's style as "mo-

12. Gabriel Marcel, *Being and Having* (London: Fontana, 1965), 109.

13. B. F. Westcott's essay, "Dionysius the Areopagite" can be found in *Essays in the History of Religious Thought in the West* (London: Macmillan, 1903), 142–93, along with studies of Plato, Aeschylus, Euripides, Origen, Browning, and Whichcote, and a couple of thematic essays.

notonously turgid. The sentences are cumbrous and involved; the words are frequently uncouth and barbarous." He speaks of his "wearisome iteration." Nevertheless, he asserts that "greater familiarity with the works reveals in them a real earnestness of purpose and many great thoughts," and he goes on to speak of the "generous and loving spirit in which he engaged in his work."[14] It is not our business here to provide an account, however brief, of Westcott's treatment of Dionysios, though this ambivalence should be noted, for it means that any criticism of Westcott is likely to find that Westcott has already noticed the point raised by the critic. And so it is with hierarchy, which concerns us here. He begins his account of hierarchy, which he rightly sees as central to the Dionysian vision, by saying that "the word 'Hierarchy' which expressed the Divine law of subordination and mutual dependence of the different ranks of beings, is one of the key-words to the whole scheme."[15] The trouble with this approach is that it introduces into a discussion of Dionysian hierarchy the modern notion of hierarchy, which is essentially concerned with rank and subordination. However, the word ἱεραρχία is a coinage of Dionysios's and would have had no prior sense of rank and subordination, as it has for us, and for Westcott. It is derived from the not-very-common classical Greek word for a high priest, ἱεράρχης, so its prior connotations are solely to do with the sacred. Dionysios defines "his" (κατ' ἐμὲ) meaning of hierarchy, which we should regard as original to him, and therefore with appropriate authority, as a sacred order and knowledge and activity, which is being assimilated to the divine likeness as much as possible and, in response to the illuminations that are given it from God, is raised to the imitation of him in its own measure.[16]

The primary purpose of hierarchy is deification, but this is achieved not by some solitary quest for the One (for all the importance that union and unification has for Dionysios), but by participation in a communion in which the celestial powers and the various orders within the church are united and, in particular, united in the celebration of sacred rites—rites performed by the whole Christian community—preeminently the Eucharist, which Dionysios calls τὸ μυστήριον συνάξεως εἴτ" οὖν κοινωνίας, the mystery of gathering together or communion.[17] Westcott recognizes the importance of what he calls "fellowship," his translation (following the nor-

14. For all these citations, see Westcott, *Essays*, 144.

15. Westcott, *Essay*, 157.

16. Dionysios, *Celestial Hierarchy* 3.1, Heil and Ritter, 17.3.

17. Dionysios, *Ecclesiastical Hierarchy* 3, Heil and Ritter, 80.8.

mal translation in the Anglican Book of Common Prayer) of κοινωνία, and indeed grasps Dionysios's conviction that the purpose of hierarchy is to lead "not indeed to a *knowledge* of the Absolute, but to a *fellowship* with it."[18]

Hierarchy and Symbolism

The way in which deification through the hierarchies takes place is largely (though not entirely) through symbolism. Dionysios's understanding of symbolism is something that he owes to Proklos, though he by no means follows him slavishly.[19] My understanding of all this has been enormously enhanced by Peter Struck's book *The Birth of the Symbol*.[20] In this book, Struck makes a distinction between what he calls the "rhetorical tradition," associated with Aristotle, and in the Latin world Horace and Quintilian, which focused on the metaphor, and saw literature, and poetry, as concerned primarily with communicating ideas to the reader, or audience, and therefore with clarity of conception, and how to communicate with the reader/audience and inspire appropriate emotions for the reception of what was being communicated: fear or pity, delight or wonder. In contrast, Struck identifies another tradition of writing and interpreting literature and poetry that sought in literature the expression of deep truths in the form of riddles or αἰνίγματα, that were veiled in a deliberate obscurity, and required patient untangling in order to yield their meaning. Struck traces this tradition from Pythagoras, through the Stoics, to the Neoplatonists. One advantage of Struck's approach is that symbolism and allegory are not presented as devices for eliciting unlikely meanings from improbable sources, as is the tendency for any literary approach that starts from the rhetorical tradition of classical and late antiquity. Rather, it is an approach to poetry and literature that values obscurity and the need for its patient unriddling, and it need hardly be said that it is a tradition that has its own place in the history of literature in many cultures, from Anglo-Saxon riddle poems, to the deliberate, veiled obscurity of the poets called "metaphysical" in English litera-

18. Westcott, *Essays*, 159. The translation of κοινωνία as "fellowship" does, however, hide one of the associations of κοινωνία for Dionysios, for it means participation, especially in the Neoplatonic sources that Dionysios draws on.

19. I made a brief attempt at exploring Dionysian symbolism and its relationship to the Neoplatonic tradition in my article "Symbolism and the Angels in Dionysios the Areopagite," *Studia Patristica* 58 (2013): 109–15, which I have drawn on in what follows.

20. Peter T. Struck, *The Birth of the Symbol: Ancient Readers at the Limits of Their Texts* (Princeton: Princeton University Press, 2004).

ture, to the Romantics, the Symbolists, and the Modernists, for all of whom difficulty, obscurity, is a necessary step to the grasp of truths beyond the trivial, and especially to truth that claims to be sacred. As Mallarmé put it: "Toute chose sacrée et qui veut demeure sacrée s'enveloppe de mystère."[21]

In his discussion of Proklos, Struck begins with a brief word about Proklos's ontology, and in particular the way in which his understanding of procession from the One bestows on matter a certain dignity, for matter, in its simplicity, participates more directly in the One than more complex beings such as plants, living beings, and even human beings. It is for this reason that, as Struck puts it, "matter now plays a pivotal role in the larger structures of the cosmos."[22] It is this that makes it possible for symbolism to provide access to divine reality: poets, through their tales and the use of symbols and divine names, sculptors and other artisans through the making of cult statues. Language-making, in the hands of the poets, is parallel to the making of cult statues: something is caught in the symbolism of the poetic language that can be traced back to the One itself, and can be a means by which lower beings are drawn up toward the higher. This focuses on the use of divine names. The way this operates, however, is not by words—the divine names—performing some kind of mimesis, imitation, but rather by words invoking the divine presence attested by the divine names. The rejection of mimesis has an important consequence, which can be seen from this passage from Proklos's commentary on the *Republic*:

> How could one call the poetry that interprets divine matters by means of symbols "imitation"? For symbols are not imitations [*mimemata*] of those things of which they are symbolic. For things could never be imitations of their opposites, the shameful of the beautiful, the unnatural of the natural. But the symbolic mode indicates the nature of things even through what is most strongly antithetical to them.[23]

Symbols can function as symbols while being quite opposite to that to which they refer. Symbols have some kind of ontological link, revealed in the divine name, and they function by being invoked, not because they resemble the reality to which they refer. The poet, then, functions as what

21. *Hérésies artistiques—"L'art pour tous,"* in Stéphane Mallarmé, *Œuvres completes*, ed. Henri Mondor and G. Jean-Aubry (Paris: Gallimard, 1945), 257.

22. Struck, *Birth of the Symbol*, 233.

23. Proklos, *In rempublicam* 1.198.13–19, in Proklos, *In rempublicam*, ed. Wilhelm Kroll (Leipzig, 1901); translation, Struck, *Birth of the Symbol*, 239.

Struck calls a "cog" in the machinery of emanation: the recitation of his poetry sets off a sort of resonance with the divine reality to which it refers and draws the one who recites or listens into a kind of communion with the divine reality referred to by the symbol. In some way, the symbol participates in that to which it refers; there is established a kind of sympathy that draws the worshiper into the divine orbit. The poet passes beyond being merely a theologian, who says something about the gods; rather his words establish a link with the gods: the poet becomes a theurgist.[24]

Even from such a bare summary, it is evident that Dionysios's understanding of symbolism is indebted to Proklos, or his tradition. The only difference seems to be that Dionysios apparently tries to keep divine names and symbols in separate compartments: the divine names are conceptual for the most past—goodness, being, life, wisdom, and so on—while the symbols are drawn from material reality. Symbols in *Celestial Hierarchy* 2 are presented as necessary props if we are to use material, sensible reality to describe the spiritual realm, whereas divine names are concepts that are used to make some sense of God, who transcends intelligible reality. But the distinction is not one that Dionysios maintains consistently: in his discussion in *Divine Names* 1.6, of how God is hymned "both as nameless and from every name," he passes seamlessly from divine names such as being, life, goodness, to a list of sensible names (or symbols) such as "sun, star, fire, water, wind, dew, cloud, rock itself and stone, all beings and none of the beings."[25] As Eric Perl points out, the metaphysical basis for his theory of symbols is the same as for his theory of divine names, for God transcends utterly both the realm of the senses and the realm of the intellect.[26] The parallel between (sensible) symbols and (intelligible) divine names is underlined by the correspondence between apophatic and kataphatic theologies (or ways of naming God) and unlike and like symbolism; in both cases the two opposites are held together and the negative form—apophatic theology and unlike symbolism—held to be more fundamentally true (or less false). So Dionysios's distinction between divine names and symbols scarcely marks him off from Proklos. To Proklos's poets correspond Diony-

24. The past few paragraphs are a rather banal summary of Struck's presentation in his chapter on Proklos: *Birth of the Symbol*, 227–53.

25. Dionysios, *Divine Names* 1.6, in *Corpus Dionysiacum*, vol. 1, *De divinis nominibus*, ed. Beate Suchla (Berlin: de Gruyter, 1990), 119.7–9.

26. Eric D. Perl, *Theophany: The Neoplatonic Philosophy of Dionysius the Areopagite* (Albany, N.Y.: State University of New York Press, 2007), chap. 7 ("Symbolism"), 101–9 passim.

sios's *theologoi*, the scriptural writers, though these are not the only people who praise God by the divine names, according to Dionysios: that is the special role of the hierarchs, not least the revered Hierotheos, and seems to be the function of any bishop when celebrating the eucharistic liturgy. Furthermore, Proklos's understanding of poetry as invocation is perfectly reflected in Dionysios's understanding of the divine names (and by extension symbols) as means by which we do not describe God (which would entail some notion of language as mimetic), so much as praise him: ὑμνεῖν. All that is true. It remains the case, however, that, although Dionysios makes effective use of Proklos's theory of language as invocation, rather than imitation, the tradition of using language as invocatory is something Dionysios inherited from within Christian practice, not something he introduced to the Christian tradition. One only need recall the opening words of the anaphora of St. John Chrysostom (which may not be Chrysostom's, but is likely to be older than Dionysios): "It is right and fitting to hymn you, to bless you, to praise you, to give you thanks, to worship you in every place of your dominion; for you are God, ineffable, incomprehensible, invisible, inconceivable, ever existing, eternally the same." My immediate point here is the affirmation of God's incomprehensibility in the anaphora of St. John Chrysostom, but I cannot help adding that the ancient anaphoras of the church have a strikingly incantatory dimension, which is often ignored by liturgical scholars.

So much for the interpretation of symbolism in Dionysios's theology, which is discussed mostly in relation to the heavenly hierarchies. But how do the hierarchies actually function in this? Hierarchy involves, as Dionysios unfolds it, a system of ranks of celestial beings ranked three by three—three ranks of three graded beings—where the threefold element expresses and effects the threefold process that leads to union with God or perfection: the process of purification, enlightenment, and union or perfection or deification. It is interesting to note that, whereas mimetic language had been set aside, in accordance with Proklos, in his discussion of unlike symbolism, here the language of mimesis once again finds a place in Dionysios's thought: hierarchy leads up ἐπὶ τὸ θεομίμητον, "to imitation of God."[27] What has happened, I think, is that the "unlike" has been incorporated in the process of purification, enlightenment, and union; purification has something of a moral dimension, but its real function is epistemological, to

27. Dionysios, *Celestial Hierarchy* 3.1, Heil and Ritter, 17.5.

prepare the created mind to receive the enlightenment that leads to union, and part of that, presumably, is recognizing the "unlike" element in symbolism, so as to interpret the symbols in the right way, that is, in the way that enables the symbols to lead one to participation in that of which they are symbols, and furthermore to acknowledge that there is no "objective" revelation in the sense of divinely guaranteed information, but rather revelation as transformative initiation. As Dionysios puts it,

> If anyone says that theophanies take place directly and immediately to certain of the holy ones, let him learn, and that clearly from the most sacred oracles, that "no one has seen," or shall see, the hiddenness itself of God as it is, and that theophanies occurred to the pious in accordance with manifestations fitting to God through certain sacred visions analogous to those who saw them. The all-wise theology naturally calls that vision, which manifests depicted in itself the divine likeness as a shaping of the shapeless, a theophany, from the leading up of those who behold towards the divine as through the divine enlightenment itself that comes upon those who behold, and from their being sacredly initiated into something of the divine.[28]

But this process, as Dionysios makes clear, is not some individual, intellectual process, but something mediated by angels, and also by the community of the church, primarily, though not, I think, exclusively, the sacred ministers. Chapters 4 to 14 of the *Celestial Hierarchy* explore various aspects of the process of assimilation to the divine mediated by the principle and reality of hierarchy, and then there follows the final chapter 15, which deals in detail with the symbolism used to understand the realm of celestial intelligible beings, and beyond that God himself. It is striking that in this final chapter all the cautions about the necessity of paying attention to unlike symbolism seem to be set on one side. All the symbols introduced, from fire onward, are interpreted in what seems to me a mimetic way. So, of fire, he says,

> The fiery, therefore, I think manifests that which is most deiform in the heavenly intellects. For the sacred theologians often describe the being beyond being and shapeless in terms of fire, as possessing many images, if one may say so, of the thearchic property, as in visible things.[29]

One finds the same in the explanation of how the parts of the (human? animal?) body are applied to God; the principle of interpretation is mimesis.

28. Dionysios, *Celestial Hierarchy* 4.3, Heil and Ritter, 22.1–10.
29. Dionysios, *Celestial Hierarchy* 15.2, Heil and Ritter, 52.7–11.

Dionysios and the Liturgy

This movement away from the apophatic/unlike symbolic to mimesis, imitation, becomes even more striking in the treatise *The Ecclesiastical Hierarchy*. Paul Rorem, in his first monograph, *Biblical and Liturgical Symbols within the Pseudo-Dionysian Synthesis*, drew attention to the apparent neglect, if not rejection, of negation and the preference for unlikeness in the treatment of symbols in the *Ecclesiastical Hierarchy*. He remarked,

> Not only are liturgical images and symbols never called incongruous or dissimilar, a silence striking by itself, but they are explicitly considered "precise" and ascribed "with appropriateness." Either the Areopagite does not apply to the liturgy his firm principles that even the loftiest images are insufficient and need interpretation including negation, or else that principle is at this point so assumed that it is never mentioned.[30]

Perhaps we should not be completely surprised, as we have already noticed that, although his understanding of the apophatic in relation to concepts and of unlike symbolism in relation to images seem based on precisely the same principles, when it comes to symbolism, Dionysios's practice seems to diverge from his theory. It is partly a matter of discernment. Take, for example, the case of the seraphim: the name ("to those who know Hebrew") indicates that they are "kindling or burning," and he goes on to explain that

> the naming of the seraphim plainly teaches their ever moving around things divine, and constancy, and warmth, and keenness, and the seething of that persistent, indomitable, and inflexible perpetual motion, and the vigorous assimilation and elevation of the subordinate, as giving new life and rekindling them to the same heat; and purifying through fire and burnt-offering, and the light-like and light-shedding characteristic which can never be concealed or consumed, and remains always the same, which destroys and dispels every kind of obscure darkness.[31]

The depiction of the seraphim as fiery beings circulating the Godhead is purified of spatial and material associations, but its symbolic associations—purifying, warmth, fervor, ceaselessness—are affirmed.

30. Paul Rorem, *Biblical and Liturgical Symbols within the Pseudo-Dionysian Synthesis* (Toronto: Pontifical Institute of Mediaeval Studies, 1984), 96. The references are to *Ecclesiastical Hierarchy* 2. *Theoria* 6, 7 (Heil and Ritter, 77.8, 24). Rorem returns to this later: 119–21.

31. Dionysios, *Celestial Hierarchy* 7.1, Heil and Ritter, 27.14–28.2; John Parker, trans., *The Works of Dionysius the Areopagite*, 2 vols. (London: Parker, 1897–1899).

With the sacraments (not a very happy term with Dionysios, who is really concerned with various sacred rites) the negative notions associated with the apophatic and unlike seem to fall away, as Rorem notes. Perhaps the reason for this is that we are moving from a fundamentally intellectual understanding of knowing to something rather different. So far, the discussion of the apophatic in relation to the conceptual and the unlike in relation of symbols and images has been concerned with an intellectual process of understanding; we are tracing an ascent of knowledge, a knowledge that proceeds beyond what we would normally count as knowledge to knowing by *unknowing*, as Dionysios puts it. Another way of putting this would be to say that we are passing beyond a notion of knowledge conceived on analogy with seeing—something very difficult to avoid in Greek, where the verbs "to know" and "to see" are so close as to become entangled. If knowing is understood on analogy with seeing, then knowing will be thought of as like seeing: there will be, ideally, clarity about the object of knowledge, which is separated from us by distance (it is over there; if we get too close we can no longer see it). But there are other senses: touch, taste, smell, hearing. Especially with the first three of these senses, we have a notion of apprehension very different from the apprehension we receive through sight: what we perceive is *present*, but often very difficult to describe. If sight suggests a form of knowing that is clear, distinct, objective, then touch, taste, and smell suggest forms of knowing that are unclear, indistinct, subjective, but nonetheless convincing, compelling. Gregory of Nyssa explored something of this, not least in his homilies on the Song of Songs. As the soul, the bride, finds herself encompassed by the divine night, she can no longer make out what or who is revealed to her, but has, nonetheless, a "certain sense of his presence" (αἴσθησιν μέν τινα … τῆς παρουσίας).[32] The Song of Songs encouraged Gregory to explore knowledge of God in terms of taste, touch, and smell: to explore a knowledge of God with the different characteristics we have already mentioned, that distinguish such apprehension from that based on sight.

When we read Dionysios on the sacraments, or sacred rites, what is striking is his lack of interest in what is said, uttered. Yes, there are hymns and prayers, but he virtually never says anything about their content (or not directly). What he pays attention to is, first of all, movement: the movement of the hierarch as he moves round the church censing it. Then the materials

32. Gregory of Nyssa, *In Cant.* 11, GNO 6:324.10–11.

used in these sacred rites: water, oil, *myron* or chrism, bread, wine, incense; he even mentions something like icons, decorations, depictions, presumably in form and color. He is no longer much interested in the conceptual, and his interest in the symbolic is no longer concerned with verbal images drawing on the visible. He is concerned directly with the material things themselves, and their symbolism. In his letter to the apostle John, he asserts that "truly visible things are manifest images of the invisible."[33] It is through engagement in the visible world—the physical world of the materials used in the sacraments, but also (implicit, I think, in his notion of hierarchies, all consisting of groups of heavenly and earthly beings) with people are their relationships with each other. The sacraments or sacred rites undergird the apophatic, for they are concerned with a form of knowing that is not conceptual, but with the knowing that comes about through participation in the material symbols—together with fellow participants—in the rites and ceremonies of the church: a knowledge that is essentially participation, and only secondarily conceptual.

To return to the episode in Acts, it is rarely, if ever, remarked on that the inscription ἀγνώστῳ θεῳ is on an *altar*, a place of worship. If I am right in my interpretation of the Areopagite's grasp of the apostle's teaching, then it would seem that Dionysios himself was very much aware of this fact. For in his understanding of the ἄγνωστος θεός it is in worship, not in philosophy, nor even in mystical rapture, that the true meaning of the unknowability of God is revealed.

33. Dionysios, *Ep.* 10, Heil and Ritter, 208.9–10.

RESPONSE

A Response to Fr. Louth on Patristic Interpretations of Acts 17

Fr. Brian E. Daley (Catholic)

Perhaps the most surprising thing about the theological interpretation of Acts 17:16–31 by the fathers of the church is that—in comparison with what they have left us on many other well-known passages in the Christian canon of Scripture—there is relatively little of it. To many modern readers, this dramatic passage in Luke's narrative of the growth of the early Christian community marks a key transition in both the content and the strategy of evangelization. Luke has previously presented Paul as going on missionary journeys that take him farther and farther from his base in Antioch—first to Cyprus and central Asia Minor with Barnabas (Acts 13–14), then back to Asia Minor with Silas and Timothy (Acts 16), and eventually on with them from there to continental Europe, where they preached the news of the risen Jesus at Philippi, Thessalonica, and Berea (Acts 16–17). Despite resistance and harsh treatment from the synagogue leaders in many of these small Greek-speaking towns, Paul's strategy seems to have remained constant: to focus his energies mainly on trying to convince the members of local Jewish communities that Jesus of Nazareth, whom the Romans had executed, was truly the Messiah Israel had so long awaited, and that God had raised him from the dead to begin his reign invisibly in glory among those who looked for his coming.

When he moves on from Berea to Athens, the intellectual capital of the Hellenistic world, however, Paul's preaching (as Luke presents it) seems to undergo a decided change. Luke tells us "his spirit was provoked [παρωξύνετο] within him, as he saw that the city was full of idols" (Acts 17:16). Rather than simply react with antipagan polemics, we hear, he began to spend time talking directly with local Greek intellectuals, as well as with the Jewish population and their gentile sympathizers. So Luke tells us Paul deliberately began to converse with Epicurean and Stoic philosophers (Acts 17:18), who were, like the stereotype of all Athenians, insatiable in their eagerness to "hear something new" (Acts 17:21). Eventually, as we know, he found himself delivering his message to a non-Jewish audience on what was arguably one of the most revered centers of Athenian culture: the Areopagus—"Mars Hill"—the traditional site Athens's court of final appeal for a variety of capital cases. Like a pro-life demonstrator in front of the U.S. Supreme Court, Paul was now engaging full-tilt in argument with the ruling elite of the Greek intellectual and religious world.

His address there, most of us would agree, is one of Luke's masterpieces. Paul begins by talking of his own experience of wandering around the Athenian agora in the days he has spent in the city, and of being struck by the number of altars honoring various deities, among them one inscribed "to an unknown god [ἀγνώστῳ θεῷ]." Citing phrases attributed to the seventh-century Cretan holy man Epimenides and the third-century Stoic poet Aratus, Paul identifies this "unknown god" as in fact the creator of all things, who is presented in the Hebrew Bible; he concludes with the proclamation that this God has sent a judge into the world—clearly Jesus—to confront all peoples with the claims of righteousness, and has already shown him to be credible by raising him from the dead. Most of his hearers are skeptical, we read, some even scornful; but among those who believe is a certain Dionysius, a member of the Areopagus court—the first high-level Athenian convert!

For most modern readers of the book of Acts, I suppose, this scene is an engaging, even a thrilling one: Paul, the archetypal wandering apostle, Jewish down to his fingertips in thought and background, speaks here to cultured, philosophically inclined Athenians in their own terms—even quotes to them a few of their own religious authors, as a way of presenting the gospel of Jesus and the message of biblical monotheism in language they might find intellectually convincing. It may even seem to us a model of cultural adaptation in proclaiming the gospel, of respecting the religious traditions of our non-Christian hearers as a way of connecting our message to their own background and aspirations. What may appear odd to us, then—what *does* seem a little surprising to me, at least—is that most of the Fathers, Greek as well as Latin, seem not to have been very interested in explaining the passage or applying it to their own situations, aside from citing in passing a few of its celebrated phrases—referring to our "groping after" God (Acts 17:27), for instance, or characterizing God as the one "in whom we live and move and are" (Acts 17:28). As Andrew Louth has shown already in his essay, when they do take it up, their response to it varies widely. Let me here simply attempt to expand a bit on his excellent summary of the material we have, from (roughly) the first six centuries of our era.

Interest in the passage is first noticeable in the last few decades of the second century, as Christian theologians struggled with the phenomenon of "Gnostic" Christianity and its tendency to retell the biblical narrative in radically altered, often anti-Jewish terms. As part of a detailed argument that the first Christian preachers did in fact proclaim Jesus the Savior within the context of the Hebrew Bible and its testimony to a single, transcendent creator, Irenaeus of Lyons—writing about 185—briefly retells the story of Acts 17, as one of many witnesses that the original content of the Christian message was clearly the traditional biblical faith, even when an evangelist like Paul goes out of his way to present the message in terms a philosophically cultured Greek might understand.[34] The content of Paul's preaching, Irenaeus emphasizes here, like the content of everything Jesus's disciples taught, was perfectly continuous with the faith of Israel, whatever the concepts may have been in which it was couched.

Irenaeus's contemporary Clement of Alexandria, himself a convert highly learned in Greek literature and philosophy, and probably a native of Athens, shows, as Louth points out, a good deal of sympathetic interest in the scene of Paul's speech on the Areopagus—perhaps more than any other early Father. In book 1 of his *Stromateis*, for instance—a book that deals mainly with the ways classical philosophy can be an aid to our coming to know God—Clement quotes Acts 17:22–28 directly, as proof that Paul "approves what was well said by the Greeks"; he even hints that God the Creator is honored among the Greeks, although in other terms, by their reverence of "the unknown God," but that "it was necessary to receive information and learn, in the way of intimate knowledge [κατ' ἐπίγνωσιν], through the Son."[35] The groping efforts of Greek religion and philosophy to grasp the reality of God at the heart of the world are only confirmed and clarified in the revelation of Jesus. So, a few lines later, Clement adds: "'The eyes of the blind [that were] opened' refers to the deep knowledge of the Father through the Son, the

34. Irenaeus, *Haer.* 3.12.9.

35. Clement of Alexandria, *Stromateis* 1.19.91.5, in *Clemens Alexandrinus*, vol. 2, *Stromata Buch I–VI*, ed. Otto Stählin and Ludwig Früchtel, Griechische christliche Schriftsteller (Berlin: Akademie-Verlag, 1985), 59.1–4.

grasp [κατάληψις] of what the Greeks had paraphrased."[36] Gospel revelation offers the fulfillment of an ongoing human search for God the mystery.

In book 5 of the *Stromateis,* Clement is dealing mainly with faith and its engagement with mysteries that are behind normal human comprehension. There, in section 12, as Louth rightly points out, Clement suggests that faith is a necessary part of our engagement with God because God is in his nature beyond what classical epistemology might identify as knowledge—"this discussion about God is surely the hardest for human discourse to handle."

> For the first and most original principle of all is difficult to demonstrate, since it is the cause of being and continuing existence for all other things. For how could something be verbalized, which is neither genus nor difference nor species nor individual thing nor number, but also is neither an accident nor something in which an accident inheres. No one could express all of this rightly.[37]

As Louth points out, the beginnings of what will later be referred to as "apophatic theology" are here expressed in Greek philosophical terms. We use all kinds of words and names for God, based on the rest of our experience; yet "we speak not as if we were uttering his name, but for want of alternatives we employ useful words, so that the thinking mind might not stray through others, but might have in them something on which to support itself." As Paul realized while strolling through the Athenian agora, Clement adds, it is the grace of divine revelation in Christ that provides the most appropriate material for support in this quest.[38]

It is no surprise that Origen, the church's first great biblical scholar, who in some way carried on the tradition of Christian intellectualism begun in Alexandria by Clement, also alludes a few times, in an appreciative way, to the story of Paul speaking to the Athenians. In his twelfth *Homily on Leviticus,* for instance, probably delivered in Caesarea in the early 240s, Origen reflects on what constitutes a holy place or temple, and concludes that it is constituted above all by our holy thoughts, where God himself dwells.

36. Clement of Alexandria, *Stromateis* 1.19.92.2, Stählin and Früchtel, 59.8–10. Κατάληψις is the usual Stoic term for full knowledge, the goal of the epistemic process.

37. Clement of Alexandria, *Stromateis* 5.12.81.4–5, Stählin and Früchtel, 380.14–19.

38. Clement of Alexandria, *Stromateis* 5.12.82.4, Stählin and Früchtel, 381.7–13. In *Stromateis* 6, the first part of Clement's long meditation on the characteristics of true Christian gnosis—the knowledge that perfects the believer and unites him or her continually to God—he again mentions the story of Paul's preaching on the Areopagus in Acts 17, to underscore that real gnosis, "being the perfection of faith, overflows beyond catechesis, in accord with the greatness of the Lord's teaching and with the church's rule [of faith]" (*Stromateis* 6.18.165.1, Stählin and Früchtel, 517.3–6). Real gnosis, in other words, is faithfully lived theology!

Doesn't it seem to you (he asks) that when Paul entered a theatre or when he went up onto the Areopagus and preached Christ to the Athenians, he was in a holy place? Even when he walked among the altars and idols of the Athenians, where he found the inscription "To an unknown god" and took the beginning of his preaching of Christ from this phrase—even strolling among pagan altars—he was in a holy place, because he was thinking of holy things.[39]

The episode of Paul's ministry in Athens illustrates for Origen that even religious instincts that are in themselves false can be an environment where God is found and worshiped rightly by the believer. This same positive interpretation of Acts 17 recurs, perhaps unexpectedly, in a fragment of Origen's *Scholia on Proverbs*, written probably in the late 240s, after his return from Athens to Caesarea. Here, as part of his explanation of the puzzling text of Proverbs 30:29–31, which celebrates four imposing animals—the lion, the cock, the he-goat, and the king—that look majestic and are all "stately in their stride," Origen identifies the *lion* with Paul's behavior in Athens, a place where many Greeks famously gave themselves airs. "So Paul spoke to the Athenians," he says, "and explained things well, as he walked around and gazed at their idols. For from the inscription 'To an unknown god,' he strode on to give a fine discourse about God."[40] The truth of Paul's preaching, in Origen's view, lent dignity to his presence among those intellectual Greeks!

Not everyone in the early church who gave attention to this section of Acts 17, however, saw it as an affirmation of the compatibility of scriptural proclamation and Greek learning in the way Clement and Origen did. As might be expected, the ever-critical Tertullian offers us the opposite interpretation. In his treatise *On the Soul*, apparently dating from the later part of his career, around 210, Tertullian attacks both philosophical and Gnostic ways of understanding the spiritual dimension of human experience, in the attempt to develop a thoroughly biblical anthropology. Near the beginning of his refutation of Greek philosophical theories of the soul, Tertullian refers to Paul's engagement with the intellectuals of Athens as his model:

If only (he writes) it were *not* "necessary that heresies exist, so that those who are genuine among you might stand out clearly" (I Cor 11.19)! Then we would also have no experience at all with philosophers concerning the soul—those patriarchs, if I

39. Origen, *Homily 12 on Leviticus* 4, in Origen, *Homélies sur le Lévitique VIII–XVI*, ed. Marcel Borret, Sources chrétiennes 287 (Paris: Cerf, 1982), 182.70–77.

40. Origen, *Questions on Proverbs*, frag. 12, from the Catena of Procopius of Gaza in Marcel Richard, ed., "Les fragments d'Origène sur Prov 30–15–31," in *Epektasis: Mélanges patristiques offerts au Cardinal J. Daniélou*, ed. Jacques Fontaine and Charles Kannengiesser (Paris: Beauchesne, 1972), 394.

may call them that, of heretics—just as, long ago philosophy was foreseen by the Apostle to be an attack on truth. For at Athens he experienced a city focused on talk, when he had a taste of all the hucksters of wisdom and eloquence who were there, and from his experience he conceived that statement of his own as a warning.[41]

Philosophical speculation and the religious arguments of the Gnostic "sects," for Tertullian, are both expressions of human resistance to truth, which itself is only available through the Scriptures. So Paul, curiously, for Tertullian is a model in this passage for Christian resistance to philosophy; his experience on the Areopagus exemplifies the unresolvable opposition between faith and secular reasoning.

This same inclination to identify the nonbiblical philosophy of the Athenians, and its cultural and religious environment as depicted in Acts 17, with human resistance to orthodox theological thinking, appears also—even more curiously—a few times a century and a half later, in the works of one of the most unashamedly Platonic of patristic thinkers, Gregory of Nyssa. Gregory seems to have seen in this passage about Paul in Athens a parallel to contemporary debates on the (philosophically counterintuitive) doctrine of God as a Trinity of persons. At the end of part 2 of book 3 of his refutation of Eunomian Arianism, for instance, written between 381 and 383,[42] Gregory remarks that these highly dialectical defenders of the creaturehood of the Son of God unjustly charge his own brother Basil with dishonoring the Son, at the same time that they, by their philosophical twists and turns, separate the Son from the divine nature altogether.

This same accusation Paul once received from the Athenians, being charged by them with proclaiming strange divinities, when he criticized the insane error of the idolaters concerning divine spirits, and tried to lead them towards the truth by preaching the resurrection in Jesus. Now these modern Stoics and Epicureans bring charges against the imitator of Paul—these "people who spend their time on nothing else," as the story says of the Athenians, "but trying to speak and to hear something new" (Acts 17.21).[43]

The Eunomian Arians, in Gregory's rhetorically charged depiction, have sacrificed the church's doctrinal tradition for flashy intellectual speculation,

41. Tertullian, *De anima* 3.1, in Tertullian, *De anima*, ed. J. H. Waszink, CCSL 2 (Turnhout: Brepols, 1954), 785. The "heretics" he mentions are, of course, members of Gnostic sects like the Valentinians.

42. For the dating of *Contra Eunomium* 3, see Pierre Maraval, "Chronology of Works [of Gregory of Nyssa]," in *The Brill Dictionary of Gregory of Nyssa*, ed. L. F. Mateo-Seco and G. Maspero (Leiden: Brill, 2010), 153.

43. Gregory of Nyssa, *Eun.* 3.2.163, GNO 2:105.26–106.6.

and so criticize the defenders of the Son's full Godhead for their lack of theological sophistication.

Similarly, in a celebrated and sharply ironic passage of his address *On the Godhead of the Son and the Holy Spirit, and on Abraham*, delivered in Constantinople during a synod in June 383, Gregory again recalls the story of Paul's experience in Acts 17, as an example of the dangers of vulgarized theological discourse, and of the constant desire of the unqualified to debate issues above their understanding. He continues:

> Surely you are not unaware of where these arguments are leading. For all around us the city is filled with such conversation: the narrow alleys, the marketplaces, the squares, the intersections—the merchants of clothing standing at their tables, the people who sell food to eat. If you ask about the price, he offers you a speculation about "begotten" and "unbegotten"; if you inquire about a piece of bread, he answers, "The Father is greater, and the Son subordinate"; and if you try to ask, "Is the bath ready?" he insists, "The Son is from non-being!" I do not know what one should call this sad situation—some delirium or madness, or some epidemic of the kind that drives people's thoughts astray![44]

In both these contexts from works of the early 380s, the story of Paul's engagement with philosophical Athenians becomes for Gregory a story of frustrated evangelization, the radical content of the gospel thwarted by those who are simply agog about the latest intellectual trends. One cannot help being reminded of similar satirical thrusts by his namesake and friend, Gregory of Nazianzus—notably in his *First Theological Oration*—against the ways Eunomian Arianism has come to dominate public discourse;[45] yet for Gregory of Nazianzus, the story of Paul in Athens seems not to have come to mind as a parallel.

In the Latin West, however, their equally cultured contemporaries Ambrose and Augustine offer arresting contrasts. So near the end of the sixth book of his *Exposition of the Gospel of Luke*, written in 390, Ambrose draws on Paul's speech to the Athenians to argue that the evangelization of intellectually sophisticated pagans should normally follow a logical sequence, first demonstrating that the world and all that is in it was created by one God, "in whom we live and move and are" (Acts 17:24), and that "we are his offspring" (Acts 17:28–29); then arguing that material idols may not be

44. Gregory of Nyssa, *De deitate Filii et Spiritus sancti, et de Abraham*, GNO 10/2:120–21. For the date of this discourse, see Maraval, "Chronology," 165.

45. Gregory of Nazianzus, *Or.* 27.

worshiped, "because the material of gold, silver, and wood cannot contain divine power"; finally, he suggests to the potential preacher, "you will declare that salvation was given to us through Christ, beginning from those things that he did in the body and describing them as divine.... For faith grows little by little, so that when he is seen to have been above man, he is believed to be God."[46] Ambrose continues:

> But perhaps too little authority and faith will be bestowed on us. Read the Apostle's sermon to the Athenians, for if he had sought from the outset to destroy the sacred rites of the idols, the ears of the Gentiles would have spurned his sermon.... For one who discusses must first consider the persons in the audience, lest he is mocked before he is heard.[47]

For Ambrose, the classical rhetor turned politician turned bishop, it seems, Paul's discourse in Acts 17 is at least an example of good oral argument, and demonstrates by its limited but real success that one needs to approach unbelievers by arguing in the right order; so "even Dionysios the Areopagite believed, and others believed in the man [presumably Jesus], so that they came to believe in God."[48] Our credibility, even as preachers of the gospel, is only enhanced by learning the techniques of argument.

Ambrose's precocious hearer and spiritual protégé Augustine was also a professional rhetorician and deeply immersed in the Platonist philosophical tradition. Although he refers to individual phrases in Paul's discourse on the Areopagus fairly often in his own sermons, and sees it above all as communicating the message of Christ's resurrection,[49] Augustine reflects more at length, in *Confessions* 7, on the positive pedagogical effect of his own reading of "the books of the Platonists"—probably Latin translations of some of Plotinus's essays—when describing the resolution of some of his major intellectual problems with Christian faith, during his time as a pro-

46. Ambrose, *Exposition of the Holy Gospel according to Luke* 6.104, in Ambrose of Milan, *Expositio Sancti Evangelii secundum Lucam*, ed. M. Adriaen, CCSL 14 (Turnhout: Brepols, 1957); 211.1130–212.1135; translation from Saint Ambrose of Milan, *Exposition of the Holy Gospel According to Saint Luke with Fragments on the Prophecy of Isaias*, trans. Theodosia Tomkinson (Etna, Calif.: Center for Traditionalist Orthodox Studies, 1998) 232.

47. Ambrose, *Exposition of Luke* 6.105, Adriaen, 14.212.1138–41; Tomkinson, 232–33.

48. Ambrose, *Exposition of Luke* 6.105, Adriaen, 14.212.1155–56; Tomkinson, 233.

49. So in his *Tractates on the Gospel of John* 109, dating from the early 420s, Augustine insists that the news that Christ had risen was the heart of the gospel preached by both Paul and all the apostles. "And in the Acts of the Apostles we read that in Christ God defined the content of faith for everyone, by raising him from the dead" (*Tractatus in Johannis Evangelium* 109.5, ed. R. Willems, CCSL 36 [Turnhout: Brepols, 1954], 621.19–20).

fessor of rhetoric in Ambrose's Milan. To find in the work of Plotinus, the Egyptian-born pagan, an aid toward his own conversion to Christ and to his decision to accept baptism seemed to Augustine to parallel the account in the Exodus story of the Israelites' bringing with them golden gifts they had begged from their Egyptian neighbors, when they fled across the Red Sea (Ex 11:2–3). So, after his engagement with "pagan" Neoplatonism had enabled the thirty-year-old Augustine, by his own account, to realize that evil is not itself a substance, and to see that nonspatial, nontemporal substances (like God and the soul) can be at least as genuine as material ones, Augustine felt himself positioned to understand for the first time how the biblical tradition really conceives of God, the beneficent and all-present Creator.

> And I had come to you from the Gentiles, and fixed my attention on the gold which you willed your people to take from Egypt—since the gold was yours, wherever it was. And through your Apostle you said to the Athenians, "In you we live and move and are, as also some whom they cultivate there have said" (Acts 17.28). And that [= Athens] is where these books [of the Platonists] come from. I did not give attention to the idols of the Egyptians, which they served with your gold.[50]

For Augustine, the story of God's command to the people Israel to take Egyptian gold with them in their exodus was a command to borrow valuable intellectual ornaments from their pagan neighbors, and to make use of these ornaments in God's service; it was a command that applied to all the good and useful products of human culture, which could and should be used in communicating the gospel. So he writes in the second book of *On Christian Learning*:

> Thus all the teachings of the nations contain not only false and superstitious inventions and the heavy burdens of superfluous labor, which each of us, as we make our exit from pagan society under Christ's leadership, should detest and avoid; but they also contain liberal branches of learning more suited to the expression of truth, as well as some highly useful moral teachings; and some true statements are found among them about how to worship the one God. This is like their gold and silver, which they have not devised themselves, but have extracted from certain mines of divine Providence, whose riches are scattered everywhere; and just as they have abused these in a wicked and damaging way to serve demons, so when the Chris-

50. Augustine, *Confessions* 7.9.15, in Augustine, *Confessions*, trans. Henry Chadwick (Oxford: Oxford University Press, 1991), 123 (altered). With Ambrose, Pelagius, and other Latin authors of the fourth century, Augustine here follows the so-called Western reading of Acts 17:28.

tian separates himself at heart from their wretched company, he should take these things away for righteous use in preaching the gospel.[51]

It is the basis of what was to become the ideal of a Christian transformation of culture, the principle of continuity between the classics of ancient learning and Christian theology.

But the possibility of such continuity and transformation seems to have been perceived relatively seldom by the major Christian theologians and biblical commentators of the first five centuries. As the Christian community moved gradually toward defining its beliefs, assumptions, and practices within the world of Hellenistic culture and Roman imperial organization, its energies seem to have been more focused on what made them *different* from their neighbors, especially those of a nonbiblical religious background, than on the deeper religious longings and instincts they may have shared. Even Gregory of Nyssa, who draws so much of his understanding of the human person from the Platonic tradition, is ready to criticize those Christians who apparently interpreted the ontological status of the Son and the Spirit in more philosophically rigorous categories than their Nicene confreres were able to do as being overly secular, sold out to intellectual fads or tied up in facile logical categories. Except for a few, like Clement of Alexandria, Ambrose, and Augustine, who were convinced of the urgent need to learn from the best of what pagan literature and philosophy had to offer, most Christian writers through the end of the fourth century seem to have felt real ambivalence about the degree to which the church could profit from studying what "the Greeks" had to say. Perhaps this is the main reason why Luke's dramatic narrative of Paul's mission to the intellectual Athenians, apart from some of its more memorable phrases, seems to have engaged early Christian thought so little.

With the writings that have come down to us under the name of Dionysius the Areopagite, of course, all of this changed radically, as Louth has so well reminded us. This mysterious ancient Christian author, whose identity and life remain unknown, but whose works have indelibly influenced mystical and sacramental theology ever since, clearly produced his writings around 500; the liturgy referred to in his *Ecclesiastical Hierarchy* locates the work in the church of fifth-century Antioch, and the contents of the corpus of his writings suggests that the author was deeply versed in the ascetical

51. Augustine, *De doctrina Christiana* 2.40.60, in Augustine, *De doctrina Christiana*, ed. J. Martin, CCSL 32 (Turnhout: Brepols, 1962). This part of *De doctrina* is contemporary with the *Confessions*.

tradition of Greek monasticism, especially the works of Evagrius.[52] Two German scholars, in 1895, separately established beyond doubt his strong literary and philosophical debt to the non-Christian Athenian Neoplatonist Proclus (ca. 410–465).[53] But while Dionysius's name and person still remains hidden, the significance of his pseudonym is powerfully telling: what he writes—laying out an elaborate vision of an ordered, interconnected cosmos in which Scripture, living creatures, and liturgical rites communicate to humans the life-giving knowledge and energies of a God who is, in his own being, beyond all creaturely knowing—is explicitly meant to be taken as the work of the cultured, philosophically literate Athenian convert and disciple of Paul, mentioned in Acts 17:34. By the author's design, these writings are to be thought of as composed by one of those religious Athenian philosophers whom Paul met, who reverenced "the unknown god" with an altar (Acts 17:23), "in the hope that they might grope after him and find him" (Acts 17:27); yet these works are also clearly meant to be taken as deriving their content from the teaching of Paul, the self-effacing mystic who was "was caught up to the third heaven . . . and heard things that cannot be told, which man may not utter" (2 Cor 12:2–3)—the one who recognized in the incarnate Christ "the mystery hidden from the ages and generations, but now made manifest to his saints, . . . which is Christ in you, your hope of glory" (Col 1:26–27). Attributing this corpus of writings to Dionysius the Areopagite was a way of both acknowledging its Greek philosophical inspiration—even its link with Proclus, the contemporary Athenian religious Platonist—and of claiming for it a central doctrinal link with New Testament teaching. Both claims are firmly rooted in the story of Acts 17, even though the pseudonymous author carefully avoids explicit references to Luke's text. The narrative itself—the story of the Athenian public's reach for the "unknown God" who is now revealed in Jesus—is the only connection.

This emphasis on the overarching significance of this work's pseudonymity—of attributing what we know as the *Corpus Dionysiacum* (CD),

52. See especially Alexander Golitzin, *Et Introibo ad Altare Dei: The Mystagogy of Dionysius Areopagita, with Special Reference to Its Predecessors in the Eastern Christian Tradition*, Analecta Vlatadon 59 (Thessaloniki: Patriarchal Institute of Patristic Studies, 1994).

53. See Hugo Koch, "Proklos als Quelle des Pseudo-Dionysius Areopagita in der Lehre vom Bösen," *Philologus* 54 (1895): 438–54; and Josef Stiglmayr, "Der Neuplatoniker Proklos als Vorlage des sogenannten Dionysius Areopagita in der Lehre vom Übel," *Historisches Jahrbuch* 16 (1895): 253–73 and 721–48. It is remarkable that two studies, one by a German Protestant theologian and one by a German Catholic, proving Dionysius's dependence on Proclus for his conception of evil, appeared in the same year in different periodicals.

by the author's design, to Paul's Athenian convert at the end of chapter 17 of Acts—has principally been the work, in recent years, of Charles Stang.[54] In an essay summarizing his longer book on Dionysius, Stang writes:

> The author of the CD literally assumes the identity of Dionysius the Areopagite. He addresses his works to other apostles and disciples; he transports himself into this apostolic community, to the point that he is present at the Dormition of Mary; he counsels John the Evangelist in exile on Patmos. And yet all the while the author is also in the fifth century: quoting—sometimes at great length, and with little cover—from Proclus' works, describing the ceremonials of Byzantine churches rather than the humbler home churches of the New Testament. The author is, in words borrowed from his description of Moses, "neither himself nor someone else," neither the contemplative from Syria who scholars assume him to be nor the Athenian judge under whose name he writes. Like the ecstatic God with whom he seeks to suffer union, as a writer he simultaneously remains where he is and stretches outside himself. . . .
>
> One should understand the entire CD as a single, coherent "mystical theology," the aim of which is "unknowing." To "unknow" the unknown God, one must contravene the Greek sages and "unknow oneself."[55]

It is here, in this "Dionysius's" remarkable collection of essays on the relationship of sacramental mediation and scriptural revelation to the God who is the pulsating source of transforming energy in the cosmos, yet who remains forever hidden from our human comprehension, that the representational and metaphysical instincts of high Greek culture encounter, without contradiction or retreat, the Christ-centered revelation of the Christian Bible, as proclaimed by Paul. What Paul is presented as doing in Acts 17—preaching the Paschal mystery of Jesus as the answer to Hellenistic culture's centuries-long, still-continuing quest to worship an "unknown god"—is, fleshed out in detail, the heart of the fifth-century Dionysius's message to the world. At last, even without being explicitly cited, Acts 17 has come theologically into its own.

54. See especially Charles Stang, *Apophasis and Pseudonymity in Dionysius the Areopagite: "No Longer I"* (Oxford: Oxford University Press, 2012); also Stang, "Dionysius, Paul, and the Significance of the Pseudonym," in *Re-thinking Dionysius the Areopagite*, ed. Sarah Coakley and Charles M. Stang (Oxford: Wiley-Blackwell, 2009), 11–25.

55. Stang, "Significance," 21.

RESPONSE

Unknowable or Unknown God?

Evangelical Tensions

Donald Fairbairn (Evangelical)

I am grateful to our hosts from the Paradosis Center at John Brown University for organizing this conference and for their gracious hospitality. It is a pleasure to respond to the paper by Fr. Andrew Louth, my old acquaintance who examined my dissertation seventeen years ago, and to respond along with Fr. Brian Daley, whom I have long known by reputation but have met in person for the first time this week. In my response to Fr. Louth, I would like to concentrate on two major points he makes in the paper. The first is the issue of whether it is appropriate to take the inscription ἀγνώστῳ θεῷ in the sense of "to an *unknowable* God" (rather than simply "to an *unknown* God"), and the second is Pseudo-Dionysius's act of inserting himself into the text of Acts 17.[56] I would like to reflect on Evangelical scholarly and popular practice related to these points, and to suggest that in both cases, there is a significant tension with evangelicalism, a tension that other Christian traditions may be able to help us navigate.

Unknown versus Unknowable

The first time I stood on top of the Areopagos in Athens, I realized that I had completely misconstrued the situation of Acts 17. I had previously envisioned a large area with many temples on it. Instead, what I beheld was not a temple mount, but a vantage point—the ideal place from which to

56. The fifth- or sixth-century Syrian writer whom Louth calls Dionysios is also called Pseudo-Dionysius or Denys, to distinguish him from the figure of Acts 17, the Dionysius who was converted as a result of Paul's speech on the Areopagus. He was the author of a corpus of mystical writings called the *Corpus Dionysiacum* or *Corpus Areopagiticum*. Because Louth's appellation "Dionysios" and the Latinized "Dionysius" are very easy to confuse, I will refer to the figure in Acts 17 as Dionysius and the fifth- or sixth-century author as Pseudo-Dionysius.

look over at the Acropolis (and of course, the Parthenon), and down in various different directions at the Temple of Zeus, the agora, and so on. The ancient Athenians, Acts 17 implies, were looking for gods to worship (or at least to avoid offending!), and their many temples paid homage to the ones that they found or knew about. In a sense, then, to stand on the Areopagos was to survey in grand panorama the results of humanity's quest for gods. As such, it was the perfect setting for the cognoscenti of the day to debate whatever gods or realities were out there and which among them most commanded our attention.

Against such a backdrop, the building of a temple "to an unknown god" in Athens might be considered the Greeks' way of covering themselves lest they miss one deity and be in danger of falling under his wrath as a result of their carelessness. This is the way all Evangelical interpreters understand the passage.[57] Indeed, Evangelical commentators, like Protestant commentators more generally, are most concerned with whether there could have been such an inscription in Athens (since the ones we have found are in the plural, rather than the singular), or whether perhaps Paul changed a plural inscription to the singular as a lead-in to his proclamation of monotheism.[58] None of the commentaries I have consulted even mention the possibility that the phrase might be taken in the sense of "to an unknowable God."

But is the possibility that the Athenians had missed a god or two really all there is to it? Or is it possible that Clement—as described by Fr. Louth—is on to something when he claims that "unknown" means "unknowable"? After all, when one stands on the Areopagos, what is *most* striking is not the beautiful temples one sees when one looks *down*, or the even more spectacular Parthenon one sees when one looks *over*, but the stunningly deep blue Athenian sky one sees when one looks *up*. That sky could rival

57. Among recent Evangelical commentaries, see, e.g., F. F. Bruce, *The Book of Acts*, New International Commentary on the New Testament (Grand Rapids: Eerdmans, 1983), 355–56; Richard N. Longenecker, *The Expositor's Bible Commentary*, vol. 9, *John–Acts* (Grand Rapids: Zondervan, 1981), 475; John B. Polhill, *Acts*, New American Commentary 26 (Nashville: Broadman & Holman, 1992), 371; Ajith Fernando, *Acts*, NIV Application Commentary (Grand Rapids: Zondervan, 1998), 475; Darrell L. Bock, *Acts*, Baker Exegetical Commentary on the New Testament (Grand Rapids: Baker Academic, 2007), 564; David G. Peterson, *The Acts of the Apostles*, Pillar New Testament Commentary (Grand Rapids: Eerdmans, 2009), 494–95; Derek H. W. Thomas, *Acts*, Reformed Expository Commentary (Phillipsburg, N.J.: P&R, 2011), 502. Cf. non-Evangelical but very influential Protestant commentaries that take the phrase the same way: C. K. Barrett, *The Acts of the Apostles*, International Critical Commentary (London: T&T Clark, 1998), 2:838; Richard I. Pervo, *Acts: A Commentary*, Hermeneia (Minneapolis: Fortress, 2009), 433.

58. See the commentaries referenced in the previous footnote.

even Montana's Big Sky country for majesty, and the eye is surely drawn upward even more readily than it is drawn down or over. An upward gaze certainly raises the possibility that there is a God dwelling in that sky, one who cannot be categorized or circumscribed to dwell in man-made temples. Such a God, if he is up there, would indeed be of a different order than the familiar deities that the Athenians could name and confine to their temples. Might not such a God be fairly described as unknowable, rather than just unknown as of yet? Might not Paul have been hinting something along these lines? Evangelical biblical scholars seem never to consider this possibility. Perhaps we should.

This brings us to the broader issue of Christian apophaticism in general, the practice of stripping one's mind of false conceptions of God, of seeking to come into his presence and be united to him rather than to gain rational knowledge about him.[59] Evangelical exegetes and theologians usually refuse to entertain the possibility that the (to us) suspicious *via negativa* might actually have some use in our approach to God. We insist that we can and must build up a positive picture of God from scriptural assertions, rather than fleeing knowledge of God in the hope that by doing so, we will come into his presence. If we know the person Fr. Louth calls Dionysios (and whom I call Pseudo-Dionysius) at all,[60] he usually scares us or annoys us rather than inspiring us. The same is true for the great Greek monastic writer Gregory Palamas in the fourteenth century or the Russian émigré theologian Vladimir Lossky in the twentieth—Evangelicals are either ignorant of them or dismiss their "mysticism" fairly quickly.[61]

Of course, we forget—if we ever knew—that behind Pseudo-Dionysius's apophatic imagery of God's filling "our sightless minds with treasures beyond all beauty"[62] lies the conviction that our contact with God must

59. Apophaticism is also called *via negativa*, the negative way of going about theology. This approach stands in contrast to kataphaticism, or *via eminentia*, the building up of a positive—usually rational—picture of God. Father Louth is one of the foremost authorities on apophaticism and mysticism more generally. For an excellent general overview, see his now classic work *The Origins of the Christian Mystical Tradition: From Plato to Denys* (Oxford: Clarendon, 1981).

60. A convenient English edition of his works is Pseudo-Dionysius, *The Complete Works*, ed. Paul Rorem, trans. Colm Luibheid, Classics of Western Spirituality (Mahwah, N.J.: Paulist Press, 1987).

61. The easiest entry point to the writings of Palamas is Gregory Palamas, *The Triads*, ed. John Meyendorff, trans. Nicholas Gendle, Classics of Western Spirituality (New York: Paulist Press, 1983). Vladimir Lossky's most famous work, and the one dealing most directly with the apophatic tradition exemplified by Pseudo-Dionysius and Palamas, is *The Mystical Theology of the Eastern Church* (Crestwood, N.Y.: St. Vladimir's Seminary Press, 1976).

62. This quote is a classic illustration of the paradoxical nature of apophatic theology. It comes from

be shaped by Scripture,[63] or that Palamas's attention to the presence of God on the other side of the darkness is in part an attempt to come to terms with Paul's experience in 2 Corinthians 12.[64] Apophaticism is not, as we often surmise, merely negative, and it is certainly not divorced from biblical revelation. But even more important than Evangelicals' superficial grasp and consequent misunderstanding of Eastern apophaticism is our failure to recognize how strong is the apophatic streak in our own midst.

I am convinced that rank-and-file Evangelical Christians are not nearly as opposed to a negative approach to theology as our professional exegetes are. In one of my recent classes, after listening to my explanations of the Trinity and other central aspects of the faith, a student asked me, "Are there any mysteries left for you?" This question was not a compliment. Indeed, the student was actually quite worried. He explained further that after listening to me in class, he had passed my explanations on to other students, and they had all agreed that my explanations were too simple, too easy to understand. Those students were only the most recent of a long line of students who have seemed positively alarmed that I might tell them too much, explain things too well, and thus ruin their faith. As I have reflected on my students' attitudes, it has begun to dawn on me that many Evangelicals are afraid of "figuring God out," as if they will have no need to worship him once they understand him completely. My stock answer to such concerns is, "Don't worry. You won't ever figure God out."

But here we seem to have our finger on a major fault line within Evangelicalism. On one hand, some or most of our academically trained scholars want no part with apophaticism, because they want to move in straight lines from text to meaning to application. They seem to fear the uncertainty that might come from bending any of those straight lines. But on the other hand, some or most of our ordinary Evangelicals don't fear uncertainty as much as they fear certainty, the elimination of all mystery and thus the elimination of any sense that God is greater than we are, beyond us. Perhaps one could say that near the heart of Evangelicalism lies an uneasy truce between Enlightenment-influenced rationalism, with its clear interpretive rules and its confidence in its ability to come up with the right answers, and pietistic

the famous poem that introduces Pseudo-Dionysius's brief work *The Mystical Theology*. See *Complete Works*, 135.

63. See Pseudo-Dionysius, *The Divine Names* 1.1–2, in *Complete Works*, 49–51.

64. Palamas, *Triads* 1.3.21, in Meyendorff, trans., 38.

mysticism,[65] which longs far more for a sense of closeness to the divine than for understanding or right answers. Apophatic theology—whether it comes from Clement, Gregory of Nyssa, Pseudo-Dionysius, Gregory Palamas, or Vladimir Lossky—is at once utterly foreign and too close to home, and thus it serves as a reminder of that uncomfortable tension within our own Evangelical tradition.

So where is an Evangelical to turn from here? I would like to suggest that the facile distinction between kataphatic and apophatic approaches to theology often simply gets in the way of our pursuit of God. Of course our contact with God needs to grow out of Scripture, and even the most radical voices within the apophatic tradition (surely Pseudo-Dionysius himself counts as a "radical" voice) affirm as much. The mystics are rarely—if ever—actually pursuing the kind of contentless absorption into God of which Evangelicals accuse them. At the same time, a more kataphatic approach to God does not—and cannot—lead to putting God in a box or getting him figured out to the point that we feel he is no longer worthy of our worship. Indeed, the more we seek to plumb the mystery of God, to plunge ourselves in the Godhead's deepest sea (to cite one of our greatest Evangelical preachers, Charles Spurgeon),[66] the more we recognize how vastly beyond our comprehension God is. Perhaps, then, what we need is a "kataphatic mysticism" based firmly on Scripture and intent on pursuing both knowledge of God and awe at how far he transcends our knowledge. We need not fear either uncertainty or knowledge, but we can pursue God, and the knowledge of God, with a confidence born out of the fact that we are his beloved children.

The Insertion of the Exegete into the Passage

I now turn to Louth's point that Pseudo-Dionysius has done reverse exegesis by inserting himself into the passage from Acts 17. Again, this is not something that Evangelical commentators would ever think of doing. None of the commentaries I have consulted consider this possibility, and only one even mentions the author of the *Corpus Dionysiacum* at all while com-

65. Some Evangelicals will bristle at my labeling of Pietism as "mysticism." But if one understands mysticism as the various Christian movements seeking experience of God rather than knowledge about him, then surely modern Evangelical Pietism is a form of mysticism.

66. From his sermon at New Park Street Chapel in London on January 7, 1855, as reported in J. I. Packer, *Knowing God* (Downers Grove, Ill.: InterVarsity Press, 1973), 14.

menting on the Dionysius in Acts 17:34.[67] In the minds of most academic Evangelicals, just as the lines must run straight from text to interpretation, so also must they run in only one direction—forward, not backward. Only after one has followed those lines from text to meaning may one address the interaction between the text and our own lives. But if we step back from pure biblical exegesis to actual practice, we find that in fact, Evangelicalism has a long history of reading ourselves into the text of Scripture.

A sophisticated early example came in the 1630s, when Rembrandt memorably painted himself among the Roman soldiers who raised Jesus up on the cross.[68] In the world of modern pietism, it has sometimes been common for the reader to open the Bible at random, hoping to gain insight for his or her life from whatever verse first appeared to the eye. And today, one of the most ubiquitous statements among Evangelicals is "what this passage means to me is . . . ," indicative of a close juxtaposition of the Word of God with whatever the reader happens to think when he or she reads the passage. From my days as a youth pastor, I remember sitting in a packed auditorium in Washington, D.C., with ten thousand youth and their leaders, listening to the speaker (Buster Soares) say, "I am not talking to the person next to you, or the person behind you. I'm talking to *you*." I daresay that I was the only one in the crowded hall who spent the next couple of minutes thinking about the fact that in reality, Soares *was* talking to the person next to me and behind me as well as to me. For everyone but me, Soares's rhetorical device was so effective they never imagined that he could be talking to anyone else. Evangelicalism, at least in its American variety, has such an individualistic focus that it inevitably leads each person to think of the biblical text in direct connection to his or her own life, regardless of what the scholars may say or what the historical background of the passage may be. It seems to me that this is quite close to the reverse exegesis that Pseudo-Dionysius does.

As was the case with the question of whether God is unknowable, so also here, we seem to have a tension between what most of the academic biblical exegetes insist on and what the rank-and-file Christians do. Academic Evangelical biblical scholarship is profoundly rational, focused on

67. Polhill, *Acts*, 378, writes simply: "Some later writings under the name of Dionysius the Areopagite exist, but these are the products of a fifth-century Syrian monk writing pseudonymously under the name of the New Testament character." Other commentaries mention the tradition given by Eusebius (*Ecclesiastical History* 3.4.11; 4.23.3) that the Dionysius of Acts 17:34 became the first bishop of Athens. See, e.g., Bruce, *Acts*, 364; Longenecker, *Acts*, 478; Polhill, *Acts*, 378; Barrett, *Acts*, 855.

68. The famous painting is *The Raising of the Cross*, one of seven paintings in the Passion Series, housed in the Alte Pinakothek in Munich.

rules and techniques, concerned deeply with the immediate historical and literary context of a given passage, always moving from background to context to text, and only then (if ever) to our contemporary situation. But ordinary Evangelical Christians habitually work backward from their own situation to the text, either reading themselves into the text (à la Pseudo-Dionysius) or reading any text from any time period as being written specifically for them. So even though Evangelical commentators would never do what Pseudo-Dionysius does here, and would be quick to criticize him for doing so if they knew about it, ordinary Evangelicals do this kind of thing all the time. And that again brings us to the question, Where is an evangelical to turn from here?

To state the obvious, this certainly does not mean that Evangelicals should lessen our commitment to serious historical and linguistic investigation of the biblical text. Such rigor is the hallmark of our movement—or at least of the scholarly wing of our movement. In my own institution—one of the leaders in Evangelical theological education—there is no question about what holds pride of place. It is biblical exegesis and exposition, and the lion's share of our M.Div. curriculum focuses explicitly on that movement from context to text to sermon. This is the way it should be. But at the same time, we as Evangelicals need to recognize that the Holy Spirit works through the Word he has inspired in a myriad of ways, and perhaps we should be willing to acknowledge that a broader construal of the relation between text and audience is permissible and even laudable, rather than cringeworthy. Perhaps our rigid distinction between what the text *means* and how it *applies* has begun to outlive its usefulness, and we can be open to reading ourselves into the text even as we read the text into ourselves. In fact, since rank-and-file Evangelicals are already doing precisely that, and doing it all the time, perhaps the Evangelical academy is overdue for some serious reflection on these popular practices, rather than simply dismissing them as mistakes or even as tacky theology. As we Evangelical academics seek guidance in navigating such nonlinear interpretive spheres that are foreign to us, and probably rather frightening, people like Pseudo-Dionysius may be able to help us, or at least to prod us into thinking about this matter more carefully.

Conclusion

The Western world, now including the United States, has dramatically moved away from its Christian roots. As we Christians face the task of living and ministering in increasingly post-Christian societies, one thing we should find is that the differences between different groups of Christians are, while still important, not as overwhelming as they once appeared to be. The fact that such a conference as this is being held, and being held at an institution that until recently has had little to do with non-Evangelical Christian traditions, is an indication of the degree to which we are recognizing that our common identity as Christians is more important than our divided identity as Evangelicals, Roman Catholics, or Eastern Orthodox. With a newly recognized sense of common identity comes a new opportunity—or at least a new willingness—to learn from one another. In connection to Fr. Louth's paper, I believe that two of the many ways Evangelicals can learn from the rest of the Christian tradition have to do with a willingness to embrace mystery rather than fleeing from it, and a willingness to construe the relation between text and reader more broadly and less exclusively linearly than our scholars typically do. I give my thanks to Paul in Acts 17, and Pseudo-Dionysius, who placed himself in the world of Acts 17 after the fact, and Fr. Louth for pointing these things out to us.

Bibliography

Acta synodalia sacrosancti concilii oecumenici Vaticani II. Vatican City: Typis Polyglottis Vaticanis, 1971.

Aelfric. *Aelfric's Catholic Homilies.* Vol. 1, *The First Series.* Edited by Peter Clemoes. Early English Text Society, s.s. 17. Oxford: Oxford University Press, 1997.

———. *Aelfric's Catholic Homilies.* Vol. 2, *The Second Series.* Edited by Malcom R. Godden. Early English Text Society, s.s. 5. London: Oxford University Press, 1979.

Ambrose of Milan. *Exposition of the Holy Gospel according to Saint Luke with Fragments on the Prophecy of Isaias.* Translated by Theodosia Tomkinson. Etna, Calif.: Center for Traditionalist Orthodox Studies, 1998.

———. *Expositio Sancti Evangelii secundum Lucam.* Edited by M. Adriaen. CCSL 14. Turnhout: Brepols, 1957.

Andrewes, Lancelot. *The Works of Lancelot Andrewes.* Edited by J. Bliss and J. P. Wilson. 11 vols. Oxford: Oxford University Press, 1841–1854.

———. *The Liturgical Sermons of Lancelot Andrewes.* Edited by Marianne Dorman. 2 vols. Edinburgh: Pentland, 1993.

Archer, Anthony. "Teach Yourself Tongue-Speaking.'" *New Blackfriars* 55, no. 651 (1974): 357–64.

Aristotle. *De anima.* Edited by W. D. Ross. Oxford: Oxford University Press, 1956.

Ashton, John. *Understanding the Fourth Gospel.* 2nd ed. Oxford: Oxford University Press, 2007.

Athanasius. *On the Incarnation.* Translated by a religious of CSMV. Crestwood, N.Y.: St. Vladimir's Seminary Press, 1993.

Attridge, Harold W. *The Epistle to the Hebrews.* Hermeneia. Minneapolis: Fortress, 1989.

Auden, W. H. *Collected Shorter Poems 1927–1957.* New York: Random House, 1966.

Augustine. *Confessions.* Translated by Henry Chadwick. Oxford: Oxford University Press, 1991.

———. *Confessions.* Translated by Maria Boulding, O.S.A. The Works of Saint Augustine: A Translation for the 21st Century. Hyde Park, N.Y.: New City Press, 1997.

———. *De doctrina Christiana.* Edited by J. Martin. CCSL 32. Turnhout: Brepols, 1962.

———. *On Genesis.* Translated by Edmund Hill. The Works of Saint Augustine: A Translation for the 21st Century. Hyde Park, N.Y.: New City Press, 2002.

———. *Responses to Miscellaneous Questions.* Translated by Boniface Ramsey. The Works of Saint Augustine: A Translation for the 21st Century. Hyde Park, N.Y.: New City Press, 2008.

———. *Tractatus in Johannis Evangelium.* Edited by R. Willems. CCSL 36. Turnhout: Brepols, 1954.

Barrett, C. K. *The Acts of the Apostles.* 2 vols. International Critical Commentary. London: T&T Clark, 1998

Barth, Karl. *Church Dogmatics*. Translated by Geoffrey W. Bromily et al. Edited by Geoffrey W. Bromiley and T. F. Torrance. 4 vols. in 14 parts. Edinburgh: T&T Clark, 1936–1977

———. *Evangelical Theology*. Translated by Grover Foley. Grand Rapids: Eerdmans, 1980.

Bauckham, Richard. *The Book of Acts in Its Palestinian Setting*. Grand Rapids: Eerdmans, 1995.

Beale, G. K. "The Descent of the Eschatological Temple in the Form of the Spirit at Pentecost." *Tyndale Bulletin* 56, no. 1 (2005): 73–102.

Bede. *The Commentary of the Venerable Bede on the Acts of the Apostles*. Translated by Lawrence T. Martin. Kalamazoo, Mich.: Cistercian, 1989.

———. *Liber hymnorum, thytthmi, varia preces*. Edited by J. Fraipont. CCSL 122. Turnhout: Brepols, 1955.

Behr, John. *The Case against Diodore and Theodore: Texts and Their Contexts*. Oxford Early Christian Texts. Oxford: Oxford University Press, 2011.

Berthold, Heinz, ed. *Makarios/Symeon, Reden und Briefe: Die Sammlung I des Vaticanus Graecus 694 (B)*. 2 vols. GCS 55–56. Berlin: Akademie-Verlag, 1973.

Best, Ernest. "The Interpretation of Tongues." In *Speaking in Tongues: A Guide to Research on Glossolalia*, edited by Watson E. Mills, 295–312. Grand Rapids: Eerdmans, 1986.

Blenkinsopp, Joseph. *Ezekiel*. Interpretation: A Bible Commentary for Teaching and Preaching. Louisville: John Knox Press, 1990.

Bock, Darrell L. *Acts*. Baker Exegetical Commentary on the New Testament. Grand Rapids: Baker Academic, 2007.

Bockmuehl, Markus. *Jewish Law in Gentile Churches*. Edinburgh: T&T Clark, 2000.

Bonaventure. *Commentary on the Gospel of Luke*. Edited by Robert J. Karris, OFM. Works of St. Bonaventure 8 part 3. St. Bonaventure, N.Y.: Franciscan Institute Publications, 2004.

Boyarin, Daniel. *The Jewish Gospels: The Story of the Jewish Christ*. New York: New Press, 2012.

Bruce, F. F. *Commentary on the Book of Acts*. New International Commentary on the New Testament. Grand Rapids: Eerdmans, 1954; 2nd ed., 1983.

———. *Commentary on the Book of Acts*. London: Marshall, Morgan and Scott, 1968.

Bucer, Martin. *On the True Reconciliation and Composition of the Churches*. Strasbourg: Wendelin Rihel, 1542.

Cabié, Robert. *La Pentecôte: l'évolution de la cinquantaine pascale au cours des cinq premiers siècles*. Tournai: Desclée, 1965.

Calvin, John. *The Acts of the Apostles*. Translated by W. J. G. McDonald. Edited by David W. Torrance and Thomas F. Torrance. Calvin's New Testament Commentaries 6. Grand Rapids: Eerdmans, 1965.

———. *Institutes of the Christian Religion*. Translated by Henry Beveridge. 2 vols. Grand Rapids: Eerdmans, 1981.

Carroll, John T. *Luke: A Commentary*. New Testament Library. Louisville: Westminster John Knox, 2012.

Cartledge, Mark J. "The Nature and Function of New Testament Glossolalia." *Evangelical Quarterly* 72, no. 2 (2000): 135–50.

———. *Charismatic Glossolalia: An Empirical Theological Study*. Aldershot: Ashgate, 2002.
Catherine of Siena. *The Dialogue*. Translated by Suzanne Noffke, OP. New York: Paulist Press, 1980.
Chavannes-Mazel, Claudine A. "Paradise and Pentecost." In *Reading Images and Texts: Medieval Images and Texts as Forms of Communication; Papers from the Third Utrecht Symposium on Medieval Literacy, Utrecht, 7–9 December 2000*, edited by Mariëlle Hageman and Marco Mostert, 121–37. Turnhout: Brepols, 2005.
Chesterton, G. K. *William Blake*. London: Duckworth, 1909. Project Gutenberg Australia, 2012. http://tinyurl.com/zmpetu9.
Claudel, Paul. "Du sens figuré de l'Écriture." In *Œuvres Complètes de Paul Claudel*. Vol. 21, *Commentaires et exegeses*, 11–36. Paris: Gallimard, 1963.
Clement of Alexandria. *Clemens Alexandrinus*. Vol. 2, *Stromata Buch I–VI*. Edited by Otto Stählin. Revised by Ludwig Früchtel. Griechische christliche Schriftsteller. Berlin: Akademie-Verlag, 1985.
———. *De deitate Filii et Spiritus sancti, et de Abraham*. Edited by E. Rhein. GNO 10/2. Leiden: Brill, 1996.
Cleopa of Romania, Elder. *The Truth of Our Faith: A Discourse from Holy Scripture on the Teachings of True Christianity*. Athens: Uncut Mountain Press, 2000.
Congar, Yves. *Divided Christendom*. London: Centenary, 1939.
———. *After Nine Hundred Years*. 1954. Reprint, New York: Fordham University Press, 1998.
———. "La théologie au Concile: Le 'théologiser' du Concile." In *Situation et tâches présentes de la théologie*, 41–56. Paris: Cerf, 1967.
———. *My Journal of the Council*. Translated by Mary John Ronayne and Mary Cecily Boulding. Collegeville, Minn.: Liturgical Press, 2012.
Conzelmann, Hans. *Acts of the Apostles*. Hermeneia. Minneapolis: Fortress, 1988.
Cooper, Christine F. "Miraculous Translation in 'The Book of Margery Kempe.'" *Studies in Philology* 101, no. 3 (2004): 270–98.
Cranz, F. Edward. *Reorientations of Western Thought from Antiquity to the Renaissance*. Edited by Nancy Struever. Aldershot: Ashgate, 2006.
Crossley, James. *The Date of Mark's Gospel: Insights from the Law in Earliest Christianity*. London: T&T Clark, 2004.
Dales, Douglas. "The Legacy of Bede." In *Alcuin: Theology and Thought*. Edinburgh: James Clarke, 2013.
Dekker, Kees. "Pentecost and Linguistic Self-Consciousness in Anglo-Saxon England: Bede and Aelfric." *Journal of English and Germanic Philology* 104, no. 3 (2005): 345–72.
Dionysius the Areopagite (Pseudo-Dionysius). *The Complete Works*. Edited by Paul Rorem. Translated by Colm Luibheid. Classics of Western Spirituality. Mahwah, N.J.: Paulist Press, 1987.
———. *Corpus Dionysiacum*. Vol. 1, *De divinis nominibus*. Edited by Beate Suchla. Berlin: de Gruyter, 1990.
———. *Corpus Dionysiacum*. Vol. 2, *De coelesti hierarchia, De ecclesiastica hierarchia,*

De mystica theologia, Epistulae. Edited by Günter Heil and Adolf Martin Ritter. Patristische Texte und Studien 67. Berlin: de Gruyter, 2012.

———. *The Works of Dionysius the Areopagite*. Translated by John Parker. 2 vols. London: Parker, 1897–1899.

Dockery, David S. "The Theology of Acts." *Criswell Theological Review* 5, no. 1 (1990): 43–55.

Donne, John. *The Complete Poetry of John Donne*. Edited by John T. Shawcross. Garden City, N.Y.: Anchor, 1967.

Dörries, Hermann, Erich Klostermann, and Matthias Kroeger, eds. *Die 50 Geistlichen Homilien des Makarios*. PTS 4. Berlin: de Gruyter, 1964.

Dunn, James D. G. *Jesus and the Holy Spirit*. London: SCM, 1975.

———. *Jesus, Paul, and the Law*. Louisville: Westminster John Knox, 1990.

———. *The Epistle to the Galatians*. Black's New Testament Commentary. Peabody, Mass.: Hendrickson, 1993.

———. "The Incident at Antioch (Gal 2:11–18)." In *The Galatians Debate*, edited by Mark D. Nanos, 199–234. Peabody, Mass.: Hendrickson, 2002.

———. *Baptism in the Holy Spirit: A Re-examination of the New Testament Teaching on the Gift of the Spirit in Relation to Pentecostalism Today*. 2nd ed. London: SCM, 2010.

Evdokimov, Paul. *Ages of the Spiritual Life*. Crestwood, N.Y.: St. Vladimir's Seminary Press, 1998.

Everts, J. "Tongues or Languages? Contextual Consistency in the Translation of Acts 2." *Journal of Pentecostal Theology* 4 (1994): 71–80.

Farrow, Douglas. *Ascension Theology*. London: Bloomsbury, 2011.

Fee, Gordon. *Pauline Christology: An Exegetical-Theological Study*. Peabody, Mass.: Hendrickson, 2007.

Fernando, Ajith. *Acts*. NIV Application Commentary. Grand Rapids: Zondervan, 1998.

Fitzmyer, Joseph A., SJ. *The Gospel according to Luke (X–XXIV)*. Garden City, N.Y.: Doubleday, 1985.

Florovsky, Georges. *Bible, Church, Tradition: An Eastern Orthodox View*. Belmont, Mass.: Norland, 1987.

Flusser, David. *Jesus*. Jerusalem: Magnes Press, 2001.

Forbes, Christopher. "Early Christian Inspired Speech and Hellenistic Popular Religion." *Novum Testamentum* 28, no. 3 (1986): 257–70.

———. *Prophecy and Inspired Speech in Early Christianity and Its Hellenistic Environment*. Peabody, Mass.: Hendrickson, 1997.

Forshall, Josiah, and Sir Frederic Madden, eds. *The Holy Bible, Containing the Old and New Testaments, with the Apocryphal Books in the Earliest English Versions Made with the Latin Vulgate of John Wycliffe and His Followers*. Oxford: Oxford University Press, 1850.

Fowl, Stephen E. *Ephesians: A Commentary*. New Testament Library. Louisville: Westminster John Knox, 2012.

Freeman, Curtis. *Undomesticated Dissent*. Waco: Baylor University Press, 2017.

Froelich, Karlfried. "Fallibility Instead of Infallibility? A Brief History of the Interpretation of Galatians 2:11–14." In *Teaching Authority and Infallibility in the Church*, edited by Paul C. Empire, T. Austin Murphy, and Joseph A. Burgess, 259–69, 351–57. Lutherans and Catholics in Dialogue 6. Minneapolis: Augsburg, 1980.

Gager, John G. *Reinventing Paul*. New York: Oxford University Press, 2000.

Gasque, W. Ward. *A History of the Interpretation of the Acts of the Apostles*. 1975. Reprint, Peabody, Mass.: Hendrickson, 1989.

Gaventa, Beverly Roberts. *Acts*. Abingdon New Testament Commentaries. Nashville: Abingdon, 2003.

Genakoplos, Deno John. *Byzantium: Church, Society, and Civilization Seen through Contemporary Eyes*. Chicago: University of Chicago Press, 1984.

Gibson, Michael Francis. *The Mill and the Cross: Peter Bruegel's "Way to Calvary."* Lausanne: Acatos, 2000.

Gilbert, Gary. "The List of Nations in Acts 2: Roman Propaganda and the Lukan Response." *Journal of Biblical Literature* 121, no. 3 (2002): 497–529.

Gilmour, S. MacLean. "Easter and Pentecost." *Journal of Biblical Literature* 81, no. 1 (1962): 62–66.

Golitzin, Alexander. *Et Introibo ad Altare Dei: The Mystagogy of Dionysius Areopagita, with Special Reference to its Predecessors in the Eastern Christian Tradition*. Analecta Vlatadon 59. Thessaloniki: Patriarchal Institute for Patristic Studies, 1994.

———. "Revisiting the 'Sudden': Epistle III in the Corpus Dionysiacum." *Studia Patristica* 37 (2001): 482–91.

———. *Mystagogy: A Monastic Reading of Dionysius Areopagita*. Cistercian Studies 250. Collegeville, Minn.: Liturgical Press, 2013.

Gootaers, Jan, ed. *Primauté et collégialité: Le dossier de Gérard Philips sur la Nota Explicativa Praevia (Lumen gentium, chap. III)*. Leuven: Leuven University Press, 1986.

Grabar, André. "Le schéma iconographique de la Pentecôte." In *L'art de la fin de l'antiquité et du Moyen Age*, 1:615–27. Paris: Klincksieck, 1968.

Gregory of Nazianzus. *On God and Christ: The Five Theological Orations and Two Letters to Cledonius*. Translated by Frederick Williams and Lionel Wickham. Popular Patristics Series. Crestwood, N.Y.: St. Vladimir's Seminary Press, 2002.

Gregory Palamas. *The Triads*. Edited by John Meyendorff. Translated by Nicholas Gendle. Classics of Western Spirituality. New York: Paulist Press, 1983.

Gregory the Great. *Homiliae in evangelia*. Edited by Raymond Étaix. CCSL 141. Turnhout: Brepols, 1999

Guarino, Thomas. "*Essentia et non gradu tantum differant*: A Note on the Priesthood and Analogical Predication." *The Thomist* 77 (2013): 559–76.

———. "Analogy and Vatican II: An Overlooked Dimension of the Council?" *Josephinum Journal of Theology* 22 (2015): 44–58.

Guite, Malcolm. "The Word and the Words: Andrewes, Donne, and the Theology of Translation." In *The King James Bible at 400: Assessing Its Genius as Bible Translation and Its Literary Influence*, edited by David G. Burke, John F. Kutsko, and Philip H. Townec, 373–84. Atlanta: Society of Biblical Literature, 2013.

Gundry, Robert H. "'Ecstatic Utterance' (N.E.B.)?" *Journal of Theological Studies*, n.s. 17, no. 2 (1966): 229–307

Halifax, Lord, ed. *The Conversations at Malines 1921–1925*. London: Philip Allan, 1930.

Hamm, Berndt. *The Early Luther: Stages in a Reformation Reorientation*. Lutheran Quarterly Books. Grand Rapids: Eerdmans, 2014.

Hayward, Paul. "Gregory the Great as 'Apostle of the English' in Post-Conquest Canterbury." *Journal of Ecclesiastical History* 55, no. 1 (2004): 19–57.

Hine, Virginia H. "Pentecostal Glossolalia: Toward a Functional Interpretation." *Journal for the Scientific Study of Religion* 8, no. 2 (1969): 211–26.

Hoehner, Harold W. *Ephesians: An Exegetical Commentary*. Grand Rapids: Baker Academic, 2002.

Hooker, Richard. *The Works of Richard Hooker*. Edited by Georges Edelen et al. 4 vols. Folger Library Edition. Cambridge, Mass.: Belknap Press of Harvard University Press, 1977–1990.

Hopko, Thomas. "The Gift, the Gifts, and Glossolalia." *Ancient Faith Podcasts*. July 10, 2011. http://www.ancientfaith.com/podcasts/hopko/the_gift_the_gifts_and_glossolalia.

Hummel, Horace D. *Ezekiel 1–20*. Saint Louis: Concordia Publishing House, 2005.

Irenaeus of Lyons. *Adversus Haereses*. 2 vols. Cambridge: Cambridge University Press, 1857.

———. *On the Apostolic Preaching*. Translated by John Behr. Popular Patristics Series. Crestwood, N.Y.: St. Vladimir's Seminary Press, 1997.

Isaac the Syrian. *The Ascetical Homilies of St. Isaac the Syrian*. Translated by Holy Transfiguration Monastery. Boston: Holy Transfiguration Monastery, 1984.

Jeffrey, David Lyle, ed. *A Dictionary of Biblical Tradition in English Literature*. Grand Rapids: Eerdmans, 1992.

———. Introduction to *English Spirituality in the Age of Wesley*, edited by David Lyle Jeffrey, 1–52. 1987. Reprint, Vancouver, B.C.: Regent College Publishing, 2000.

Jenkins, Gary W. "Dinner with Raphael: The Prolegomena of Peter Martyr Vermigli's Eucharistic Intellections." *Zwingliana* 36 (2009): 103–13.

John Chrysostom. "In Praise of St. Paul." In *Chrysostom and His Message: A Selection from the Sermons of St. John Chrysostom of Antioch and Constantinople*. Edited and translated by Stephen Neill. New York: Association Press, 1962.

John of Damascus. *Three Treatises on the Divine Images*. Translated by Andrew Louth. Crestwood, N.Y.: St. Vladimir's Seminary Press, 2003.

Johnson, Luke Timothy. *The Writings of the New Testament: An Interpretation*. Philadelphia: Fortress, 1986.

———. *The Acts of the Apostles*. Sacra Pagina. Collegeville, Minn.: Liturgical Press, 1992.

———. "Glossolalia and the Embarrassments of Experience." *Princeton Seminary Bulletin* 18, no. 2 (1997): 113–34.

———. *Hebrews: A Commentary*. New Testament Library. Louisville: Westminster John Knox, 2006.

Johnson, S. Lewis. "A Symposium on the Tongues Movement Part II: The Gift of Tongues and the Book of Acts." *Bibliotheca Sacra* 120 (1963): 309–11

Kasper, Walter Cardinal. *That They Might All Be One: The Call to Unity Today*. London: Continuum, 2004.

Keener, Craig S. *Acts: An Exegetical Commentary*. Vol. 1, *Introduction and 1:1–2:47*. Grand Rapids: Baker Academic, 2012.

———. *Acts: An Exegetical Commentary*. Vol. 2, *3:1–14:28*. Grand Rapids: Baker Academic, 2013.

Kierkegaard, Søren. *"Fear and Trembling: A Dialectical Lyric" and "The Sickness unto Death."* Translated by Walter Lowrie. Princeton: Princeton University Press, 1941.

Kirby, W. J. Torrance. *Hooker: Reformer and Platonist*. Aldershot: Ashgate, 2013.

Kitson, Michael. *The Complete Paintings of Caravaggio*. New York: Harry N. Abrams, 1967.

Koch, Hugo, "Proklos als Quelle des Pseudo-Dionysius Areopagita in der Lehre vom Bösen." *Philologus* 54 (1895): 438–54.

Lake, Kirsopp. *Earlier Epistles of St. Paul: Their Motive and Origin*. London: Rivingtons, 1914.

Leithart, Peter. *The End of Protestantism: Pursuing Unity in a Fragmented Church*. Grand Rapids: Baker Academic, 2016.

Levenson, Jon D. *The Death and Resurrection of the Beloved Son: The Transformation of Child Sacrifice in Judaism and Christianity*. New Haven: Yale University Press, 1993.

Levison, John R. *Filled with the Spirit*. Grand Rapids: Eerdmans, 2009.

Levy, Ian Christopher, ed. *The Letter to the Galatians*. The Bible in Medieval Tradition. Grand Rapids: Eerdmans, 2011.

Lewis, C. S. *The Weight of Glory and Other Addresses*. New York: Macmillan, 1949.

Lightfoot, J. B. *St. Paul's Epistle to the Galatians*. London: Macmillan, 1880.

———. *The Acts of the Apostles: A Newly Discovered Commentary*. Edited by Ben Witherington III and Todd D. Still. Downers Grove, IL: IVP Academic, 2014.

Longenecker, Richard N. *The Expositor's Bible Commentary*. Vol. 9, *John–Acts*. Grand Rapids: Zondervan, 1981.

———. *Acts*. Expositor's Bible Commentary. Grand Rapids: Zondervan, 1995.

———. *The Expositor's Bible Commentary*. Vol. 10, *Luke-Acts*, edited by Tremper Longman III and David E. Garland. Rev. ed. Grand Rapids: Zondervan, 2007.

Lossky, Vladimir. *The Mystical Theology of the Eastern Church*. Crestwood, N.Y.: St. Vladimir's Seminary Press, 1976.

———. *Vision of God*. Translated by Ashleigh Moorehouse. Crestwood, N.Y.: St. Vladimir's Seminary Press, 1983.

———. *Essai sur la théologie mystique de l'Eglise d'Orient*. Paris: Cerf, 2005.

Louth, Andrew. *The Origins of the Christian Mystical Tradition: From Plato to Denys*. Oxford: Clarendon, 1981.

———. "Apophatic and Cataphatic Theology." In *Cambridge Companion to Christian Mysticism*, edited by Amy Hollywood and Patricia Z. Beckman, 137–46. Cambridge: Cambridge University Press, 2012.

———. "Constructing the Apostolic Past: The Case of Dionysius the Areopagite." In *The Church on Its Past*, edited by Peter D. Clarke and Charlotte Methuen, 42–51. Studies in Church History 49. Woodbridge: Boydell Press, 2013.

———. "Symbolism and the Angels in Dionysios the Areopagite." *Studia Patristica* 58 (2013): 109–15.

Lubac, Henri de. *The Drama of Atheistic Humanism*. Translated by Edith M. Rile. London: Sheed and Ward, 1949.

———. *The Mystery of the Supernatural*. Translated by Rosemary Sheed. New York: Crossroad, 1998.

Lumiansky, R. M., and David Mills, eds. *The Chester Mystery Cycle*. 2 vols. Early English Text Society, s.s. 3. London: Oxford University Press, 1974.
Luther, Martin. *Commentary on Galatians*. Grand Rapids: Fleming H. Revell, 1988.
Mallarmé, Stéphane. *Œuvres completes*. Edited by Henri Mondor and G. Jean-Aubry. Paris: Gallimard, 1945.
Maraval, Pierre. "Chronology of Works [of Gregory of Nyssa]." In *The Brill Dictionary of Gregory of Nyssa*, edited by L. F. Mateo-Seco and G. Maspero, 153–69. Leiden: Brill, 2010.
Marcel, Gabriel. *Being and Having*. London: Fontana, 1965.
Martin, Francis, in collaboration with Evan Smith. *Acts*. Ancient Christian Commentary on Scripture: New Testament 5. Downers Grove, Ill.: InterVarsity Press, 2006.
Matera, Frank. *God's Saving Grace: A Pauline Theology*. Grand Rapids: Eerdmans, 2012.
Maximus the Confessor. *On the Cosmic Mystery of Jesus Christ*. Translated by Paul M. Blowers and Robert Louis Wilken. Crestwood, N.Y.: St. Vladimir's Seminary Press, 2003.
———. *On Difficulties in the Church Fathers*. Vol. 1, *The Ambigua*. Translated by Nicholas Constas. Dumbarton Oaks Medieval Library. Cambridge, Mass.: Harvard University Press, 2014.
———. *Two Hundred Chapters on Theology*. Translated by Joshua Sales. Popular Patristics Series. Crestwood, N.Y.: St. Vladimir's Seminary Press, 2015.
Melanchthon, Philip. *Loci communes*. Edited by C. G. Bretschneider and H. E. Bindseil. Corpus Reformatorum 21. Brunswick, 1854.
Menzies, Robert P. *The Development of Early Christian Pneumatology, with Special Reference to Luke-Acts*. Journal for the Study of the New Testament Supplement Series 54. Sheffield: Sheffield Academic, 1991.
———. "Luke's Understanding of Baptism in the Holy Spirit: A Pentecostal Dialogue with the Reformed Tradition." *Journal of Pentecostal Theology* 16 (2008): 86–101.
Metzger, Bruce M. "Ancient Astrological Geography and Acts 2:9–11." In *Apostolic History and the Gospel: Biblical and Historical Essays Presented to F. F. Bruce*, edited by W. Ward Gasque and Ralph P. Martin, 124–33. Exeter: Paternoster, 1970.
Meyendorff, John. *Christ in Eastern Christian Thought*. Crestwood, N.Y.: St. Vladimir's Seminary Press, 1975.
Murray, Paul D. "Receptive Ecumenism and Catholic Learning—Establishing the Agenda." In *Receptive Ecumenism and the Call to Catholic Learning: Exploring a Way for Contemporary Ecumenism*, edited by Paul D. Murray, 5–25. Oxford: Oxford University Press, 2008.
Nanos, Mark. "Rethinking the 'Paul *and* Judaism' Paradigm: Why Not 'Paul's *Judaism*'?" Mark Nanos personal website. May 28, 2008. http://www.marknanos.com/Paul%27sJudaism-5-28-08.pdf.
———. "The Myth of the 'Law-Free' Paul Standing between Christians and Jews." Mark Nanos personal website. December 10, 2008. http://www.marknanos.com/Myth-Lawfree-12-3-08.pdf.
———. "Paul and the Jewish Tradition: The Ideology of the Shema." In *Celebrating Paul: Festschrift in Honor of J. A. Fitzmyer and J. Murphy-O'Connor*, edited by Peter Spitaler, 62–80. Washington, D.C.: Catholic Biblical Association of America, 2009.

Nassif, Bradley, ed. *New Perspectives on Historical Theology: Essays in Memory of John Meyendorff*. Grand Rapids: Eerdmans, 1997.

———. "'Authority' in the Eastern Orthodox Tradition." In *By What Authority? The Vital Questions of Religious Authority in Christianity*, edited by Robert Millett, 45–50. Macon, Ga.: Mercer University Press, 2010.

———. "Tradition, 'Catholicity,' and the Mind of the Church." In *The Mission of God: Studies in Orthodox and Evangelical Mission*, edited by Mark Oxbrow and Tim Grass, 215–23. Eugene, Ore.: Wipf and Stock, 2016.

Nelson, R. David, and Charles Raith II. *Ecumenism: A Guide for the Perplexed*. London: Bloomsbury T&T Clark, 2017.

Nickelsburg, George W. E., and James C. VanderKam, trans. *First Enoch: A New Translation*. Minneapolis: Fortress, 2004.

Nicozisin, George. "Speaking in Tongues: An Orthodox Perspective." Greek Orthodox Archdiocese of America. September 3, 2005. http://www.goarch.org/ourfaith/ourfaith7112.

Nietzsche, Friedrich. *The Portable Nietzsche*. Edited and translated by Walter Kaufmann. New York: Viking, 1954.

———. *The Gay Science*. Translated by Walter Kaufmann. New York: Vintage, 1974.

———. *Ecce Homo*. Translated by R. J. Hollingdale. New York: Penguin, 1979.

Oberman, Heiko. *The Dawn of the Reformation*. Grand Rapids: Eerdmans, 1992.

O'Malley, John W. *What Happened at Vatican II*. Cambridge, Mass.: Belknap Press of Harvard University Press, 2008.

Origen. *Homélies sur le Lévitique VIII–XVI*. Edited by Marcel Borret, Sources chrétiennes 287. Paris: Cerf, 1982.

———. *On First Principles*. Edited and translated by John Behr. Oxford Early Christian Texts. Oxford: Oxford University Press, 2018.

Packer, J. I. *Knowing God*. Downers Grove, Ill.: InterVarsity Press, 1973.

Parsons, Mikeal C. *Acts*. Paideia Commentaries on the New Testament. Grand Rapids: Baker Academic, 2008.

———. *Luke*. Paideia Commentaries on the New Testament. Grand Rapids: Baker Academic, 2015.

Pelikan, Jaroslav. *Fools for Christ. Essays on the True, the Good, and the Beautiful; Impressions of Kierkegaard, Paul, Dostoevsky, Luther, Nietzsche, Bach*. Philadelphia: Muhlenberg, 1955.

———. *Acts*. Brazos Theological Commentary on the Bible. Grand Rapids: Brazos, 2005.

Pentiuc, Eugen J. *The Old Testament in Eastern Orthodox Tradition*. Oxford: Oxford University Press, 2014.

Perl, Eric D. *Theophany: The Neoplatonic Philosophy of Dionysius the Areopagite*. Albany, N.Y.: State University of New York Press, 2007.

Pervo, Richard I. *Acts: A Commentary*. Hermeneia. Minneapolis: Fortress, 2009.

Peterson, David G. *The Acts of the Apostles*. Pillar New Testament Commentary. Grand Rapids: Eerdmans, 2009.

Philips, Gérard. *L'Église et son Mystère*. 2 vols. Paris: Desclée, 1968.

Pieper, Josef. *An Anthology*. Translated by Margareta Svjagintsev et al. San Francisco: Ignatius, 1989.

Polhill, John B. *Acts*. New American Commentary 26. Nashville: Broadman & Holman, 1992.

Possidius. *The Life of Saint Augustine*. Translated by Herbert T. Weiskotten. Merchantville, N.J.: Evolution Publishing, 2008.

Proklos. *In Rem publicam*. Edited by Wilhelm Kroll. Leipzig, 1901.

Ramage, Matthew J. *Dark Passages of the Bible: Engaging Scripture with Benedict XVI and Thomas Aquinas*. Washington, D.C.: The Catholic University of America Press, 2013.

Reno, R. R. "The Debilitation of the Churches." In *The Ecumenical Future*, edited by Carl E. Braaten and Robert W. Jenson, 46–72. Grand Rapids: Eerdmans, 2004.

Richard, Marcel, ed. "Les fragments d'Origène sur Prov 30,15–31." In *Epektasis: Mélanges patristiques offerts au Cardinal J. Daniélou*, edited by Jacques Fontaine and Charles Kannengiesser, 385–94. Paris: Beauchesne, 1972.

Robinson, Thomas. *Ignatius of Antioch and the Parting of the Ways: Early Jewish-Christian Relations*. Peabody, Mass.: Hendrickson, 2009.

Rorem, Paul. *Biblical and Liturgical Symbols within the Pseudo-Dionysian Synthesis*. Toronto: Pontifical Institute of Mediaeval Studies, 1984.

Rowe, C. Kavin. *Early Narrative Christology: The Lord in the Gospel of Luke*. Berlin: de Gruyter, 2006.

Rudolph, David. "Jesus and the Food Laws." *Evangelical Quarterly* 74, no. 4 (2002): 291–311.

———. *A Jew to the Jews: Jewish Contours of Pauline Flexibility in 1 Corinthians 9:19–23*. Tübingen: Mohr Siebeck, 2011.

Schäfer, Christian. *The Philosophy of Dionysius the Areopagite: An Introduction to the Structure and the Content of the Treatise "On the Divine Names."* Leiden: Brill, 2006.

Schall, James V., SJ. *The Regensburg Lecture*. South Bend, Ind.: St. Augustine's Press, 2007.

Schmemann, Alexander. "Towards a Theology of Councils." In *Church, World, Mission*, 159–78. Crestwood, N.Y.: St. Vladimir's Seminary Press, 1979.

Seccombe, David P. "The New People of God." In *Witness to the Gospel: The Theology of Acts*, edited by I. Howard Marshall and David Peterson, 349–72. Grand Rapids: Eerdmans, 1998.

Simmons, Thomas Frederick, ed. *The Lay Folks Mass Book; or, the manner of hearing Mass, with rubrics and devotions for the people in four texts, and offices in English according to the use of York, from manuscripts of the Xth to XVth century*. Early English Text Society. London: Trübner, 1879.

Simmons, Thomas Frederick, and H. E. Nolloth, eds. *The Lay Folks' Catechism; or, the English and Latin versions of Archbishop's instructions for the people....* Early English Text Society. London: Kegan Paul, Trench and Trübner, 1901.

Simut, Corneliu. "Richard Hooker's Epistemology of Faith in the 'A Learned and Comfortable Sermon of the Certaintie and Perpetuitie of Faith in the Elect' (1585)." *Annales Philosophici* 2 (2011): 87–95.

Stang, Charles. "Dionysius, Paul, and the Significance of the Pseudonym." In *Re-thinking Dionysius the Areopagite*, edited by Sarah Coakley and Charles M. Stang, 11–25. Oxford: Wiley-Blackwell, 2009.

———. *Apophasis and Pseudonymity in Dionysius the Areopagite: "No Longer I."* New York: Oxford University Press, 2012.

Stanton, Robert. *The Culture of Translation in Anglo-Saxon England.* Cambridge: D. S. Brewer, 2002.

Stebbins, Madeleine F. "Looking at a Masterpiece: St. Paul's Conversion on the Way to Damascus." *Catholics United for the Faith.* May/June 2009. http://www.cuf.org/2009/05/looking-at-a-masterpiece-st-pauls-conversion-on-the-way-to-damascus/.

Stewart-Sykes, Alistair, trans. *Tertullian, Cyprian, and Origen, On the Lord's Prayer.* Popular Patristics Series. Crestwood, N.Y.: St. Vladimir's Seminary Press, 2004.

Stiglmayr, Josef, "Der Neuplatoniker Proklos als Vorlage des sogenannten Dionysius Areopagita in der Lehre vom Übel." *Historisches Jahrbuch* 16 (1895): 253–73 and 721–48.

Stormon, E. J., ed. *Towards the Healing of Schism.* Mahwah, N.J.: Paulist Press, 1987.

Strelan, Rick. "'We Hear Them Telling in Our Own Tongues the Mighty Works of God' (Acts 2:10)." *Neotestamentica* 40, no. 2 (2006): 295–319.

Stronstad, Roger. *The Charismatic Theology of St. Luke: Trajectories from the Old Testament to Luke-Acts.* 2nd ed. Grand Rapids: Baker Academic, 2012.

Struck, Peter T. *The Birth of the Symbol: Ancient Readers at the Limits of Their Texts.* Princeton: Princeton University Press, 2004.

Suchla, Beate. *Dionysius Areopagite: Leben—Werk—Wirkung.* Freiburg im Breisgau: Herder, 2008.

Symeon the New Theologian. *Divine Eros: Hymns of St Symeon the New Theologian.* Translated by Daniel K. Griggs. Popular Patristics Series. Crestwood, N.Y.: St. Vladimir's Seminary Press, 2011.

Tanner, Norman P., SJ, ed. *Decrees of the Ecumenical Councils.* 2 vols. Washington, D.C.: Georgetown University Press, 1990.

Tertullian. *De anima.* Edited by J. Waszink. CCSL 2. Turnhout: Brepols, 1954.

Thérel, Marie-Louise. *Les symboles de l' "Ecclesia" dans la création iconographique de l'art chrétien du IIIe au VIe siècle.* Rome: Edizioni di Storia e Letteratura, 1973.

Thielman, Frank. *From Plight to Solution: A Jewish Framework for Understanding Paul's View of the Law in Galatians and Romans.* Eugene, Ore.: Wipf and Stock, 2007.

Thiselton, Anthony C. "The 'Interpretation' of Tongues: A New Suggestion in the Light of Greek Usage in Philo and Josephus." *Journal of Theological Studies* 30 (1979): 15–36.

Thomas, Derek H. W. *Acts.* Reformed Expository Commentary. Phillipsburg, N.J.: P and R, 2011.

Thompson, Richard P. "Luke-Acts: The Gospel of Luke and the Acts of the Apostles." In *The Blackwell Companion to the New Testament,* edited by David Aune, 319–43. Oxford: Wiley-Blackwell, 2010.

Tolkien, J. R. R. *The History of Middle-Earth.* Vol. 10, *Morgoth's Ring: The Later Silmarillion, Part One.* Edited by Christopher Tolkien. London: HarperCollins, 1993.

Tugwell, Simon. "The Gift of Tongues in the New Testament." *Expository Times* 84 (1973): 137–40.

Turner, Max. *Power from on High: The Spirit in Israel's Restoration and Witness in Luke-Acts.* Sheffield: Sheffield Academic, 2000.

Twelftree, Graham H. *People of the Spirit: Exploring Luke's View of the Church.* Grand Rapids: Baker Academic, 2009.

Ware, Kallistos. "Personal Experience of the Holy Spirit according to the Greek Fathers." Paper presented at the European Pentecostal/Charismatic Research Conference, Prague, September 10–14, 1997. Posted online at *Silouan.* August 5, 2008. http://silouanthompson.net/2008/08/personal-experience/.

Weinandy, Thomas G. *In the Likeness of Sinful Flesh: An Essay on the Humanity of Christ.* Edinburg: T&T Clark, 1993.

Weitzmann, Kurt. "*Loca Sancta* and the Representational Arts of Palestine." *Dumbarton Oaks Papers* 28 (1974): 31–55.

———. *The Monastery of Saint Catherine at Mount Sinai: The Icons.* Vol. 1, *From the Sixth to the Tenth Century.* Princeton: Princeton University Press, 1976.

Westcott, B. F. "Dionysius the Areopagite." In *Essays in the History of Religious Thought in the West,* 142–93. London: Macmillan, 1903.

Wiesel, Elie. *From the Kingdom of Memory: Reminiscences.* New York: Summit, 1990.

Wilkin, Karen. "A Transfiguring Moment: Caravaggio's Potent, Astonishing 'Conversion of Saul.'" *Wall Street Journal.* March 6, 2010. http://tinyurl.com/jc9e9k8.

Williams, Rowan. "Rowan Williams on Poetry." *Dr Rowan Williams 104th Archbishop of Canterbury* (website). January 20, 2009. http://rowanwilliams.archbishopofcanterbury.org/articles.php/1752/rowan-williams-on-poetry.

———. "'The Human Form Divine': Revelation and Orthodoxy in William Blake." In *Radical Christians Voices and Practice: Essays in Honour of Christopher Rowland,* edited by Zoë Bennett and David B. Gowler, 151–64. Oxford: Oxford University Press, 2012.

Witherington, Ben, III. *The Acts of the Apostles: A Socio-rhetorical Commentary.* Grand Rapids: Eerdmans, 1998.

Wyclif, John. *De veritate sacrae scripturae.* Edited by R. Buddenseig. 3 vols. London: Wyclif Society, Trübner, 1905–1907.

Wyschogrod, Michael. "The Impact of Dialogue with Christianity on My Self-Understanding as a Jew." In *Abraham's Promise: Judaism and Jewish-Christian Relations,* 225–36. Edited by R. Kendall Soulen. Grand Rapids: Eerdmans, 2004.

Yeago, David S. "The Spirit, the Church, and the Scriptures: Biblical Inspiration and Interpretation Revisited." In *Knowing the Triune God: The Work of the Spirit in the Practices of the Church,* edited by James J. Buckley and David S. Yeago, 49–93. Grand Rapids: Eerdmans, 2001.

Zacharias, Archimandrite. "On the Gift of Speaking in Tongues." In *The Hidden Man of the Heart (1 Peter 3:4): The Cultivation of the Heart in Orthodox Christian Anthropology.* Dalton, Pa.: Mount Thabor Publishing, 2008; Orthodox Christian Information Center, http://orthodoxinfo.com/inquirers/on-the-gift-of-speaking-in-tongues.aspx.

Ziccardi, Costantino Antonio. *The Relationship of Jesus and the Kingdom of God according to Luke-Acts.* Rome: Gregorian University Press, 2008.

Contributors

FR. JOHN BEHR is the dean of St. Vladimir's Seminary and professor of patristics, and distinguished lecturer in patristics at Fordham University. He is author of *St Irenaeus of Lyons: Identifying Christianity* and is working on a new translation of Origen's *On First Principles*.

HANS BOERSMA is the J. I. Packer Professor of Theology at Regent College in Vancouver, Canada. He is author of *Heavenly Participation: The Weaving of a Sacramental Tapestry* and *Nouvelle Théologie and Sacramental Ontology*. He is a participant in Evangelicals and Catholics Together.

DALE M. COULTER is associate professor at Regent University School of Divinity. He is coeditor of *The Spirit, the Affections, and the Christian Tradition* and coeditor of *PNEUMA: The Journal of the Society for Pentecostal Studies*. He is a participant in Evangelicals and Catholics Together.

FR. BRIAN E. DALEY is the Catherine F. Huisking Professor of Theology at the University of Notre Dame. He is also the executive secretary of the Catholic-Orthodox Consultation for North America. He is author of *On the Dormition of Mary: Early Patristic Homilies*.

DONALD FAIRBAIRN is Robert E. Cooley Professor of Early Christianity at Gordon-Conwell Theological Seminary, Charlotte. He is author of *Grace and Christology in the Early Church* and *Eastern Orthodoxy through Western Eyes*.

DOUGLAS FARROW is professor of Christian thought and current holder of the Kennedy Smith Chair in Catholic Studies at McGill University in Montreal. He is author of *Ascension Theology* and *Desiring a Better Country: Forays in Political Theology*. He is a participant in Evangelicals and Catholics Together.

MSGR. THOMAS G. GUARINO is professor of systematic theology at Seton Hall University. He recently coedited a volume of the nine statements issued by the working group Evangelicals and Catholics Together, titled *Evangelicals and Catholics Together at Twenty: Vital Statements on Contested Topics*. He is a participant in Evangelicals and Catholics Together.

DAVID LYLE JEFFREY is distinguished professor of literature and humanities at Baylor University. He is also professor emeritus of English literature at the University of Ottawa, guest professor at Peking University (Beijing), and honorary professor at the University of International Business and Economics (Beijing). He is author of the theological commentary on Luke for the Brazos Theological Commentary on the Bible series.

GARY W. JENKINS is the John H. Van Gorden Professor in History at Eastern University and the director of the Center for Orthodox Thought and Culture at Eastern University.

MATTHEW LEVERING is James N. and Mary D. Perry Jr. Chair of Theology at Mundelein Seminary, and codirector of the Chicago Theological Initiative. He is author of the theological commentary on Ezra-Nehemiah for the Brazos Theological Commentary on the Bible series. He is a participant in Evangelicals and Catholics Together.

FR. ANDREW LOUTH is emeritus professor of patristic and Byzantine studies at Durham University. He is author of *Introducing Eastern Orthodoxy* and *Greek East and the Latin West: The Church, AD 681–1071*.

GERALD R. MCDERMOTT is the Anglican professor of divinity at Beeson Divinity School. He is author of *The New Christian Zionism: Fresh Perspectives on Israel and the Land* and *A Trinitarian Theology of Religions: An Evangelical Proposal*. He is a participant in Evangelicals and Catholics Together.

BRADLEY NASSIF is professor of biblical and theological studies at North Park University and a theologian of the Patriarchate of Antioch, Syria, and America. He is coeditor of *The Philokalia: A Classic Text of Orthodox Spirituality*.

FR. EUGEN J. PENTIUC is associate dean for academic affairs and professor of Old Testament and Semitic languages at Holy Cross Orthodox Theological Seminary. He is author of *The Old Testament in Eastern Orthodox Tradition* and is an editor in chief of *The Orthodox Study Bible*.

MARCUS PLESTED is associate professor of Greek patristic and Byzantine theology at Marquette University. He is the author of *The Macarian Legacy: The Place of Macarius-Symeon in the Eastern Christian Tradition* and *Orthodox Readings of Aquinas*.

CHARLES RAITH II, editor, is assistant professor of religion and theology at John Brown University.

FR. THOMAS G. WEINANDY, OFM, CAP., has taught in a number of Catholic universities in the United States and was the warden of Greyfriars, Oxford. He is author of *Jesus: Essays in Christology* and *The Father's Spirit of Sonship: Reconceiving the Trinity*.

ROBERT LOUIS WILKEN is William R. Kenan Jr. Professor of the History of Christianity Emeritus at the University of Virginia. He is the author of *The First Thousand Years: A Global History of Christianity* and general editor of The Church's Bible series.

RALPH C. WOOD is university professor of theology and literature at Baylor University. He is author of *Literature and Theology* and *Tolkien among the Moderns*.

Index